# Internet of Things

## A Hands-On Approach

Arshdeep Bahga, Vijay Madisetti

Internet of Things: A Hands-On Approach

Published by Arshdeep Bahga & Vijay Madisetti

ISBN: 978-0996025515

Book Website: www.internet-of-things-book.com

# Contents

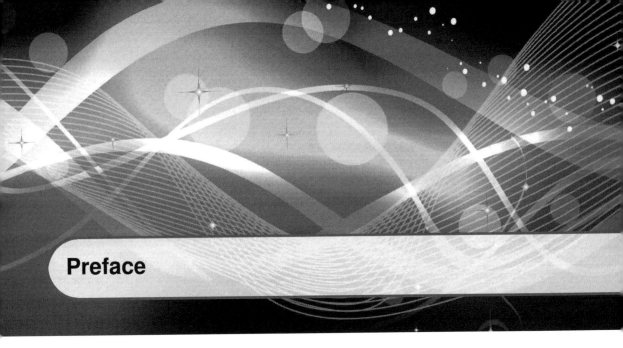

# Preface

## About This Book

Internet of Things (IOT) refers to physical and virtual objects that have unique identities and are connected to the internet to facilitate intelligent applications that make energy, logistics, industrial control, retail, agriculture and many other domains "smarter". Internet of Things is a new revolution of the Internet that is rapidly gathering momentum driven by the advancements in sensor networks, mobile devices, wireless communications, networking and cloud technologies. Experts forecast that by the year 2020 there will be a total of 50 billion devices/things connected to the internet.

This book is written as a textbook on Internet of Things for educational programs at colleges and universities, and also for IoT vendors and service providers who may be interested in offering a broader perspective of Internet of Things to accompany their own customer and developer training programs. The typical reader is expected to have completed a couple of courses in programming using traditional high-level languages at the college-level, and is either a senior or a beginning graduate student in one of the science, technology, engineering or mathematics (STEM) fields.

Like our companion book on Cloud Computing, we have tried to write a comprehensive book that transfers knowledge through an immersive "hands on" approach, where the reader is provided the necessary guidance and knowledge to develop working code for real-world IoT applications. Concurrent development of practical applications that accompanies traditional instructional material within the book further enhances the learning process, in our opinion. Please also check out the accompanying website for this book that contains additional support for instruction and learning.

The book is organized into 3 main parts, comprising of a total of 11 chapters. Part I covers the building blocks of Internet of Things (IoTs) and their characteristics. A taxonomy of IoT systems is proposed comprising of various IoT levels with increasing levels of complexity. Domain specific Internet of Things and their real-world applications are described. A generic design methodology for IoT is proposed. An IoT system management approach using NETCONF-YANG is described.

Part II introduces the reader to the programming aspects of Internet of Things with a view towards rapid prototyping of complex IoT applications. We chose Python as the primary programming language for this book, and an introduction to Python is also included within the text to bring readers to a common level of expertise. Other languages, besides Python, may also be easily used within the methodology outlined in this book. We describe packages, frameworks and cloud services including the WAMP-AutoBahn, Xively cloud and Amazon Web Services which can be used for developing IoT systems. We chose the Raspberry Pi device for the examples in this book. Raspberry Pi supports Python and allows rapid prototyping of practical IoT applications. Reference architectures for different levels of IoT applications are examined in detail. Case studies with complete source code for various IoT domains including home automation, smart environment, smart cities, logistics, retail, smart energy, smart agriculture, industrial control and smart health, are described.

Part III introduces the reader to advanced topics on IoT including IoT data analytics and Tools for IoT. Case studies on collecting and analyzing data generated by Internet of Things in the cloud are described.

Through generous use of hundreds of figures and tested code samples, we have attempted to provide a rigorous "no hype" guide to Internet of Things. It is expected that diligent readers of this book can use these exercises to develop their own IoT applications. We adopted an informal approach to describing well-known concepts primarily because these topics are covered well in existing textbooks, and our focus instead is on getting the reader firmly on track to developing robust IoT applications as opposed to more theory.

While we frequently refer to offerings from commercial vendors, such as Xively, Amazon, Google and Microsoft, this book is not an endorsement of their products or services, nor is any portion of our work supported financially (or otherwise) by these vendors. A ll trademarks and products belong to their respective owners and the underlying principles and approaches, we believe, are applicable to other vendors as well. The opinions in this book are those of the authors alone.

## Chapter-1: Introduction to Internet of Things

Provides an overview of Internet of Things, building blocks of IoT, IoT enabling technologies, characteristics of IoT systems and IoT levels.

## Chapter-2: Domain Specific IoTs

Describes the characteristics and applications of domain-specific IoTs including home automation, smart environment, smart cities, logistics, retail, smart energy, smart agriculture, industrial control and smart health.

## Chapter-3: IoT and M2M

Describes the differences and similarities between and IoT and M2M and applications of SDN and NFV in IoT.

### Chapter-4: IoT System Management with NETCONF-YANG

Describes NETCONF protocol, YANG data modeling language, and an approach for IoT system management using Netopeer tools.

### Chapter-5: IoT Platforms Design Methodology

Describes a generic design methodology for Internet of Things.

### Chapter-6: IoT Systems - Logical Design using Python

Provides an introduction to Python, installing Python, Python data types & data structures, control flow, functions, modules, packages, file input/output, data/time operations and classes.

### Chapter-7: IoT Physical Devices & Endpoints

Provides an introduction to Raspberry Pi device, programming Raspberry Pi with Python, interfacing sensors and actuators with Raspberry Pi.

### Chapter-8: IoT Physical Servers & Cloud Offerings

Provides an introduction to the use of cloud platforms and frameworks such as WAMP-AutoBahn, Xively and AWS for developing IoT applications.

### Chapter-9: Case Studies Illustrating IoT Design

Provides instruction on the design of several case studies based on Python and Raspberry Pi including home automation, smart environment, smart cities, logistics, retail, smart energy, smart agriculture, industrial control and smart health.

### Chapter-10: Data Analytics for IoT

Describes approaches for collecting and analyzing data generated by IoT systems in the cloud.

### Chapter-11: Tools for IoT

Describes various tools for IoT including Chef, Puppet, NETCONF-YANG and IoT Code Generator.

## Book Website

For more information on the book, copyrighted source code of all examples in the book, lab exercises, and instructor material, visit the book website: www.internet-of-things-book.com

## Acknowledgments

*From Arshdeep Bahga*
I would like to thank my father, Sarbjit Bahga, for inspiring me to write a book and sharing his valuable insights and experiences on authoring books. This book could not have been completed without the support of my mother Gurdeep Kaur, wife Navsangeet Kaur, and brother Supreet Bahga, who have always motivated me and encouraged me to explore my interests.

*From Vijay Madisetti*
I thank my family, especially Anitha and Jerry (Raj), and my parents for their support.

## About the Authors

**Arshdeep Bahga**
Arshdeep Bahga is a Research Scientist with Georgia Institute of Technology. His research interests include cloud computing and big data analytics. Arshdeep has authored several scientific publications in peer-reviewed journals in the areas of cloud computing and big data.

**Vijay Madisetti**
Vijay Madisetti is a Professor of Electrical and Computer Engineering at Georgia Institute of Technology. Vijay is a Fellow of the IEEE, and received the 2006 Terman Medal from the American Society of Engineering Education and HP Corporation.

# Part I

# INTRODUCTION & CONCEPTS

# 1 - Introduction to Internet of Things

This Chapter Covers

- Definition & Characteristics of IoT
- Physical Design of IoT
- Logical Design of IoT
- IoT Enabling Technologies
- IoT Levels & Deployment Templates

## 1.1   Introduction

Internet of Things (IoT) comprises things that have unique identities and are connected to the Internet. While many existing devices, such as networked computers or 4G-enabled mobile phones, already have some form of unique identities and are also connected to the Internet, the focus on IoT is in the configuration, control and networking via the Internet of devices or "things" that are traditionally not associated with the Internet. These include devices such as thermostats, utility meters, a bluetooth-connected headset, irrigation pumps and sensors, or control circuits for an electric car's engine. Internet of Things is a new revolution in the capabilities of the endpoints that are connected to the Internet, and is being driven by the advancements in capabilities (in combination with lower costs) in sensor networks, mobile devices, wireless communications, networking and cloud technologies. Experts forecast that by the year 2020 there will be a total of 50 billion devices/things connected to the Internet. Therefore, the major industry players are excited by the prospects of new markets for their products. The products include hardware and software components for IoT endpoints, hubs, or control centers of the IoT universe.

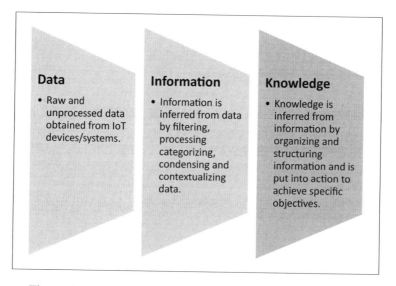

Figure 1.1: Inferring information and knowledge from data

The scope of IoT is not limited to just connecting things (devices, appliances, machines) to the Internet. IoT allows these things to communicate and exchange data (control & information, that could include data associated with users) while executing meaningful applications towards a common user or machine goal. Data itself does not have a meaning until it is contextualized processed into useful information. Applications on IoT networks extract and create information from lower level data by filtering, processing, categorizing, condensing and contextualizing the data. This information obtained is then organized and structured to infer knowledge about the system and/or its users, its environment, and its operations and progress towards its objectives, allowing a smarter performance, as shown in Figure 1.1. For example, consider a series of raw sensor measurements ((72,45) ; (84, 56)) generated by a weather monitoring station, which by themselves do not have any meaning or context. To give meaning to the data, a context is added, which in this example can be that

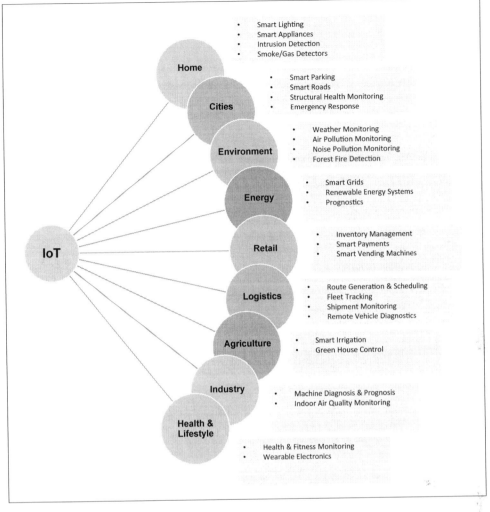

Figure 1.2: Applications of IoT

each tuple in data represents the temperature and humidity measured every minute. With this context added we know the meaning (or information) of the measured data tuples. Further information is obtained by categorizing, condensing or processing this data. For example, the average temperature and humidity readings for last five minutes is obtained by averaging the last five data tuples. The next step is to organize the information and understand the relationships between pieces of information to infer knowledge which can be put into action. For example, an alert is raised if the average temperature in last five minutes exceeds 120F, and this alert may be conditioned on the user's geographical position as well.

The applications of Internet of Things span a wide range of domains including (but not limited to) homes, cities, environment, energy systems, retail, logistics, industry, agriculture and health as listed in Figure 1.2. For homes, IoT has several applications such as smart lighting that adapt the lighting to suit the ambient conditions, smart appliances that can be remotely monitored and controlled, intrusion detection systems, smart smoke detectors, etc. For cities, IoT has applications such as smart parking systems that provide status updates on available slots, smart lighting that helps in saving energy, smart roads that provide information on driving conditions and structural health monitoring systems. For environment, IoT has applications such as weather monitoring, air and noise pollution, forest fire detection and river flood detection systems. For energy systems, IoT has applications such as including smart grids, grid integration of renewable energy sources and prognostic health management systems. For retail domain, IoT has applications such as inventory management, smart payments and smart vending machines. For agriculture domain, IoT has applications such as smart irrigation systems that help in saving water while enhancing productivity and green house control systems. Industrial applications of IoT include machine diagnosis and prognosis systems that help in predicting faults and determining the cause of faults and indoor air quality systems. For health and lifestyle, IoT has applications such as health and fitness monitoring systems and wearable electronics.

### 1.1.1  Definition & Characteristics of IoT

The Internet of Things (IoT) has been defined as [1]:

> **Definition:** A dynamic global network infrastructure with self-configuring capabilities based on standard and interoperable communication protocols where physical and virtual "things" have identities, physical attributes, and virtual personalities and use intelligent interfaces, and are seamlessly integrated into the information network, often communicate data associated with users and their environments.

Let us examine this definition of IoT further to put some of the terms into perspective.

- **Dynamic & Self-Adapting:** IoT devices and systems may have the capability to dynamically adapt with the changing contexts and take actions based on their operating conditions, user's context, or sensed environment. For example, consider a surveillance system comprising of a number of surveillance cameras. The surveillance cameras can adapt their modes (to normal or infra-red night modes) based on whether it is day or night. Cameras could switch from lower resolution to higher resolution modes when any motion is detected and alert nearby cameras to do the same. In this example, the surveillance system is adapting itself based on the context and changing (e.g., dynamic) conditions.

- **Self-Configuring:** IoT devices may have self-configuring capability, allowing a large number of devices to work together to provide certain functionality (such as weather monitoring). These devices have the ability configure themselves (in association with the IoT infrastructure), setup the networking, and fetch latest software upgrades with minimal manual or user intervention.

- **Interoperable Communication Protocols:** IoT devices may support a number of interoperable communication protocols and can communicate with other devices and also with the infrastructure. We describe some of the commonly used communication protocols and models in later sections.

- **Unique Identity:** Each IoT device has a unique identity and a unique identifier (such as an IP address or a URI). IoT systems may have intelligent interfaces which adapt based on the context, allow communicating with users and the environmental contexts. IoT device interfaces allow users to query the devices, monitor their status, and control them remotely, in association with the control, configuration and management infrastructure.

- **Integrated into Information Network:** IoT devices are usually integrated into the information network that allows them to communicate and exchange data with other devices and systems. IoT devices can be dynamically discovered in the network, by other devices and/or the network, and have the capability to describe themselves (and their characteristics) to other devices or user applications. For example, a weather monitoring node can describe its monitoring capabilities to another connected node so that they can communicate and exchange data. Integration into the information network helps in making IoT systems "smarter" due to the collective intelligence of the individual devices in collaboration with the infrastructure. Thus, the data from a large number of connected weather monitoring IoT nodes can be aggregated and analyzed to predict the weather.

## 1.2   Physical Design of IoT

### 1.2.1   Things in IoT

The "Things" in IoT usually refers to IoT devices which have unique identities and can perform remote sensing, actuating and monitoring capabilities. IoT devices can exchange data with other connected devices and applications (directly or indirectly), or collect data from other devices and process the data either locally or send the data to centralized servers or cloud-based application back-ends for processing the data, or perform some tasks locally and other tasks within the IoT infrastructure, based on temporal and space constraints (i.e., memory, processing capabilities, communication latencies and speeds, and deadlines).

Figure 1.3 shows a block diagram of a typical IoT device. An IoT device may consist of several interfaces for connections to other devices, both wired and wireless. These include (i) I/O interfaces for sensors, (ii) interfaces for Internet connectivity, (iii) memory and storage interfaces and (iv) audio/video interfaces. An IoT device can collect various types of data from the on-board or attached sensors, such as temperature, humidity, light intensity. The sensed data can be communicated either to other devices or cloud-based servers/storage. IoT devices can be connected to actuators that allow them to interact with other physical entities (including non-IoT devices and systems) in the vicinity of the device. For example, a relay switch connected to an IoT device can turn an appliance on/off based on the commands sent to the IoT device over the Internet.

IoT devices can also be of varied types, for instance, wearable sensors, smart watches, LED lights, automobiles and industrial machines. Almost all IoT devices generate data in some form or the other which when processed by data analytics systems leads to useful information to guide further actions locally or remotely. For instance, sensor data generated by a soil moisture monitoring device in a garden, when processed can help in determining the optimum watering schedules. Figure 1.4 shows different types of IoT devices.

### 1.2.2   IoT Protocols

**Link Layer**

Link layer protocols determine how the data is physically sent over the network's physical layer or medium (e.g., copper wire, coaxial cable, or a radio wave). The scope of the link

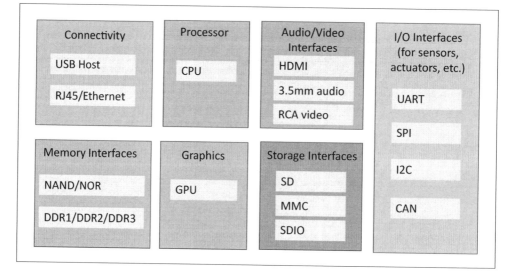

Figure 1.3: Generic block diagram of an IoT Device

layer is the local network connection to which host is attached. Hosts on the same link exchange data packets over the link layer using link layer protocols. Link layer determines how the packets are coded and signaled by the hardware device over the medium to which the host is attached (such as a coaxial cable). Let us now look at some link layer protocols which are relevant in the context of IoT.

- **802.3 - Ethernet :** IEEE 802.3 is a collection of wired Ethernet standards for the link layer. For example, 802.3 is the standard for 10BASE5 Ethernet that uses coaxial cable as a shared medium, 802.3.i is the standard for 10BASE-T Ethernet over copper twisted-pair connections, 802.3.j is the standard for 10BASE-F Ethernet over fiber optic connections, 802.3ae is the standard for 10 Gbit/s Ethernet over fiber, and so on. These standards provide data rates from 10 Mb/s to 40 Gb/s and higher. The shared medium in Ethernet can be a coaxial cable, twisted-pair wire or an optical fiber. The shared medium (i.e., broadcast medium) carries the communication for all the devices on the network, thus data sent by one device can received by all devices subject to propagation conditions and transceiver capabilities. The specifications of the 802.3 standards are available on the IEEE 802.3 working group website [2].
- **802.11 - WiFi :** IEEE 802.11 is a collection of wireless local area network (WLAN) communication standards, including extensive description of the link layer. For example, 802.11a operates in the 5 GHz band, 802.11b and 802.11g operate in the 2.4 GHz band, 802.11n operates in the 2.4/5 GHz bands, 802.11ac operates in the 5 GHz band and 802.11ad operates in the 60 GHz band. These standards provide data rates from 1 Mb/s to upto 6.75 Gb/s. The specifications of the 802.11 standards are available on the IEEE 802.11 working group website [3]
- **802.16 - WiMax :** IEEE 802.16 is a collection of wireless broadband standards, including extensive descriptions for the link layer (also called WiMax). WiMax standards provide data rates from 1.5 Mb/s to 1 Gb/s. The recent update (802.16m) provides data rates of 100 Mbit/s for mobile stations and 1 Gbit/s for fixed stations.

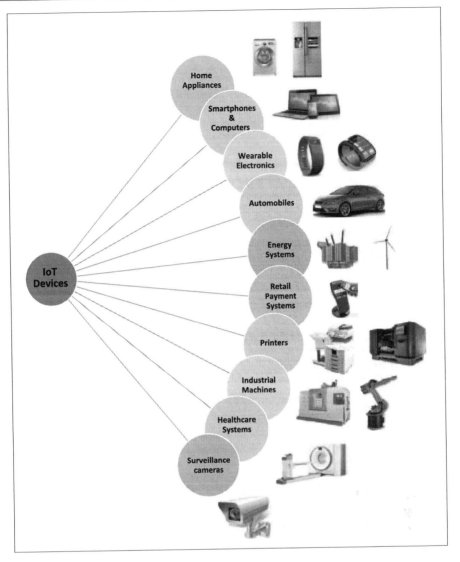

Figure 1.4: IoT Devices

The specifications of the 802.11 standards are readily available on the IEEE 802.16 working group website [4]

- **802.15.4 - LR-WPAN :** IEEE 802.15.4 is a collection of standards for low-rate wireless personal area networks (LR-WPANs). These standards form the basis of specifications for high level communication protocols such as ZigBee. LR-WPAN standards provide data rates from 40 Kb/s 250 Kb/s. These standards provide low-cost and low-speed communication for power constrained devices. The specifications of the 802.15.4 standards are available on the IEEE 802.15 working group website [5]

- **2G/ 3G/ 4G - Mobile Communication :** There are different generations of mobile communication standards including second generation (2G including GSM and CDMA), third generation (3G - including UMTS and CDMA2000) and fourth generation (4G - including LTE). IoT devices based on these standards can communicate over cellular

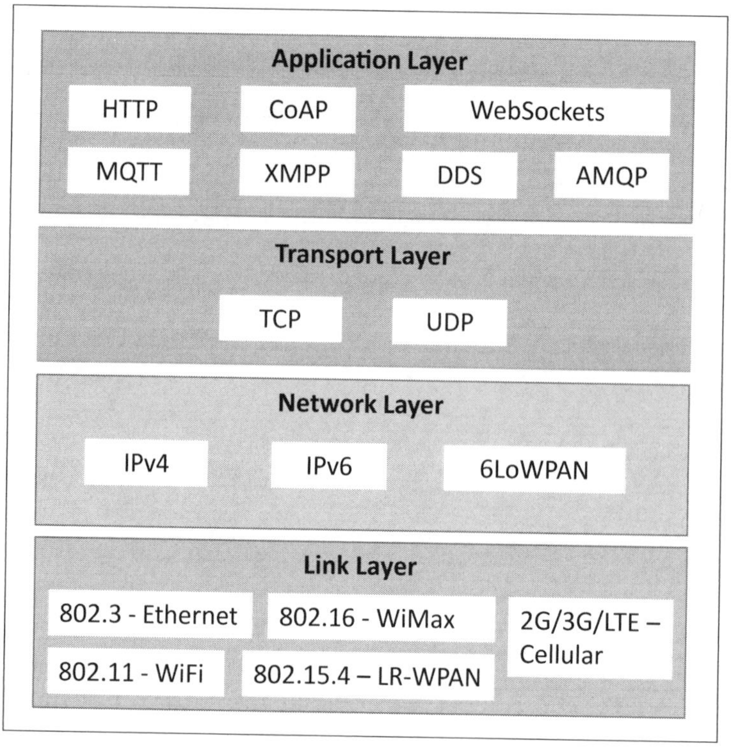

Figure 1.5: IoT Protocols

networks. Data rates for these standards range from 9.6 Kb/s (for 2G) to upto 100 Mb/s (for 4G) and are available from the 3GPP websites.

**Network/Internet Layer**

The network layers are responsible for sending of IP datagrams from the source network to the destination network. This layer performs the host addressing and packet routing. The datagrams contain the source and destination addresses which are used to route them from the source to destination across multiple networks. Host identification is done using hierarchical IP addressing schemes such as IPv4 or IPv6.

- **IPv4 :** Internet Protocol version 4 (IPv4) is the most deployed Internet protocol that is used to identify the devices on a network using a hierarchical addressing scheme. IPv4 uses a 32-bit address scheme that allows total of $2^{32}$ or 4,294,967,296 addresses. As more and more devices got connected to the Internet, these addresses got exhausted in the year 2011. IPv4 has been succeeded by IPv6. The IP protocols establish connections on packet networks, but do not guarantee delivery of packets. Guaranteed delivery and data integrity are handled by the upper layer protocols (such as TCP). IPv4 is formally described in RFC 791 [6].

- **IPv6 :** Internet Protocol version 6 (IPv6) is the newest version of Internet protocol and successor to IPv4. IPv6 uses 128-bit address scheme that allows total of $2^{128}$ or $3.4 \times 10^{38}$ addresses. IPv4 is formally described in RFC 2460 [7].

- **6LoWPAN :** 6LoWPAN (IPv6 over Low power Wireless Personal Area Networks) brings IP protocol to the low-power devices which have limited processing capability.

6LoWPAN operates in the 2.4 GHz frequency range and provides data transfer rates of 250 Kb/s. 6LoWPAN works with the 802.15.4 link layer protocol and defines compression mechanisms for IPv6 datagrams over IEEE 802.15.4-based networks [8].

**Transport Layer**

The transport layer protocols provide end-to-end message transfer capability independent of the underlying network. The message transfer capability can be set up on connections, either using handshakes (as in TCP) or without handshakes/acknowledgements (as in UDP). The transport layer provides functions such as error control, segmentation, flow control and congestion control.

- **TCP :** Transmission Control Protocol (TCP) is the most widely used transport layer protocol, that is used by web browsers (along with HTTP, HTTPS application layer protocols), email programs (SMTP application layer protocol) and file transfer (FTP). TCP is a connection oriented and stateful protocol. While IP protocol deals with sending packets, TCP ensures reliable transmission of packets in-order. TCP also provides error detection capability so that duplicate packets can be discarded and lost packets are retransmitted. The flow control capability of TCP ensures that rate at which the sender sends the data is not too high for the receiver to process. The congestion control capability of TCP helps in avoiding network congestion and congestion collapse which can lead to degradation of network performance. TCP is described in RFC 793 [9].

- **UDP :** Unlike TCP, which requires carrying out an initial setup procedure, UDP is a connectionless protocol. UDP is useful for time-sensitive applications that have very small data units to exchange and do not want the overhead of connection setup. UDP is a transaction oriented and stateless protocol. UDP does not provide guaranteed delivery, ordering of messages and duplicate elimination. Higher levels of protocols can ensure reliable delivery or ensuring connections created are reliable. UDP is described in RFC 768 [10].

**Application Layer**

Application layer protocols define how the applications interface with the lower layer protocols to send the data over the network. The application data, typically in files, is encoded by the application layer protocol and encapsulated in the transport layer protocol which provides connection or transaction oriented communication over the network. Port numbers are used for application addressing (for example port 80 for HTTP, port 22 for SSH, etc.). Application layer protocols enable process-to-process connections using ports.

- **HTTP :** Hypertext Transfer Protocol (HTTP) is the application layer protocol that forms the foundation of the World Wide Web (WWW). HTTP includes commands such as GET, PUT, POST, DELETE, HEAD, TRACE, OPTIONS, etc. The protocol follows a request-response model where a client sends requests to a server using the HTTP commands. HTTP is a stateless protocol and each HTTP request is independent of the other requests. An HTTP client can be a browser or an application running on the client (e.g., an application running on an IoT device, a mobile application or other software). HTTP protocol uses Universal Resource Identifiers (URIs) to identify HTTP resources. HTTP is described in RFC 2616 [11].

- **CoAP :** Constrained Application Protocol (CoAP) is an application layer protocol for machine-to-machine (M2M) applications, meant for constrained environments with constrained devices and constrained networks. Like HTTP, CoAP is a web transfer protocol and uses a request-response model, however it runs on top of UDP instead of TCP. CoAP uses a client-server architecture where clients communicate with servers using connectionless datagrams. CoAP is designed to easily interface with HTTP. Like HTTP, CoAP supports methods such as GET, PUT, POST, and DELETE. CoAP draft specifications are available on IEFT Constrained environments (CoRE) Working Group website [12].

- **WebSocket :** WebSocket protocol allows full-duplex communication over a single socket connection for sending messages between client and server. WebSocket is based on TCP and allows streams of messages to be sent back and forth between the client and server while keeping the TCP connection open. The client can be a browser, a mobile application or an IoT device. WebSocket is described in RFC 6455 [13].

- **MQTT :** Message Queue Telemetry Transport (MQTT) is a light-weight messaging protocol based on the publish-subscribe model. MQTT uses a client-server architecture where the client (such as an IoT device) connects to the server (also called MQTT Broker) and publishes messages to topics on the server. The broker forwards the messages to the clients subscribed to topics. MQTT is well suited for constrained environments where the devices have limited processing and memory resources and the network bandwidth is low. MQTT specifications are available on IBM developerWorks [14].

- **XMPP :** Extensible Messaging and Presence Protocol (XMPP) is a protocol for real-time communication and streaming XML data between network entities. XMPP powers wide range of applications including messaging, presence, data syndication, gaming, multi-party chat and voice/video calls. XMPP allows sending small chunks of XML data from one network entity to another in near real-time. XMPP is a decentralized protocol and uses a client-server architecture. XMPP supports both client-to-server and server-to-server communication paths. In the context of IoT, XMPP allows real-time communication between IoT devices. XMPP is described in RFC 6120 [15].

- **DDS :** Data Distribution Service (DDS) is a data-centric middleware standard for device-to-device or machine-to-machine communication. DDS uses a publish-subscribe model where publishers (e.g. devices that generate data) create topics to which subscribers (e.g., devices that want to consume data) can subscribe. Publisher is an object responsible for data distribution and the subscriber is responsible for receiving published data. DDS provides quality-of-service (QoS) control and configurable reliability. DDS is described in Object Management Group (OMG) DDS specification [16].

- **AMQP :** Advanced Message Queuing Protocol (AMQP) is an open application layer protocol for business messaging. AMQP supports both point-to-point and publisher/subscriber models, routing and queuing. AMQP brokers receive messages from publishers (e.g., devices or applications that generate data) and route them over connections to consumers (applications that process data). Publishers publish the messages to exchanges which then distribute message copies to queues. Messages are either delivered by the broker to the consumers which have subscribed to the queues or the consumers can pull the messages from the queues. AMQP specification is available on the AMQP working group website [17].

## 1.3 Logical Design of IoT

Logical design of an IoT system refers to an abstract representation of the entities and processes without going into the low-level specifics of the implementation. In this section we describe the functional blocks of an IoT system and the communication APIs that are used for the examples in this book. The steps in logical design are described in additional detail in Chapter-5.

### 1.3.1 IoT Functional Blocks

An IoT system comprises of a number of functional blocks that provide the system the capabilities for identification, sensing, actuation, communication, and management as shown in Figure 1.6. These functional blocks are described as follows:

- **Device :** An IoT system comprises of devices that provide sensing, actuation, monitoring and control functions. You learned about IoT devices in section 1.2.
- **Communication :** The communication block handles the communication for the IoT system. You learned about various protocols used for communication by IoT systems in section 1.2.
- **Services :** An IoT system uses various types of IoT services such as services for device monitoring, device control services, data publishing services and services for device discovery.
- **Management :** Management functional block provides various functions to govern the IoT system.
- **Security** Security functional block secures the IoT system and by providing functions such as authentication, authorization, message and content integrity, and data security.
- **Application :** IoT applications provide an interface that the users can use to control and monitor various aspects of the IoT system. Applications also allow users to view the system status and view or analyze the processed data.

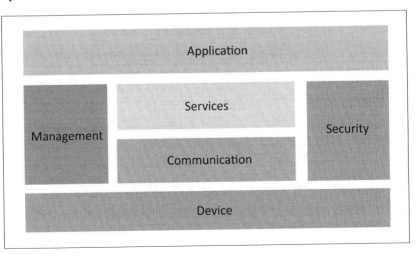

Figure 1.6: Functional Blocks of IoT

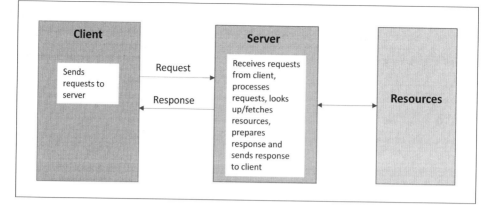

Figure 1.7: Request-Response communication model

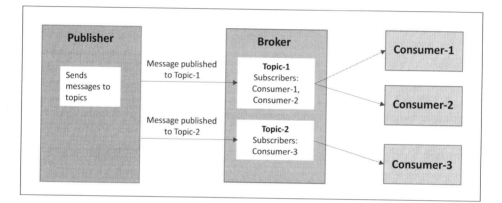

Figure 1.8: Publish-Subscribe communication model

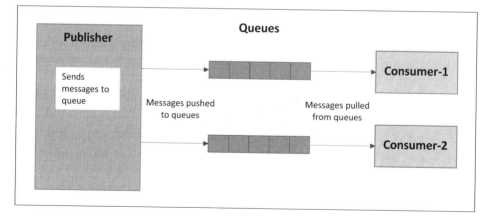

Figure 1.9: Push-Pull communication model

## 1.3.2  IoT Communication Models

- **Request-Response :** Request-Response is a communication model in which the client sends requests to the server and the server responds to the requests. When the server receives a request, it decides how to respond, fetches the data, retrieves

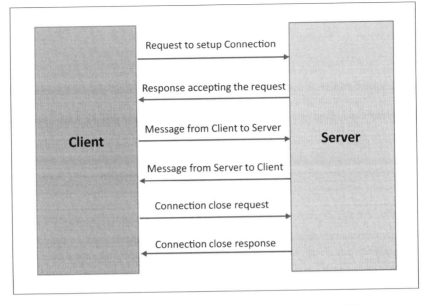

Figure 1.10: Exclusive Pair communication model

resource representations, prepares the response, and then sends the response to the client. Request-Response model is a stateless communication model and each request-response pair is independent of others. Figure 1.7 shows the client-server interactions in the request-response model.

- **Publish-Subscribe :** Publish-Subscribe is a communication model that involves publishers, brokers and consumers. Publishers are the source of data. Publishers send the data to the topics which are managed by the broker. Publishers are not aware of the consumers. Consumers subscribe to the topics which are managed by the broker. When the broker receives data for a topic from the publisher, it sends the data to all the subscribed consumers. Figure 1.8 shows the publisher-broker-consumer interactions in the publish-subscribe model.

- **Push-Pull :** Push-Pull is a communication model in which the data producers push the data to queues and the consumers pull the data from the queues. Producers do not need to be aware of the consumers. Queues help in decoupling the messaging between the producers and consumers. Queues also act as a buffer which helps in situations when there is a mismatch between the rate at which the producers push data and the rate rate at which the consumers pull data. Figure 1.9 shows the publisher-queue-consumer interactions in the push-pull model.

- **Exclusive Pair :** Exclusive Pair is a bi-directional, fully duplex communication model that uses a persistent connection between the client and server. Once the connection is setup it remains open until the client sends a request to close the connection. Client and server can send messages to each other after connection setup. Exclusive pair is a stateful communication model and the server is aware of all the open connections. Figure 1.10 shows the client-server interactions in the exclusive pair model.

### 1.3.3 IoT Communication APIs

In the previous section you learned about various communication models. In this section you will learn about two specific communication APIs which are used in the examples in this book.

#### REST-based Communication APIs

Representational State Transfer (REST) [88] is a set of architectural principles by which you can design web services and web APIs that focus on a system's resources and how resource states are addressed and transferred. REST APIs follow the request-response communication model described in previous section. The REST architectural constraints apply to the components, connectors, and data elements, within a distributed hypermedia system. The REST architectural constraints are as follows:

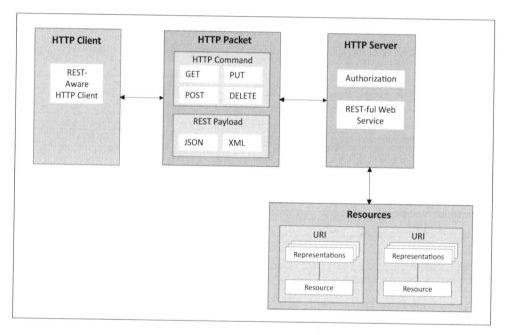

Figure 1.11: Communication with REST APIs

- **Client-Server**: The principle behind the client-server constraint is the separation of concerns. For example, clients should not be concerned with the storage of data which is a concern of the server. Similarly, the server should not be concerned about the user interface, which is a concern of the client. Separation allows client and server to be independently developed and updated.
- **Stateless**: Each request from client to server must contain all the information necessary to understand the request, and cannot take advantage of any stored context on the server. The session state is kept entirely on the client.
- **Cache-able**: Cache constraint requires that the data within a response to a request be implicitly or explicitly labeled as cache-able or non-cache-able. If a response is cache-able, then a client cache is given the right to reuse that response data for later, equivalent requests. Caching can partially or completely eliminate some interactions and improve efficiency and scalability.

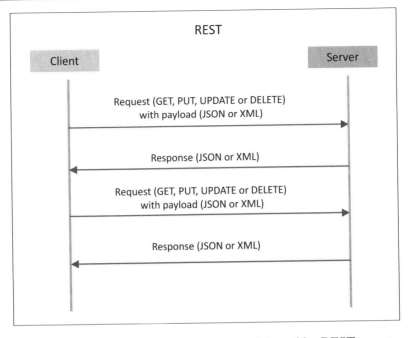

Figure 1.12: Request-response model used by REST

- **Layered System**: Layered system constraint, constrains the behavior of components such that each component cannot see beyond the immediate layer with which they are interacting. For example, a client cannot tell whether it is connected directly to the end server, or to an intermediary along the way. System scalability can be improved by allowing intermediaries to respond to requests instead of the end server, without the client having to do anything different.
- **Uniform Interface**: Uniform Interface constraint requires that the method of communication between a client and a server must be uniform. Resources are identified in the requests (by URIs in web based systems) and are themselves separate from the representations of the resources that are returned to the client. When a client holds a representation of a resource it has all the information required to update or delete the resource (provided the client has required permissions). Each message includes enough information to describe how to process the message.
- **Code on demand**: Servers can provide executable code or scripts for clients to execute in their context. This constraint is the only one that is optional.

A RESTful web service is a "web API" implemented using HTTP and REST principles. Figure 1.11 shows the communication between client and server using REST APIs. Figure 1.12 shows the interactions in the request-response model used by REST. RESTful web service is a collection of resources which are represented by URIs. RESTful web API has a base URI (e.g. http://example.com/api/tasks/). The clients send requests to these URIs using the methods defined by the HTTP protocol (e.g., GET, PUT, POST, or DELETE), as shown in Table 1.1. A RESTful web service can support various Internet media types (JSON being the most popular media type for RESTful web services). IP for Smart Objects Alliance (IPSO Alliance) has published an Application Framework that defines a RESTful design for use in

| HTTP Method | Resource Type | Action | Example |
|---|---|---|---|
| GET | Collection URI | List all the resources in a collection | http://example.com/api/tasks/ (list all tasks) |
| GET | Element URI | Get information about a resource | http://example.com/api/tasks/1/ (get information on task-1) |
| POST | Collection URI | Create a new resource | http://example.com/api/tasks/ (create a new task from data provided in the request) |
| POST | Element URI | Generally not used | |
| PUT | Collection URI | Replace the entire collection with another collection | http://example.com/api/tasks/ (replace entire collection with data provided in the request) |
| PUT | Element URI | Update a resource | http://example.com/api/tasks/1/ (update task-1 with data provided in the request) |
| DELETE | Collection URI | Delete the entire collection | http://example.com/api/tasks/ (delete all tasks) |
| DELETE | Element URI | Delete a resource | http://example.com/api/tasks/1/ (delete task-1) |

Table 1.1: HTTP request methods and actions

IP smart object systems [18].

**WebSocket-based Communication APIs**

WebSocket APIs allow bi-directional, full duplex communication between clients and servers. WebSocket APIs follow the exclusive pair communication model described in previous section and as shown in Figure 1.13. Unlike request-response APIs such as REST, the WebSocket APIs allow full duplex communication and do not require a new connection to be setup for each message to be sent. WebSocket communication begins with a connection setup request sent by the client to the server. This request (called a WebSocket handshake) is sent over HTTP and the server interprets it as an upgrade request. If the server supports WebSocket protocol, the server responds to the WebSocket handshake response. After the connection is setup, the client and server can send data/messages to each other in full-duplex mode. WebSocket APIs reduce the network traffic and latency as there is no overhead for connection setup and termination requests for each message. WebSocket is suitable for IoT applications that have low latency or high throughput requirements.

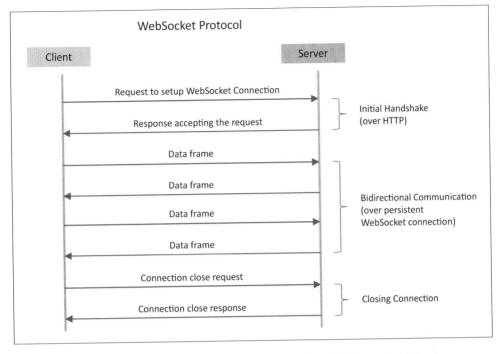

Figure 1.13: Exclusive pair model used by WebSocket APIs

## 1.4  IoT Enabling Technologies

IoT is enabled by several technologies including wireless sensor networks, cloud computing, big data analytics, embedded systems, security protocols and architectures, communication protocols, web services, mobile Internet, and semantic search engines. This section provides an overview of some of these technologies which play a key-role in IoT.

### 1.4.1  Wireless Sensor Networks

A Wireless Sensor Network (WSN) comprises of distributed devices with sensors which are used to monitor the environmental and physical conditions. A WSN consist of a number of end-nodes and routers and a coordinator. End nodes have several sensors attached to them. End nodes can also act as routers. Routers are responsible for routing the data packets from end-nodes to the coordinator. The coordinator collects the data from all the nodes. Coordinator also acts as a gateway that connects the WSN to the Internet. Some examples of WSNs used in IoT systems are described as follows:

- Weather monitoring systems use WSNs in which the nodes collect temperature, humidity and other data, which is aggregated and analyzed.
- Indoor air quality monitoring systems use WSNs to collect data on the indoor air quality and concentration of various gases.
- Soil moisture monitoring systems use WSNs to monitor soil moisture at various locations.
- Surveillance systems use WSNs for collecting surveillance data (such as motion detection data)
- Smart grids use WSNs for monitoring the grid at various points.

- Structural health monitoring systems use WSNs to monitor the health of structures (buildings, bridges) by collecting vibration data from sensor nodes deployed at various points in the structure.

WSNs are enabled by wireless communication protocols such as IEEE 802.15.4. ZigBee is one of the most popular wireless technologies used by WSNs. ZigBee specifications are based on IEEE 802.15.4. ZigBee operates at 2.4 GHz frequency and offers data rates upto 250 KB/s and range from 10 to 100 meters depending on the power output and environmental conditions. The power of WSNs lies in their ability to deploy large number of low-cost and low-power sensing nodes for continuous monitoring of environmental and physical conditions. WSNs are self-organizing networks. Since WSNs have large number of nodes, manual configuration for each node is not possible. The self-organizing capability of WSN makes the network robust. In the event of failure of some nodes or addition of new nodes to the network, the network can reconfigure itself.

## 1.4.2  Cloud Computing

Cloud computing is a transformative computing paradigm that involves delivering applications and services over the Internet. Cloud computing involves provisioning of computing, networking and storage resources on demand and providing these resources as metered services to the users, in a "pay as you go" model. Cloud computing resources can be provisioned on-demand by the users, without requiring interactions with the cloud service provider. The process of provisioning resources is automated. Cloud computing resources can be accessed over the network using standard access mechanisms that provide platform-independent access through the use of heterogeneous client platforms such as workstations, laptops, tablets and smart-phones. The computing and storage resources provided by cloud service providers are pooled to serve multiple users using multi-tenancy. Multi-tenant aspects of the cloud allow multiple users to be served by the same physical hardware. Users are assigned virtual resources that run on top of the physical resources.

Cloud computing services are offered to users in different forms (see the authors' companion book on Cloud Computing, for instance):

- **Infrastructure-as-a-Service (IaaS) :** IaaS provides the users the ability to provision computing and storage resources. These resources are provided to the users as virtual machine instances and virtual storage. Users can start, stop, configure and manage the virtual machine instances and virtual storage. Users can deploy operating systems and applications of their choice on the virtual resources provisioned in the cloud. The cloud service provider manages the underlying infrastructure. Virtual resources provisioned by the users are billed based on a pay-per-use paradigm.
- **Platform-as-a-Service (PaaS) :** PaaS provides the users the ability to develop and deploy application in the cloud using the development tools, application programming interfaces (APIs), software libraries and services provided by the cloud service provider. The cloud service provider manages the underlying cloud infrastructure including servers, network, operating systems and storage. The users, themselves, are responsible for developing, deploying, configuring and managing applications on the cloud infrastructure.
- **Software-as-a-Service (SaaS) :** SaaS provides the users a complete software application or the user interface to the application itself. The cloud service provider manages

the underlying cloud infrastructure including servers, network, operating systems, storage and application software, and the user is unaware of the underlying architecture of the cloud. Applications are provided to the user through a thin client interface (e.g., a browser). SaaS applications are platform independent and can be accessed from various client devices such as workstations, laptop, tablets and smart-phones, running different operating systems. Since the cloud service provider manages both the application and data, the users are able to access the applications from anywhere.

### 1.4.3  Big Data Analytics

Big data is defined as collections of data sets whose volume, velocity (in terms of its temporal variation), or variety, is so large that it is difficult to store, manage, process and analyze the data using traditional databases and data processing tools. Big data analytics involves several steps starting from data cleansing, data munging (or wrangling), data processing and visualization. Some examples of big data generated by IoT systems are described as follows:

- Sensor data generated by IoT systems such as weather monitoring stations.
- Machine sensor data collected from sensors embedded in industrial and energy systems for monitoring their health and detecting failures.
- Health and fitness data generated by IoT devices such as wearable fitness bands.
- Data generated by IoT systems for location and tracking of vehicles.
- Data generated by retail inventory monitoring systems.

The underlying characteristics of big data include:

- **Volume:** Though there is no fixed threshold for the volume of data to be considered as big data, however, typically, the term big data is used for massive scale data that is difficult to store, manage and process using traditional databases and data processing architectures. The volumes of data generated by modern IT, industrial, and health-care systems, for example, is growing exponentially driven by the lowering costs of data storage and processing architectures and the need to extract valuable insights from the data to improve business processes, efficiency and service to consumers.
- **Velocity:**  Velocity is another important characteristic of big data and the primary reason for exponential growth of data. Velocity of data refers to how fast the data is generated and how frequently it varies. Modern IT, industrial and other systems are generating data at increasingly higher speeds.
- **Variety:**  Variety refers to the forms of the data. Big data comes in different forms such as structured or unstructured data, including text data, image, audio, video and sensor data.

### 1.4.4  Communication Protocols

Communication protocols form the backbone of IoT systems and enable network connectivity and coupling to applications. Communication protocols allow devices to exchange data over the network. In section 1.2.2 you learned about various link, network, transport and application layer protocols. These protocols define the data exchange formats, data encoding, addressing schemes for devices and routing of packets from source to destination. Other functions of the protocols include sequence control (that helps in ordering packets determining lost packets), flow control (that helps in controlling the rate at which the sender is sending the data so that the receiver or the network is not overwhelmed) and retransmission of lost packets.

### 1.4.5  Embedded Systems

An Embedded System is a computer system that has computer hardware and software embedded to perform specific tasks. In contrast to general purpose computers or personal computers (PCs) which can perform various types of tasks, embedded systems are designed to perform a specific set of tasks.  Key components of an embedded system include, microprocessor or microcontroller, memory (RAM, ROM, cache), networking units (Ethernet, WiFi adapters), input/output units (display, keyboard, etc.)  and storage (such as flash memory).  Some embedded systems have specialized processors such as digital signal processors (DSPs), graphics processors and application specific processors.  Embedded systems run embedded operating systems such as real-time operating systems (RTOS). Embedded systems range from low-cost miniaturized devices such as digital watches to devices such as digital cameras, point of sale terminals, vending machines, appliances (such as washing machines), etc. In the next chapter we describe how such devices form an integral part of IoT systems.

## 1.5   IoT Levels & Deployment Templates

In this section we define various levels of IoT systems with increasing completely. An IoT system comprises of the following components:

- **Device:** An IoT device allows identification, remote sensing, actuating and remote monitoring capabilities. You learned about various examples of IoT devices in section 1.2.1.
- **Resource:**  Resources are software components on the IoT device for accessing, processing, and storing sensor information, or controlling actuators connected to the device.  Resources also include the software components that enable network access for the device.
- **Controller Service:**  Controller service is a native service that runs on the device and interacts with the web services. Controller service sends data from the device to the web service and receives commands from the application (via web services) for controlling the device.
- **Database:** Database can be either local or in the cloud and stores the data generated by the IoT device.
- **Web Service:**  Web services serve as a link between the IoT device, application, database and analysis components. Web service can be either implemented using HTTP and REST principles (REST service) or using WebSocket protocol (WebSocket service). A comparison of REST and WebSocket is provided below:
    - **Stateless/Stateful:** REST services are stateless in nature. Each request contains all the information needed to process it. Requests are independent of each other. WebSocket on the other hand is stateful in nature where the server maintains the state and is aware of all the open connections.
    - **Uni-directional/Bi-directional:**  REST services operate over HTTP and are uni-directional. Request is always sent by a client and the server responds to the

requests. On the other hand, WebSocket is a bi-directional protocol and allows both client and server to send messages to each other.

- **Request-Response/Full Duplex:** REST services follow a request-response communication model where the client sends requests and the server responds to the requests. WebSocket on the other hand allow full-duplex communication between the client and server, i.e., both client and server can send messages to each other independently.

- **TCP Connections:** For REST services, each HTTP request involves setting up a new TCP connection. WebSocket on the other hand involves a single TCP connection over which the client and server communicate in a full-duplex mode.

- **Header Overhead:** REST services operate over HTTP, and each request is independent of others. Thus each request carries HTTP headers which is an overhead. Due the overhead of HTTP headers, REST is not suitable for real-time applications. WebSocket on the other hand does not involve overhead of headers. After the initial handshake (that happens over HTTP), the client and server exchange messages with minimal frame information. Thus WebSocket is suitable for real-time applications.

- **Scalability:** Scalability is easier in the case of REST services as requests are independent and no state information needs to be maintained by the server. Thus both horizontal (scaling-out) and vertical scaling (scaling-up) solutions are possible for REST services. For WebSockets, horizontal scaling can be cumbersome due to the stateful nature of the communication. Since the server maintains the state of a connection, vertical scaling is easier for WebSockets than horizontal scaling.

- **Analysis Component:** The Analysis Component is responsible for analyzing the IoT data and generate results in a form which are easy for the user to understand. Analysis of IoT data can be performed either locally or in the cloud. Analyzed results are stored in the local or cloud databases.

- **Application:** IoT applications provide an interface that the users can use to control and monitor various aspects of the IoT system. Applications also allow users to view the system status and view the processed data.

### 1.5.1 IoT Level-1

A level-1 IoT system has a single node/device that performs sensing and/or actuation, stores data, performs analysis and hosts the application as shown in Figure 1.14. Level-1 IoT systems are suitable for modeling low-cost and low-complexity solutions where the data involved is not big and the analysis requirements are not computationally intensive.

Let us now consider an example of a level-1 IoT system for home automation. The system consists of a single node that allows controlling the lights and appliances in a home remotely. The device used in this system interfaces with the lights and appliances using electronic relay switches. The status information of each light or appliance is maintained in a local database. REST services deployed locally allow retrieving and updating the state of each light or appliance in the status database. The controller service continuously monitors the state of each light or appliance (by retrieving state from the database) and triggers the relay switches accordingly. The application which is deployed locally has a user interface for controlling the lights or appliances. Since the device is connected to the Internet, the application can be accessed remotely as well.

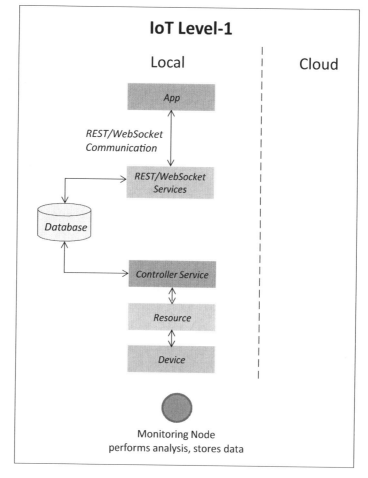

Figure 1.14: IoT Level-1

## 1.5.2   IoT Level-2

A level-2 IoT system has a single node that performs sensing and/or actuation and local analysis as shown in Figure 1.15. Data is stored in the cloud and application is usually cloud-based. Level-2 IoT systems are suitable for solutions where the data involved is big, however, the primary analysis requirement is not computationally intensive and can be done locally itself.

Let us consider an example of a level-2 IoT system for smart irrigation. The system consists of a single node that monitors the soil moisture level and controls the irrigation system. The device used in this system collects soil moisture data from sensors. The controller service continuously monitors the moisture levels. If the moisture level drops below a threshold, the irrigation system is turned on. For controlling the irrigation system actuators such as solenoid valves can be used. The controller also sends the moisture data to the computing cloud. A cloud-based REST web service is used for storing and retrieving moisture data which is stored in the cloud database. A cloud-based application is used for visualizing the moisture levels over a period of time, which can help in making decisions about irrigation schedules.

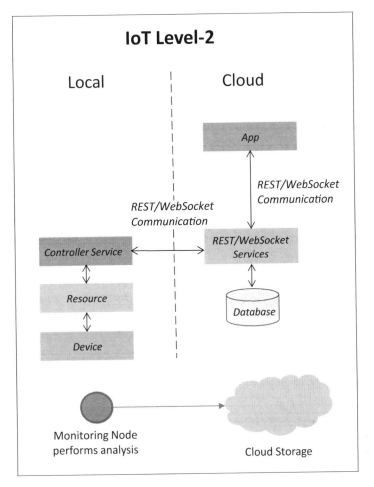

Figure 1.15: IoT Level-2

### 1.5.3  IoT Level-3

A level-3 IoT system has a single node. Data is stored and analyzed in the cloud and application is cloud-based as shown in Figure 1.16. Level-3 IoT systems are suitable for solutions where the data involved is big and the analysis requirements are computationally intensive.

Let us consider an example of a level-2 IoT system for tracking package handling. The system consists of a single node (for a package) that monitors the vibration levels for a package being shipped. The device in this system uses accelerometer and gyroscope sensors for monitoring vibration levels. The controller service sends the sensor data to the cloud in real-time using a WebSocket service. The data is stored in the cloud and also visualized using a cloud-based application. The analysis components in the cloud can trigger alerts if the vibration levels become greater than a threshold. The benefit of using WebSocket service instead of REST service in this example is that, the sensor data can be sent in real time to the cloud. Moreover, cloud based applications can subscribe to the sensor data feeds for viewing the real-time data.

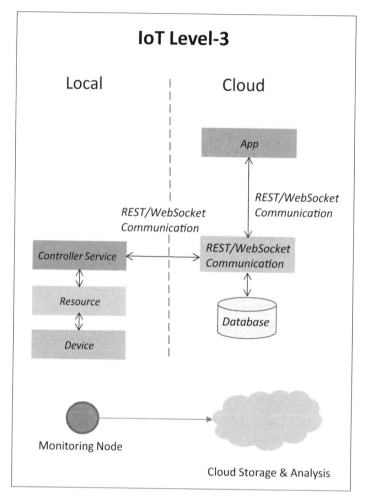

Figure 1.16: IoT Level-3

### 1.5.4   IoT Level-4

A level-4 IoT system has multiple nodes that perform local analysis. Data is stored in the cloud and application is cloud-based as shown in Figure 1.17. Level-4 contains local and cloud-based observer nodes which can subscribe to and receive information collected in the cloud from IoT devices. Observer nodes can process information and use it for various applications, however, observer nodes do not perform any control functions. Level-4 IoT systems are suitable for solutions where multiple nodes are required, the data involved is big and the analysis requirements are computationally intensive.

Let us consider an example of a level-4 IoT system for noise monitoring. The system consists of multiple nodes placed in different locations for monitoring noise levels in an area. The nodes in this example are equipped with sound sensors. Nodes are independent of each other. Each node runs its own controller service that sends the data to the cloud. The data is stored in a cloud database. The analysis of data collected from a number of nodes is done in the cloud. A cloud-based application is used for visualizing the aggregated data.

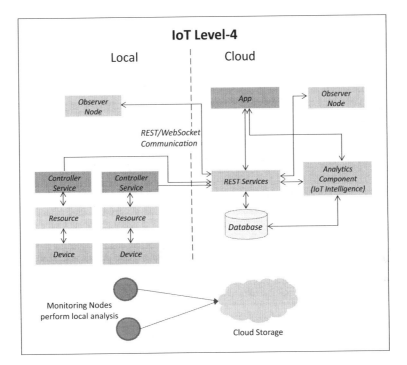

Figure 1.17: IoT Level-4

## 1.5.5   IoT Level-5

A level-5 IoT system has multiple end nodes and one coordinator node as shown in Figure 1.18. The end nodes that perform sensing and/or actuation. Coordinator node collects data from the end nodes and sends to the cloud. Data is stored and analyzed in the cloud and application is cloud-based. Level-5 IoT systems are suitable for solutions based on wireless sensor networks, in which the data involved is big and the analysis requirements are computationally intensive.

Let us consider an example of a level-5 IoT system for forest fire detection. The system consists of multiple nodes placed in different locations for monitoring temperature, humidity and carbon dioxide ($CO_2$) levels in a forest. The end nodes in this example are equipped with various sensors (such as temperature, humidity and $CO_2$). The coordinator node collects the data from the end nodes and acts as a gateway that provides Internet connectivity to the IoT system. The controller service on the coordinator device sends the collected data to the cloud. The data is stored in a cloud database. The analysis of data is done in the computing cloud to aggregate the data and make predictions. A cloud-based application is used for visualizing the data.

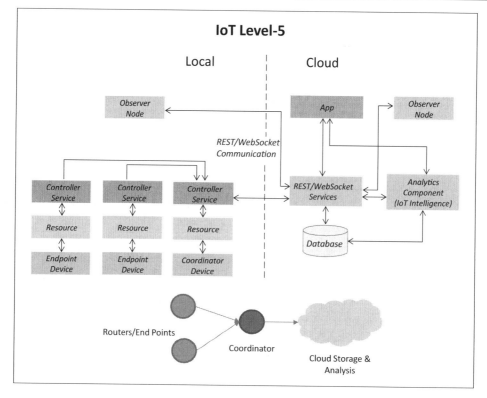

Figure 1.18: IoT Level-5

### 1.5.6   IoT Level-6

A level-6 IoT system has multiple independent end nodes that perform sensing and/or actuation and send data to the cloud. Data is stored in the cloud and application is cloud-based as shown in Figure 1.19. The analytics component analyzes the data and stores the results in the cloud database. The results are visualized with the cloud-based application. The centralized controller is aware of the status of all the end nodes and sends control commands to the nodes.

Let us consider an example of a level-6 IoT system for weather monitoring. The system consists of multiple nodes placed in different locations for monitoring temperature, humidity and pressure in an area. The end nodes are equipped with various sensors (such as temperature, pressure and humidity). The end nodes send the data to the cloud in real-time using a WebSocket service. The data is stored in a cloud database. The analysis of data is done in the cloud to aggregate the data and make predictions. A cloud-based application is used for visualizing the data.

### Summary

Internet of Things (IoT) refers to physical and virtual objects that have unique identities and are connected to the Internet. This allows the development of intelligent applications that make energy, logistics, industrial control, retail, agriculture and many other domains of human endeavour "smarter". IoT allows different types of devices, appliances, users and

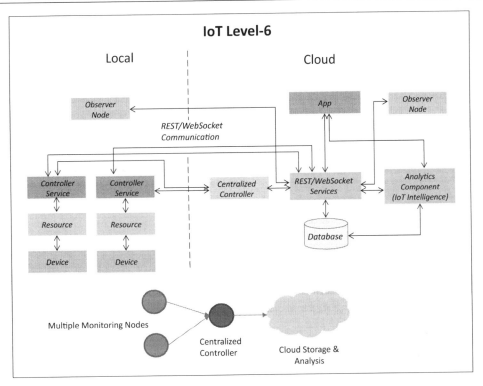

Figure 1.19: IoT Level-6

machines to communicate and exchange data. The applications of Internet of Things (IoT) span a wide range of domains including (but not limited to) homes, cities, environment, energy systems, retail, logistics, industry, agriculture and health. Things in IoT refers to IoT devices which have unique identities and allow remote sensing, actuating and remote monitoring capabilities. Almost all IoT devices generate data in some form or the other which when processed by data analytics systems leads to useful information to guide further actions. You learned about IoT protocols for link, network, transport and application layers. Link layer protocols determine how the data is physically sent over the network. The network/internet layers is responsible for sending of IP datagrams from the source network to the destination network. The transport layer protocols provides end-to-end message transfer capability independent of the underlying network. Application layer protocols define how the applications interface with the lower layer protocols to send the data over the network. You learned about functional blocks of an IoT system including device communication, services, management, security and application blocks. You learned about IoT communication models such as request-response, publish-subscribe, push-pull and exclusive pair. You learned about REST-based and WebSocket-based communication APIs. REST is a set of architectural principles by which you can design web services and web APIs that focus on a system's resources and how resource states are addressed and transferred. A RESTful web service is a web API implemented using HTTP and REST principles. WebSocket APIs allow bi-directional, full duplex communication between clients and servers. You learned about enabling technologies of IoT such as wireless sensor networks, cloud computing, big data analytics, communication protocols and embedded systems. Finally, you learned about IoT levels. A level-1 IoT system has a single node/device that performs sensing and/or actuation, stores data, performs analysis and hosts the application. A level-2 IoT system has a single node that performs sensing and/or actuation and local analysis. A level-3 IoT system has a single node. Data is stored and analyzed in the cloud and application is cloud-based. A level-4 IoT system has multiple nodes that perform local analysis. Data is stored in the cloud and application is cloud-based. A level-5 IoT system has multiple end nodes and one coordinator node. A level-6 IoT system has multiple independent end nodes that perform sensing and/or actuation and send data to the cloud.

## Review Questions

1. Describe an example of an IoT system in which information and knowledge are inferred from data.
2. Why do IoT systems have to be self-adapting and self-configuring?
3. What is the role of things and Internet in IoT?
4. What is the function of communication functional block in an IoT system?
5. Describe an example of IoT service that uses publish-subscribe communication model.
6. Describe an example of IoT service that uses WebSocket-based communication.
7. What are the architectural constraints of REST?
8. What is the role of a coordinator in wireless sensor network?
9. What is the role of a controller service in an IoT system?

# 2 - Domain Specific IoTs

This Chapter Covers

IoT Applicatins for:
- Home
- Cities
- Environment
- Energy Systems
- Retail
- Logistics
- Industry
- Agriculture
- Health & Lifestyle

## 2.1  Introduction

The Internet of Things (IoT) applications span a wide range of domains including (but not limited to) homes, cities, environment, energy systems, retail, logistics, industry, agriculture and health. This chapter provides an overview of various types of IoT applications for each of these domains. In the later chapters the reader is guided through detailed implementations of several of these applications.

## 2.2  Home Automation

### 2.2.1  Smart Lighting

Smart lighting for homes helps in saving energy by adapting the lighting to the ambient conditions and switching on/off or dimming the lights when needed. Key enabling technologies for smart lighting include solid state lighting (such as LED lights) and IP-enabled lights. For solid state lighting solutions both spectral and temporal characteristics can be configured to adapt illumination to various needs. Smart lighting solutions for home achieve energy savings by sensing the human movements and their environments and controlling the lights accordingly. Wireless-enabled and Internet connected lights can be controlled remotely from IoT applications such as a mobile or web application. Smart lights with sensors for occupancy, temperature, lux level, etc., can be configured to adapt the lighting (by changing the light intensity, color, etc.) based on the ambient conditions sensed, in order to provide a good ambiance. In [19] controllable LED lighting system is presented that is embedded with ambient intelligence gathered from a distributed smart wireless sensor network to optimize and control the lighting system to be more efficient and user-oriented. A solid state lighting model is described in  [20] and implemented on a wireless sensor network that provides services for sensing illumination changes and dynamically adjusting luminary brightness according to user preferences.  In chapter-9 we provide a case study on a smart lighting system.

### 2.2.2  Smart Appliances

Modern homes have a number of appliances such as TVs, refrigerators, music systems, washer/dryers, etc. Managing and controlling these appliances can be cumbersome, with each appliance having its own controls or remote controls. Smart appliances make the management easier and also provide status information to the users remotely. For example, smart washer/dryers that can be controlled remotely and notify when the washing/drying cycle is complete. Smart thermostats allow controlling the temperature remotely and can learn the user preferences [22]. Smart refrigerators can keep track of the items stored (using RFID tags) and send updates to the users when an item is low on stock. Smart TVs allows users to search and stream videos and movies from the Internet on a local storage drive, search TV channel schedules and fetch news, weather updates and other content from the Internet. OpenRemote [21] is an open source automation platform for homes and buildings. OpenRemote is platform agnostic and works with standard hardware. With OpenRemote, users can control various appliances using mobile or web applications. OpenRemote comprises of three components - a Controller that manages scheduling and runtime integration between devices, a Designer that allows you to create both configurations for the controller and create user interface designs and Control Panels that allow you to interact with devices and control them. An IoT-based appliance control system for smart homes is described in [23], that uses a smart central controller to set up a wireless sensor and actuator network and control modules for appliances.

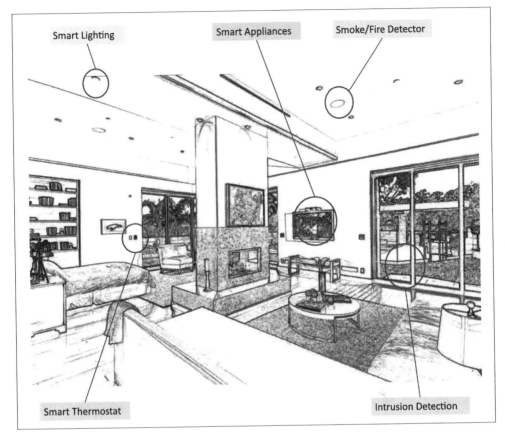

Figure 2.1: Applications of IoT for homes

### 2.2.3  Intrusion Detection

Home intrusion detection systems use security cameras and sensors (such as PIR sensors and door sensors) to detect intrusions and raise alerts. Alerts can be in the form of an SMS or an email sent to the user. Advanced systems can even send detailed alerts such as an image grab or a short video clip sent as an email attachment. A cloud controlled intrusion detection system is described in [24] that uses location-aware services, where the geo-location of each node of a home automation system is independently detected and stored in the cloud. In the event of intrusions, the cloud services alert the accurate neighbors (who are using the home automation system) or local police. In [25], an intrusion detection system based on UPnP technology is described. The system uses image processing to recognize the intrusion and extract the intrusion subject and generate Universal-Plug-and-Play (UPnP-based) instant messaging for alerts. In chapter-9 we provide a case study on an intrusion detection system.

### 2.2.4 Smoke/Gas Detectors

Smoke detectors are installed in homes and buildings to detect smoke that is typically an early sign of fire. Smoke detectors use optical detection, ionization or air sampling techniques to detect smoke. Alerts raised by smoke detectors can be in the form of signals to a fire alarm system. Gas detectors can detect the presence of harmful gases such as carbon monoxide (CO), liquid petroleum gas (LPG), etc. A smart smoke/gas detector [22] can raise alerts in human voice describing where the problem is, send or an SMS or email to the user or the local fire safety department and provide visual feedback on its status (healthy, battery-low, etc.). In [26], the design of a system that detects gas leakage and smoke and gives visual level indication, is described.

## 2.3 Cities

### 2.3.1 Smart Parking

Finding a parking space during rush hours in crowded cities can be time consuming and frustrating. Furthermore, drivers blindly searching for parking spaces create additional traffic congestion. Smart parking make the search for parking space easier and convenient for drivers. Smart parking are powered by IoT systems that detect the number of empty parking slots and send the information over the Internet to smart parking application back-ends. These applications can be accessed by the drivers from smart-phones, tablets and in-car navigation systems. In smart parking, sensors are used for each parking slot, to detect whether the slot is empty or occupied. This information is aggregated by a local controller and then sent over the Internet to the database. In [29], Polycarpou *et. al.* describe latest trends in parking availability monitoring, parking reservation and dynamic pricing schemes. Design and implementation of a prototype smart parking system based on wireless sensor network technology with features like remote parking monitoring, automated guidance, and parking reservation mechanism is described in [30]. In chapter-9 we provide a case study on a smart parking system.

### 2.3.2 Smart Lighting

Smart lighting systems for roads, parks and buildings can help in saving energy. According to an IEA report [27], lighting is responsible for 19% of global electricity use and around 6% of global greenhouse gas emissions. Smart lighting allows lighting to be dynamically controlled and also adaptive to the ambient conditions. Smart lights connected to the Internet can be controlled remotely to configure lighting schedules and lighting intensity. Custom lighting configurations can be set for different situations such as a foggy day, a festival, etc. Smart lights equipped with sensors can communicate with other lights and exchange information on the sensed ambient conditions to adapt the lighting. Castro *et. al.* [28] describe the need for smart lighting system in smart cities, smart lighting features and how to develop interoperable smart lighting solutions.

### 2.3.3 Smart Roads

Smart roads equipped with sensors can provide information on driving conditions, travel time estimates and alerts in case of poor driving conditions, traffic congestions and accidents. Such

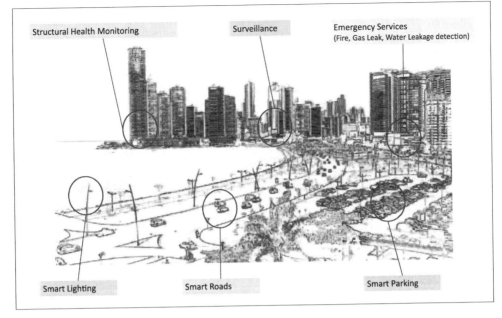

Figure 2.2: Applications of IoT for cities

information can help in making the roads safer and help in reducing traffic jams. Information sensed from the roads can be communicated via Internet to cloud-based applications and social media and disseminated to the drivers who subscribe to such applications. In [31], a distributed and autonomous system of sensor network nodes for improving driving safety on public roads in proposed. The system can provide the drivers and passengers with a consistent view of the road situation a few hundred meters ahead of them or a few dozen miles away, so that they can react to potential dangers early enough.

### 2.3.4 Structural Health Monitoring

Structural Health Monitoring systems use a network of sensors to monitor the vibration levels in the structures such as bridges and buildings. The data collected from these sensors is analyzed to assess the health of the structures. By analyzing the data it is possible to detect cracks and mechanical breakdowns, locate the damages to a structure and also calculate the remaining life of the structure. Using such systems, advance warnings can be given in the case of imminent failure of the structure. An environmental effect removal based structural health monitoring scheme in an IoT environment is proposed in [32]. Since structural health monitoring systems use large number of wireless sensor nodes which are powered by traditional batteries, researchers are exploring energy harvesting technologies to harvesting ambient energy, such as mechanical vibrations, sunlight, and wind [33, 34].

### 2.3.5 Surveillance

Surveillance of infrastructure, public transport and events in cities is required to ensure safety and security. City wide surveillance infrastructure comprising of large number of distributed and Internet connected video surveillance cameras can be created. The video feeds from surveillance cameras can be aggregated in cloud-based scalable storage solutions.

Cloud-based video analytics applications can be developed to search for patterns or specific events from the video feeds. In [35] a smart city surveillance system is described that leverages benefits of cloud data stores.

### 2.3.6  Emergency Response

IoT systems can be used for monitoring the critical infrastructure in cities such as buildings, gas and water pipelines, public transport and power substations. IoT systems for fire detection, gas and water leakage detection can help in generating alerts and minimizing their effects on the critical infrastructure. IoT systems for critical infrastructure monitoring enable aggregation and sharing of information collected from large number of sensors. Using cloud-based architectures, multi-modal information such as sensor data, audio, video feeds can be analyzed in near real-time to detect adverse events. Response to alerts generated by such systems can be in the form of alerts sent to the public, re-routing of traffic, evacuations of the affected areas, etc. In [36] Attwood *et. al.* describe critical infrastructure response framework for smart cities. A Traffic Management System for emergency services is described in [37]. The system adapts by dynamically adjusting traffic lights, changing related driving policies, recommending behavior change to drivers, and applying essential security controls. Such systems can reduce the latency of emergency services for vehicles such as ambulances and police cars while minimizing disruption of regular traffic.

## 2.4  Environment

### 2.4.1  Weather Monitoring

IoT-based weather monitoring systems can collect data from a number of sensor attached (such as temperature, humidity, pressure, etc.) and send the data to cloud-based applications and storage back-ends. The data collected in the cloud can then be analyzed and visualized by cloud-based applications. Weather alerts can be sent to the subscribed users from such applications. AirPi [38] is a weather and air quality monitoring kit capable of recording and uploading information about temperature, humidity, air pressure, light levels, UV levels, carbon monoxide, nitrogen dioxide and smoke level to the Internet. In [39], a pervasive weather monitoring system is described that is integrated with buses to measure weather variables like humidity, temperature and air quality during the bus path. In [40], a weather monitoring system based on wireless sensor networks is described. In chapter-9 we provide a case study on a weather monitoring system.

### 2.4.2  Air Pollution Monitoring

IoT based air pollution monitoring systems can monitor emission of harmful gases ($CO_2$, $CO$, $NO$, $NO_2$, etc.) by factories and automobiles using gaseous and meteorological sensors. The collected data can be analyzed to make informed decisions on pollutions control approaches. In [41], a real-time air quality monitoring system is presented that comprises of several distributed monitoring stations that communicate via wireless with a back-end server using machine-to-machine communication. In [42], an air pollution system is described that integrates a single-chip microcontroller, several air pollution sensors, GPRS-Modem, and a GPS module. In chapter-9 we provide a case study on an air pollution monitoring system.

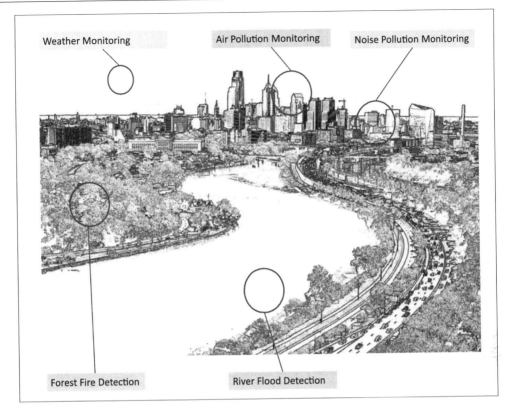

Figure 2.3: Applications of IoT for environment

### 2.4.3 Noise Pollution Monitoring

Due to growing urban development, noise levels in cities have increased and even become alarmingly high in some cities. Noise pollution can cause health hazards for humans due to sleep disruption and stress. Noise pollution monitoring can help in generating noise maps for cities. Urban noise maps can help the policy makers in urban planning and making policies to control noise levels near residential areas, schools and parks. IoT based noise pollution monitoring systems use a number of noise monitoring stations that are deployed at different places in a city. The data on noise levels from the stations is collected on servers or in the cloud. The collected data is then aggregated to generate noise maps. In [43], a noise mapping study for a city is presented which revealed that the city suffered from serious noise pollution. In [44], the design of smart phone application is described that allows the users to continuously measure noise levels and send to a central server where all generated information is aggregated and mapped to a meaningful noise visualization map.

### 2.4.4 Forest Fire Detection

Forest fires can cause damage to natural resources, property and human life. There can be different causes of forest fires including lightening, human negligence, volcanic eruptions and sparks from rock falls. Early detection of forest fires can help in minimizing the damage. IoT based forest fire detection systems use a number of monitoring nodes deployed at different locations in a forest. Each monitoring node collects measurements on ambient conditions including temperature, humidity, light levels, etc. A system for early detection of forest fires is described in [45] that provides early warning of a potential forest fire and estimates the scale and intensity of the fire if it materializes. In [46], a forest fire detection system based on wireless sensor networks in presented. The system uses multi-criteria detection which is implemented by the artificial neural network (ANN). The ANN fuses sensing data corresponding to multiple attributes of a forest fire (such as temperature, humidity, infrared and visible light) to detect forest fires.

### 2.4.5 River Floods Detection

River floods can cause extensive damage to the natural and human resources and human life. River floods occur due to continuous rainfall which cause the river levels to rise and flow rates to increase rapidly. Early warnings of floods can be given by monitoring the water level and flow rate. IoT based river flood monitoring system use a number of sensor nodes that monitor the water level (using ultrasonic sensors) and flow rate (using the flow velocity sensors). Data from a number of such sensor nodes is aggregated in a server or in the cloud. Monitoring applications raise alerts when rapid increase in water level and flow rate is detected. In [47], a river flood monitoring system in described that measures river and weather conditions through wireless sensor nodes equipped with different sensors. In [48], a motes-based sensor network for river flood monitoring is described. The system includes a water level monitoring module, network video recorder module, and data processing module that provides flood information in the form of raw data, predicted data, and video feed.

## 2.5 Energy

### 2.5.1 Smart Grids

Smart Grid is a data communications network integrated with the electrical grid that collects and analyzes data captured in near-real-time about power transmission, distribution, and consumption. Smart Grid technology provides predictive information and recommendations to utilities, their suppliers, and their customers on how best to manage power. Smart Grids collect data regarding electricity generation (centralized or distributed), consumption (instantaneous or predictive), storage (or conversion of energy into other forms), distribution and equipment health data. Smart grids use high-speed, fully integrated, two-way communication technologies for real-time information and power exchange. By using IoT based sensing and measurement technologies, the health of equipment and the integrity of the grid can be evaluated. Smart meters can capture almost real-time consumption, remotely control the consumption of electricity and remotely switch off supply when required. Power thefts can be prevented using smart metering. By analyzing the data on power generation, transmission and consumption smart girds can improve efficiency throughout the electric system. Storage collection and analysis of smarts grids data in the cloud can help in dynamic optimization of system operations, maintenance, and planning. Cloud-based monitoring of smart grids data can improve energy usage levels via energy feedback to users coupled with real-time pricing information. Real-time demand response and management strategies can be used for lowering peak demand and overall load via appliance control and energy storage mechanisms. Condition monitoring data collected from power generation and transmission systems can help in detecting faults and predicting outages. In [49], application of IoT in smart grid power transmission is described.

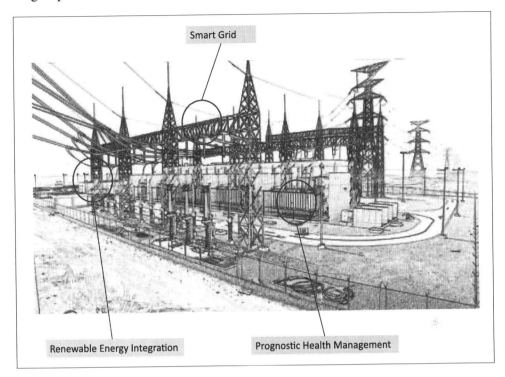

Figure 2.4: Applications of IoT for energy systems

## 2.5.2   Renewable Energy Systems

Due to the variability in the output from renewable energy sources (such as solar and wind), integrating them into the grid can cause grid stability and reliability problems. Variable output produces local voltage swings that can impact power quality. Existing grids were designed to handle power flows from centralized generation sources to the loads through transmission and distribution lines. When distributed renewable energy sources are integrated into the grid, they create power bi-directional power flows for which the grids were not originally designed. IoT based systems integrated with the transformers at the point of interconnection measure the electrical variables and how much power is fed into the grid. To ensure the grid stability, one solution is to simply cut off the overproduction. For wind energy systems, closed-loop controls can be used to regulate the voltage at point of interconnection which coordinate wind turbine outputs and provides reactive power support [52].

## 2.5.3   Prognostics

Energy systems (smart grids, power plants, wind turbine farms, for instance) have a large number of critical components that must function correctly so that the systems can perform their operations correctly. For example, a wind turbine has a number of critical components, e.g., bearings, turning gears, for instance, that must be monitored carefully as wear and tear in such critical components or sudden change in operating conditions of the machines can result in failures. In systems such as power grids, real-time information is collected using specialized electrical sensors called Phasor Measurement Units (PMU) at the substations. The information received from PMUs must be monitored in real-time for estimating the state of the system and for predicting failures. Energy systems have thousands of sensors that gather real-time maintenance data continuously for condition monitoring and failure prediction purposes. IoT based prognostic real-time health management systems can predict performance of machines or energy systems by analyzing the extent of deviation of a system from its normal operating profiles. Analyzing massive amounts of maintenance data collected from sensors in energy systems and equipment can provide predictions for the impending failures (potentially in real-time) so that their reliability and availability can be improved. Prognostic health management systems have been developed for different energy systems. OpenPDC [50] is a set of applications for processing of streaming time-series data collected from Phasor Measurement Units (PMUs) in real-time. A generic framework for storage, processing and analysis of massive machine maintenance data, collected from a large number of sensors embedded in industrial machines, in a cloud computing environment was proposed in [51].

## 2.6 Retail

### 2.6.1 Inventory Management

Inventory management for retail has become increasingly important in the recent years with the growing competition. While over-stocking of products can result in additional storage expenses and risk (in case of perishables), under-stocking can lead to loss of revenue. IoT systems using Radio Frequency Identification (RFID) tags can help in inventory management and maintaining the right inventory levels. RFID tags attached to the products allow them to be tracked in real-time so that the inventory levels can be determined accurately and products which are low on stock can be replenished. Tracking can be done using RFID readers attached to the retail store shelves or in the warehouse. IoT systems enable remote monitoring of inventory using the data collected by the RFID readers. In [53], an RFID data-based inventory management system for time-sensitive materials is described.

### 2.6.2 Smart Payments

Smart payment solutions such as contact-less payments powered by technologies such as Near field communication (NFC) and Bluetooh. Near field communication (NFC) is a set of standards for smart-phones and other devices to communicate with each other by bringing them into proximity or by touching them. Customers can store the credit card information in their NFC-enabled smart-phones and make payments by bringing the smart-phones near the point of sale terminals. NFC maybe used in combination with Bluetooh, where NFC (which offers low speeds) initiates initial pairing of devices to establish a Bluetooh connection while the actual data transfer takes place over Bluetooh. The applications of NFC for contact-less payments are described in [54, 55].

### 2.6.3 Smart Vending Machines

Smart vending machines connected to the Internet allow remote monitoring of inventory levels, elastic pricing of products, promotions, and contact-less payments using NFC. Smart-phone applications that communicate with smart vending machines allow user preferences to be remembered and learned with time. When a user moves from one vending machine to the other and pairs the smart-phone with the vending machine, a user specific interface is presented. Users can save their preferences and favorite products. Sensors in a smart vending machine monitor its operations and send the data to the cloud which can be used for predictive maintenance. Smart vending machines can communicate with other vending machines in their vicinity and share their inventory levels so that the customers can be routed to the nearest machine in case a product goes out of stock in a machine. For perishable items, the smart vending machines can reduce the price as the expiry date nears. New products can be recommended to the customers based on the purchase history and preferences.

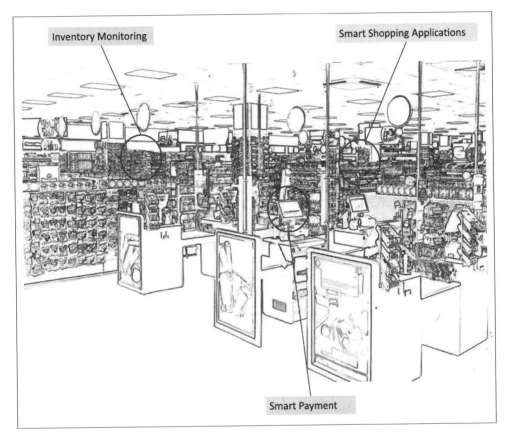

Figure 2.5: Applications of IoT for retail

## 2.7  Logistics

### 2.7.1  Route Generation & Scheduling

Modern transportation systems are driven by data collected from multiple sources which is processed to provide new services to the stakeholders. By collecting large amount of data from various sources and processing the data into useful information, data-driven transportation systems can provide new services such as advanced route guidance [62, 63], dynamic vehicle routing [64], anticipating customer demands for pickup and delivery problem, for instance. Route generation and scheduling systems can generate end-to-end routes using combination of route patterns and transportation modes and feasible schedules based on the availability of vehicles. As the transportation network grows in size and complexity, the number of possible route combinations increases exponentially. IoT based systems backed by the cloud can provide fast response to the route generation queries and can be scaled up to serve a large transportation network.

### 2.7.2 Fleet Tracking

Vehicle fleet tracking systems use GPS technology to track the locations of the vehicles in real-time. Cloud-based fleet tracking systems can be scaled up on demand to handle large number of vehicles. Alerts can be generated in case of deviations in planned routes. The vehicle locations and routes data can be aggregated and analyzed for detecting bottlenecks in the supply chain such as traffic congestions on routes, assignments and generation of alternative routes, and supply chain optimization. In [58], a fleet tracking system for commercial vehicles is described. The system can analyze messages sent from the vehicles to identify unexpected incidents and discrepancies between actual and planned data, so that remedial actions can be taken.

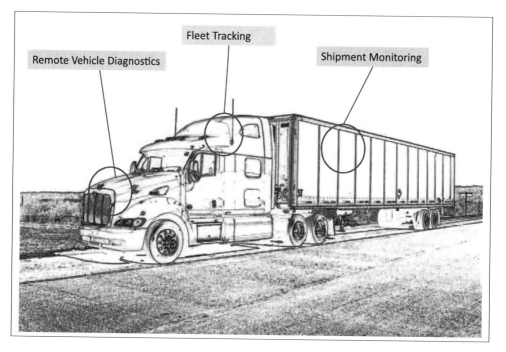

Figure 2.6: Applications of IoT for logistics

### 2.7.3 Shipment Monitoring

Shipment monitoring solutions for transportation systems allow monitoring the conditions inside containers. For example, containers carrying fresh food produce can be monitored to prevent spoilage of food. IoT based shipment monitoring systems use sensors such as temperature, pressure, humidity, for instance, to monitor the conditions inside the containers and send the data to the cloud, where it can be analyzed to detect food spoilage. The analysis and interpretation of data on the environmental conditions in the container and food truck positioning can enable more effective routing decisions in real time. Therefore, it is possible to take remedial measures such as - the food that has a limited time budget before it gets rotten can be re-routed to a closer destinations, alerts can be raised to the driver and the distributor about the transit conditions, such as container temperature exceeding the allowed limit, humidity levels going out of the allowed limit, for instance, and corrective actions can be taken before the food gets damaged. A cloud-based framework for real-time fresh food supply tracking and monitoring was proposed in [61]. For fragile products, vibration levels during shipments can be tracked using accelerometer and gyroscope sensors attached to IoT devices. In [59], a system for monitoring container integrity and operating conditions is described. The system monitors the vibration patterns of a container and its contents to reveal information related to its operating environment and integrity during transport, handling and storage.

### 2.7.4 Remote Vehicle Diagnostics

Remote vehicle diagnostic systems can detect faults in the vehicles or warn of impending faults. These diagnostic systems use on-board IoT devices for collecting data on vehicle operation (such as speed, engine RPM, coolent temperature, fault code number) and status of various vehicle sub-systems. Such data can be captured by integrating on-board diagnostic systems with IoT devices using protocols such as CAN bus. Modern commercial vehicles support on-board diagnostic (OBD) standards such as OBD-II. OBD systems provide real-time data on the status of vehicle sub-systems and diagnostic trouble codes which allow rapidly identifying the faults in the vehicle. IoT based vehicle diagnostic systems can send the vehicle data to centralized servers or the cloud where it can be analyzed to generate alerts and suggest remedial actions. In [60], a real-time online vehicle diagnostics and early fault estimation system is described. The system makes use of on-board vehicle diagnostics device and expert system to achieve real-time vehicle diagnostics and fault warning.

## 2.8 Agriculture

### 2.8.1 Smart Irrigation

Smart irrigation systems can improve crop yields while saving water. Smart irrigation systems use IoT devices with soil moisture sensors to determine the amount of moisture in the soil and release the flow of water through the irrigation pipes only when the moisture levels go below a predefined threshold. Smart irrigation systems also collect moisture level measurements on a server or in the cloud where the collected data can be analyzed to plan watering schedules. Cultivar's RainCloud [56] is a device for smart irrigation that uses water valves, soil sensors and a WiFi enabled programmable computer.

### 2.8.2 Green House Control

Green houses are structures with glass or plastic roofs that provide conducive environment for growth of plants. The climatological conditions inside a green house can be monitored and controlled to provide the best conditions for growth of plants. The temperature, humidity, soil moisture, light and carbon dioxide levels are monitored using sensors and the climatological conditions are controlled automatically using actuation devices (such as valves for releasing

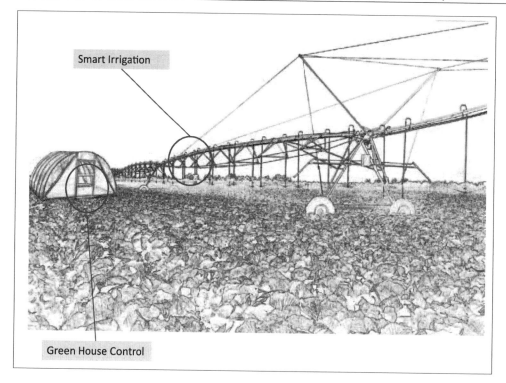

Figure 2.7: Applications of IoT for agriculture

water and switches for controlling fans). IoT systems play an important role in green house control and help in improving productivity. The data collected from various sensors is stored on centralized servers or in the cloud where analysis is performed to optimize the control strategies and also correlate the productivity with different control strategies. In [57], the design of a wireless sensing and control system for precision green house management is described. The system uses wireless sensor network to monitor and control the agricultural parameters like temperature and humidity in real time for better management and maintenance of agricultural production.

## 2.9   Industry

### 2.9.1   Machine Diagnosis & Prognosis

Machine prognosis refers to predicting the performance of a machine by analyzing the data on the current operating conditions and how much deviations exist from the normal operating conditions. Machine diagnosis refers to determining the cause of a machine fault. IoT plays a major role in both prognosis and diagnosis of industrial machines. Industrial machines have a large number of components that must function correctly for the machine to perform its operations. Sensors in machines can monitor the operating conditions such as (temperature and vibration levels). The sensor data measurements are done on timescales of few milliseconds to few seconds, which leads to generation of massive amount of data. IoT based systems integrated with cloud-based storage and analytics back-ends can help in storage, collection and analysis of such massive scale machine sensor data. A number of methods

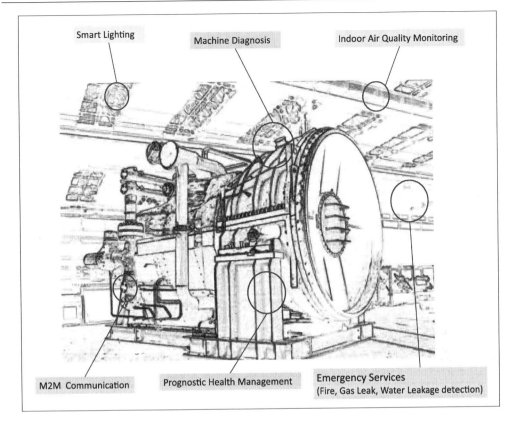

Figure 2.8: Applications of IoT for industry

have been proposed for reliability analysis and fault prediction in machines. Case-based reasoning (CBR) is a commonly used method that finds solutions to new problems based on past experience. This past experience is organized and represented as cases in a case-base. CBR is an effective technique for problem solving in the fields in which it is hard to establish a quantitative mathematical model, such as machine diagnosis and prognosis. Since for each machine, data from a very large number of sensors is collected, using such high dimensional data for creation of case library reduces the case retrieval efficiency. Therefore, data reduction and feature extraction methods are used to find the representative set of features which have the same classification ability as the complete of features. A CBR based machine fault diagnosis and prognosis approach is described in [51]. A survey on recent trends in machine diagnosis and prognosis algorithms is presented in [65].

### 2.9.2  Indoor Air Quality Monitoring

Monitoring indoor air quality in factories is important for health and safety of the workers. Harmful and toxic gases such as carbon monoxide ($CO$), nitrogen monoxide ($NO$), Nitrogen Dioxide ($NO_2$), etc., can cause serious health problems. IoT based gas monitoring systems can help in monitoring the indoor air quality using various gas sensors. The indoor air quality can vary for different locations. Wireless sensor networks based IoT devices can identify the hazardous zones, so that corrective measures can be taken to ensure proper ventilation. In [66] a hybrid sensor system for indoor air quality monitoring is presented, which contains both stationary sensors (for accurate readings and calibration) and mobile sensors (for coverage). In [67] a wireless solution for indoor air quality monitoring is described that measures the environmental parameters like temperature, humidity, gaseous pollutants, aerosol and particulate matter to determine the indoor air quality.

Figure 2.9: Applications of IoT for health

## 2.10   Health & Lifestyle

### 2.10.1   Health & Fitness Monitoring

Wearable IoT devices that allow non-invasive and continuous monitoring of physiological parameters can help in continuous health and fitness monitoring. These wearable devices may can be in various forms such as belts and wrist-bands. The wearable devices form a type of wireless sensor networks called body area networks in which the measurements from a number of wearable devices are continuous sent to a master node (such as a smart-phone) which then sends the data to a server or a cloud-based back-end for analysis and archiving. Health-care providers can analyze the collected health-care data to determine any health conditions or anomalies. Commonly uses body sensors include: body temperature, heart rate, pulse oximeter oxygen saturation (SPo2), blood pressure, electrocardiogram (ECG), movement (with accelerometers), and electroencephalogram (EEG). An ubiquitous mobility approach for body sensor networks in health-care is proposed in [72]. In [73], a wearable ubiquitous health-care monitoring system is presented that uses integrated electrocardiogram (ECG), accelerometer and oxygen saturation (SpO2) sensors. Fitbit wristband [74] is a wearable device that tracks steps, distance, and calories burned during the day and sleep quality at night.

### 2.10.2  Wearable Electronics

Wearable electronics such as wearable gadgets (smart watches, smart glasses, wristbands, etc.) and fashion electronics (with electronics integrated in clothing and accessories, (e.g., Google Glass or Moto 360 smart watch) provide various functions and features to assist us in our daily activities and making us lead healthy lifestyles. Smart watches that run mobile operating systems (such as Android) provide enhanced functionality beyond just timekeeping. With smart watches, the users can search the Internet, play audio/video files, make calls (with or without paired mobile phones), play games and use various kinds of mobile applications [68]. Smart glasses allows users to take photos and record videos, get map directions, check flight status, and search the Internet by using voice commands [69]. Smart shoes monitor the walking or running speeds and jumps with the help of embedded sensors and be paired with smart-phones to visualize the data [70]. Smart wristbands can track the daily exercise and calories burnt [71].

## Summary

In this chapters you learned about domain specific applications of Internet of Things (IoT). For homes, IoT has several applications such as smart lighting that adapt the lighting to suit the ambient conditions, smart appliances that can be remotely monitored and controlled, intrusion detection systems and smart smoke detectors. For cities, applications of IoT include smart parking systems that provide status updates on available slots, smart lighting that helps in saving energy, smart roads that provide information on driving conditions and structural health monitoring systems. For environment, you learned about IoT applications including weather monitoring, air and noise pollution, forest fire detection and river flood detection systems. You learned about IoT applications for energy systems including smart grids, grid integration of renewable energy sources and prognostic health management systems. For retail domain, you learned about IoT applications such as inventory management, smart payments and smart vending machines. For agriculture domain, you learned about smart irrigation systems that help in saving water while enhancing productivity and green house control systems. You learned about the industrial applications of IoT including machine diagnosis and prognosis systems that help in predicting faults and determining the cause of faults and indoor air quality systems. You learned about IoT applications for health and lifestyle such as health and fitness monitoring systems and wearable electronics. The applications generate much value to the end users and also provide new revenue opportunities to service and systems providers when integrated to rating, billing and financial applications.

## Review Questions

1. Determine the IoT-levels for designing home automation IoT systems including smart lighting and intrusion detection.
2. Determine the IoT-levels for designing structural health monitoring system.
3. Determine the various communication models that can be used for weather monitoring system. Which is a more appropriate model for this system. Describe the pros and cons.
4. Determine the types of data generated by a forest fire detection system? Describe alternative approaches for storing the data. What type of analysis is required for forest fire detection from the data collected?

# 3 - IoT and M2M

This Chapter Covers

- M2M
- Differences and Similarities between M2M and IoT
- SDN and NFV for IoT

## 3.1 Introduction

In Chapter-1, you learned about the definition and characteristics of Internet of Things (IoT). Another term which is often used synonymously with IoT is Machine-to-Machine (M2M). Though IoT and M2M are often used interchangeably, these terms have evolved from different backgrounds. This chapter describes some of the differences and similarities between IoT and M2M.

## 3.2 M2M

Machine-to-Machine (M2M) refers to networking of machines (or devices) for the purpose of remote monitoring and control and data exchange. Figure 3.1 shows the end-to-end architecture for M2M systems comprising of M2M area networks, communication network and application domain. An M2M area network comprises of machines (or M2M nodes) which have embedded hardware modules for sensing, actuation and communication. Various communication protocols can be used for M2M local area networks such as ZigBee, Bluetooh, ModBus, M-Bus, Wirless M-Bus, Power Line Communication (PLC), 6LoWPAN, IEEE 802.15.4, etc. These communication protocols provide connectivity between M2M nodes within an M2M area network. The communication network provides connectivity to remote M2M area networks. The communication network can use either wired or wireless networks (IP-based). While the M2M area networks use either proprietary or non-IP based communication protocols, the communication network uses IP-based networks. Since non-IP based protocols are used within M2M area networks, the M2M nodes within one network cannot communicate with nodes in an external network. To enable the communication between remote M2M area networks, M2M gateways are used.

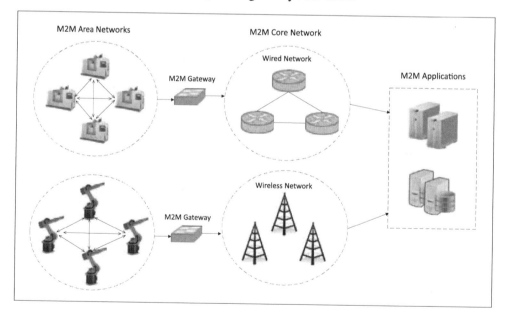

Figure 3.1: M2M system architecture

Figure 3.2 shows a block diagram of an M2M gateway. The communication between the M2M nodes and the M2M gateway is based on the communication protocols which are native to the M2M area network. M2M gateway performs protocol translations to enable IP-connectivity for M2M area networks. M2M gateway acts as a proxy performing translations from/to native protocols to/from Internet Protocol (IP). With an M2M gateway, each node in an M2M area network appears as a virtualized node for external M2M area networks.

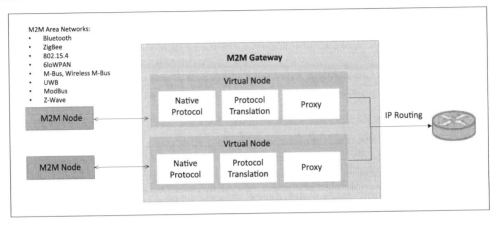

Figure 3.2: Block diagram of an M2M gateway

The M2M data is gathered into point solutions such as enterprise applications, service management applications, or remote monitoring applications. M2M has various application domains such as smart metering, home automation, industrial automation, smart grids, etc. M2M solution designs (such as data collection and storage architectures and applications) are specific to the M2M application domain.

## 3.3  Difference between IoT and M2M

Though both M2M and IoT involve networking of machines or devices, they differ in the underlying technologies, systems architectures and types of applications.

The differences between M2M and IoT are described as follows:
- **Communication Protocols:** M2M and IoT can differ in how the communication between the machines or devices happens. M2M uses either proprietary or non-IP based communication protocols for communication within the M2M area networks. Commonly uses M2M protocols include ZigBee, Bluetooh, ModBus, M-Bus, Wirless M-Bus, Power Line Communication (PLC), 6LoWPAN, IEEE 802.15.4, Z-Wave, etc. The focus of communication in M2M is usually on the protocols below the network layer. The focus of communication in IoT is usually on the protocols above the network layer such as HTTP, CoAP, WebSockets, MQTT, XMPP, DDS, AMQP, etc., as shown in Figure 3.3.
- **Machines in M2M vs Things in IoT:** The "Things" in IoT refers to physical objects that have unique identifiers and can sense and communicate with their external environment (and user applications) or their internal physical states. The unique identifiers for the things in IoT are the IP addresses (or MAC addresses). Things have software components for accessing, processing, and storing sensor information, or controlling actuators connected. IoT systems can have heterogeneous things (e.g., a

home automation IoT system can include IoT devices of various types, such as fire alarms, door alarms, lighting control devices, etc.) M2M systems, in contrast to IoT, typically have homogeneous machine types within an M2M area network.

- **Hardware vs Software Emphasis:** While the emphasis of M2M is more on hardware with embedded modules, the emphasis of IoT is more on software. IoT devices run specialized software for sensor data collection, data analysis and interfacing with the cloud through IP-based communication. Figure 3.4 shows the various components of IoT systems including the things, the Internet, communication infrastructure and the applications.

- **Data Collection & Analysis:** M2M data is collected in point solutions and often in on-premises storage infrastructure. In contrast to M2M, the data in IoT is collected in the cloud (can be public, private or hybrid cloud). Figure 3.5 shows the various IoT-levels, and the IoT components deployed in the cloud. The analytics component analyzes the data and stores the results in the cloud database. The IoT data and analysis results are visualized with the cloud-based applications. The centralized controller is aware of the status of all the end nodes and sends control commands to the nodes. Observer nodes can process information and use it for various applications, however, observer nodes do not perform any control functions.

- **Applications:** M2M data is collected in point solutions and can be accessed by on-premises applications such as diagnosis applications, service management applications, and on-premisis enterprise applications. IoT data is collected in the cloud and can be accessed by cloud applications such as analytics applications, enterprise applications, remote diagnosis and management applications, etc. Since the scale of data collected in IoT is so massive, cloud-based real-time and batch data analysis frameworks are used for data analysis.

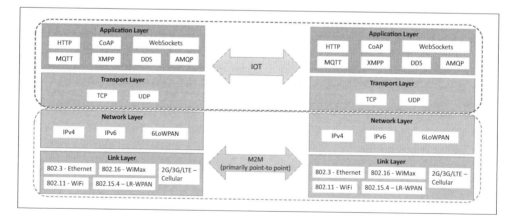

Figure 3.3: Communication in IoT is IP-based whereas M2M uses non-IP based networks. Communication within M2M area networks is based on protocols below the network layer whereas IoT is based on protocols above the network layer.

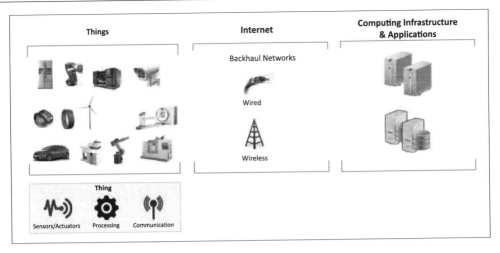

Figure 3.4: IoT components

## 3.4   SDN and NFV for IoT

In this section you will learn about Software Defined Networking (SDN) and Network Function Virtualization (NFV) and their applications for IoT.

### 3.4.1   Software Defined Networking

Software-Defined Networking (SDN) is a networking architecture that separates the control plane from the data plane and centralizes the network controller. Figure 3.6 shows the conventional network architecture built with specialized hardware (switches, routers, etc.). Network devices in conventional network architectures are getting exceedingly complex with the increasing number of distributed protocols being implemented and the use of proprietary hardware and interfaces. In the conventional network architecture the control plane and data plane are coupled. Control plane is the part of the network that carries the signaling and routing message traffic while the data plane is the part of the network that carries the payload data traffic.

The limitations of the conventional network architectures are as follows:

- **Complex Network Devices**: Conventional networks are getting increasingly complex with more and more protocols being implemented to improve link speeds and reliability. Interoperability is limited due to the lack of standard and open interfaces. Network devices use proprietary hardware and software and have slow product life-cycles limiting innovation. The conventional networks were well suited for static traffic patterns and had a large number of protocols designed for specific applications. For IoT applications which are deployed in cloud computing environments, the traffic patterns are more dynamic. Due to the complexity of conventional network devices, making changes in the networks to meet the dynamic traffic patterns has become increasingly difficult.

- **Management Overhead**: Conventional networks involve significant management overhead. Network managers find it increasingly difficult to manage multiple network devices and interfaces from multiple vendors. Upgradation of network requires

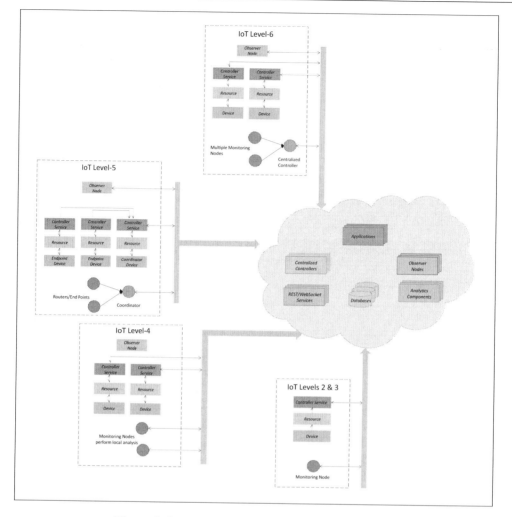

Figure 3.5: IoT levels and IoT cloud components

configuration changes in multiple devices (switches, routers, firewalls, etc.)

- **Limited Scalability**: The virtualization technologies used in cloud computing environments has increased the number of virtual hosts requiring network access. IoT applications hosted in the cloud are distributed across multiple virtual machines that require exchange of traffic. The analytics components of IoT applications run distributed algorithms on a large number of virtual machines that require huge amounts of data exchange between virtual machines. Such computing environments require highly scalable and easy to manage network architectures with minimal manual configurations, which is becoming increasingly difficult with conventional networks.

SDN attempts to create network architectures that are simpler, inexpensive, scalable, agile and easy to manage. Figures 3.7 and 3.8 show the SDN architecture and the SDN layers in which the control and data planes are decoupled and the network controller is centralized. Software-based SDN controllers maintain a unified view of the network and make configuration, management and provisioning simpler. The underlying infrastructure in SDN

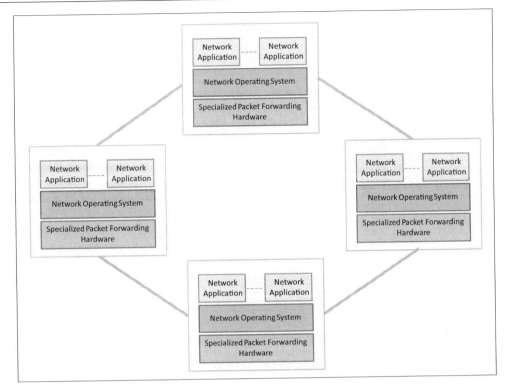

Figure 3.6: Conventional network architecture

uses simple packet forwarding hardware as opposed to specialized hardware in conventional networks. The underlying network infrastructure is abstracted from the applications. Network devices become simple with SDN as they do not require implementations of a large number of protocols. Network devices receive instructions from the SDN controller on how to forward the packets. These devices can be simpler and cost less as they can be built from standard hardware and software components.

Key elements of SDN are as follows:

- **Centralized Network Controller**: With decoupled control and data planes and centralized network controller, the network administrators can rapidly configure the network. SDN applications can be deployed through programmable open APIs. This speeds up innovation as the network administrators no longer need to wait for the device vendors to embed new features in their proprietary hardware.

- **Programmable Open APIs**: SDN architecture supports programmable open APIs for interface between the SDN application and control layers (Northbound interface). With these open APIs various network services can be implemented, such as routing, quality of service (QoS), access control, etc.

- **Standard Communication Interface (OpenFlow)**: SDN architecture uses a standard communication interface between the control and infrastructure layers (Southbound interface). OpenFlow, which is defined by the Open Networking Foundation (ONF) is the broadly accepted SDN protocol for the Southbound interface. With OpenFlow, the forwarding plane of the network devices can be directly accessed and manipulated.

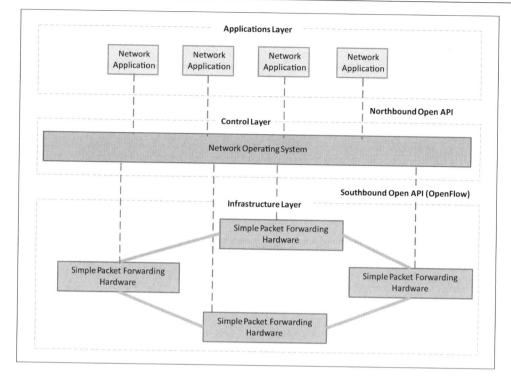

Figure 3.7: SDN architecture

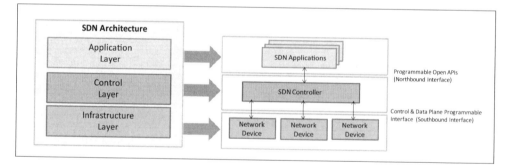

Figure 3.8: SDN layers

OpenFlow uses the concept of flows to identify network traffic based on pre-defined match rules. Flows can be programmed statically or dynamically by the SDN control software. Figure 3.9 shows the components of an OpenFlow switch comprising of one or more flow tables and a group table, which perform packet lookups and forwarding, and OpenFlow channel to an external controller. OpenFlow protocol is implemented on both sides of the interface between the controller and the network devices. The controller manages the switch via the OpenFlow switch protocol. The controller can add, update, and delete flow entries in flow tables. Figure 3.10 shows an example of an OpenFlow flow table. Each flow table contains a set of flow entries. Each flow entry consists of match fields, counters, and a set of instructions to apply to matching packets. Matching starts at the first flow table and may continue to additional flow tables of the pipeline [83].

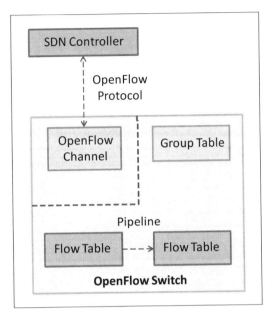

Figure 3.9: OpenFlow switch

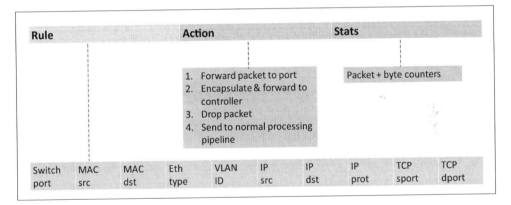

Figure 3.10: OpenFlow flow table

### 3.4.2 Network Function Virtualization

Network Function Virtualization (NFV) is a technology that leverages virtualization to consolidate the heterogeneous network devices onto industry standard high volume servers, switches and storage. NFV is complementary to SDN as NFV can provide the infrastructure on which SDN can run. NFV and SDN are mutually beneficial to each other but not dependent. Network functions can be virtualized without SDN, similarly, SDN can run without NFV.

Figure 3.11 shows the NFV architecture, as being standardized by the European Telecommunications Standards Institute (ETSI) [82]. Key elements of the NFV architecture are as follows:

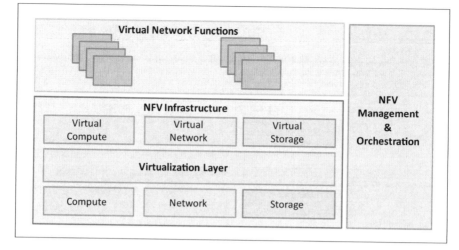

Figure 3.11: NFV architecture

- **Virtualized Network Function (VNF)**: VNF is a software implementation of a network function which is capable of running over the NFV Infrastructure (NFVI).
- **NFV Infrastructure (NFVI)**: NFVI includes compute, network and storage resources that are virtualized.
- **NFV Management and Orchestration**: NFV Management and Orchestration focuses on all virtualization-specific management tasks and covers the orchestration and life-cycle management of physical and/or software resources that support the infrastructure virtualization, and the life-cycle management of VNFs.

NFV comprises of network functions implemented in software that run on virtualized resources in the cloud. NFV enables separation of network functions which are implemented in software from the underlying hardware. Thus network functions can be easily tested and upgraded by installing new software while the hardware remains the same. Virtualizing network functions reduces the equipment costs and also reduces power consumption. The multi-tenanted nature of the cloud allows virtualized network functions to be shared for multiple network services. NFV is applicable only to data plane and control plane functions in fixed and mobile networks.

Let us look at an example of how NFV can be used for virtualization of the home networks. Figure 3.12 shows a home network with a Home Gateway that provides Wide Area Network (WAN) connectivity to enable services such as Internet, IPTV, VoIP, etc. The Home Gateway performs various functions including - Dynamic Host Configuration Protocol (DHCP) server, Network Address Translation (NAT), application specific gateway and Firewall. The Home Gateway provides private IP addresses to each connected device in the home. The Home Gateway provides routing capabilities and translates the private IP addresses to one public address (NAT function). The gateway also provides application specific routing for applications such as VoIP and IPTV.

Figure 3.13 shows how NFV can be used to virtualize the Home Gateway. The NFV infrastructure in the cloud hosts a virtualized Home Gateway. The virtualized gateway provides private IP addresses to the devices in the home. The virtualized gateway also connects to network services such as VoIP and IPTV.

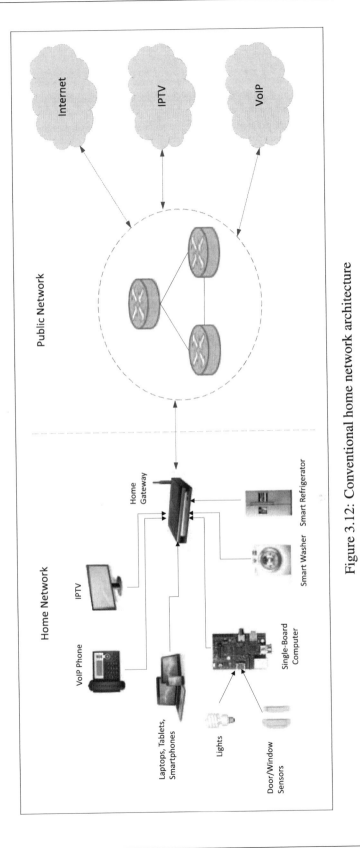

Figure 3.12: Conventional home network architecture

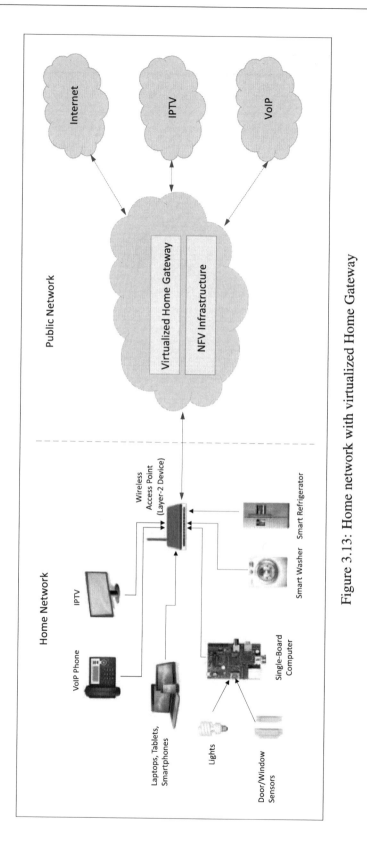

Figure 3.13: Home network with virtualized Home Gateway

## Summary

In this chapter you learned about the differences and similarities between IoT and M2M. Machine-to-Machine (M2M) typically refers to networking of machines (or devices) for the purpose of remote monitoring and control and data exchange. An M2M area network comprises of machines (or M2M nodes) which have embedded hardware modules for sensing, actuation and communication. M2M and IoT differ in how the communication between the machines or devices happens. While M2M uses either proprietary or non-IP based communication protocols for communica-tion within the M2M area networks, IoT uses IP-based protocols for communication. While IoT systems can have heterogeneous things M2M systems usually have the same machine types within an M2M area network. The emphasis of M2M is more on hardware with embedded modules, whereas, the emphasis of IoT is more on software. M2M data is collected in point solutions and can be accessed by on-premisis applications. IoT is collected in the cloud. You also learned about Software Defined Networking (SDN) and Network Function Virtualization (NFV) and their applications for IoT. Software-Defined Networking (SDN) is a networking architecture that separates the control plane from the data plane and centralizes the network controller. Key elements of SDN include centralized network controller, programmable open APIs and a standard communication interface. NFV is complementary to SDN and leverages virtualization to consolidate the heterogeneous network devices onto industry standard high volume servers, switches and storage.

## Review Questions

1. Which communication protocols are used for M2M local area networks?
2. What are the differences between Machines in M2M and Things in IoT?
3. How do data collection and analysis approaches differ in M2M and IoT?
4. What are the differences between SDN and NFV?
5. Describe how SDN can be used for various levels of IoT?
6. What is the function of a centralized network controller in SDN?
7. Describe how NFV can be used for virtualizing IoT devices?

# 4 - IoT System Management with NETCONF-YANG

This Chapter Covers

- Need for IoT Systems Management
- SNMP
- Network Operator Requirements
- NETCONF
- YANG
- IoT Systems Management with NETCONF-YANG

## 4.1   Need for IoT Systems Management

Internet of Things (IoT) systems can have complex software, hardware and deployment designs including sensors, actuators, software and network resources, data collection and analysis services and user interfaces. IoT systems can have distributed deployments comprising of a number of IoT devices which collect data from sensors or perform actuation. Managing multiple devices within a single system requires advanced management capabilities. The need for managing IoT systems is described as follows:

- **Automating Configuration**: IoT system management capabilities can help in automating the system configurations. System management interfaces provide predictable and easy to use management capability and the ability to automate system configuration. Automation becomes even more important when a system consists of multiple devices or nodes. In such cases automating the system configuration ensures that all devices have the same configuration and variations or errors due to manual configurations are avoided.
- **Monitoring Operational & Statistical Data**: Operational data is the data which is related to the system's operating parameters and is collected by the system at runtime. Statistical data is the data which describes the system performance (e.g. CPU and memory usage). Management systems can help in monitoring operational and statistical data of a system. This data can be used for fault diagnosis or prognosis.
- **Improved Reliability**: A management system that allows validating the system configurations before they are put into effect can help in improving the system reliability.
- **System Wide Configuration**: For IoT systems that consist of multiple devices or nodes, ensuring system-wide configuration can be critical for the correct functioning of the system. Management approaches in which each device is configured separately (either through a manual or automated process) can result in system faults or undesirable outcomes. This happens when some devices are running on an old configuration while others start running on new configuration. To avoid this, system wide configuration is required where all devices are configured in a single atomic transaction. This ensures that the configuration changes are either applied to all devices or to none. In the event of a failure in applying the configuration to one or more devices, the configuration changes are rolled back. This 'all or nothing' approach ensures that the system works as expected.
- **Multiple System Configurations**: For some systems it may be desirable to have multiple valid configurations which are applied at different times or in certain conditions.
- **Retrieving & Reusing Configurations**: Management systems which have the capability of retrieving configurations from devices can help in reusing the configurations for other devices of the same type. For example, for an IoT system which has multiple devices and requires same configuration for all devices, it is important to ensure that when a new device is added, the same configuration is applied. For such cases, the management system can retrieve the current configuration from a device and apply the same to the new devices.

## 4.2   Simple Network Management Protocol (SNMP)

SNMP is a well-known and widely used network management protocol that allows monitoring and configuring network devices such as routers, switches, servers, printers, etc. Figure 4.1 shows the components of the entities involved in managing a device with SNMP, including the Network Management Station (NMS), Managed Device, Management Information Base (MIB) and the SNMP Agent that runs on the device. NMS executes SNMP commands to monitor and configure the Managed Device. The Managed Device contains the MIB which has all the information of the device attributes to be managed. MIBs use the Structure of Management Information (SMI) notation for defining the structure of the management data. The structure of management data is defined in the form of variables which are identified by object identifiers (OIDs), which have a hierarchical structure. Management applications can either get or set the values of these variables. SNMP is an application layer protocol that uses User Datagram Protocol (UDP) as the transport protocol.

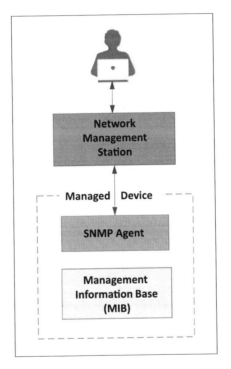

Figure 4.1: Managing a device with SNMP

### 4.2.1   Limitations of SNMP

While Simple Network Management Protocol (SNMP) has been the most popular protocol for network management, it has several limitations which may make it unsuitable for configuration management.

- SNMP was designed to provide a simple management interface between the management applications and the managed devices. SNMP is stateless in nature and each SNMP request contains all the information to process the request. The application needs to be intelligent to manage the device. For a sequence of SNMP interactions, the application needs to maintain state and also to be smart enough to roll back the device into a consistent state in case of errors or failures in configuration.

- SNMP is a connectionless protocol which uses UDP as the transport protocol, making it unreliable as there was no support for acknowledgement of requests.
- MIBs often lack writable objects without which device configuration is not possible using SNMP. With the absence of writable objects, SNMP can be used only for device monitoring and status polling.
- It is difficult to differentiate between configuration and state data in MIBs.
- Retrieving the current configuration from a device can be difficult with SNMP. SNMP does not support easy retrieval and playback of configurations.
- Earlier versions of SNMP did not have strong security features making the management information vulnerable to network intruders. Though security features were added in the later versions of SNMP, it increased the complexity a lot.

## 4.3  Network Operator Requirements

To address the limitations of the existing network management protocols and plan the future work on network management, the Internet Architecture Board (IAB), which oversees the Internet Engineering Task Force (IETF) held a workshop on network management in 2002 that brought together network operators and protocol developers. Based on the inputs from operators, a list of operator requirements was prepared [122]. The following points provide a brief overview of the operator requirements.

- **Ease of use**: From the operators point of view, ease of use is the key requirement for any network management technology.
- **Distinction between configuration and state data**: Configuration data is the set of writable data that is required to transform the system from its initial state to its current state. State data is the data which is not configurable. State data includes operational data which is collected by the system at runtime and statistical data which describes the system performance. For an effective management solution, it is important to make a clear distinction between configuration and state data.
- **Fetch configuration and state data separately**: In addition to making a clear distinction between configuration and state data, it should be possible to fetch the configuration and state data separately from the managed device. This is useful when the configuration and state data from different devices needs to be compared.
- **Configuration of the network as a whole**: It should be possible for operators to configure the network as a whole rather than individual devices. This is important for systems which have multiple devices and configuring them within one network wide transaction is required to ensure the correct operation of the system.
- **Configuration transactions across devices**: Configuration transactions across multiple devices should be supported.
- **Configuration deltas**: It should be possible to generate the operations necessary for going from one configuration state to another. The devices should support configuration deltas with minimal state changes.
- **Dump and restore configurations**: It should be possible to dump configurations from devices and restore configurations to devices.

- **Configuration validation**: It should be possible to validate configurations.
- **Configuration database schemas**: There is a need for standardized configuration database schemas or data models across operators.
- **Comparing configurations**: Devices should not arbitrarily reorder data, so that it is possible to use text processing tools such as *diff* to compare configurations.
- **Role-based access control**: Devices should support role-based access control model, so that a user is given the minimum access necessary to perform a required task.
- **Consistency of access control lists**: It should be possible to do consistency checks of access control lists across devices.
- **Multiple configuration sets**: There should be support for multiple configurations sets on devices. This way a distinction can be provided between candidate and active configurations.
- **Support for both data-oriented and task-oriented access control**: While SNMP access control is data-oriented, CLI access control is usually task oriented. There should be support for both types of access control.

## 4.4   NETCONF

Network Configuration Protocol (NETCONF) is a session-based network management protocol. NETCONF allows retrieving state or configuration data and manipulating configuration data on network devices [123, 136].

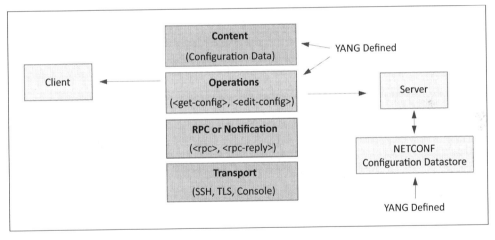

Figure 4.2: NETCONF protocol layers

Figure 4.2 shows the layered architecture of NETCONF protocol. For network management architecture based on NETCONF, the terms client and management system and the terms server and device are often used interchangeably. NETCONF works on SSH transport protocol. In addition to Secure Shell Transport Layer Protocol (SSH), NETCONF implementations can support other transport mappings such as Blocks Extensible Exchange Protocol (BEEP). Transport layer provides end-to-end connectivity and ensure reliable delivery of messages. NETCONF uses XML-encoded Remote Procedure Calls (RPCs) for framing request and response messages. The RPC layer provides mechanism for encoding of RPC calls and notifications. NETCONF provides various operations to retrieve and edit configuration data from network devices. Table 4.1 provides a list of some commonly used NETCONF operations. The Content Layer consists of configuration and state data which is XML-encoded. The schema of the configuration and state data is defined in a data modeling language called YANG. NETCONF provides a clear separation of the configuration and state data. For example, the NETCONF operation <get-config> retrieves the configuration data only, while the operation <get> retrieves the configuration and state data.

The configuration data resides within a NETCONF configuration datastore on the server. The NETCONF server resides on the network device. The management application plays the role of a NETCONF client. For managing a network device the client establishes a NETCONF session with the server. When a session is established the client and server exchange 'hello' messages which contain information on their capabilities. Client can then send multiple requests to the server for retrieving or editing the configuration data. NETCONF allows the management client to discover the capabilities of the server (on the device). NETCONF gives access to the native capabilities of the device.

NETCONF defines one or more configuration datastores. A configuration store contains all the configuration information to bring the device from its initial state to the operational state. By default a <running> configuration store is present. Additional configuration datastores such as <startup> and <candidate> can be defined in the capabilities.

NETCONF is a connection oriented protocol and NETCONF connection persists between protocol operations. For authentication, data integrity, and confidentiality, NETCONF depends on the transport protocol, e.g., SSH or TLS. NETCONF overcomes the limitations of SNMP and is suitable not only for monitoring state information, but also for configuration management.

## 4.5  YANG

YANG is a data modeling language used to model configuration and state data manipulated by the NETCONF protocol [137, 124]. YANG modules contain the definitions of the configuration data, state data, RPC calls that can be issued and the format of the notifications. YANG modules defines the data exchanged between the NETCONF client and server. A module comprises of a number of 'leaf' nodes which are organized into a hierarchical tree structure. The 'leaf' nodes are specified using the 'leaf' or 'leaf-list' constructs. Leaf nodes are organized using 'container' or 'list' constructs. A YANG module can import definitions from other modules. Constraints can be defined on the data nodes, e.g. allowed values. YANG can model both configuration data and state data using the 'config' statement. YANG defines four types of nodes for data modeling as shown in Table 4.2.

Let us now look at an example of a YANG module. Box 4.1 shows a YANG module for a "network-enabled toaster". This YANG module is a YANG version of the toaster Management Information Base (MIB). We use the Toaster MIB since it has been widely used as an example in introductory tutorials on SNMP to explain how SNMP can be used for managing a network-connected toaster. A YANG module has several sections starting from header information, followed by imports and includes, type definitions, configuration and operational data declarations, and RPC and notification declarations. The toaster YANG module begins with the header information followed by identity declarations which define various bread types. The leaf nodes ('toasterManufacturer', 'toasterModelNumber' and

| Operation | Description |
|---|---|
| connect | Connect to a NETCONF server |
| get | Retrieve the running configuration and state information |
| get-config | Retrieve all or a portion of a configuration datastore |
| edit-config | Loads all or part of a specified configuration to the specified target configuration |
| copy-config | Create or replace an entire target configuration datastore with a complete source configuration |
| delete-config | Delete the contents of a configuration datastore |
| lock | Lock a configuration datastore for exclusive edits by a client |
| unlock | Release the lock on a configuration datastore |
| get-schema | This operation is used to retrieve a schema from the NETCONF server |
| commit | Commit the candidate configuration as the device's new current configuration |
| close-session | Gracefully terminate a NETCONF session |
| kill-session | Forcefully terminate a NETCONF session |

Table 4.1: List of commonly used NETCONF RPC methods

'toasterStatus') are defined in the 'toaster' container. Each leaf node definition has a type and optionally a description and default value. The module has two RPC definitions ('make-toast' and 'cancel-toast'). A tree representation of the toaster YANG module is shown in Figure 4.3.

■ **Box 4.1: YANG version of the Toaster-MIB**

```
module toaster {

   yang-version 1;

   namespace
     "http://example.com/ns/toaster";

   prefix toast;

   revision "2009-11-20" {
    description
      "Toaster module";
   }

   identity toast-type {
    description
      "Base for all bread types";
   }
```

| Node Type | Description |
|-----------|-------------|
| Leaf Nodes | Contains simple data structures such as an integer or a string. Leaf has exactly one value of a particular type and no child nodes. |
| Leaf-List Nodes | Is a sequence of leaf nodes with exactly one value of a particular type per leaf. |
| Container Nodes | Used to group related nodes in a subtree. A container has only child nodes and no value. A container may contain any number of child nodes of any type (including leafs, lists, containers, and leaf-lists). |
| List Nodes | Defines a sequence of list entries. Each entry is like a structure or a record instance, and is uniquely identified by the values of its key leafs. A list can define multiple key leafs and may contain any number of child nodes of any type. |

Table 4.2: YANG Node Types

```
identity white-bread {
  base toast:toast-type;
}

identity wheat-bread {
  base toast-type;
}

identity wonder-bread {
  base toast-type;
}

identity frozen-waffle {
  base toast-type;
}

identity frozen-bagel {
  base toast-type;
}

identity hash-brown {
  base toast-type;
}

typedef DisplayString {
  type string {
    length "0 .. 255";
  }
}

container toaster {
  presence
    "Indicates the toaster service is available";
```

```
  description
    "Top-level container for all toaster database objects.";
  leaf toasterManufacturer {
    type DisplayString;
    config false;
    mandatory true;
  }

  leaf toasterModelNumber {
    type DisplayString;
    config false;
    mandatory true;
  }

  leaf toasterStatus {
    type enumeration {
      enum "up" {
        value 1;
      }
      enum "down" {
        value 2;
      }
    }
    config false;
    mandatory true;
  }
}

rpc make-toast {
  input {
    leaf toasterDoneness {
      type uint32 {
        range "1 ..  10";
      }
      default '5';
    }

    leaf toasterToastType {
      type identityref {
        base toast:toast-type;
      }
      default 'wheat-bread';
    }
  }
}

rpc cancel-toast {
  description
    "Stop making toast, if any is being made.";
}

notification toastDone {
  leaf toastStatus {
    type enumeration {
```

```
            enum "done" {
              value 0;
              description "The toast is done.";
            }
            enum "cancelled" {
              value 1;
              description
               "The toast was cancelled.";
            }
            enum "error" {
              value 2;
              description
               "The toaster service was disabled or
                   the toaster is broken.";
            }
          }
        }
      }
    }
```

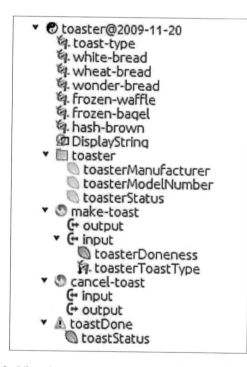

Figure 4.3: Visual representation of the Toaster YANG Module

Let us look at another example of a YANG module. Box 4.2 shows a YANG module for configuring a HAProxy load balancer for a commercial website. The module includes containers for global, defaults, frontend and backend sections of an HAProxy configuration. In the global container the leaf nodes for configuration data such as max-connections and mode are defined. In the defaults container the leaf nodes for configuration data such as retries, *contimeout*, etc. are defined. The front-end port bindings are defined in the frontend container. The backend container has definitions on the servers to load balance. A reusable tree structure called 'server-list' is used for the server definitions. The 'server-list' structure is defined using the 'grouping' construct in the module. A tree representation of the HAProxy YANG module is shown in Figure 4.4.

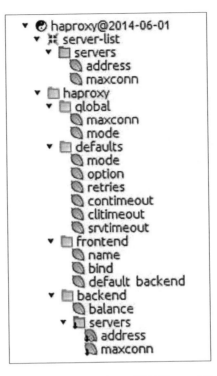

Figure 4.4: Visual representation of HAProxy YANG Module

■ **Box 4.2: YANG Module for HAProxy configuration**

```
module haproxy {
   yang-version 1;

   namespace "http://example.com/ns/haproxy";

   prefix haproxy;

   import ietf-inet-types { prefix inet; }

   description
   "YANG version of the ";

   revision "2014-06-01" {
      description
      "HAProxy module";
   }

container haproxy {
   description
```

```
"configuration parameters for a HAProxy load balancer";

    container global {
      leaf maxconn {
      type uint32;
      default 4096;
      }

      leaf mode {
      type string;
      default 'daemon';
      }
    }

    container defaults {
      leaf mode {
      type string;
      default 'http';
      }

      leaf option {
      type string;
      default 'redispatch';
      }

      leaf retries {
      type uint32;
      default 3;
      }

      leaf contimeout {
      type uint32;
      default 5000;
      }

      leaf clitimeout {
      type uint32;
      default 50000;
      }

      leaf srvtimeout {
      type uint32;
      default 50000;
      }
    }


    container frontend {

      leaf name {
      type string;
      default 'http-in';
      }
```

```
    leaf bind {
    type string;
    default '*:80';
    }

    leaf default_backend {
    type string;
    default 'webfarm';
    }
}

container backend {
    leaf balance   {
    type string;
    default 'roundrobin';
    }
    uses server-list;
}
}

grouping server-list {
description "List of servers to load balance";
    list servers {
    key address;
    leaf address {
        type inet:ip-address;
    }

    leaf maxconn {
        type uint32;
        default 255;
    }

    }
    }
}
```

## 4.6  IoT Systems Management with NETCONF-YANG

In this section you will learn how to manage IoT systems with NECONF and YANG. Figure 4.5 shows the generic approach of IoT device management with NETCONF-YANG.

Let is look at the roles of the various components:

- **Management System**: The operator uses a Management System to send NETCONF messages to configure the IoT device and receives state information and notifications from the device as NETCONF messages.
- **Management API**: Management API allows management applications to start NETCONF sessions, read and write configuration data, read state data, retrieve configurations, and invoke RPCs, programmatically, in the same way as an operator can.
- **Transaction Manager**: Transaction Manager executes all the NETCONF transactions and ensures that the ACID (Atomicity, Consistency, Isolation, Durability) properties hold true for the transactions. Atomicity property ensures that a transaction is executed

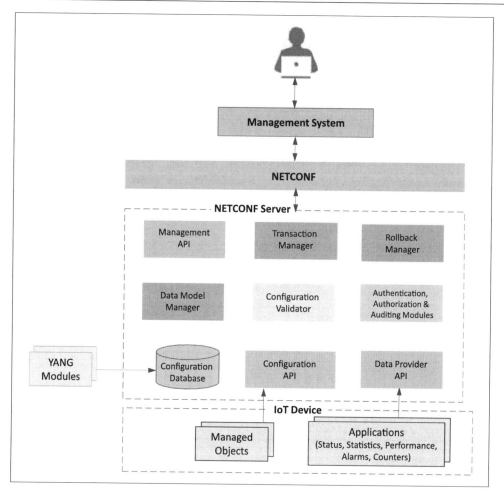

Figure 4.5: IoT device management with NETCONF-YANG - a generic approach

either completely or not at all. Consistency property ensures that a transaction brings the device configuration from one valid state to another. Isolation property ensures that concurrent execution of transactions results in the same device configuration as if transactions were executed serially in order. Durability property ensures that a transaction once committed will persist.

- **Rollback Manager** : Rollback manager is responsible for generating all the transactions necessary to rollback a current configuration to its original state.

- **Data Model Manager**: The Data Model manager keeps track of all the YANG data models and the corresponding managed objects. The Data Model manager also keeps track of the applications which provide data for each part of a data model.

- **Configuration Validator**: Configuration validator checks if the resulting configuration after applying a transaction would be a valid configuration.

- **Configuration Database**: This database contains both the configuration and operational data.

- **Configuration API**: Using the configuration API the applications on the IoT device can read configuration data from the configuration datastore and write operational data

to the operational datastore.
- **Data Provider API**: Applications on the IoT device can register for callbacks for various events using the Data Provider API. Through the Data Provider API, the applications can report statistics and operational data.

## 4.6.1 NETOPEER

While the previous section described a generic approach of IoT device management with NETCONF-YANG, this section describes a specific implementation based on the Netopeer tools [125]. Netopeer is set of open source NETCONF tools built on the Libnetconf library [126]. Figure 4.6 shows how to manage an IoT device using the Netopeer tools. The Netopeer tools include:

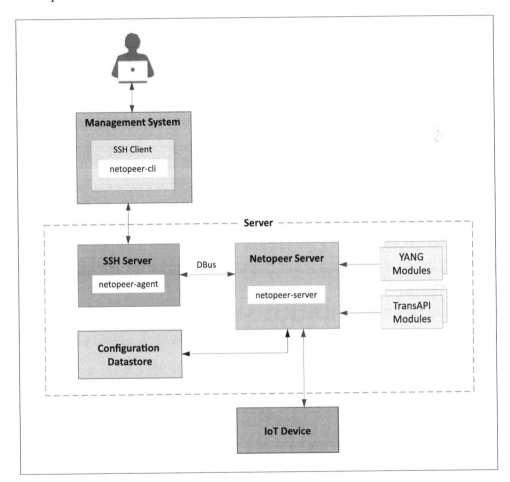

Figure 4.6: IoT device management with NETCONF - a specific approach based on Netopeer tools

- **Netopeer-server**: Netopeer-server is a NETCONF protocol server that runs on the managed device. Netopeer-server provides an environment for configuring the device using NETCONF RPC operations and also retrieving the state data from the device.
- **Netopeer-agent**: Netopeer-agent is the NETCONF protocol agent running as a

SSH/TLS subsystem. Netopeer-agent accepts incoming NETCONF connection and passes the NETCONF RPC operations received from the NETCONF client to the Netopeer-server.

- **Netopeer-cli**: Netopeer-cli is a NETCONF client that provides a command line interface for interacting with the Netopeer-server. The operator can use the Netopeer-cli from the management system to send NETCONF RPC operations for configuring the device and retrieving the state information.
- **Netopeer-manager**: Netopeer-manager allows managing the YANG and Libnetconf Transaction API (TransAPI) modules on the Netopeer-server. With Netopeer-manager modules can be loaded or removed from the server.
- **Netopeer-configurator**: Netopeer-configurator is a tool that can be used to configure the Netopeer-server.

### Steps for IoT device Management with NETCONF-YANG

1. Create a YANG model of the system that defines the configuration and state data of the system.
2. Compile the YANG model with the 'lnctool' which comes with Libnetconf.
Libnetconf provides a framework called Transaction API (TransAPI) that provides a mechanism of reflecting the changes in the configuration file in the actual device. The 'lnctool' generates a TransAPI module (callbacks C file). Whenever a change is made in the configuration file using the NETCONF operations, the corresponding callback function is called. The callback functions contain the code for making the changes on the device.
3. Fill in the IoT device management code in the TransAPI module (callbacks C file). This file includes configuration callbacks, RPC callbacks and state data callbacks.
4. Build the callbacks C file to generate the library file (.so).
5. Load the YANG module (containing the data definitions) and the TransAPI module (.so binary) into the Netopeer server using the Netopeer manager tool.
6. The operator can now connect from the management system to the Netopeer server using the Netopeer CLI.
7. Operator can issue NETCONF commands from the Netopeer CLI. Commands can be issued to change the configuration data, get operational data or execute an RPC on the IoT device.

In Chapter 11, detailed case studies on IoT device Management using the above steps are provided.

## Summary

In this chapter you learned about the need for IoT systems management. IoT system management capabilities can help in automating the system configurations. Management systems can collect operational and statistical data from IoT devices which can be used for fault diagnosis or prognosis. For IoT systems that consist of multiple devices, system wide configuration is important to ensure that all devices are configured within one transaction and the transactions are atomic. It is desirable for devices to have multiple configurations with one of them being the active and running configuration. Management systems which have the capability of retrieving configurations from devices can help in reusing the configurations for other devices of the same type. SNMP has been a popular network management protocol, however it has several limitations which make it unsuitable for IoT device management. Network Configuration Protocol (NETCONF), which is a session-based network management protocol, is more suitable for IoT device management. NETCONF works on SSH transport protocol and provides various operations to retrieve and edit configuration data from devices. The configuration data resides within a NETCONF configuration datastore on the server. The NETCONF server resides on the network device. The device configuration and state data is modeled using the YANG data modeling language. There is a clear separation of configuration and state data in the YANG models. You learned about a generic approach for IoT device management and the roles of various components such as the Management API, Transaction Manager, Rollback Manager, Data Model Manager, Configuration Validator, Configuration Database, Configuration API and Data Provider API. You learned about the Netopeer tools for NETCONF and the steps for IoT device Management using these tools.

## Review Questions

1. Why is network wide configuration important for IoT systems with multiple nodes?
2. Which limitations make SNMP unsuitable for IoT systems?
3. What is the difference between configuration and state data?
4. What is the role of a NETCONF server?
5. What is the function of a data model manager?
6. Describe the roles of YANG and TransAPI modules in device management?

# Part II

# DEVELOPING INTERNET OF THINGS

# 5 - IoT Platforms Design Methodology

This Chapter Covers
IoT Design Methodology that includes:
- Purpose & Requirements Specification
- Process Specification
- Domain Model Specification
- Information Model Specification
- Service Specifications
- IoT Level Specification
- Functional View Specification
- Operational View Specification
- Device & Component Integration
- Application Development

## 5.1  Introduction

IoT systems comprise of multiple components and deployment tiers. In Chapter-1, we defined six IoT system levels. Each level is suited for different applications and has different component and deployment configurations. Designing IoT systems can be a complex and challenging task as these systems involve interactions between various components such as IoT devices and network resources, web services, analytics components, application and database servers. Due to a wide range of choices available for each of these components, IoT system designers may find it difficult to evaluate the available alternatives. IoT system designers often tend to design IoT systems keeping specific products/services in mind. Therefore, these designs are tied to specific product/service choices made. This leads to product, service or vendor lock-in, which while satisfactory to the dominant vendor, is unacceptable to the customer. For such systems, updating the system design to add new features or replacing a particular product/service choice for a component becomes very complex, and in many cases may require complete re-design of the system.

In this Chapter, we propose a generic design methodology for IoT system design which is independent of specific product, service or programming language. IoT systems designed with the proposed methodology have reduced design, testing and maintenance time, better interoperability and reduced complexity. With the proposed methodology, IoT system designers can compare various alternatives for the IoT system components. The methodology described in this Chapter is generally based on the IoT-A reference model [75], but is broad enough to embrace other industry efforts as well. Later chapters in this book describe the implementation aspects of various steps in the proposed methodology.

## 5.2  IoT Design Methodology

Figure 5.1 shows the steps involved in the IoT system design methodology. Each of these steps is explained in the sections that follow. To explain these steps, we use the example of a smart IoT-based home automation system.

### 5.2.1  Step 1: Purpose & Requirements Specification

The first step in IoT system design methodology is to define the purpose and requirements of the system. In this step, the system purpose, behavior and requirements (such as data collection requirements, data analysis requirements, system management requirements, data privacy and security requirements, user interface requirements, ...) are captured.

Applying this to our example of a smart home automation system, the purpose and requirements for the system may be described as follows:

- **Purpose :** A home automation system that allows controlling of the lights in a home remotely using a web application.
- **Behavior :** The home automation system should have auto and manual modes. In auto mode, the system measures the light level in the room and switches on the light when it gets dark. In manual mode, the system provides the option of manually and remotely switching on/off the light.
- **System Management Requirement :** The system should provide remote monitoring and control functions.
- **Data Analysis Requirement :** The system should perform local analysis of the data.

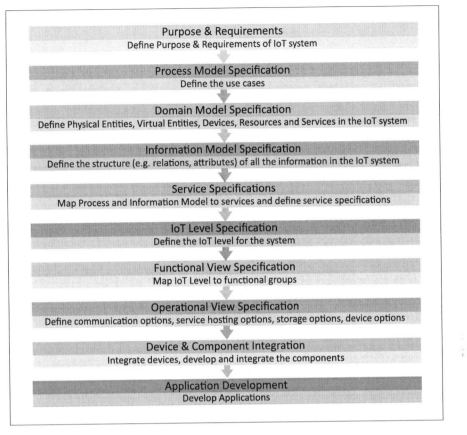

Figure 5.1: Steps involved in IoT system design methodology

- **Application Deployment Requirement :** The application should be deployed locally on the device, but should be accessible remotely.
- **Security Requirement :** The system should have basic user authentication capability.

### 5.2.2   Step 2: Process Specification

The second step in the IoT design methodology is to define the process specification. In this step, the use cases of the IoT system are formally described based on and derived from the purpose and requirement specifications. Figure 5.2 shows the process diagram for the home automation system. The process diagram shows the two modes of the system - auto and manual. In a process diagram, the circle denotes the start of a process, diamond denotes a decision box and rectangle denotes a state or attribute. When the auto mode is chosen, the system monitors the light level. If the light level is low, the system changes the state of the light to "on". Whereas, if the light level is high, the system changes the state of the light to "off". When the manual mode is chosen, the system checks the light state set by the user. If the light state set by the user is "on", the system changes the state of light to "on". Whereas, if the light state set by the user is "off", the system changes the state of light to "off".

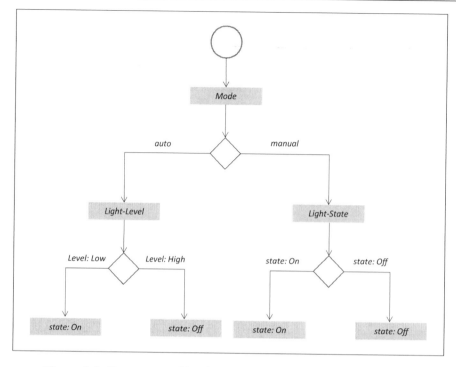

Figure 5.2: Process specification for home automation IoT system

## 5.2.3   Step 3: Domain Model Specification

The third step in the IoT design methodology is to define the Domain Model. The domain model describes the main concepts, entities and objects in the domain of IoT system to be designed. Domain model defines the attributes of the objects and relationships between objects. Domain model provides an abstract representation of the concepts, objects and entities in the IoT domain, independent of any specific technology or platform. With the domain model, the IoT system designers can get an understanding of the IoT domain for which the system is to be designed. Figure 5.3 shows the domain model for the home automation system example. The entities, objects and concepts defined in the domain model include:

- **Physical Entity :** Physical Entity is a discrete and identifiable entity in the physical environment (e.g. a room, a light, an appliance, a car, etc.). The IoT system provides information about the Physical Entity (using sensors) or performs actuation upon the Physical Entity (e.g., switching on a light). In the home automation example, there are two Physical Entities involved - one is the room in the home (of which the lighting conditions are to be monitored) and the other is the light appliance to be controlled.
- **Virtual Entity :** Virtual Entity is a representation of the Physical Entity in the digital world. For each Physical Entity, there is a Virtual Entity in the domain model. In the home automation example, there is one Virtual Entity for the room to be monitored, another for the appliance to be controlled.
- **Device :** Device provides a medium for interactions between Physical Entities and Virtual Entities. Devices are either attached to Physical Entities or placed near Physical Entities. Devices are used to gather information about Physical Entities (e.g., from

sensors), perform actuation upon Physical Entities (e.g. using actuators) or used to identify Physical Entities (e.g., using tags). In the home automation example, the device is a single-board mini computer which has light sensor and actuator (relay switch) attached to it.

- **Resource :** Resources are software components which can be either "on-device" or "network-resources". On-device resources are hosted on the device and include software components that either provide information on or enable actuation upon the Physical Entity to which the device is attached. Network resources include the software components that are available in network (such as a database). In the home automation example, the on-device resource is the operating system that runs on the single-board mini computer.

- **Service :** Services provide an interface for interacting with the Physical Entity. Services access the resources hosted on the device or the network resources to obtain information about the Physical Entity or perform actuation upon the Physical Entity. In the home automation example, there are three services: (1) a service that sets mode to auto or manual, or retrieves the current mode; (2) a service that sets the light appliance state to on/off, or retrieves the current light state; and (3) a controller service that runs as a native service on the device. When in auto mode, the controller service monitors the light level and switches the light on/off and updates the status in the status database. When in manual mode, the controller service retrieves the current state from the database and switches the light on/off. The process of deriving the services from the process specification and information model is described in the later sections.

### 5.2.4 Step 4: Information Model Specification

The fourth step in the IoT design methodology is to define the Information Model. Information Model defines the structure of all the information in the IoT system, for example, attributes of Virtual Entities, relations, etc. Information model does not describe the specifics of how the information is represented or stored. To define the information model, we first list the Virtual Entities defined in the Domain Model. Information model adds more details to the Virtual Entities by defining their attributes and relations. In the home automation example, there are two Virtual Entities - a Virtual Entity for the light appliance (with attribute - light state) and a Virtual Entity for the room (with attribute - light level). Figure 5.4 shows the Information Model for the home automation system example.

### 5.2.5 Step 5: Service Specifications

The fifth step in the IoT design methodology is to define the service specifications. Service specifications define the services in the IoT system, service types, service inputs/output, service endpoints, service schedules, service preconditions and service effects.

You learned about the Process Specification and Information Model in the previous sections. Figure 5.5 shows an example of deriving the services from the process specification and information model for the home automation IoT system. From the process specification and information model, we identify the states and attributes. For each state and attribute we define a service. These services either change the state or attribute values or retrieve the current values. For example, the Mode service sets mode to auto or manual or retrieves the current mode. The State service sets the light appliance state to on/off or retrieves the current

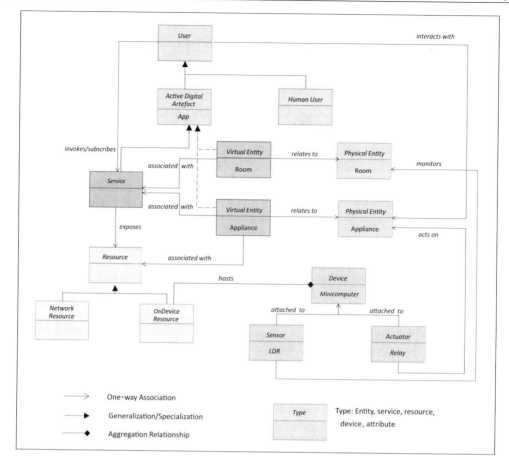

Figure 5.3: Domain model of the home automation IoT system

Figure 5.4: Information model of the home automation IoT system

light state. The Controller service monitors the light level in auto mode and switches the light on/off and updates the status in the status database. In manual mode, the controller service, retrieves the current state from the database and switches the light on/off.

Figures 5.6, 5.7 and 5.8 show specifications of the controller, mode and state services of

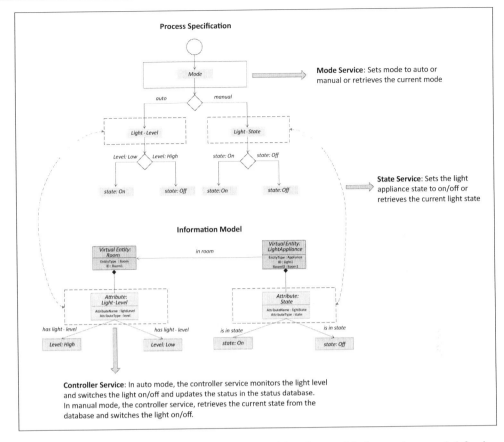

Figure 5.5: Deriving services from process specification and information model for home automation IoT system

the home automation system. The Mode service is a RESTful web service that sets mode to auto or manual (PUT request), or retrieves the current mode (GET request) . The mode is updated to/retrieved from the database. The State service is a RESTful web service that sets the light appliance state to on/off (PUT request), or retrieves the current light state (GET request). The state is updated to/retrieved from the status database. The Controller service runs as a native service on the device. When in auto mode, the controller service monitors the light level and switches the light on/off and updates the status in the status database. When in manual mode, the controller service, retrieves the current state from the database and switches the light on/off.

## 5.2.6   Step 6: IoT Level Specification

The sixth step in the IoT design methodology is to define the IoT level for the system. In Chapter-1, we defined five IoT deployment levels. Figure 5.9 shows the deployment level of the home automation IoT system, which is level-1.

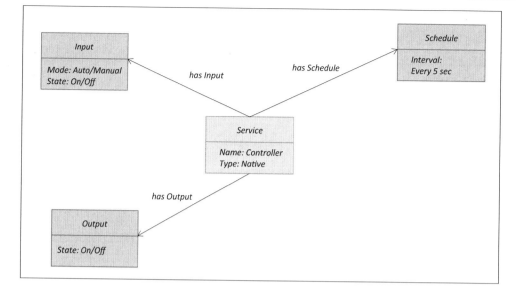

Figure 5.6: Controller service of the home automation IoT system

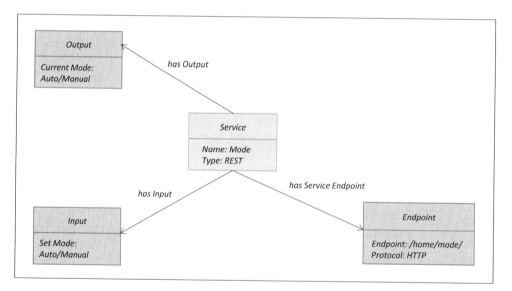

Figure 5.7: Service specification for home automation IoT system - mode service

### 5.2.7   Step 7: Functional View Specification

The seventh step in the IoT design methodology is to define the Functional View. The Functional View (FV) defines the functions of the IoT systems grouped into various Functional Groups (FGs). Each Functional Group either provides functionalities for interacting with instances of concepts defined in the Domain Model or provides information related to these concepts.

The Functional Groups (FG) included in a Functional View include:

- **Device :** The device FG contains devices for monitoring and control. In the home automation example, the device FG includes a single board mini-computer, a light

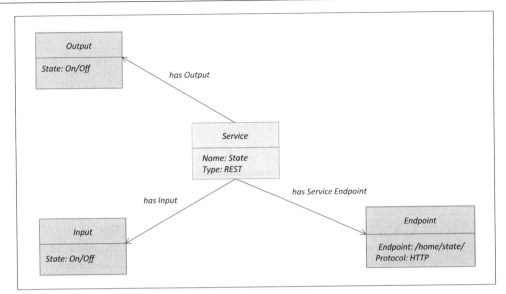

Figure 5.8: Service specification for home automation IoT system - state service

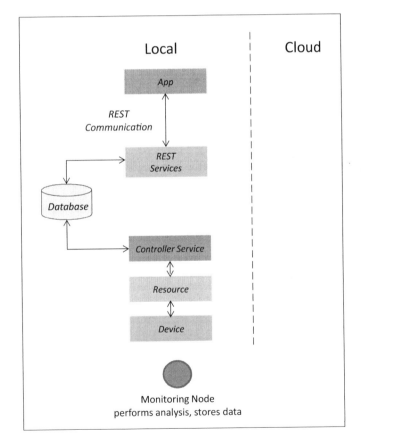

Figure 5.9: Deployment design of the home automation IoT system

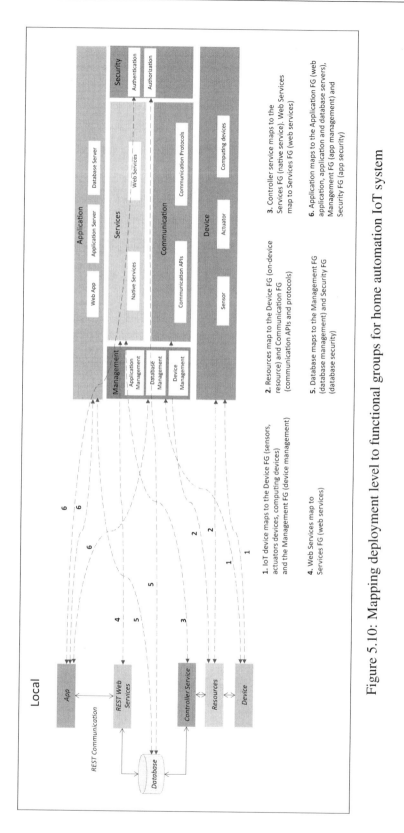

Figure 5.10: Mapping deployment level to functional groups for home automation IoT system

sensor and a relay switch (actuator).

- **Communication :** The communication FG handles the communication for the IoT system. The communication FG includes the communication protocols that form the backbone of IoT systems and enable network connectivity. You learned about various link, network, transport and application layer protocols in Chapter-1. The communication FG also includes the communication APIs (such as REST and WebSocket) that are used by the services and applications to exchange data over the network. In the home automation example the communication protocols include - 802.11 (link layer), IPv4/IPv6 (network layer), TCP (transport layer), and HTTP (application layer). The communication API used in the home automation examples is a REST-based API.

- **Services :** The service FG includes various services involved in the IoT system such as services for device monitoring, device control services, data publishing services and services for device discovery. In the home automation example, there are two REST services (mode and state service) and one native service (controller service).

- **Management :** The management FG includes all functionalities that are needed to configure and manage the IoT system.

- **Security :** The security FG includes security mechanisms for the IoT system such as authentication, authorization, data security, etc.

- **Application :** The application FG includes applications that provide an interface to the users to control and monitor various aspects of the IoT system. Applications also allow users to view the system status and the processed data.

Figure 5.10 shows an example of mapping deployment level to functional groups for home automation IoT system.

IoT device maps to the Device FG (sensors, actuators devices, computing devices) and the Management FG (device management). Resources map to the Device FG (on-device resource) and Communication FG (communication APIs and protocols). Controller service maps to the Services FG (native service). Web Services map to Services FG . Database maps to the Management FG (database management) and Security FG (database security). Application maps to the Application FG (web application, application and database servers), Management FG (app management) and Security FG (app security).

### 5.2.8   Step 8: Operational View Specification

The eighth step in the IoT design methodology is to define the Operational View Specifications. In this step, various options pertaining to the IoT system deployment and operation are defined, such as, service hosting options, storage options, device options, application hosting options, etc.

Figure 5.11 shows an example of mapping functional groups to operational view specifications for home automation IoT system.

Operational View specifications for the home automation example are as follows:

- Devices: Computing device (Raspberry Pi), light dependent resistor (sensor), relay switch (actuator).
- Communication APIs: REST APIs
- Communication Protocols: Link Layer - 802.11, Network Layer - IPv4/IPv6, Transport - TCP, Application - HTTP.
- Services:

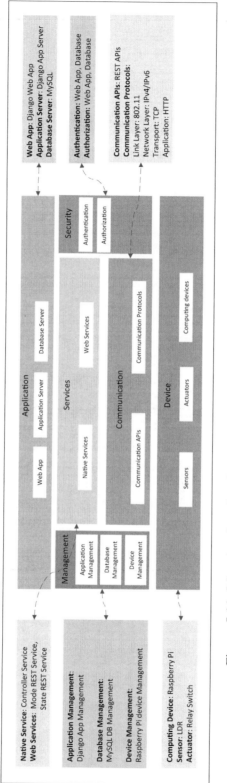

Figure 5.11: Mapping functional groups to operational view for home automation IoT system

1. Controller Service - Hosted on device, implemented in Python and run as a native service.
2. Mode service - REST-ful web service, hosted on device, implemented with Django-REST Framework.
3. State service - REST-ful web service, hosted on device, implemented with Django-REST Framework.

- Application:
  Web Application - Django Web Application,
  Application Server - Django App Server,
  Database Server - MySQL.
- Security:
  Authentication: Web App, Database
  Authorization: Web App, Database

- Management:
  Application Management - Django App Management
  Database Management - MySQL DB Management,
  Device Management - Raspberry Pi device Management.

### 5.2.9   Step 9: Device & Component Integration

The ninth step in the IoT design methodology is the integration of the devices and components. Figure 5.12 shows a schematic diagram of the home automation IoT system. The devices and components used in this example are Raspberry Pi mini computer, LDR sensor and relay switch actuator. A detailed description of Raspberry Pi board and how to interface sensors and actuators with the board is provided in later chapters.

### 5.2.10   Step 10: Application Development

The final step in the IoT design methodology is to develop the IoT application. Figure 5.13 shows a screenshot of the home automation web application. The application has controls for the mode (auto on or auto off) and the light (on or off). In the auto mode, the IoT system controls the light appliance automatically based on the lighting conditions in the room. When auto mode is enabled the light control in the application is disabled and it reflects the current state of the light. When the auto mode is disabled, the light control is enabled and it is used for manually controlling the light.

## 5.3   Case Study on IoT System for Weather Monitoring

In this section we present a case study on design of an IoT system for weather monitoring using the IoT design methodology. The purpose of the weather monitoring system is to collect data on environmental conditions such as temperature, pressure, humidity and light in an area using multiple end nodes. The end nodes send the data to the cloud where the data is aggregated and analyzed.

Figure 5.14 shows the process specification for the weather monitoring system. The process specification shows that the sensors are read after fixed intervals and the sensor measurements are stored.

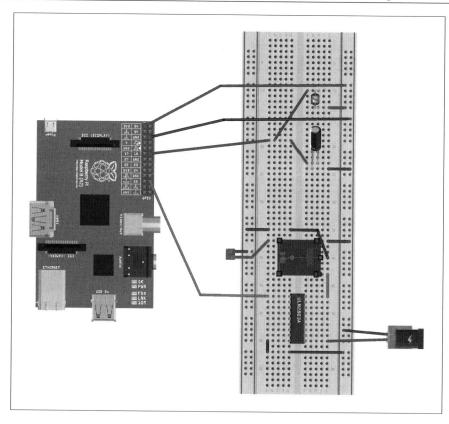

Figure 5.12: Schematic diagram of the home automation IoT system showing the device, sensor and actuator integrated

Figure 5.13: Home automation web application screenshot

Figure 5.15 shows the domain model for the weather monitoring system. In this domain model the physical entity is the environment which is being monitored. There is a virtual entity for the environment. Devices include temperature sensor, pressure sensor, humidity sensor, light sensor and single-board mini computer. Resources are software components which can be either on-device or network-resources. Services include the controller service that monitors the temperature, pressure, humidity and light and sends the readings to the

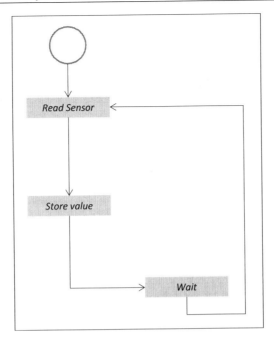

Figure 5.14: Process specification for weather monitoring IoT system

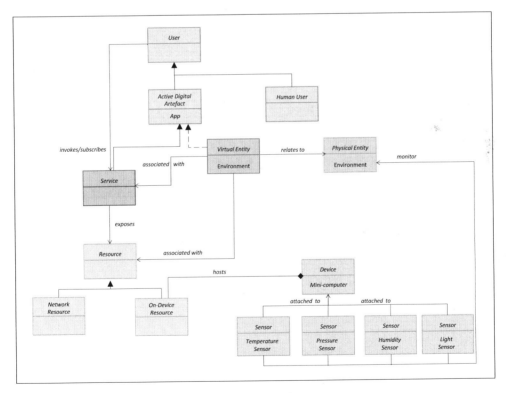

Figure 5.15: Domain model for weather monitoring IoT system

cloud.

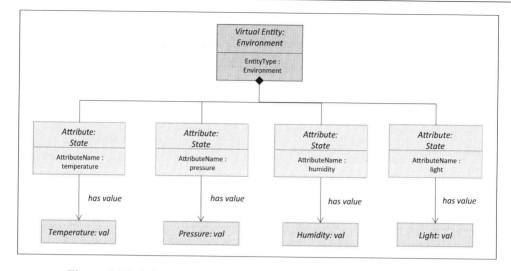

Figure 5.16: Information model for weather monitoring IoT system

Figure 5.16 shows the information model for the weather monitoring system. In this example, there is one virtual entity for the environment being sensed. The virtual entity has attributes - temperature, pressure, humidity and light. Figure 5.17 shows an example of deriving the services from the process specification and information model for the weather monitoring system.

Figure 5.18 shows the specification of the controller service for the weather monitoring system. The controller service runs as a native service on the device and monitors temperature, pressure, humidity and light once every 15 seconds. The controller service calls the REST service to store these measurements in the cloud. In Chapter-8 we describe a Platform-as-a-Service called Xively that can be used for creating solutions for Internet of Things. An implementation of a controller service that calls the Xively REST API to store data in Xively cloud is described in Chapter-9.

Figure 5.19 shows the deployment design for the system. The system consists of multiple nodes placed in different locations for monitoring temperature, humidity and pressure in an area. The end nodes are equipped with various sensors (such as temperature, pressure, humidity and light). The end nodes send the data to the cloud and the data is stored in a cloud database. The analysis of data is done in the cloud to aggregate the data and make predictions. A cloud-based application is used for visualizing the data. The centralized controller can send control commands to the end nodes, for example, to configure the monitoring interval on the end nodes.

Figure 5.20 shows an example of mapping deployment level to functional groups for the weather monitoring system. Figure 5.21 shows an example of mapping functional groups to operational view specifications for the weather monitoring system.

Figure 5.22 shows a schematic diagram of the weather monitoring system. The devices and components used in this example are Raspberry Pi mini computer, temperature sensor, humidity sensor, pressure sensor and LDR sensor.

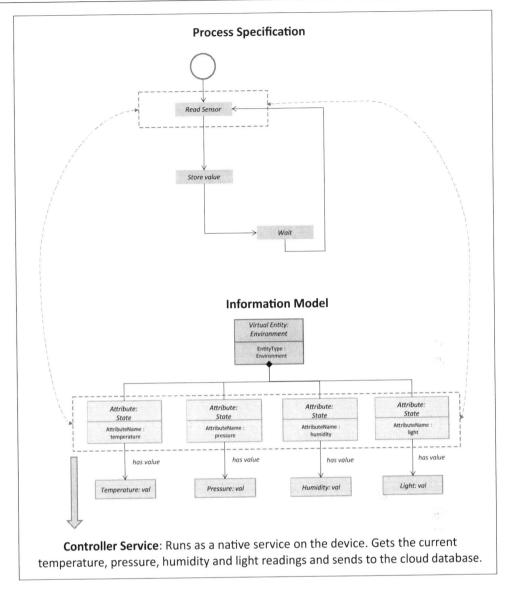

Figure 5.17: Deriving services from process specification and information model for weather monitoring IoT system

## 5.4  Motivation for Using Python

This book uses the Python language for all the examples, though the basic principles apply to other high level languages. In this section we explain the motivation for using Python for developing IoT systems. Python is a minimalistic language with English-like keywords and fewer syntactical constructions as compared to other languages. This makes Python easier to learn and understand. Moreover, Python code is compact as compared to other languages. Python is an interpreted language and does not require an explicit compilation step. The Python interpreter converts the Python code to the intermediate byte code, specific to the system. Python is supported on wide range of platforms, hence Python code is easily

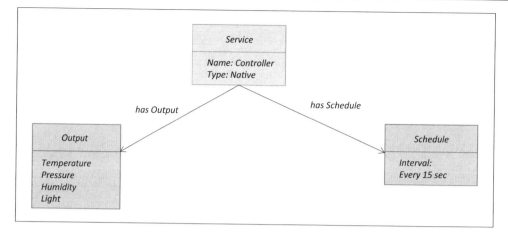

Figure 5.18: Controller service of the weather monitoring IoT system

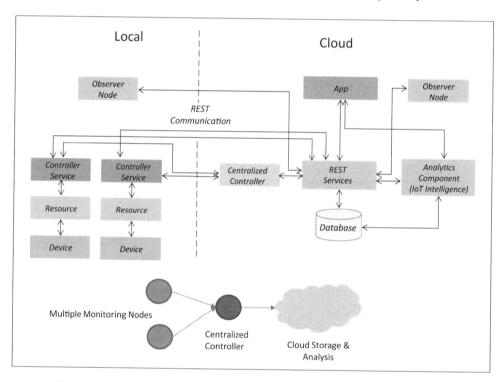

Figure 5.19: Deployment design of the weather monitoring IoT system

portable. The wide library support available for Python makes it an excellent choice for IoT systems. Python can be used for end-to-end development of IoT systems from IoT device code (e.g. code for capturing sensor data), native services (e.g., a controller service implemented in Python), web services (e.g. a RESTful web service implemented in Python), web applications (e.g., Python web applications developed with Python web frameworks such as Django) and analytics components (e.g. machine learning components developed using Python libraries such as scikit-learn). In the next chapter you will learn the basics of Python language amd all the related packages of interest that are used in the examples in this

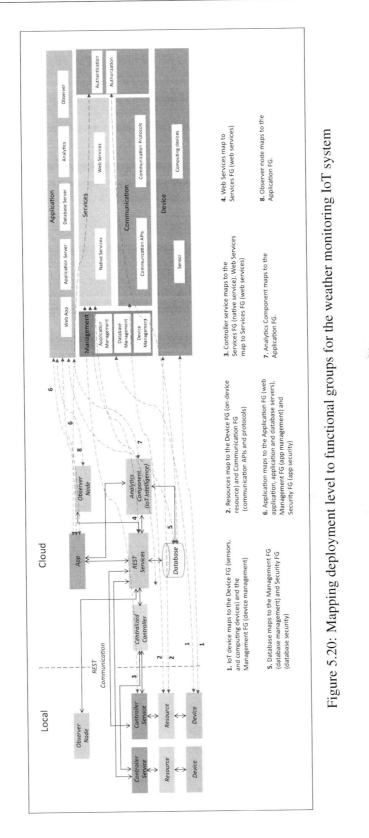

Figure 5.20: Mapping deployment level to functional groups for the weather monitoring IoT system

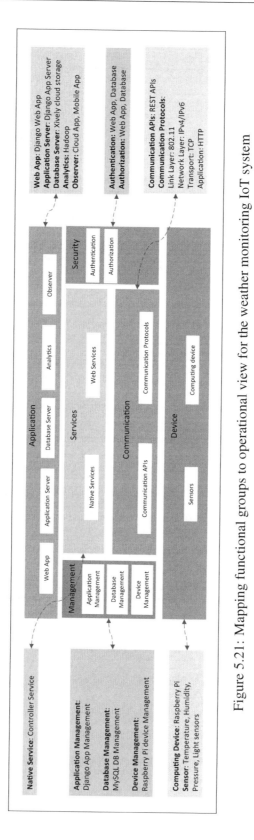

Figure 5.21: Mapping functional groups to operational view for the weather monitoring IoT system

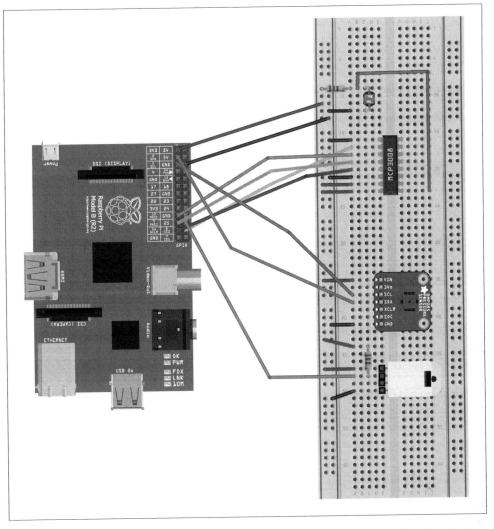

Figure 5.22: Schematic diagram of a weather monitoring end-node showing the device and sensors

book.

## Summary

In this chapter you learned about generic design methodology for IoT system design which is independent of specific product, service or programming language. The first step in IoT system design methodology is to define the purpose and requirements of the system. In the second step, the use cases of the IoT system are formally described based on the purpose and requirement specifications. The third step is to define the Domain Model which describes the main concepts, entities and objects in the domain of IoT system to be designed. The fourth step is to define the Information Model which defines the structure of all the information in the IoT system. The fifth step is to define the Functional View which defines the functions of the IoT systems grouped into various Functional Groups. The sixth step is to define the service specifications which define the services in the IoT system, service types, service inputs/output, service endpoints, service schedules, service preconditions and service effects. The seventh step is to define the Deployment & Operational View Specifications in which various options pertaining to the IoT system deployment and operation are defined. The eight step is the integration of the devices and components. The final step in the IoT design methodology is to develop the IoT application.

## Review Questions

1. What is the difference between a physical and virtual entity?
2. What is an IoT device?
3. What is the purpose of information model?
4. What are the various service types?
5. What is the need for a controller service?

# 6 - IoT Systems - Logical Design using Python

This Chapter covers

- Introduction to Python
- Installing Python
- Python Data Types & Data Structures
- Control Flow
- Functions
- Modules
- Packages
- File Input/Output
- Date/Time Operations
- Classes

## 6.1  Introduction

This book uses Python as the primary programming languages for examples. This chapter will help you in understanding the basics of Python programming and the Python packages that are used in examples in this book.

Python is a general-purpose high level programming language. Python 2.0 was released in the year 2000 and Python 3.0 was released in the year 2008. The 3.0 version is not backward compatible with earlier releases. The most recent release of Python is version 3.3. Currently, there is limited library support for the 3.x versions with operating systems such as Linux and Mac still using Python 2.x as default language. The exercises and examples in this book have been developed with Python version 2.7. The main characteristics of Python are:

### Multi-paradigm programming language

Python supports more than one programming paradigms including object-oriented programming and structured programming

### Interpreted Language

Python is an interpreted language and does not require an explicit compilation step. The Python interpreter executes the program source code directly, statement by statement, as a processor or scripting engine does.

### Interactive Language

Python provides an interactive mode in which the user can submit commands at the Python prompt and interact with the interpreter directly.

The key benefits of Python are:

### Easy-to-learn, read and maintain

Python is a minimalistic language with relatively few keywords, uses English keywords and has fewer syntactical constructions as compared to other languages. Reading Python programs is easy with pseudo-code like constructs. Python is easy to learn yet an extremely powerful language for a wide range of applications. Due to its simplicity, programs written in Python are generally easy to maintain.

### Object and Procedure Oriented

Python supports both procedure-oriented programming and object-oriented programming. Procedure oriented paradigm allows programs to be written around procedures or functions that allow reuse of code. Procedure oriented paradigm allows programs to be written around objects that include both data and functionality.

### Extendable

Python is an extendable language and allows integration of low-level modules written in languages such as C/C++. This is useful when you want to speed up a critical portion of a program.

### Scalable

Due to the minimalistic nature of Python, it provides a manageable structure for large programs.

## Portable

Since Python is an interpreted language, programmers do not have to worry about compilation, linking and loading of programs. Python programs can be directly executed from source code and copied from one machine to other without worrying about portability. The Python interpreter converts the source code to an intermediate form called byte codes and then translates this into the native language of your specific system and then runs it.

## Broad Library Support

Python has a broad library support and works on various platforms such as Windows, Linux, Mac, etc. There are a large number of Python packages available for various applications such as machine learning, image processing, network programming, cryptography, etc.

## 6.2   Installing Python

Python is a highly portable language that works on various platforms such as Windows, Linux, Mac, etc. This section describes the Python installation steps for Windows and Linux:

### Windows

Python binaries for Windows can be downloaded from http://www.python.org/getit . For the examples and exercise in this book, you would require Python 2.7 which can be directly downloaded from: http://www.python.org/ftp/python/2.7.5/python-2.7.5.msi Once the python binary is installed you can run the python shell at the command prompt using
> python

### Linux

Box 6.1 provides the commands for installing Python on Ubuntu.

```
■ Box 6.1: Installing Python on Ubuntu Linux

#Install Dependencies
sudo apt-get install build-essential
sudo apt-get install libreadline-gplv2-dev libncursesw5-dev
libssl-dev libsqlite3-dev tk-dev libgdbm-dev libc6-dev libbz2-dev

#Download Python
wget http://python.org/ftp/python/2.7.5/Python-2.7.5.tgz
tar -xvf Python-2.7.5.tgz
cd Python-2.7.5

#Install Python
./configure
make
sudo make install
```

## 6.3   Python Data Types & Data Structures

### 6.3.1   Numbers

Number data type is used to store numeric values. Numbers are immutable data types, therefore changing the value of a number data type results in a newly allocated object.

Box 6.2 shows some examples of working with numbers.

---

**■ Box 6.2: Working with Numbers in Python**

```
#Integer
>>>a=5
>>>type(a)
<type 'int'>

#Floating Point
>>>b=2.5
>>>type(b)
<type 'float'>

#Long
>>>x=9898878787676L
>>>type(x)
<type 'long'>

#Complex
>>>y=2+5j
>>>y
(2+5j)
>>>type(y)
<type 'complex'>
>>>y.real
2
>>>y.imag
5

#Addition
>>>c=a+b
>>>c
7.5
>>>type(c)
<type 'float'>

#Subtraction
>>>d=a-b
>>>d
2.5
>>>type(d)
<type 'float'>

#Multiplication
>>>e=a*b
>>>e
12.5
>>>type(e)
<type 'float'>

#Division
>>>f=b/a
>>>f
```

```
0.5
>>>type(f)
<type 'float'>

#Power
>>>g=a**2
>>>g
25
```

## 6.3.2  Strings

A string is simply a list of characters in order. There are no limits to the number of characters you can have in a string. A string which has zero characters is called an empty string. Box 6.3 shows examples of working with strings.

**■ Box 6.3:  Working with Strings in Python**

```
#Create string
>>>s="Hello World!"
>>>type(s)
<type 'str'>

#String concatenation
>>>t="This is sample program."
>>>r = s+t
>>>r
'Hello World!This is sample program.'

#Get length of string
>>>len(s)
12

#Convert string to integer
>>>x="100"
>>>type(s)
<type 'str'>
>>>y=int(x)
>>>y
100

#Print string
>>>print s
Hello World!

#Formatting output
>>>print "The string (%s) has %d characters" % (s,len(s))
The string (Hello World!)  has 12 characters

#Convert to upper/lower case
>>>s.upper()
'HELLO WORLD!'
>>>s.lower()
'hello world!'
```

```
#Accessing sub-strings
>>>s[0]
'H'
>>>s[6:]
'World!'
>>>s[6:-1]
'World'

#strip:  Returns a copy of the string with
#the leading and trailing characters removed.
>>>s.strip("!")
'Hello World'
```

### 6.3.3  Lists

List is a compound data type used to group together other values. List items need not all
have the same type. A list contains items separated by commas and enclosed within square
brackets. Box 6.4 shows examples of working with lists.

#### ■ Box 6.4:  Working with Lists in Python

```
>>>fruits=['apple','orange','banana','mango']
>>>type(fruits)
<type 'list'>
>>>len(fruits)
4

>>>fruits[1]
'orange'
>>>fruits[1:3]
['orange', 'banana']
>>>fruits[1:]
['orange', 'banana', 'mango']

#Appending an item to a list
>>>fruits.append('pear')
>>>fruits
['apple', 'orange', 'banana', 'mango', 'pear']

#Removing an item from a list
>>>fruits.remove('mango')
>>>fruits
['apple', 'orange', 'banana', 'pear']

#Inserting an item to a list
>>>fruits.insert(1,'mango')
>>>fruits
['apple', 'mango', 'orange', 'banana', 'pear']

#Combining lists
>>>vegetables=['potato','carrot','onion','beans','radish']
>>>vegetables
['potato', 'carrot', 'onion', 'beans', 'radish']
```

```
>>>eatables=fruits+vegetables
>>>eatables
['apple', 'mango', 'orange', 'banana', 'pear',
'potato', 'carrot', 'onion', 'beans', 'radish']

#Mixed data types in a list
>>>mixed=['data',5,100.1,8287398L]
>>>type(mixed)
<type 'list'>
>>>type(mixed[0])
<type 'str'>
>>>type(mixed[1])
<type 'int'>
>>>type(mixed[2])
<type 'float'>
>>>type(mixed[3])
<type 'long'>

#It is possible to change individual elements of a list
>>>mixed[0]=mixed[0]+" items"
>>>mixed[1]=mixed[1]+1
>>>mixed[2]=mixed[2]+0.05
>>>mixed
['data items', 6, 100.14999999999999, 8287398L]

#Lists can be nested
>>>nested=[fruits,vegetables]
>>>nested
[['apple', 'mango', 'orange', 'banana', 'pear'],
['potato', 'carrot', 'onion', '
beans', 'radish']]
```

## 6.3.4  Tuples

A tuple is a sequence data type that is similar to the list. A tuple consists of a number of values separated by commas and enclosed within parentheses. Unlike lists, the elements of tuples cannot be changed, so tuples can be thought of as read-only lists. Box 6.5 shows examples of working with tuples.

### ■ Box 6.5: Working with Tuples in Python

```
>>>fruits=("apple","mango","banana","pineapple")
>>>fruits
('apple', 'mango', 'banana', 'pineapple')
>>>type(fruits)
<type 'tuple'>

#Get length of tuple
>>>len(fruits)
4

#Get an element from a tuple
>>>fruits[0]
```

```
'apple'
>>>fruits[:2]
('apple', 'mango')

#Combining tuples
>>>vegetables=('potato','carrot','onion','radish')
>>>eatables=fruits+vegetables
>>>eatables
('apple', 'mango', 'banana', 'pineapple',
'potato', 'carrot', 'onion', 'radish')
```

### 6.3.5 Dictionaries

Dictionary is a mapping data type or a kind of hash table that maps keys to values. Keys in a dictionary can be of any data type, though numbers and strings are commonly used for keys. Values in a dictionary can be any data type or object. Box 6.6 shows examples on working with dictionaries.

■ **Box 6.6: Working with Dictionaries in Python**

```
>>>student={'name':'Mary','id':'8776','major':'CS'}
>>>student
{'major': 'CS', 'name': 'Mary', 'id': '8776'}
>>>type(student)
<type 'dict'>

#Get length of a dictionary
>>>len(student)
3

#Get the value of a key in dictionary
>>>student['name']
'Mary'

#Get all items in a dictionary
>>>student.items()
[('major', 'CS'), ('name', 'Mary'), ('id', '8776')]

#Get all keys in a dictionary
>>>student.keys()
[ 'major', 'name', 'id']

#Get all values in a dictionary
>>>student.values()
[ 'CS', 'Mary', '8776']

>>>student
{ 'major': 'CS', 'name': 'Mary', 'id': '8776'}

#A value in a dictionary can be another dictionary
>>>student1={'name':'David','id':'9876','major':'ECE'}
>>>students={'1': student,'2':student1}
>>>students
```

```
{'1':   {'major':   'CS', 'name':   'Mary', 'id':   '8776'},
'2':   {'major':   'ECE', 'name':   'David', 'id':   '9876'}}

#Check if dictionary has a key
>>>student.has_key('name')
True
>>>student.has_key('grade')
False
```

### 6.3.6   Type Conversions

Box 6.7 shows examples of type conversions.

■ **Box 6.7:  Type conversion examples**

```
#Convert to string
>>>a=10000
>>>str(a)
'10000'

#Convert to int
>>>b="2013"
>>>int(b)
2013

#Convert to float
>>>float(b)
2013.0

#Convert to long
>>>long(b)
2013L

#Convert to list
>>>s="aeiou"
>>>list(s)
['a', 'e', 'i', 'o', 'u']

#Convert to set
>>>x=['mango','apple','banana','mango','banana']
>>>set(x)
set(['mango', 'apple', 'banana'])
```

## 6.4   Control Flow

Lets us look at the control flow statements in Python.

### 6.4.1   if

The *if* statement in Python is similar to the *if* statement in other languages. Box 6.8 shows some examples of the *if* statement.

■ **Box 6.8: if statement examples**

```
>>>a = 25**5
>>>if a>10000:
  print "More"
else:
  print "Less"

More

>>>if a>10000:
  if a<1000000:
    print "Between 10k and 100k"
  else:
    print "More than 100k"
elif a==10000:
  print "Equal to 10k"
else:
  print "Less than 10k"

More than 100k

>>>s="Hello World"
>>>if "World" in s:
  s=s+"!"
  print s

Hello World!

>>>student={'name':'Mary','id':'8776'}
>>>if not student.has_key('major'):
student['major']='CS'
>>>student
{'major': 'CS', 'name': 'Mary', 'id': '8776'}
```

### 6.4.2 for

The *for* statement in Python iterates over items of any sequence (list, string, etc.) in the order in which they appear in the sequence. This behavior is different from the *for* statement in other languages such as C in which an initialization, incrementing and stopping criteria are provided. Box 6.9 shows examples of the *for* statement.

■ **Box 6.9: for statement examples**

```
helloString = "Hello World"
fruits=['apple','orange','banana','mango']
student = 'name': 'Mary', 'id': '8776', 'major': 'CS'

#Looping over characters in a string
for c in helloString:
  print c
```

```
#Looping over items in a list
i=0
for item in fruits:
    print "Fruit-%d:  %s" % (i,item)
    i=i+1

#Looping over keys in a dictionary
for key in student:
    print "%s:  %s" % (key,student[key])
```

### 6.4.3   while

The *while* statement in Python executes the statements within the *while* loop as long as the *while* condition is true. Box 6.10 shows a *while* statement example.

■ **Box 6.10: while statement examples**

```
#Prints even numbers upto 100
>>> i = 0
>>> while i<=100:
if i%2 == 0:
print i
i = i+1
```

### 6.4.4   range

The *range* statement in Python generates a list of numbers in arithmetic progression. Examples of *range* statement are shown in Box 6.11.

■ **Box 6.11: range examples**

```
#Generate a list of numbers from 0 - 9
>>>range (10)
[0, 1, 2, 3, 4, 5, 6, 7, 8, 9]

#Generate a list of numbers from 10 - 100 with increments of 10
>>>range(10,110,10)
[10, 20, 30, 40, 50, 60, 70, 80, 90,100]
```

### 6.4.5   break/continue

The *break* and *continue* statements in Python are similar to the statements in C. The *break* statement breaks out of the for/while loop whereas the *continue* statement continues with the next iteration. Box 6.12 shows examples of *break* and *continue* usage.

■ **Box 6.12: break/continue examples**

```
#Break statement example
>>>y=1
>>>for x in range(4,256,4):
    y = y * x
```

```
        if y > 512:
            break
        print y

4
32
384


#Continue statement example
>>>fruits=['apple','orange','banana','mango']
>>>for item in fruits:
    if item == "banana":
        continue
    else:
        print item

apple
orange
mango
```

### 6.4.6 pass

The *pass* statement in Python is a null operation. The *pass* statement is used when a statement is required syntactically but you do not want any command or code to execute. Box 6.13 shows an example of *pass* statement.

■ **Box 6.13: pass statement example**

```
fruits=['apple','orange','banana','mango']
for item in fruits:
    if item == "banana":
        pass
    else:
        print item

apple
orange
mango
```

## 6.5  Functions

A function is a block of code that takes information in (in the form of parameters), does some computation, and returns a new piece of information based on the parameter information. A function in Python is a block of code that begins with the keyword *def* followed by the function name and parentheses. The function parameters are enclosed within the parenthesis. The code block within a function begins after a colon that comes after the parenthesis enclosing the parameters. The first statement of the function body can optionally be a documentation string or docstring. Box 6.14 shows an example of a function that computes the average grade given a dictionary containing student records.

■ **Box 6.14: Example of a function in Python**

```
students = { '1':  {'name':  'Bob', 'grade':  2.5},
    '2':  {'name':  'Mary', 'grade':  3.5},
    '3':  {'name':  'David', 'grade':  4.2},
    '4':  {'name':  'John', 'grade':  4.1},
    '5':  {'name':  'Alex', 'grade':  3.8}}


def averageGrade(students):
    "This function computes the average grade"
    sum = 0.0
    for key in students:
        sum = sum + students[key]['grade']
        average = sum/len(students)
        return average

avg = averageGrade(students)
print "The average garde is:  %0.2f" % (avg)
```

Functions can have default values of the parameters. If a function with default values is called with fewer parameters or without any parameter, the default values of the parameters are used as shown in the example in Box 6.15.

■ **Box 6.15: Example of function with default arguments**

```
>>>def displayFruits(fruits=['apple','orange']):
    print "There are %d fruits in the list" % (len(fruits))
    for item in fruits:
        print item

#Using default arguments
>>>displayFruits()
apple
orange

>>>fruits = ['banana', 'pear', 'mango']
>>>displayFruits(fruits)
banana
pear
mango
```

All parameters in the Python functions are passed by reference. Therefore, if a parameter is changed within a function the change also reflected back in the calling function. Box 6.16 shows an example of parameter passing by reference.

■ **Box 6.16: Example of passing by reference**

```
>>>def displayFruits(fruits):
    print "There are %d fruits in the list" % (len(fruits))
    for item in fruits:
```

```
      print item
   print "Adding one more fruit"
   fruits.append('mango')


>>>fruits = ['banana', 'pear', 'apple']
>>>displayFruits(fruits)
There are 3 fruits in the list
banana
pear
apple
Adding one more fruit

>>>print "There are %d fruits in the list" % (len(fruits))
There are 4 fruits in the list
```

Functions can also be called using keyword arguments that identify the arguments by the parameter name when the function is called. Box 6.17 shows examples of keyword arguments.

■ **Box 6.17: Examples of keyword arguments**

```
>>>def printStudentRecords(name,age=20,major='CS'):
   print "Name:   " + name
   print "Age:   " + str(age)
   print "Major:   " + major

#This will give error as name is required argument
>>>printStudentRecords()
Traceback (most recent call last):
File "<stdin>", line 1, in <module>
TypeError: printStudentRecords() takes at least 1 argument (0 given)

>>>printStudentRecords(name='Alex')
Name:  Alex
Age:  20
Major:  CS

>>>printStudentRecords(name='Bob',age=22,major='ECE')
Name:  Bob
Age:  22
Major:  ECE

>>>printStudentRecords(name='Alan',major='ECE')
Name:  Alan
Age:  20
Major:  ECE

#name is a formal argument.
#**kwargs is a keyword argument that receives all
#arguments except the formal argument as a dictionary.
>>>def student(name, **kwargs):
   print "Student Name:   " + name
   for key in kwargs:
```

```
      print key + ': '  + kwargs[key]


>>>student(name='Bob', age='20', major = 'CS')
Student Name:  Bob
age:  20
major:  CS
```

Python functions can have variable length arguments. These variable length arguments are passed as a tuple to the function with an argument prefixed with asterix (*) as shown in Box 6.18.

**■ Box 6.18: Example of variable length arguments**

```
def student(name, *varargs):
   print "Student Name:  " + name
   for item in varargs:
     print item

>>>student('Nav')
Student Name:  Nav

>>>student('Amy', 'Age:  24')
Student Name:  Amy
Age:  24

>>>student('Bob', 'Age:  20', 'Major:  CS')
Student Name:  Bob
Age:  20
Major:  CS
```

## 6.6  Modules

Python allows organizing of the program code into different modules which improves the code readability and management. A module is a Python file that defines some functionality in the form of functions or classes. Modules can be imported using the import keyword. Modules to be imported must be present in the search path. Box 6.19 shows the example of a student module that contains two functions and Box 6.20 shows an example of importing the student module and using it.

**■ Box 6.19: Module student**

```
def averageGrade(students):
   sum = 0.0
   for key in students:
     sum = sum + students[key]['grade']
   average = sum/len(students)
   return average

def printRecords(students):
```

```
    print "There are %d students" %(len(students))
    i=1
    for key in students:
      print "Student-%d:  " % (i)
      print "Name:   " + students[key]['name']
      print "Grade:  " + str(students[key]['grade'])
      i = i+1
```

■ **Box 6.20: Using module student**

```
>>>import student

>>>students =  '1':  'name':  'Bob',  'grade':  2.5,
        '2':  'name':  'Mary',  'grade':  3.5,
        '3':  'name':  'David', 'grade':  4.2,
        '4':  'name':  'John',  'grade':  4.1,
        '5':  'name':  'Alex',  'grade':  3.8

>>>student.printRecords(students)
There are 5 students
Student-1:
Name:  Bob
Grade:  2.5

Student-2:
Name:  David
Grade:  4.2

Student-3:
Name:  Mary
Grade:  3.5

Student-4:
Name:  Alex
Grade:  3.8

Student-5:
Name:  John
Grade:  4.1

>>>avg = student. averageGrade(students)
>>>print "The average garde is:  %0.2f" % (avg)
3.62
```

The import keyword followed by the module name imports all the functions in the module. If you want to use only a specific function it is recommended to import only that function using the keyword *from* as shown in the example in Box 6.21.

■ **Box 6.21: Importing a specific function from a module**

```
»>from student import averageGrade
```

```
>>>students = '1': 'name': 'Bob', 'grade': 2.5,
        '2': 'name': 'Mary', 'grade': 3.5,
        '3': 'name': 'David', 'grade': 4.2,
        '4': 'name': 'John', 'grade': 4.1,
        '5': 'name': 'Alex', 'grade': 3.8

>>>avg = averageGrade(students)
>>>print "The average garde is: %0.2f" % (avg)
3.62
```

Python comes with a number of standard modules such as system related modules (sys), OS related module (os), mathematical modules (math, fractions, etc.), Internet related modules (email, json. etc), etc. The complete list of standard modules is available in the Python documentation [87]. Box 6.22 shows an example of listing all names defined in a module using the built-in dir function.

■ **Box 6.22: Listing all names defined in a module**

```
>>>import email

>>>dir (email)
['Charset', 'Encoders', 'Errors', 'FeedParser', 'Generator', 'Header',
'Iterators', 'LazyImporter', 'MIMEAudio', 'MIMEBase', 'MIMEImage',
'MIMEMessage', 'MIMEMultipart', 'MIMENonMultipart', 'MIMEText',
'Message', 'Parser', 'Utils', '_LOWERNAMES', '_MIMENAMES',
'__all__', '__builtins__', '__doc__', '__file__',
'__name__', '__package__', '__path__', '__version__',
'_name', 'base64MIME', 'email', 'importer', 'message_from_file',
'message_from_string', 'mime', 'quopriMIME', 'sys']
```

## 6.7  Packages

Python package is hierarchical file structure that consists of modules and subpackages. Packages allow better organization of modules related to a single application environment. For example, Box 6.23 shows the listing of the skimage package that provides image processing algorithms. The package is organized into a root directory (skimage) with sub-directories (color, draw, etc) which are sub-packages within the skimage package. Each directory contains a special file named __init__.py which tells Python to treat directories as packages. This file can either be an empty file or contain some initialization code for the package.

■ **Box 6.23: skimage package listing**

```
skimage/                        Top level package
    __init__.py                     Treat directory as a package
    color/                      color subpackage
        __init__.py
        colorconv.py
```

```
            colorlabel.py
            rgb_colors.py
        draw/                          draw subpackage
            __init__.py
            draw.py
            setup.py
        exposure/                      exposure subpackage
            __init__.py
            _adapthist.py
            exposure.py
        feature/                       feature subpackage
            __init__.py
            _brief.py
            _daisy.py
            ...
    ...
```

## 6.8   File Handling

Python allows reading and writing to files using the file object. The open(filename, mode) function is used to get a file object. The mode can be read (r), write (w), append (a), read and write (r+ or w+), read-binary (rb), write-binary (wb), etc. Box 6.24 shows an example of reading an entire file with read function. After the file contents have been read the close function is called which closes the file object.

■ **Box 6.24:  Example of reading an entire file**

```
>>>fp = open('file.txt','r')
>>>content = fp.read()
>>>print content
Python supports more than one programming paradigms
including object-oriented programming and structured
programming
Python is an interpreted language and does
not require an explicit compilation
step.  >>>fp.close()
```

Box 6.25 shows an example of reading line by line from a file using the readline function.

■ **Box 6.25:  Example of reading line by line**

```
>>>fp.close()
>>>fp = open('file.txt','r')
>>>print "Line-1:  " + fp.readline()
Line-1:  Python supports more than one programming paradigms
including object-oriented programming and structured
programming

>>>print "Line-2:  " + fp.readline()
Line-2:  Python is an interpreted language and does not
require an explicit compilation step.
```

```
>>>fp.close()
```

Box 6.26 shows an example of reading lines of a file in a loop using the readlines function.

■ **Box 6.26: Example of reading lines in a loop**

```
>>>fp = open('file.txt','r')
>>>lines = fp.readlines()
>>>for line in lines:
   print line

Python supports more than one programming paradigms including
object-oriented programming and structured programming

Python is an interpreted language and does not
require an explicit compilation step.
```

Box 6.27 shows an example of reading a certain number of bytes from a file using the read(size) function.

■ **Box 6.27: Example of reading a certain number of bytes**

```
>>>fp = open('file.txt','r')
>>>fp.read(10)
'Python sup'
>>>fp.close()
```

Box 6.28 shows an example of getting the current position of read using the tell function.

■ **Box 6.28: Example of getting the current position of read**

```
>>>fp = open('file.txt','r')
>>>fp.read(10)
'Python sup'
>>>currentpos = fp.tell
>>>print currentpos
<built-in method tell of file object at 0x0000000002391390>
>>>fp.close()
```

Box 6.29 shows an example of seeking to a certain position in a file using the seek function.

■ **Box 6.29: Example of seeking to a certain position**

```
>>>fp = open('file.txt','r')
>>>fp.seek(10,0)
>>>content = fp.read(10)
>>>print content
ports more
```

```
>>>fp.close()
```

Box 6.30 shows an example of writing a file using the write function.

**■ Box 6.30: Example of writing to a file**

```
>>>fo = open('file1.txt','w')
>>>content='This is an example of writing to a file in Python.'
>>>fo.write(content)
>>>fo.close()
```

## 6.9   Date/Time Operations

Python provides several functions for date and time access and conversions. The datetime module allows manipulating date and time in several ways. Box 6.31 shows examples of manipulating with date.

**■ Box 6.31: Examples of manipulating with date**

```
>>>from datetime import date
>>>now = date.today()
>>>print "Date:   " + now.strftime("%m-%d-%y")
Date:   07-24-13
>>>print "Day of Week:   " + now.strftime("%A")
Day of Week:   Wednesday
>>>print "Month:   " + now.strftime("%B")
Month:   July
>>>
>>>then = date(2013, 6, 7)
>>>timediff = now - then
>>>timediff.days
47
```

The time module in Python provides various time-related functions. Box 6.32 shows examples of manipulating with time.

**■ Box 6.32: Examples of manipulating with time**

```
>>>import time
>>>nowtime = time.time()
>>>time.localtime(nowtime)
time.struct_time(tm_year=2013, tm_mon=7, tm_mday=24, tm_
ec=51, tm_wday=2, tm_yday=205, tm_isdst=0)
>>>time.asctime(time.localtime(nowtime))
'Wed Jul 24 16:14:51 2013'

>>>time.strftime("The date is %d-%m-%y.
Today is a %A. It is %H hours, %M minutes and %S seconds now.")
'The date is 24-07-13.  Today is a Wednesday.  It is 16 hours,
15 minutes and 14 seconds now.'
```

## 6.10   Classes

Python is an Object-Oriented Programming (OOP) language. Python provides all the standard features of Object Oriented Programming such as classes, class variables, class methods, inheritance, function overloading, and operator overloading. Let us briefly look at these OOP concepts:

### Class

A class is simply a representation of a type of object and user-defined prototype for an object that is composed of three things: a name, attributes, and operations/methods.

### Instance/Object

Object is an instance of the data structure defined by a class.

### Inheritance

Inheritance is the process of forming a new class from an existing class or base class.

### Function overloading

Function overloading is a form of polymorphism that allows a function to have different meanings, depending on its context.

### Operator overloading

Operator overloading is a form of polymorphism that allows assignment of more than one function to a particular operator.

### Function overriding

Function overriding allows a child class to provide a specific implementation of a function that is already provided by the base class. Child class implementation of the overridden function has the same name, parameters and return type as the function in the base class.

Box 6.33 shows an example of a Class. The variable *studentCount* is a class variable that is shared by all instances of the class *Student* and is accessed by *Student.studentCount*. The variables *name*, *id* and *grades* are instance variables which are specific to each instance of the class. There is a special method by the name *__init__()* which is the class constructor. The class constructor initializes a new instance when it is created. The function *__del__()* is the class destructor.

■ **Box 6.33: Examples of a class**

```
>>>class Student:
  studentCount = 0
  def __init__(self, name, id):
    print "Constructor called"
    self.name = name
    self.id = id
    Student.studentCount = Student.studentCount + 1
    self.grades=

  def __del__(self):
    print "Destructor called"
```

```
    def getStudentCount(self):
        return Student.studentCount

    def addGrade(self,key,value):
        self.grades[key]=value

    def getGrade(self,key):
        return self.grades[key]

    def printGrades(self):
        for key in self.grades:
            print key + ":   " + self.grades[key]
>>>s = Student('Steve','98928')
Constructor called
>>>s.addGrade('Math','90')
>>>s.addGrade('Physics','85')
>>>s.printGrades()
Physics:   85
Math:   90
>>>mathgrade = s.getGrade('Math')
>>>print mathgrade
90
>>>count = s.getStudentCount()
>>>print count
1
>>>del s
Destructor called
```

Box 6.34 shows an example of class inheritance. In this example *Shape* is the base class and *Circle* is the derived class. The class *Circle* inherits the attributes of the *Shape* class. The child class *Circle* overrides the methods and attributes of the base class (eg. *draw()* function defined in the base class *Shape* is overridden in child class *Circle*). It is possible to hide some class attributes by naming them with a *double underscore* prefix. For example, __label attribute is hidden and cannot be directly accessed using the object (*circ.__label* gives an error). To hide the attributes with double underscore prefix, Python changes their names internally and prefixes the class name (e.g. __label is changed to _Circle__label).

■ **Box 6.34: Examples of class inheritance**

```
>>>class Shape:
    def __init__(self):
        print "Base class constructor"
        self.color = 'Green'
        self.lineWeight = 10.0
    def draw(self):
        print "Draw - to be implemented"
    def setColor(self, c):
        self.color = c
    def getColor(self):
        return self.color
```

```
    def setLineWeight(self,lwt):
       self.lineWeight = lwt
    def getLineWeight(self):
       return self.lineWeight

>>>class Circle(Shape):
    def __init__(self, c,r):
       print "Child class constructor"
       self.center = c
       self.radius = r
       self.color = 'Green'
       self.lineWeight = 10.0
       self.__label = 'Hidden circle label'
    def setCenter(self,c):
       self.center = c
    def getCenter(self):
       return self.center
    def setRadius(self,r):
       self.radius = r
    def getRadius(self):
       return self.radius
    def draw(self):
       print "Draw Circle (overridden function)"

>>>class Point:
    def __init__(self, x, y):
       self.xCoordinate = x
       self.yCoordinate = y

    def setXCoordinate(self,x):
       self.xCoordinate = x
    def getXCoordinate(self):
       return self.xCoordinate
    def setYCoordinate(self,y):
       self.yCoordinate = y
    def getYCoordinate(self):
       return self.yCoordinate

>>>p = Point(2,4)
>>>circ = Circle(p,7)
Child class constructor
>>>circ.getColor()
'Green'
>>>circ.setColor('Red')
>>>circ.getColor()
'Red'

>>>circ.getLineWeight()
10.0
>>>circ.getCenter().getXCoordinate()
2
>>>circ.getCenter().getYCoordinate()
4
```

```
>>>circ.draw()
Draw Circle (overridden function)

>>>circ.radius
7
>>>circ.__label
Traceback (most recent call last):
File "<stdin>", line 1, in <module>
AttributeError:  Circle instance has no attribute '__label'

>>>circ._Circle__label
'Hidden circle label'
```

## 6.11    Python Packages of Interest for IoT

### 6.11.1    JSON

JavaScript Object Notation (JSON) is an easy to read and write data-interchange format. JSON is used as an alternative to XML and is is easy for machines to parse and generate. JSON is built on two structures - a collection of name-value pairs (e.g. a Python dictionary) and ordered lists of values (e.g.. a Python list).

JSON format is often used for serializing and transmitting structured data over a network connection, for example, transmitting data between a server and web application. Box 6.35 shows an example of a Twitter tweet object encoded as JSON.

■ **Box 6.35:  JSON Example - A Twitter tweet object**

```
{
    "created_at":
    "Sat Jun 01 11:39:43 +0000 2013",
    "id":340794787059875841,
    "text":"What a bright and sunny day today!",
    "truncated":false,
    "in_reply_to_status_id":null,
    "user":{
        "id":383825039,
        "name":"Harry",
        "followers_count":316,
        "friends_count":298,
        "listed_count":0,
        "created_at":"Sun Oct 02 15:51:16 +0000 2011",
        "favorites_count":251,
        "statuses_count":1707,
        :
        "notifications":null
        },
    "geo":{
        "type":"Point",
        "coordinates":[26.92782727,75.78908449]
        },
    "coordinates":{
        "type":"Point",
```

```
      "coordinates":[75.78908449,26.92782727]
      },
  "place":null,
  "contributors":null,
  "retweet_count":0,
  "favorite_count":0,
  "entities":{
    "hashtags":[],
    "symbols":[],
    "urls":[],
    "user_mentions":[]
    },
  "favorited":false,
  "retweeted":false,
  "filter_level":"medium",
  "lang":"nl"
}
```

Exchange of information encoded as JSON involves encoding and decoding steps. The Python JSON package [109] provides functions for encoding and decoding JSON.

Box 6.36 shows an example of JSON encoding and decoding.

---

**■ Box 6.36: Encoding & Decoding JSON in Python**

```
>>>import json

>>>message = {
  "created":  "Wed Jun 31 2013",
  "id":"001",
  "text":"This is a test message.",
}

>>>json.dumps(message)
'{"text":  "This is a test message.", "id":  "001",
"created":  "Wed Jun 31 2013"}'


>>>decodedMsg = json.loads( '{"text":  "This is a
test message.", "id":  "001", "created":  "Wed Jun 31 2013"}')

>>>decodedMsg['created']
u'Wed Jun 31 2013'
>>>decodedMsg['text']
u'This is a test message.'
```

---

## 6.11.2   XML

XML (Extensible Markup Language) is a data format for structured document interchange. Box 6.37 shows an example of an XML file. In this section you will learn how to parse, read and write XML with Python. The Python *minidom* library provides a minimal implementation of the Document Object Model interface and has an API similar to that in other languages. Box 6.38 shows a Python program for parsing an XML file.  Box 6.39 shows a Python program for creating an XML file.

### ■ Box 6.37: XML example

```
<?xml version="1.0"?>
<catalog>
< plant id='1' >
<common>Bloodroot</common>
<botanical>Sanguinaria canadensis</botanical>
<zone>4</zone>
<light>Mostly Shady</light>
<price> 2.44 </price>
<availability>031599</availability>
</plant>
<plant id='2' >
<common>Columbine</common>
<botanical>Aquilegia canadensis</botanical>
<zone>3</zone>
<light>Mostly Shady</light>
<price> 9.37</price >
<availability>030699</availability>
</plant>
<plant id='3' >
<common>Marsh Marigold</common>
<botanical>Caltha palustris</botanical>
<zone>4</zone>
<light>Mostly Sunny</light>
<price> 6.81</price>
<availability>051799</availability>
</plant>
</catalog>
```

### ■ Box 6.38: Parsing an XML file in Python

```
from xml.dom.minidom import parse
dom = parse("test.xml")
for node in dom.getElementsByTagName('plant'):
   id=node.getAttribute('id')
   print "Plant ID:", id
   common=node.getElementsByTagName('common')[0]
      .childNodes[0].nodeValue
   print "Common:", common
   botanical=node.getElementsByTagName('botanical')[0]
      .childNodes[0].nodeValue
   print "Botanical:", botanical
   zone=node.getElementsByTagName('zone')[0]
      .childNodes[0].nodeValue
   print "Zone:", zone
```

---

■ **Box 6.39: Creating an XML file with Python**

```
#Python example to create the following XML:
#' <?xml version="1.0" ?> <Class> <Student>
#<Name>Alex</Name> <Major>ECE</Major> </Student > </Class>

from xml.dom.minidom import Document
doc = Document()

# create base element
base = doc.createElement('Class')
doc.appendChild(base)

# create an entry element
entry = doc.createElement('Student')
base.appendChild(entry)

# create an element and append to entry element
name = doc.createElement('Name')
nameContent = doc.createTextNode('Alex')
name.appendChild(nameContent)
entry.appendChild(name)

# create an element and append to entry element
major = doc.createElement('Major')
majorContent = doc.createTextNode('ECE')
major.appendChild(majorContent)
entry.appendChild(major)

fp = open('foo.xml','w')
doc.writexml()
fp.close()
```

---

### 6.11.3  HTTPLib & URLLib

HTTPLib2 and URLLib2 are Python libraries used in network/internet programming [111, 112]. HTTPLib2 is an HTTP client library and URLLib2 is a library for fetching URLs.

Box 6.40 shows an example of an HTTP GET request using the HTTPLib. The variable *resp* contains the response headers and *content* contains the content retrieved from the URL.

---

■ **Box 6.40: HTTP GET request example using HTTPLib**

```
>>> import httplib2
>>> h = httplib2.Http()
>>> resp, content = h.request("http://example.com", "GET")
>>> resp
{'status': '200', 'content-length': '1270', 'content-location':
'http://example.com', 'x-cache': 'HIT', 'accept-ranges':
'bytes', 'server': 'ECS
(cpm/F858)', 'last-modified': 'Thu,
25 Apr 2013 16:13:23 GMT', 'etag':
```

---

```
'"780602-4f6-4db31b2978ec0"', 'date':  'Wed, 31 Jul 2013 12:36:05 GMT',
'content-type':  'text/html; charset=UTF-8'}

>>> content
'<!doctype html>\n<html>\n<head>\n
<title>Example Domain</title>\n\n
<meta charset="utf-8" />\n
:
```

Box 6.41 shows an HTTP request example using URLLib2. A request object is created by calling *urllib2.Request* with the URL to fetch as input parameter. Then *urllib2.urlopen* is called with the request object which returns the response object for the requested URL. The response object is read by calling *read* function.

■ **Box 6.41: HTTP request example using URLLib2**

```
>>> import urllib2
>>>
>>> req = urllib2.Request('http://example.com')
>>> response = urllib2.urlopen(req)
>>> response_page = response.read()
>>> response_page
'<!doctype html>\n<html>\n<head>\n
<title>Example Domain</title>\n\n
<meta charset="utf-8" />\n
```

Box 6.42 shows an example of an HTTP POST request. The data in the POST body is encoded using the *urlencode* function from urllib.

■ **Box 6.42: HTTP POST example using HTTPLib2**

```
>>> import httplib2
>>> import urllib
>>> h = httplib2.Http()
>>> data = {'title':  'Cloud computing'}
>>> resp, content =
h.request("http://www.htmlcodetutorial.com/cgi-bin/mycgi.pl", "POST",
urllib.urlencode(data))
>>> resp
{'status':  '200', 'transfer-encoding':  'chunked',
'server':  'Apache/2.0.64 (Unix) mod_ssl/2.0.64 OpenSSL/0.9.7a
mod_auth_passthrough/2.1 mod_bwlimited/1.4 FrontPage/5.0.2.2635
PHP/5.3.10', 'connection':  'close', 'date':  'Wed, 31 Jul 2013
12:41:20 GMT', 'content-type':  'text/html; charset=ISO-8859-1'}

>>> content
'<HTML>\n<HEAD>\n<TITLE>Idocs Guide to
HTML: My CGI</TITLE>\n</HEAD>
:
```

Box 6.43 shows an example of sending data to a URL using URLLib2 (e.g. an HTML form submission). This example is similar to the HTTP POST example in Box 6.42 and uses URLLib2 request object instead of HTTPLib2.

---

**■ Box 6.43: Example of sending data to a URL**

```
>>> import urllib
>>> import urllib2
>>>
>>> url = 'http://www.htmlcodetutorial.com/cgi-bin/mycgi.pl'
>>> values = {'title' : 'Cloud Computing',
... 'language' : 'Python' }
>>>
>>> data = urllib.urlencode(values)
>>> req = urllib2.Request(url, data)
>>> response = urllib2.urlopen(req)
>>> the_page = response.read()
>>> the_page
'<HTML>\n<HEAD>\n<TITLE>Idocs Guide to
HTML: My CGI</TITLE>\n</HEAD>
:
```

---

### 6.11.4 SMTPLib

Simple Mail Transfer Protocol (SMTP) is a protocol which handles sending email and routing e-mail between mail servers. The Python smtplib module provides an SMTP client session object that can be used to send email [113].

Box 6.44 shows a Python example of sending email from a Gmail account. The string *message* contains the email message to be sent. To send email from a Gmail account the Gmail SMTP server is specified in the *server* string.

To send an email, first a connection is established with the SMTP server by calling *smtplib.SMTP* with the SMTP server name and port. The user name and password provided are then used to login into the server. The email is then sent by calling *server.sendmail* function with the from address, to address list and message as input parameters.

---

**■ Box 6.44: Python example of sending email**

```
import smtplib

from_email = '<enter-gmail-address>'
recipients_list = ['<enter-sender-email>']
cc_list = [ ]
subject = 'Hello'
message = 'This is a test message.'
username = '<enter-gmail-username>'
password = '<enter-gmail-password>'
server = 'smtp.gmail.com:587'

def sendemail(from_addr, to_addr_list, cc_addr_list,
subject, message,
login, password,
```

---

```
smtpserver):

header = 'From:   %s\n' % from_addr
header += 'To:    %s\n' % ','.join(to_addr_list)
header += 'Cc:    %s\n' % ','.join(cc_addr_list)
header += 'Subject:   %s\n\n' % subject
message = header + message

server = smtplib.SMTP(smtpserver)
server.starttls()
server.login(login,password)
problems = server.sendmail(from_addr, to_addr_list, message)
server.quit()

#Send email
sendemail(from_email, recipients_list, cc_list, subject,
message, username, password, server)
```

## Summary

In this chapter you learned the essentials of the Python programming language. Python is a general-purpose, high level programming language that supports more than one programming paradigms including object-oriented programming and structured programming. Python is an interpreted language and does not require an explicit compilation step. Python provides an interactive mode in which the user can submit commands at the Python prompt and interact with the interpreter directly. Python supports both procedure-oriented programming and object-oriented programming. Python programs can be directly executed from source code and copied from one machine to another without worrying about portability. Python Data Types & Data Structures include Numbers, Strings, Lists, Tuples and Dictionaries. Control flow statements in Python include $if$, $for$, $while$, $break$, $continue$, $range$ and $pass$. A function in Python is a block of code that begins with the keyword $def$ followed by the function name and parentheses. Python allows organizing the program code into different modules which improves the code readability and makes it easy to manage. Python packages allow better organization of modules related to a single application environment. Python provides all the standard features of Object Oriented Programming such as classes, class variables, class methods, inheritance, function overloading, and operator overloading.

## Review Questions

1. What is the difference between procedure-oriented programming and object-oriented programming?
2. What is an interpreted language?
3. Describe a use case of Python dictionary?
4. What is a keyword argument in Python?
5. What are variable length arguments?
6. What is the difference between a Python module and a package?
7. How is function overriding implemented in Python?

## Lab Exercises

1. In this exercise you will create a Python program to compute document statistics. Follow the steps below:

   - Create a text file with some random text.
   - Create a Python program with functions for reading the file, computing word count and top 10 words. Use the template below:

     ```
     def readFile(filename):
     #Implement this

     def wordCount(contents):
     #Implement this

     def topTenWords(wordCountDict):
     #Implement this

     def main():
         filename = sys.argv[1]
         contents = readFile(filename)
         wordCountDict=wordCount(contents)
         topTenWords(wordCountDict)

     if __name__ == '__main__':
         main()
     ```

   - Run the Python program as follows:
     python documentstats.py filename.txt

   - Extend Exercise-1 to compute top 10 keywords in a file. To ignore stop-words (commonly occurring words such as 'an', 'the', 'how', etc) create a list of stop-words. Ignore stop-words when computing top 10 keywords.

# 7 - IoT Physical Devices & Endpoints

This Chapter covers

- Basic building blocks of an IoT Device
- Exemplary Device: Raspberry Pi
- Raspberry Pi interfaces
- Programming Raspberry Pi with Python
- Other IoT devices

## 7.1    What is an IoT Device

As described earlier, a "Thing" in Internet of Things (IoT) can be any object that has a unique identifier and which can send/receive data (including user data) over a network (e.g., smart phone, smart TV, computer, refrigerator, car, etc. ). IoT devices are connected to the Internet and send information about themselves or about their surroundings (e.g. information sensed by the connected sensors) over a network (to other devices or servers/storage) or allow actuation upon the physical entities/environment around them remotely. Some examples of IoT devices are listed below:

- A home automation device that allows remotely monitoring the status of appliances and controlling the appliances.
- An industrial machine which sends information abouts its operation and health monitoring data to a server.
- A car which sends information about its location to a cloud-based service.
- A wireless-enabled wearable device that measures data about a person such as the number of steps walked and sends the data to a cloud-based service.

### 7.1.1    Basic building blocks of an IoT Device

An IoT device can consist of a number of modules based on functional attributes, such as:

- Sensing: Sensors can be either on-board the IoT device or attached to the device. IoT device can collect various types of information from the on-board or attached sensors such as temperature, humidity, light intensity, etc. The sensed information can be communicated either to other devices or cloud-based servers/storage.
- Actuation: IoT devices can have various types of actuators attached that allow taking actions upon the physical entities in the vicinity of the device. For example, a relay switch connected to an IoT device can turn an appliance on/off based on the commands sent to the device.
- Communication: Communication modules are responsible for sending collected data to other devices or cloud-based servers/storage and receiving data from other devices and commands from remote applications.
- Analysis & Processing: Analysis and processing modules are responsible for making sense of the collected data.

The representative IoT device used for the examples in this book is the widely used single-board mini computer called Raspberry Pi (explained in later sections). The use of Raspberry Pi is intentional since these devices are widely accessible, inexpensive, and available from multiple vendors. Furthermore, extensive information is available on their programming and use both on the Internet and in other textbooks. The principles we teach in this book are just as applicable to other (including proprietary) IoT endpoints, in addition to Raspberry Pi. Before we look at the specifics of Raspberry Pi, let us first look at the building blocks of a generic single-board computer (SBC) based IoT device.

Figure 7.1 shows a generic block diagram of a single-board computer (SBC) based IoT device that includes CPU, GPU, RAM, storage and various types of interfaces and peripherals.

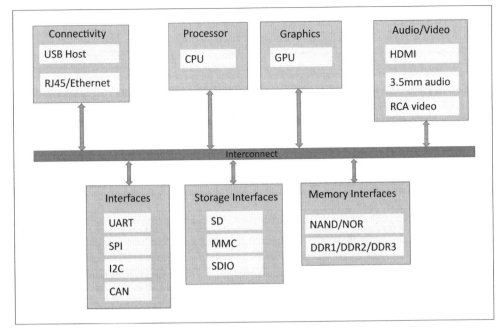

Figure 7.1: Block diagram of an IoT Device

## 7.2  Exemplary Device: Raspberry Pi

Raspberry Pi [104] is a low-cost mini-computer with the physical size of a credit card. Raspberry Pi runs various flavors of Linux and can perform almost all tasks that a normal desktop computer can do. In addition to this, Raspberry Pi also allows interfacing sensors and actuators through the general purpose I/O pins. Since Raspberry Pi runs Linux operating system, it supports Python "out of the box".

## 7.3  About the Board

Figure 7.2 shows the Raspberry Pi board with the various components/peripherals labeled.
- **Processor & RAM** : Raspberry Pi is based on an ARM processor. The latest version of Raspberry Pi (Model B, Revision 2) comes with 700 MHz Low Power ARM1176JZ-F processor and 512 MB SDRAM.
- **USB Ports** : Raspberry Pi comes with two USB 2.0 ports. The USB ports on Raspberry Pi can provide a current upto 100mA. For connecting devices that draw current more than 100mA, an external USB powered hub is required.
- **Ethernet Ports** : Raspberry Pi comes with a standard RJ45 Ethernet port. You can connect an Ethernet cable or a USB Wifi adapter to provide Internet connectivity.
- **HDMI Output** : The HDMI port on Raspberry Pi provides both video and audio output. You can connect the Raspberry Pi to a monitor using an HDMI cable. For monitors that have a DVI port but no HDMI port, you can use an HDMI to DVI adapter/cable.
- **Composite Video Output** : Raspberry Pi comes with a composite video output with an RCA jack that supports both PAL and NTSC video output. The RCA jack can be

used to connect old televisions that have an RCA input only.

- **Audio Output** : Raspberry Pi has a 3.5mm audio output jack. This audio jack is used for providing audio output to old televisions along with the RCA jack for video. The audio quality from this jack is inferior to the HDMI output.

- **GPIO Pins** : Raspberry Pi comes with a number of general purpose input/ouput pins. Figure 7.3 shows the Raspberry Pi GPIO headers. There are four types of pins on Raspberry Pi - true GPIO pins, I2C interface pins, SPI interface pins and serial Rx and Tx pins.

- **Display Serial Interface (DSI)** : The DSI interface can be used to connect an LCD panel to Raspberry Pi.

- **Camera Serial Interface (CSI)** : The CSI interface can be used to connect a camera module to Raspberry Pi.

- **Status LEDs** : Raspberry Pi has five status LEDs. Table 7.1 lists Raspberry Pi status LEDs and their functions.

- **SD Card Slot** : Raspberry Pi does not have a built in operating system and storage. You can plug-in an SD card loaded with a Linux image to the SD card slot. Appendix-A provides instructions on setting up New Out-of-the-Box Software (NOOBS) on Raspberry Pi. You will require atleast an 8GB SD card for setting up NOOBS.

- **Power Input** : Raspberry Pi has a micro-USB connector for power input.

| Status LED | Function |
|------------|----------|
| ACT | SD card access |
| PWR | 3.3V Power is present |
| FDX | Full duplex LAN connected |
| LNK | Link/Network activity |
| 100 | 100 Mbit LAN connected |

Table 7.1: Raspberry Pi Status LEDs

## 7.4   Linux on Raspberry Pi

Raspberry Pi supports various flavors of Linux including:

- **Raspbian** Raspbian Linux is a Debian Wheezy port optimized for Raspberry Pi. This is the recommended Linux for Raspberry Pi. Appendix-1 provides instructions on setting up Raspbian on Raspberry Pi.

- **Arch** : Arch is an Arch Linux port for AMD devices.

- **Pidora** : Pidora Linux is a Fedora Linux optimized for Raspberry Pi.

- **RaspBMC** : RaspBMC is an XBMC media-center distribution for Raspberry Pi.

- **OpenELEC** : OpenELEC is a fast and user-friendly XBMC media-center distribution.

- **RISC OS** : RISC OS is a very fast and compact operating system.

Figure 7.4 shows the Raspbian Linux desktop on Raspberry Pi. Figure 7.5 shows the default file explorer on Raspbian. Figure 7.6 shows the default console on Raspbian. Figure 7.7 shows the default browser on Raspbian. To configure Raspberry Pi, the raspi-config tool is used which can be launched from command line as ($raspi-config) as shown in

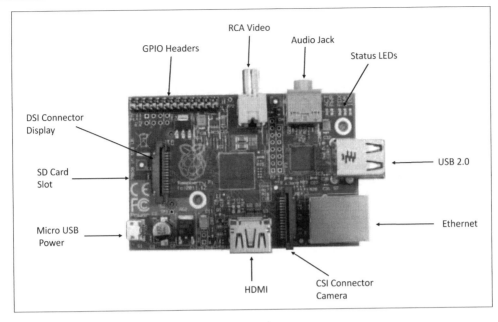

Figure 7.2: Raspberry Pi board

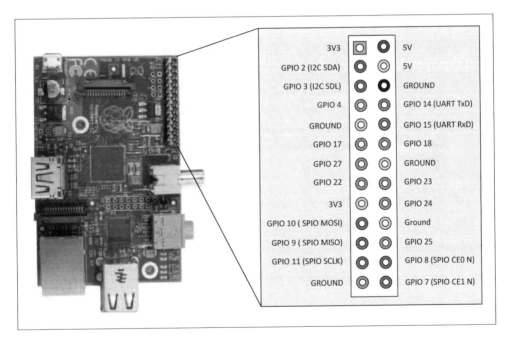

Figure 7.3: Raspberry Pi GPIO headers

Figure 7.8. Using the configuration tool you can expand root partition to fill SD card, set keyboard layout, change password, set locale and timezone, change memory split, enable or disable SSH server and change boot behavior. It is recommended to expand the root file-system so that you can use the entire space on the SD card.

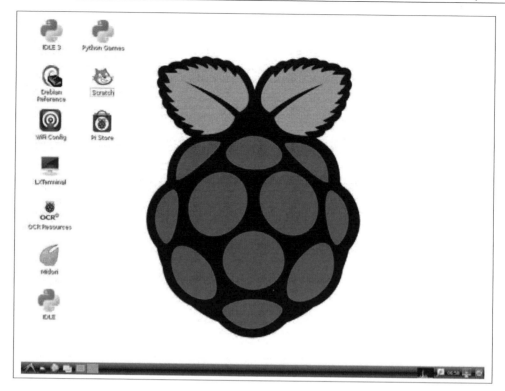

Figure 7.4: Rasbian Linux desktop

Though Raspberry Pi comes with an HDMI output, it is more convenient to access the device with a VNC connection or SSH. This does away with the need for a separate display for Raspberry Pi and you can use Raspberry Pi from your desktop or laptop computer. Appendix-A provides instructions on setting up VNC server on Raspberry Pi and the instructions to connect to Raspberry Pi with SSH. Table 7.2 lists the frequently used commands on Raspberry Pi.

Figure 7.5: File explorer on Raspberry Pi

Figure 7.6: Console on Raspberry Pi

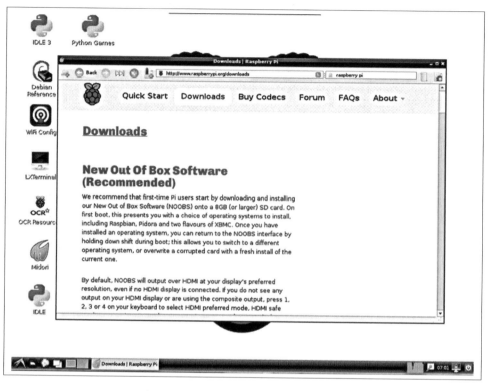

Figure 7.7: Browser on Raspberry Pi

Figure 7.8: Raspberry Pi configuration tool

| Command | Function | Example |
|---|---|---|
| cd | Change directory | cd /home/pi |
| cat | Show file contents | cat file.txt |
| ls | List files and folders | ls /home/pi |
| locate | Search for a file | locate file.txt |
| lsusb | List USB devices | lsusb |
| pwd | Print name of present working directory | pwd |
| mkdir | Make directory | mkdir /home/pi/new |
| mv | Move (rename) file | mv sourceFile.txt destinationFile.txt |
| rm | Remove file | rm file.txt |
| reboot | Reboot device | sudo reboot |
| shutdown | Shutdown device | sudo shutdown -h now |
| grep | Print lines matching a pattern | grep -r "pi" /home/ |
| df | Report file system disk space usage | df -Th |
| ifconfig | Configure a network interface | ifconfig |
| netstat | Print network connections, routing tables, interface statistics | netstat -lntp |
| tar | Extract/create archive | tar -xzf foo.tar.gz |
| wget | Non-interactive network downloader | wget http://example.com/file.tar.gz |

Table 7.2: Raspberry Pi frequently used commands

## 7.5   Raspberry Pi Interfaces

Raspberry Pi has serial, SPI and I2C interfaces for data transfer as shown in Figure 7.3.

### 7.5.1   Serial

The serial interface on Raspberry Pi has receive (Rx) and transmit (Tx) pins for communication with serial peripherals.

### 7.5.2   SPI

Serial Peripheral Interface (SPI) is a synchronous serial data protocol used for communicating with one or more peripheral devices. In an SPI connection, there is one master device and one or more peripheral devices. There are five pins on Raspberry Pi for SPI interface:

- **MISO (Master In Slave Out)** : Master line for sending data to the peripherals.
- **MOSI (Master Out Slave In)** : Slave line for sending data to the master.
- **SCK (Serial Clock)** : Clock generated by master to synchronize data transmission
- **CE0 (Chip Enable 0)** : To enable or disable devices.
- **CE0 (Chip Enable 1)** : To enable or disable devices.

### 7.5.3   I2C

The I2C interface pins on Raspberry Pi allow you to connect hardware modules. I2C interface allows synchronous data transfer with just two pins - SDA (data line) and SCL (clock line).

## 7.6   Programming Raspberry Pi with Python

In this section you will learn how to get started with developing Python programs on Raspberry Pi. Raspberry Pi runs Linux and supports Python out of the box. Therefore, you can run any Python program that runs on a normal computer. However, it is the general purpose input/output capability provided by the GPIO pins on Raspberry Pi that makes it useful device for Internet of Things. You can interface a wide variety of sensor and actuators with Raspberry Pi using the GPIO pins and the SPI, I2C and serial interfaces. Input from the sensors connected to Raspberry Pi can be processed and various actions can be taken, for instance, sending data to a server, sending an email, triggering a relay switch.

### 7.6.1   Controlling LED with Raspberry Pi

Let us start with a basic example of controlling an LED from Raspberry Pi. Figure 7.9 shows the schematic diagram of connecting an LED to Raspberry Pi. Box 7.1 shows how to turn the LED on/off from command line. In this example the LED is connected to GPIO pin 18. You can connect the LED to any other GPIO pin as well.

Box 7.2 shows a Python program for blinking an LED connected to Raspberry Pi every second. The program uses the RPi. GPIO module to control the GPIO on Raspberry Pi. In this program we set pin 18 direction to output and then write *True/False* alternatively after a delay of one second.

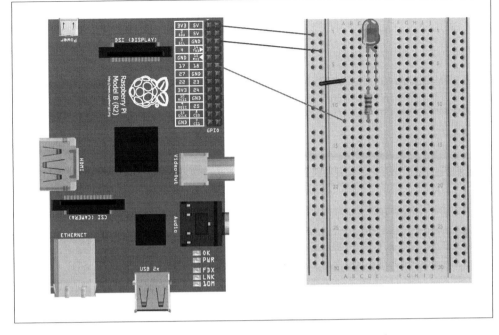

Figure 7.9: Controlling LED with Raspberry Pi

■ **Box 7.1: Switching LED on/off from Raspberry Pi console**

```
$echo 18 > /sys/class/gpio/export
$cd /sys/class/gpio/gpio18

#Set pin 18 direction to out
$echo out > direction

#Turn LED on
$echo 1 > value
#Turn LED off
$echo 0 > value
```

■ **Box 7.2: Python program for blinking LED**

```
import RPi.GPIO as GPIO
import time

GPIO.setmode(GPIO.BCM)
GPIO.setup(18, GPIO.OUT)

while True:
    GPIO.output(18, True)
    time.sleep(1)
    GPIO.output(18, False)
    time.sleep(1)
```

### 7.6.2   Interfacing an LED and Switch with Raspberry Pi

Now let us look at a more detailed example involving an LED and a switch that is used to control the LED.

Figure 7.10 shows the schematic diagram of connecting an LED and switch to Raspberry Pi. Box 7.3 shows a Python program for controlling an LED with a switch. In this example the LED is connected to GPIO pin 18 and switch is connected to pin 25. In the infinite while loop the value of pin 25 is checked and the state of LED is toggled if the switch is pressed. This example shows how to get input from GPIO pins and process the input and take some action. The action in this example is toggling the state of an LED. Let us look at another example, in which the action is an email alert. Box 7.4 shows a Python program for sending an email on switch press. Note that the structure of this program is similar to the program in Box 7.3. This program uses the Python SMTP library for sending an email when the switch connected to Raspberry Pi is pressed.

■ **Box 7.3: Python program for controlling an LED with a switch**

```python
from time import sleep
import RPi.GPIO as GPIO

GPIO.setmode(GPIO.BCM)

#Switch Pin
GPIO.setup(25, GPIO.IN)

#LED Pin
GPIO.setup(18, GPIO.OUT)

state=false

def toggleLED(pin):
   state = not state
   GPIO.output(pin, state)

while True:
   try:
      if (GPIO.input(25) == True):
         toggleLED(pin)
      sleep(.01)
   except KeyboardInterrupt:
      exit()
```

■ **Box 7.4: Python program for sending an email on switch press**

```python
import smtplib
from time import sleep
import RPi.GPIO as GPIO
from sys import exit
```

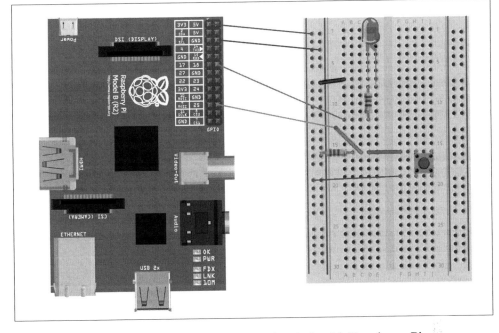

Figure 7.10: Interfacing LED and switch with Raspberry Pi

```
from_email = '<my-email>'
receipients_list = ['<receipient-email>']
cc_list = []
subject = 'Hello'
message = 'Switch pressed on Raspberry Pi'
username = '<Gmail-username>'
password = '<password>'
server = 'smtp.gmail.com:587'

GPIO.setmode(GPIO.BCM)
GPIO.setup(25, GPIO.IN)


def sendemail(from_addr, to_addr_list, cc_addr_list,
    subject, message,
    login, password,
    smtpserver):

  header = 'From: %s \n' % from_addr
  header += 'To: %s \n' % ','.join(to_addr_list)
  header += 'Cc: %s \n' % ','.join(cc_addr_list)
  header += 'Subject: %s \n \n' % subject
  message = header + message

  server = smtplib.SMTP(smtpserver)
  server.starttls()
  server.login(login,password)
  problems = server.sendmail(from_addr, to_addr_list, message)
  server.quit()
```

```
while True:
  try:
    if (GPIO.input(25) == True):
      sendemail(from_email, receipients_list,
          cc_list, subject, message,
          username, password, server)
    sleep(.01)
  except KeyboardInterrupt:
    exit()
```

### 7.6.3   Interfacing a Light Sensor (LDR) with Raspberry Pi

So far you have learned how to interface LED and switch with Raspberry Pi. Now let us look at an example of interfacing a Light Dependent Resistor (LDR) with Raspberry Pi and turning an LED on/off based on the light-level sensed.

Figure 7.11 shows the schematic diagram of connecting an LDR to Raspberry Pi. Connect one side of LDR to 3.3V and other side to a $1\mu$F capacitor and also to a GPIO pin (pin 18 in this example). An LED is connected to pin 18 which is controlled based on the light-level sensed.

Box 7.5 shows the Python program for the LDR example. The *readLDR()* function returns a count which is proportional to the light level. In this function the LDR pin is set to output and low and then to input. At this point the capacitor starts charging through the resistor (and a counter is started) until the input pin reads high (this happens when capacitor voltage becomes greater than 1.4V). The counter is stopped when the input reads high. The final count is proportional to the light level as greater the amount of light, smaller is the LDR resistance and greater is the time taken to charge the capacitor.

■ **Box 7.5:  Python program for switching LED/Light based on reading LDR reading**

```
import RPi.GPIO as GPIO
import time

GPIO.setmode(GPIO.BCM)
ldr_threshold = 1000
LDR_PIN = 18
LIGHT_PIN = 25

def readLDR(PIN):
  reading=0
  GPIO.setup(LIGHT_PIN, GPIO.OUT)
  GPIO.output(PIN, False)
  time.sleep(0.1)
  GPIO.setup(PIN, GPIO.IN)
  while (GPIO.input(PIN)==False):
    reading=reading+1
  return reading

def switchOnLight(PIN):
  GPIO.setup(PIN, GPIO.OUT)
```

```
    GPIO.output(PIN, True)

def switchOffLight(PIN):
  GPIO.setup(PIN, GPIO.OUT)
  GPIO.output(PIN, False)


while True:
  ldr_reading = readLDR(LDR_PIN)
  if ldr_reading < ldr_threshold:
    switchOnLight(LIGHT_PIN)
  else:
    switchOffLight(LIGHT_PIN)

  time.sleep(1)
```

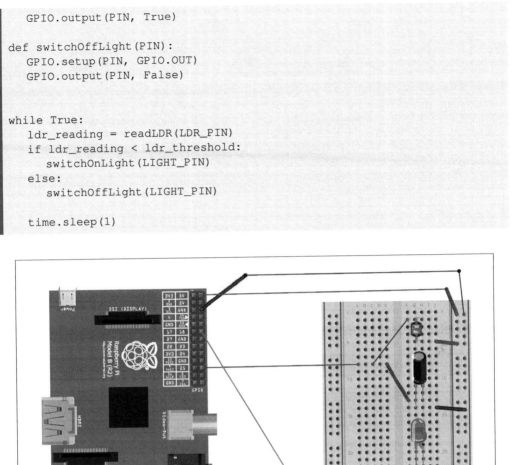

Figure 7.11: Interfacing LDR with Raspberry Pi

## 7.7  Other IoT Devices

Let us look at single-board mini-computers which are alternatives to Raspberry Pi. Table 7.3
provides a comparison of some single-board mini-computers that can be used for IoT.

### 7.7.1  pcDuino

pcDuino [105] is an Arduino-pin compatible single board mini-computer that comes with a 1
GHz ARM Cortex-A8 processor. pcDuino is a high performance and cost effective device
that runs PC like OS such as Ubuntu and Android ICS. Like, Raspberry Pi, it has an HDMI
video/audio interface. pcDuino supports various programming languages including C, C++
(with GNU tool chain), Java (with standard Android SDK) and Python.

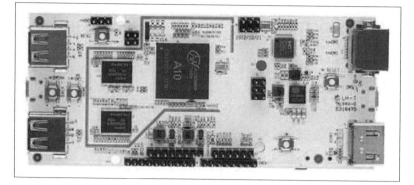

Figure 7.12: pcDuino

Figure 7.13: Beaglebone Black

### 7.7.2  BeagleBone Black

BeagleBone Black[106] is similar to Raspberry Pi, but a more powerful device. It comes with a 1 GHz ARM Cortex-A8 processor and supports both Linux and Android operating systems. Like Raspberry Pi, it has HDMI video/audio interface, USB and Ethernet ports.

### 7.7.3  Cubieboard

Cubieboard [107] is powered by a dual core ARM Cortex A7 processor and has a range of input/output interfaces including USB, HDMI, IR, serial, Ethernet, SATA, and a 96 pin extended interface. Cubieboard also provides SATA support. The board can run both Linux and Android operating systems.

## Summary

In this chapter you learned about Raspberry Pi which is a low-cost mini-computer. Raspberry Pi supports various flavors of Linux operating system. The official recommended operating system is Raspbian Linux. Raspberry Pi has an ARM processor, 512MB RAM, two USB

Figure 7.14: Cubieboard

ports, HDMI, RCA and audio outputs, Ethernet port, SD card slot and DSI and CSI interfaces. Raspberry Pi has serial, SPI and I2C interfaces for data transfer. Raspberry Pi supports Python. You learned how to develop Python programs that run on Raspberry Pi. You learned how to interface LED, switch and LDR with Raspberry Pi.

## Review Questions

1. How is Raspberry Pi different from a desktop computer?
2. What is the use of GPIO pins?
3. What is the use of SPI and I2C interfaces on Raspberry Pi?

| | Raspberry Pi | pcDuino | BeagleBone Black | Cubieboard |
|---|---|---|---|---|
| CPU | 700 MHz ARM1176JZ-F Processor | 1GHz ARM Cortex A8 | AM335x 1GHz ARM Cortex-A8 | Dual core 1GHz ARM Cortex-A7 |
| GPU | Dual Core VideoCore IV Multimedia Co-Processor | Mali 400 | PowerVR SGX530 | Dual core ARM Mali 400 MP2 |
| Memory | 512MB | 1GB | 512MB | 1GB |
| Storage | - | 2GB Flash (ATmega328) | 2GB on-board flash storage | 4GB NAND Flash |
| Networking | 10/100M Ethernet | 10/100M Ethernet | 10/100M Ethernet | 10/100M Ethernet |
| Input/Output | 2 USB, SD, MMC, SDIO card slot | - | 4+1 USB, MicroSD slot | 2 USB, MicroSD slot, SATA, IR sensor |
| Interfaces | GPIO, SPI, I2C, serial | Serial, ADC, PWM, GPIO, I2C, SPI | 69 pin GPIO, SPI, I2C, 4 serial, CAN, GPMC, AIN, MMC, XDMA | 96 extend pin interface, including I2C, SPI, RGB/LVDS, CSI/TS, FM-IN, ADC, CVBS, VGA, SPDIF-OUT, R-TP |
| OS | Rasbian, Pidora, RISC OS, Arch Linux | Ubuntu, Android | Angstrom Linux, Android, Ubuntu | Android, Official Linux distribution |
| Video | HDMI, Composite RCA (PAL and NTSC) | HDMI | HDMI | HDMI |
| Audio | 3.5mm jack, HDMI | HDMI | HDMI | HDMI |
| Power | 5VDC/700mA | 5V/2A | 5VDC/460mA | 5VDC/2A |

Table 7.3: Comparison of single board mini-computers

# 8 - IoT Physical Servers & Cloud Offerings

This Chapter Covers

- Cloud Storage Models & Communication APIs
- Web Application Messaging Protocol (WAMP)
- Xively cloud for IoT
- Python web application framework - Django
- Developing applications with Django
- Developing REST web services
- Amazon Web Services for IoT
- SkyNet IoT Messaging Platform

## 8.1   Introduction to Cloud Storage Models & Communication APIs

Cloud computing is a transformative computing paradigm that involves delivering applications and services over the Internet. NIST defines cloud computing as [77] - Cloud computing is a model for enabling ubiquitous, convenient, on-demand network access to a shared pool of configurable computing resources (e.g., networks, servers, storage, applications, and services) that can be rapidly provisioned and released with minimal management effort or service provider interaction. The interested reader may want to refer to the companion book on Cloud Computing by your authors.

In this chapter you will learn how to use cloud computing for Internet of Things (IoT). You will learn about the Web Application Messaging Protocol (WAMP), Xively's Platform-as-a-Service (PaaS) which provides tools and services for developing IoT solutions. You will also learn about the Amazon Web Services (AWS) and their applications for IoT.

## 8.2   WAMP - AutoBahn for IoT

Web Application Messaging Protocol (WAMP) is a sub-protocol of Websocket which provides publish-subscribe and remote procedure call (RPC) messaging patterns. WAMP enables distributed application architectures where the application components are distributed on multiple nodes and communicate with messaging patterns provided by WAMP.

Let us look at the key concepts of WAMP:

- **Transport:** Transport is channel that connects two peers. The default transport for WAMP is WebSocket. WAMP can run over other transports as well which support message-based reliable bi-directional communication.
- **Session:** Session is a conversation between two peers that runs over a transport.
- **Client:** Clients are peers that can have one or more roles. In publish-subscribe model client can have following roles:
    - **Publisher:** Publisher publishes events (including payload) to the topic maintained by the Broker.
    - **Subscriber:** Subscriber subscribes to the topics and receives the events including the payload.
  In RPC model client can have following roles:
    - **Caller:** Caller issues calls to the remote procedures along with call arguments.
    - **Callee:** Callee executes the procedures to which the calls are issued by the caller and returns the results back to the caller.
- **Router:** Routers are peers that perform generic call and event routing. In publish-subscribe model Router has the role of a Broker:
    - **Broker:** Broker acts as a router and routes messages published to a topic to all subscribers subscribed to the topic.
      In RPC model Router has the role of a Broker:
    - **Dealer:** Dealer acts a router and routes RPC calls from the Caller to the Callee and routes results from Callee to Caller.
- **Application Code:** Application code runs on the Clients (Publisher, Subscriber, Callee or Caller).

Figure 8.1 shows a WAMP Session between Client and Router, established over a Transport. Figure 8.2 shows the WAMP protocol interactions between peers. In this figure the WAMP transport used is WebSocket. Recall the WebSocket protocol diagram explained in Chapter-1. WAMP sessions are established over WebSocket transport within the lifetime of WebSocket transport.

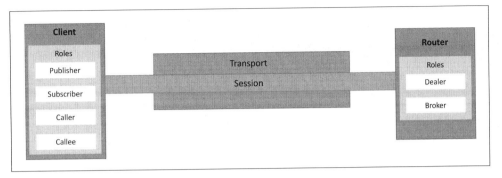

Figure 8.1: WAMP Session between Client and Router

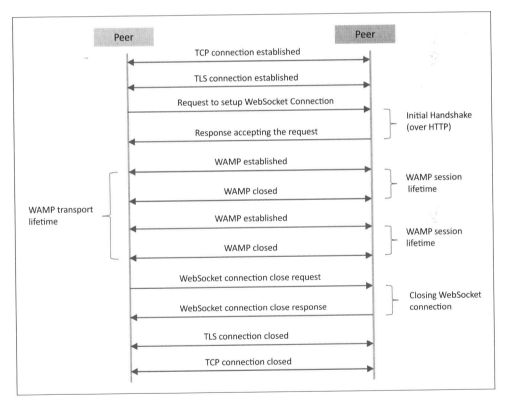

Figure 8.2: WAMP protocol

For the examples in this hands-on book we use the AutoBahn framework which provides open-source implementations of the WebSocket and WAMP protocols [100].

Figure 8.3 shows the communication between various components of a typical WAMP-AutoBahn deployment. The Client (in Publisher role) runs a WAMP application component that publishes messages to the Router. The Router (in Broker role) runs on the

Server and routes the messages to the Subscribers. The Router (in Broker role) decouples the Publisher from the Subscribers. The communication between Publisher - Broker and Broker - Subscribers happens over a WAMP-WebSocket session.

Let us look at an example of a WAMP publisher and subscriber implemented using AutoBahn. Box 8.1 shows the commands for installing AutoBahn-Python.

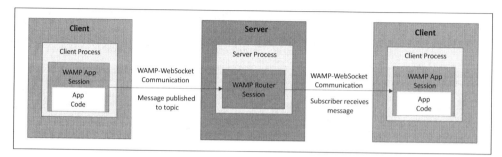

Figure 8.3: Publish-subscribe messaging using WAMP-AutoBahn

---

■ **Box 8.1: Commands for installing AutoBahn**

```
#Setup Autobahn
sudo apt-get install python-twisted python-dev
sudo apt-get install python-pip
sudo pip install -upgrade twisted
sudo pip install -upgrade autobahn
```

---

After installing AutoBahn, clone AutobahnPython from GitHub as follows:

■ git clone https://github.com/tavendo/AutobahnPython.git

Create a WAMP publisher component as shown in Box 8.2. The publisher component publishes a message containing the current time-stamp to a topic named 'test-topic'. Next, create a WAMP subscriber component as shown in Box 8.3. The subscriber component that subscribes to the 'test-topic'. Run the application router on a WebSocket transport server as follows:

■ python AutobahnPython/examples/twisted/wamp/basic/server.py

Run the publisher component over a WebSocket transport client as follows:

■ python AutobahnPython/examples/twisted/wamp/basic/client.py –component "publisherApp.Component"

Run the subscriber component over a WebSocket transport client as follows:

■ python AutobahnPython/examples/twisted/wamp/basic/client.py –component "subscriberApp.Component"

---

**■ Box 8.2: Example of a WAMP Publisher implemented using AutoBahn framework - publisherApp.py**

```python
from twisted.internet import reactor
from twisted.internet.defer import inlineCallbacks
from autobahn.twisted.util import sleep
from autobahn.twisted.wamp import ApplicationSession
import time,datetime

def getData():
    #Generate message
    timestamp = datetime.datetime.fromtimestamp(
    time.time()).strftime('%Y-%m-%d%H:%M:%S')
    data = "Message at time-stamp:  "+str(timestamp)
    return data

#An application component that publishes an event every second.
class Component(ApplicationSession):
    @inlineCallbacks
    def onJoin(self, details):
        while True:
            data = getData()
            self.publish('test-topic', data)
            yield sleep(1)
```

---

**■ Box 8.3: Example of a WAMP Subscriber implemented using AutoBahn framework - subscriberApp.py**

```python
from twisted.internet import reactor
from twisted.internet.defer import inlineCallbacks
from autobahn.twisted.wamp import ApplicationSession

#An application component that subscribes and receives events
class Component(ApplicationSession):
    @inlineCallbacks
    def onJoin(self, details):
        self.received = 0

        def on_event(data):
            print "Received message:  " + data
            yield self.subscribe(on_event, 'test-topic')

    def onDisconnect(self):
        reactor.stop()
```

While you can setup the server and client processes on a local machine for trying out the publish-subscribe example, in production environment, these components run on separate machines. The server process (the brains or the "Thing Tank"!) is setup on a cloud-based instance while the client processes can run either on local hosts/devices or in the cloud.

---

## 8.3   Xively Cloud for IoT

Xively is a commercial Platform-as-a-Service that can be used for creating solutions for Internet of Things. With Xively cloud, IoT developers can focus on the front-end infrastructure and devices for IoT (that generate the data), while the backend data collection infrastructure is managed by Xively.

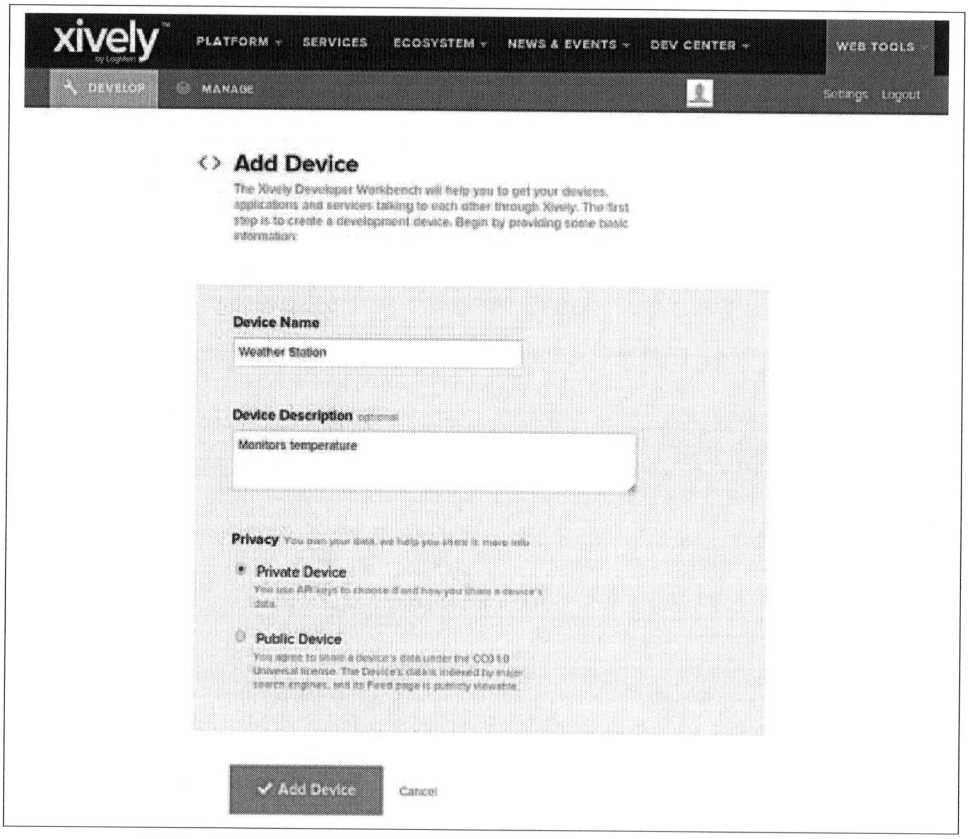

Figure 8.4: Screenshot of Xively dashboard - creating a new device

Xively platform comprises of a message bus for real-time message management and routing, data services for time series archiving, directory services that provides a search-able directory of objects and business services for device provisioning and management. Xively provides an extensive support for various languages and platforms. The Xively libraries leverage standards-based API over HTTP, Sockets and MQTT for connecting IoT devices to the Xively cloud. In this chapter we will describe how to use the Xively Python library.

To start using Xively, you have to register for a developer account. You can then create development devices on Xively. Figures 8.4 shows screenshot of how to create a new device from the Xively dashboard. When you create a device, Xively automatically creates a Feed-ID and an API Key to connect to the device as shown in Figures 8.5. Each device has a unique Feed-ID. Feed-ID is a collection of channels or datastreams defined for a device and the associated meta-data. API keys are used to provide different levels of permissions. The default API key has read, update, create and delete permissions.

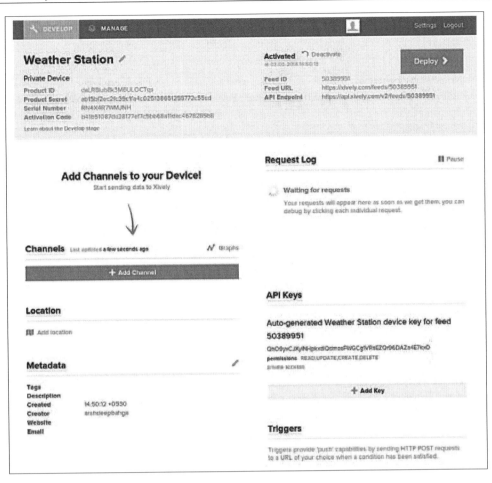

Figure 8.5: Screenshot of Xively dashboard - device details

Xively devices have one or more channels. Each channel enables bi-directional communication between the IoT devices and the Xively cloud. IoT devices can send data to a channel using the Xively APIs. For each channel, you can create one or more triggers. A trigger specification includes a channel to which the trigger corresponds, trigger condition (e.g. channel value less than or greater than a certain value) and an HTTP POST URL to which the request is sent when the trigger fires. Triggers are used for integration with third-party applications.

Let us look at an example of using Xively cloud for an IoT system that monitors temperature and sends the measurements to a Xively channel. The temperature monitoring device can be built with the Raspberry Pi board and a temperature sensor connected to the board. The Raspberry Pi runs a controller program that reads the sensor values every few seconds and sends the measurements to a Xively channel. Box 8.4 shows the Python program for the sending temperature data to Xively Cloud. This example uses the Xively Python library. To keep the program simple and without going into the details of the temperature sensor we use synthetic data (generated randomly in *readTempSensor*() function). The complete implementation of the *readTempSensor*() function is described in the next chapter.

In this controller program, a feed object is created by providing the API key and Feed-ID. Then a channel named *temperature* is created (if not existing) or retrieved. The temperature data is sent to this channel in the *runController()* function every 10 seconds. Figures 8.6 shows the temperature channel in the Xively dashboard. In this example we created a single Xively device with one channel. In real-world scenario each Xively device can have multiple channels and you can have multiple devices in a production batch.

■ **Box 8.4: Python program sending data to Xively Cloud**

```
import time
import datetime
import requests
import xively
from random import randint
global temp_datastream
#Initialize Xively Feed
FEED_ID = "<enter feed-id>"
API_KEY = "<enter api-key>"
api = xively.XivelyAPIClient(API_KEY)

#Function to read Temperature Sensor
def readTempSensor():
   #Return random value
   return randint(20,30)

#Controller main function
def runController():
   global temp_datastream
   temperature=readTempSensor()
   temp_datastream.current_value = temperature
   temp_datastream.at = datetime.datetime.utcnow()

   print "Updating Xively feed with Temperature:  %s" % temperature
   try:
      temp_datastream.update()
   except requests.HTTPError as e:
      print "HTTPError(0):  1".format(e.errno, e.strerror)

#Function to get existing or
#create new Xively data stream for temperature
def get_tempdatastream(feed):
   try:
      datastream = feed.datastreams.get("temperature")
      return datastream
   except:
      datastream = feed.datastreams.create("temperature",
      tags="temperature")
      return datastream

#Controller setup function
def setupController():
   global temp_datastream
   feed = api.feeds.get(FEED_ID)
```

```
    feed.location.lat="30.733315"
    feed.location.lon="76.779418"
    feed.tags="Weather"
    feed.update()

    temp_datastream = get_tempdatastream(feed)
    temp_datastream.max_value = None
    temp_datastream.min_value = None
setupController()
while True:
    runController()
    time.sleep(10)
```

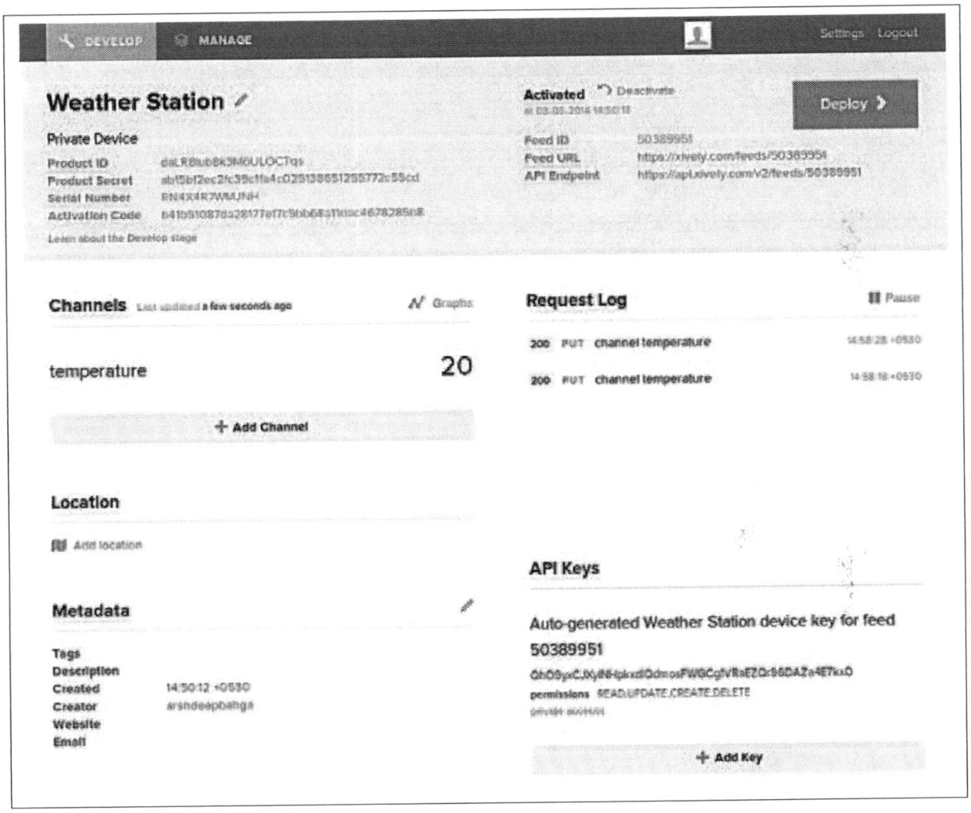

Figure 8.6: Screenshot of Xively dashboard - data sent to channel

## 8.4   Python Web Application Framework - Django

In the previous section, you learned about the Xively PaaS for collecting and processing data from IoT systems in the cloud. You learned how to use the Xively Python library. To build IoT applications that are a backed by Xively cloud or any other data collection systems, you would require some type of web application framework. In this section you will learn about a Python-based web application framework called Django.

Django is an open source web application framework for developing web applications in Python [116]. A "web application framework" in general is a collection of solutions, packages and best practices that allows development of web applications and dynamic websites. Django is based on the well-known Model-Template-View architecture and provides a separation of the data model from the business rules and the user interface. Django provides a unified API to a database backend. Therefore, web applications built with Django can work with different databases without requiring any code changes. With this flexibility in web application design combined with the powerful capabilities of the Python language and the Python ecosystem, Django is best suited for IoT applications. Django, concisely stated, consists of an object-relational mapper, a web templating system and a regular-expression-based URL dispatcher.

## 8.4.1  Django Architecture

Django is a Model-Template-View (MTV) framework wherein the roles of model, template and view, respectively, are:

### Model

The model acts as a definition of some stored data and handles the interactions with the database. In a web application, the data can be stored in a relational database, non-relational database, an XML file, etc. A Django model is a Python class that outlines the variables and methods for a particular type of data.

### Template

In a typical Django web application, the template is simply an HTML page with a few extra placeholders. Django's template language can be used to create various forms of text files (XML, email, CSS, Javascript, CSV, etc.)

### View

The view ties the model to the template. The view is where you write the code that actually generates the web pages. View determines what data is to be displayed, retrieves the data from the database and passes the data to the template.

## 8.4.2  Starting Development with Django

Appendix C provides the instructions for setting up Django. In this section you will learn how to start developing web applications with Django.

### Creating a Django Project and App

Box 8.5 provides the commands for creating a Django project and an application within a project.

When you create a new django project a number of files are created as described below:
- __init__.py: This file tells Python that this folder is a Python package
- manage.py: This file contains an array of functions for managing the site.
- settings.py: This file contains the website's settings
- urls.py: This file contains the URL patterns that map URLs to pages.

A Django project can have multiple applications ("apps"). Apps are where you write the code that makes your website function. Each project can have multiple apps and each app can be part of multiple projects.

When a new application is created a new directory for the application is also created which has a number of files including:

- model.py: This file contains the description of the models for the application.
- views.py: This file contains the application views.

■ **Box 8.5: Creating a new Django project and an app in the project**

```
#Create a new project
django-admin.py startproject blogproject

#Create an application within the project
python mangage.py startapp myapp

#Starting development server
python manage.py runserver

#Django uses port 8000 by default
#The project can be viewed at the URL:
#http://localhost:8000
```

Django comes with a built-in, lightweight Web server that can be used for development purposes. When the Django development server is started the default project can be viewed at the URL: http://localhost:8000. Figure 8.7 shows a screenshot of the default project.

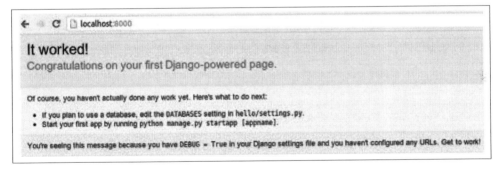

Figure 8.7: Django default project

**Configuring a Database**

Till now you have learned how to create a new Django project and an app within the project. Most web applications have a database backend. Developers have a wide choice of databases that can be used for web applications including both relational and non-relational databases. Django provides a unified API for database backends thus giving the freedom to choose the database. Django supports various relational database engines including MySQL, PostgreSQL, Oracle and SQLite3. Support for non-relational databases such as MongoDB can be added by installing additional engines (e.g. Django-MongoDB engine for MongoDB).

Let us look at examples of setting up a relational and a non-relational database with a Django project. The first step in setting up a database is to install and configure a database server. After installing the database, the next step is to specify the database settings in the setting.py file in the Django project.

Box 8.6 shows the commands to setup MySQL. Box 8.7 shows the database setting to use MySQL with a Django project.

### ■ Box 8.6: Setting up MySQL database

```
#Install MySQL
sudo apt-get install mysql-server mysql-client
sudo mysqladmin -u root -h localhost password 'mypassword'
```

### ■ Box 8.7: Configuring MySQL with Django - settings.py

```
DATABASES = {
  'default':  {
    'ENGINE': 'django.db.backends.mysql',
    'NAME': '<database-name>'
    'USER': 'root'
    'PASSWORD': 'mypassword'
    'HOST': '<hostname>', # set to empty for localhost
    'PORT': '<port>', #set to empty for default port
}
}
```

Box 8.8 shows the commands to setup MongoDB and the associated Django-MongoDB engine. Box 8.9 shows the database setting to use MongoDB within a Django project.

### ■ Box 8.8: Setting up MongoDB and Django-MongoDB engine

```
#Install MongoDB
sudo apt-key adv -keyserver keserver.ubuntu.com -recv 7F0CEB10
echo 'deb http://downloads-distro.mongodb.org/repo/ubuntu-upstart
dist 10gen' | sudo tee /etc/apt/sources.list.d/10gen.list

sudo apt-get update
sudo apt-get install mongodb-10gen

#Setup Django MongoDB Engine
sudo pip install
https://bitbucket.org/wkornewald/django-nonrel/get/tip.tar.gz
sudo pip install
https://bitbucket.org/wkornewald/djangotoolbox/get/tip.tar.gz
sudo pip install
https://github.com/django-nonrel/mongodb-engine/tarball/master
```

---

**■ Box 8.9: Configuring MongoDB with Django - settings.py**

```
DATABASES = {
   'default':  {
      'ENGINE': 'django_mongodb_engine',
      'NAME': '<database-name>'
      'HOST': '<mongodb-hostname>', # set to empty for localhost
      'PORT': '<mongodb-port>', #set to empty for default port
   }
}
```

---

### Defining a Model

A Model acts as a definition of the data in the database. In this section we will explain Django with the help of a weather station application that displays the temperature data collected by an IoT device. Box 8.10 shows an example of a Django model for *TemperatureData*. The *TemperatureData* table in the database is defined as a Class in the Django model.

Each class that represents a database table is a subclass of *django.db.models.Model* which contains all the functionality that allows the models to interact with the database. The *TemperatureData* class has fields timestamp, temperature, lat and lon all of which are *CharField*. To sync the models with the database simply run the following command:
>python manage.py syncdb

When the *syncdb* command is run for the first time, it creates all the tables defined in the Django model in the configured database. For more information about the Django models refer to the Django documentation [117].

---

**■ Box 8.10:  Example of a Django model**

```
from django.db import models

class TemperatureData(models.Model):
   timestamp = models.CharField(max_length=10)
   temperature = models.CharField(max_length=5)
   lat = models.CharField(max_length=10)
   lon = models.CharField(max_length=10)
   def __unicode__(self):
      return self.timestamp
```

---

### Django Admin Site

Django provides an administration system that allows you to manage the website without writing additional code. This "admin" system reads the Django model and provides an interface that can be used to add content to the site. The Django admin site is enabled by adding *django.contrib.admin* and *django.contrib.admindocs* to the INSTALLED_APPS section in the settings.py file. The admin site also requires URL pattern definitions in the urls.py file described later in the URLs sections.

---

To define which of your application models should be editable in the admin interface, a new file named admin.py is created in the application folder as shown in Box 8.11.

■ **Box 8.11: Enabling admin for Django models**

```
from django.contrib import admin
from myapp.models import TemperatureData

admin.site.register(TemperatureData)
```

Figure 8.8 shows a screenshot of the default admin interface. You can see all the tables corresponding to the Django models in this screenshot. Figure 8.9 shows how to add new items in the TemperatureData table using the admin site.

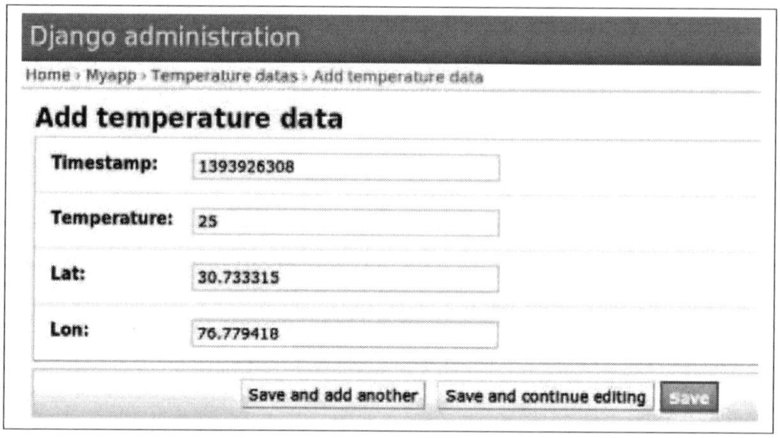

Figure 8.8: Screenshot of default Django admin interface

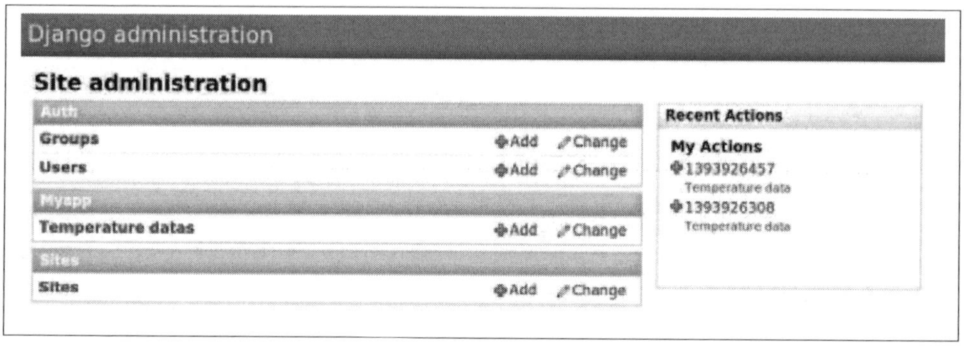

Figure 8.9: Adding data to table from Django admin interface

### Defining a View

The View contains the logic that glues the model to the template. The view determines the data to be displayed in the template, retrieves the data from the database and passes it to the template. Conversely, the view also extracts the data posted in a form in the template and inserts it in the database. Typically, each page in the website has a separate view, which is basically a Python function in the views.py file. Views can also perform additional tasks such as authentication, sending emails, etc.

Box 8.12 shows an example of a Django view for the Weather Station app. This view corresponds to the webpage that displays latest entry in the TemperatureData table. In this view the Django's built in object-relational mapping API is used to retrieve the data from the TemperatureData table. The object-relational mapping API allows the developers to write generic code for interacting with the database without worrying about the underlying database engine. So the same code for database interactions works with different database backends. You can optionally choose to use a Python library specific to the database backend used (e.g. MySQLdb for MYSQL, PyMongo for MongoDB, etc.) to write database backed specific code. For more information about the Django views refer to the Django documentation [118].

In the view shown in Box 8.12, the $TemperatureData.objects.order\_by('-id')[0]$ query returns the latest entry in the table. To retrieve all entries, you can use $table.objects.all()$. To retrieve specific entries, you can use $table.objects.filter(**kwargs)$ to filter out queries that match the specified condition. To render the retrieved entries in the template, the $render\_to\_response$ function is used. This function renders a given template with a given context dictionary and returns an $HttpResponse$ object with that rendered text. Box 8.13 shows an alternative view that retrieves data from the Xively cloud.

■ **Box 8.12: Example of a Django view**

```
from django.shortcuts import render_to_response
from myapp.models import *
from django.template import RequestContext

def home(request):
   tempData = TemperatureData.objects.order_by('-id')[0]
   temperature = tempData.temperature
   lat = tempData.lat
   lon = tempData.lon


   return render_to_response('index.html','temperature':temperature,
   'lat':  lat, 'lon':  lon, context_instance=RequestContext(request))
```

■ **Box 8.13: Alternative Django View that retrieves data from Xively**

```
from django.shortcuts import render_to_response
from django.template import RequestContext
import requests
import xively

FEED_ID = "<enter-id>"
API_KEY = "<enter-key>"
api = xively.XivelyAPIClient(API_KEY)

feed = api.feeds.get(FEED_ID)
temp_datastream = feed.datastreams.get("temperature")
```

```
def home(request):
    temperature=temp_datastream.current_value
    lat=feed.location.lat
    lon=feed.location.lon

    return render_to_response('index.html','temperature':temperature,
    'lat':  lat, 'lon':  lon, context_instance=RequestContext(request))
```

## Defining a Template

A Django template is typically an HTML file (though it can be any sort of text file such as XML, email, CSS, Javascript, CSV, etc.). Django templates allow separation of the presentation of data from the actual data by using placeholders and associated logic (using template tags). A template receives a context from the view and presents the data in context variables in the placeholders. Box 8.14 shows an example of a template for the Weather Station app. In the previous section you learned how the data is retrieved from the database in the view and passed to the template in the form of a context dictionary. In the example shown in Box 8.14, the variables containing the retrieved temperature, latitude and longitude are passed to the template. For more information about the Django templates refer to the Django documentation [119].

### ■ Box 8.14: Example of a Django template

```
<html>
<head>
<meta charset="utf-8">
<link href="/static/css/bootstrap-responsive.css" rel="stylesheet">
<script type="text/javascript"
src="http://maps.google.com/maps/api/js?sensor=false"></script>
<script type="text/javascript">
function initialize()
    var latlng = new google.maps.LatLng(lat,lon);
    var settings =
    zoom:  11,
    center:  latlng,
    mapTypeControl:  false,
    mapTypeControlOptions:  style:
google.maps.MapTypeControlStyle.DROPDOWN_MENU,
    navigationControl:  true,
    navigationControlOptions:  style:
google.maps.NavigationControlStyle.SMALL,
    mapTypeId:  google.maps.MapTypeId.TERRAIN
    ;

var map = new google.maps.Map(document.getElementById("map_canvas"),
settings);
var wespiMarker = new google.maps.Marker(
    position:  latlng,
    map:  map,
```

```
    title:"CityName, "
    );
    startws ();

</script>
<title>Weather Station</title>
</head>
<body onload="initialize()">

<div class="container">
    <center><h1>Weather Station</h1></center>
    <h3>CityName</h3>
    <div class='row'>
    <div class='span3'><h4>Temperature</h4></div>
    <div class='span3'>
<h4 id='temperature'>{{temperature}}</h4></div></div>
    <div class="span6" style="height:435px">
    <div id = "map_canvas">
    </div>
    </div>
</div>

</body>
</html>
```

Figure 8.10 shows the home page for the Weather Station app. The home page is rendered from the template shown in Box 8.14.

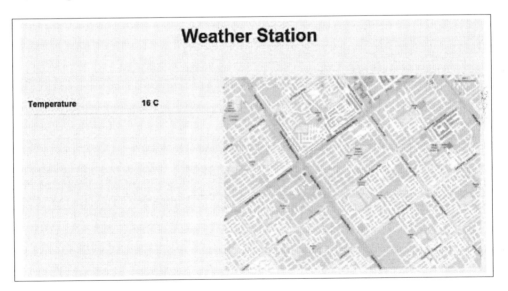

Figure 8.10: Screenshot of a temperature monitoring web application

**Defining the URL Patterns**

URL Patterns are a way of mapping the URLs to the views that should handle the URL requests. The URLs requested by the user are matched with the URL patterns and the view corresponding to the pattern that matches the URL is used to handle the request. Box 8.15 shows an example of the URL patterns for the Weather Station project. As seen in this example, the URL patterns are constructed using regular expressions. The simplest regular expression (r' $^\wedge$ $') corresponds to the root of the website or the home page. For more information about the Django URL patterns refer to the Django documentation [120].

■ **Box 8.15: Example of a URL configuration**

```
from django.conf.urls.defaults import *
from django.contrib import admin
admin.autodiscover()

urlpatterns = patterns('',
   url(r'^$', 'myapp.views.home', name='home'),
   url(r'^admin/doc/', include('django.contrib.admindocs.urls')),
   url(r'^admin/', include(admin.site.urls)),
)
```

With the models, views, templates and URL patterns defined for the Django project, the application is finally run with the commands shown in Box 8.16.

■ **Box 8.16: Running a Django application**

```
#cd into the project root
$cd weatherStationProject

#Sync the database
$ python manage.py syncdb

#Run the application
$ python manage.py runserver
```

## 8.5   Designing a RESTful Web API

In this section you will learn how to develop a RESTful web API. The example in this section uses the Django REST framework [89] introduced earlier for building a REST API. With the Django framework already installed, the Django REST framework can be installed as follows:

```
■ pip install djangorestframework
pip install markdown
pip install django-filter
```

After installing the Django REST framework, let us create a new Django project named *restfulapi*, and then start a new app called *myapp*, as follows:

```
■ django-admin.py startproject restfulapi
cd restfulapi
```

```
python manage.py startapp myapp
```

The REST API described in this section allows you to create, view, update and delete a collection of resources where each resource represents a sensor data reading from a weather monitoring station. Box 8.17 shows the Django model for such a station. The station model contains four fields - station name, timestamp, temperature, latitude and longitude. Box 8.18 shows the Django views for the REST API. ViewSets are used for the views that allow you to combine the logic for a set of related views in a single class.

Box 8.19 shows the serializers for the REST API. Serializers allow complex data (such as querysets and model instances) to be converted to native Python datatypes that can then be easily rendered into JSON, XML or other content types. Serializers also provide de-serialization, allowing parsed data to be converted back into complex types, after first validating the incoming data.

Box 8.20 shows the URL patterns for the REST API. Since ViewSets are used instead of views, we can automatically generate the URL conf for our API, by simply registering the viewsets with a router class. Routers automatically determining how the URLs for an application should be mapped to the logic that deals with handling incoming requests. Box 8.21 shows the settings for the REST API Django project.

■ **Box 8.17: Django model for Weather Station - models.py**

```
from django.db import models

class Station(models.Model):
    name = models.CharField(max_length=10)
    timestamp = models.CharField(max_length=10)
    temperature = models.CharField(max_length=5)
    lat = models.CharField(max_length=10)
    lon = models.CharField(max_length=10)
```

■ **Box 8.18: Django views for Weather Station REST API - views.py**

```
from myapp.models import Station
from rest_framework import viewsets
from django.shortcuts import render_to_response
from django.template import RequestContext
from myapp.serializers import StationSerializer
import requests
import json

class StationViewSet(viewsets.ModelViewSet):
    queryset = Station.objects.all()
    serializer_class = StationSerializer

def home(request):
    r=requests.get('http://127.0.0.1:8000/station/',
    auth=('username', 'password'))
```

```
    result=r.text
    output = json.loads(result)
    count=output['count']
    count=int(count)-1

    name=output['results'][count]['name']
    temperature=output['results'][count]['temperature']
    lat=output['results'][count]['lat']
    lon=output['results'][count]['lon']

    return render_to_response('index.html','name':name,
    'temperature':temperature, 'lat': lat, 'lon': lon,
    context_instance=RequestContext(request))
```

■ **Box 8.19:  Serializers for Weather Station REST API - serializers.py**

```
from myapp.models import Station
from rest_framework import serializers

class StationSerializer(serializers.HyperlinkedModelSerializer):
  class Meta:
    model = Station
    fields = ('url', 'name','timestamp','timestamp',
    'temperature','lat','lon')
```

■ **Box 8.20:  Django URL patterns example - urls.py**

```
from django.conf.urls import patterns, include, url
from django.contrib import admin
from rest_framework import routers
from myapp import views

admin.autodiscover()

router = routers.DefaultRouter()
router.register(r'station', views.StationViewSet)

urlpatterns = patterns('',
url(r'^', include(router.urls)),
url(r'^api-auth/', include('rest_framework.urls',
namespace='rest_framework')),
url(r'^admin/', include(admin.site.urls)),
url(r'^home/', 'myapp.views.home'),
)
```

■ **Box 8.21:  Django project settings example - settings.py**

```
DATABASES = {
'default': {
'ENGINE': 'django.db.backends.mysql',
'NAME': 'weatherstation',
'USER': 'root',
'PASSWORD': 'password',
'HOST': '',
'PORT': '',
}
}
REST_FRAMEWORK = {
    'DEFAULT_PERMISSION_CLASSES':
    ('rest_framework.permissions.IsAdminUser',),
    'PAGINATE_BY': 10
}

INSTALLED_APPS = (
    'django.contrib.admin',
    'django.contrib.auth',
    'django.contrib.contenttypes',
    'django.contrib.sessions',
    'django.contrib.messages',
    'django.contrib.staticfiles',
    'myapp',
    'rest_framework',
)
```

After creating the Station REST API source files, the next step is to setup the database and then run the Django development web server as follows:

```
■ python manage.py syncdb
python manage.py runserver
```

■ **Box 8.22: Using the Station REST API - CURL examples**

```
#------POST Example-------
$ curl -i -H "Content-Type: application/json" -H
"Accept:application/json; indent=4" -X POST -d
'"name": "CityName", "timestamp": "1393926310",
"temperature": "28", "lat": "30.733315", "lon":
"76.779418"' -u arshdeep http://127.0.0.1:8000/station/
Enter host password for user 'arshdeep':
HTTP/1.0 201 CREATED
Date: Tue, 04 Mar 2014 11:21:29 GMT
Server: WSGIServer/0.1 Python/2.7.3
Vary: Accept, Cookie
Content-Type: application/json; indent=4
Location: http://127.0.0.1:8000/station/4/
Allow: GET, POST, HEAD, OPTIONS
```

```
      "url":  "http://127.0.0.1:8000/station/4/",
      "name":  "CityName",
      "timestamp":  "1393926310",
      "temperature":  "28",
      "lat":  "30.733315",
      "lon":  "76.779418"


#-----GET Examples-------
$ curl -i -H "Accept: application/json; indent=4" -u arsheep
http://127.0.0.1:8000/station/
Enter host password for user 'arshdeep':
HTTP/1.0 200 OK
Date:  Tue, 04 Mar 2014 11:21:56 GMT
Server:  WSGIServer/0.1 Python/2.7.3
Vary:  Accept, Cookie
Content-Type:  application/json; indent=4
Allow:  GET, POST, HEAD, OPTIONS


   "count":  2,
   "next":  null,
   "previous":  null,
   "results":  [

        "url":  "http://127.0.0.1:8000/station/1/",
        "name":  "CityName",
        "timestamp":  "1393926457",
        "temperature":  "20",
        "lat":  "30.733315",
        "lon":  "76.779418"
     ,

        "url":  "http://127.0.0.1:8000/station/2/",
        "name":  "CityName",
        "timestamp":  "1393926310",
        "temperature":  "28",
        "lat":  "30.733315",
        "lon":  "76.779418"

   ]


$ curl -i -H "Accept: application/json; indent=4" -u arsheep
http://127.0.0.1:8000/station/1/
Enter host password for user 'arshdeep':
HTTP/1.0 200 OK
Date:  Tue, 04 Mar 2014 11:23:08 GMT
Server:  WSGIServer/0.1 Python/2.7.3
Vary:  Accept, Cookie
Content-Type:  application/json; indent=4
Allow:  GET, PUT, PATCH, DELETE, HEAD, OPTIONS
```

```
        "url":   "http://127.0.0.1:8000/station/1/",
        "name":   "CityName",
        "timestamp":  "1393926457",
        "temperature":   "20",
        "lat":  "30.733315",
        "lon":  "76.779418"



#------PUT Example-------
$ curl -i -H "Content-Type:  application/json" -H
"Accept:  pplication/json; indent=4" -X PUT -d
'"name":  "CityName", "timestamp":  "1393926310",
"temperature":   "29", "lat":  "30.733315",
"lon":  "76.779418"' -u arshdeep
http://127.0.0.1:8000/station/1/
Enter host password for user 'arshdeep':
HTTP/1.0 200 OK
Date:  Tue, 04 Mar 2014 11:24:14 GMT
Server:  WSGIServer/0.1 Python/2.7.3
Vary:  Accept, Cookie
Content-Type:  application/json
Allow:  GET, PUT, PATCH, DELETE, HEAD, OPTIONS

    "url":  "http://127.0.0.1:8000/station/1/",
    "name":  "CityName", "timestamp":  "1393926310",
    "temperature":  "29", "lat":  "30.733315", "lon":   "76.779418"

#------DELETE Example-------
$curl -i -X DELETE -H "Accept:  application/json; indent=4" -u arshdeep
http://127.0.0.1:8000/station/2/
Enter host password for user 'arshdeep':
HTTP/1.0 204 NO CONTENT
Date:  Tue, 04 Mar 2014 11:24:55 GMT
Server:  WSGIServer/0.1 Python/2.7.3
Vary:  Accept, Cookie
Content-Length:  0
Allow:  GET, PUT, PATCH, DELETE, HEAD, OPTIONS
```

Box 8.22 shows examples of interacting with the Station REST API using CURL. The HTTP POST method is used to create a new resource, GET method is used to obtain information about a resource, PUT method is used to update a resource and DELETE method is used to delete a resource. Figure 8.11 shows the screenshots from the web browsable Station REST API.

## 8.6 Amazon Web Services for IoT

In this section you will learn how to use Amazon Web Services for IoT.

### 8.6.1 Amazon EC2

Amazon EC2 is an Infrastructure-as-a-Service (IaaS) provided by Amazon. EC2 delivers scalable, pay-as-you-go compute capacity in the cloud. EC2 is a web service that provides computing capacity in the form of virtual machines that are launched in Amazon's cloud

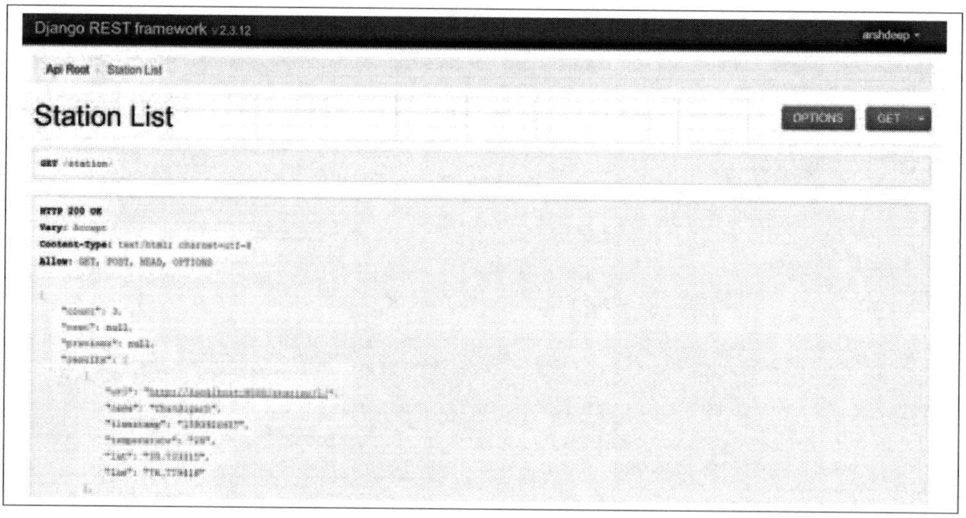

Figure 8.11: Screenshot from the web browsable Station REST API

computing environment. EC2 can be used for several purposes for IoT systems. For example, IoT developers can deploy IoT applications (developed in frameworks such as Django) on EC2, setup IoT platforms with REST web services, etc.

Let us look at some examples of using EC2. Box 8.23 shows the Python code for launching an EC2 instance. In this example, a connection to EC2 service is first established by calling *boto.ec2.connect_to_region*. The EC2 region, AWS access key and AWS secret key are passed to this function. After connecting to EC2 , a new instance is launched using the *conn.run_instances* function. The AMI-ID, instance type, EC2 key handle and security group are passed to this function. This function returns a reservation. The instances associated with the reservation are obtained using *reservation.instances*. Finally the status of an instance associated with a reservation is obtained using the *instance.update* function. In the example shown in Box 8.23, the program waits till the status of the newly launched instance becomes *running* and then prints the instance details such as public DNS, instance IP, and launch time.

■ **Box 8.23: Python program for launching an EC2 instance**

```
import boto.ec2
from time import import sleep

ACCESS_KEY="<enter access key>"
SECRET_KEY="<enter secret key>"

REGION="us-east-1"
AMI_ID = "ami-d0f89fb9"
EC2_KEY_HANDLE = "<enter key handle>"
INSTANCE_TYPE="t1.micro"
SECGROUP_HANDLE="default"

print "Connecting to EC2"
```

```
conn = boto.ec2.connect_to_region(REGION,
   aws_access_key_id=ACCESS_KEY,
   aws_secret_access_key=SECRET_KEY)

print "Launching instance with AMI-ID %s, with keypair
%s, instance type %s, security group
%s"%(AMI_ID,EC2_KEY_HANDLE,INSTANCE_TYPE,SECGROUP_HANDLE)

reservation = conn.run_instances(image_id=AMI_ID,
        key_name=EC2_KEY_HANDLE,
        instance_type=INSTANCE_TYPE,
        security_groups = [ SECGROUP_HANDLE, ] )

instance = reservation.instances[0]

print "Waiting for instance to be up and running"

status = instance.update()
while status == 'pending':
   sleep(10)
   status = instance.update()

if status == 'running':
   print " \n Instance is now running.  Instance details are:"
   print "Intance Size:  " + str(instance.instance_type)
   print "Intance State:  " + str(instance.state)
   print "Intance Launch Time:  " + str(instance.launch_time)
   print "Intance Public DNS: " + str(instance.public_dns_name)
   print "Intance Private DNS: " + str(instance.private_dns_name)
   print "Intance IP: " + str(instance.ip_address)
   print "Intance Private IP: " + str(instance.private_ip_address)
```

Box 8.24 shows the Python code for stopping an EC2 instance. In this example the *conn.get_all_instances* function is called to get information on all running instances. This function returns reservations. Next, the IDs of instances associated with each reservation are obtained. The instances are stopped by calling *conn.stop_instances* function to which the IDs of the instances to stop are passed.

■ **Box 8.24: Python program for stopping an EC2 instance**

```
import boto.ec2
from time import sleep


ACCESS_KEY="<enter access key>"
SECRET_KEY="<enter secret key>"

REGION="us-east-1"

print "Connecting to EC2"
```

```
conn = boto.ec2.connect_to_region(REGION,
    aws_access_key_id=ACCESS_KEY,
    aws_secret_access_key=SECRET_KEY)

print "Getting all running instances"
reservations = conn.get_all_instances()
print reservations

instance_rs = reservations[0].instances
instance = instance_rs[0]
instanceid=instance_rs[0].id
print "Stopping instance with ID: " + str(instanceid)

conn.stop_instances(instance_ids=[instanceid])

status = instance.update()
while not status == 'stopped':
    sleep(10)
    status = instance.update()

print "Stopped instance with ID: " + str(instanceid)
```

### 8.6.2  Amazon AutoScaling

Amazon AutoScaling allows automatically scaling Amazon EC2 capacity up or down according to user defined conditions. Therefore, with AutoScaling users can increase the number of EC2 instances running their applications seamlessly during spikes in the application workloads to meet the application performance requirements and scale down capacity when the workload is low to save costs. AutoScaling can be used for auto scaling IoT applications and IoT platforms deployed on Amazon EC2.

Let us now look at some examples of using AutoScaling. Box 8.25 shows the Python code for creating an AutoScaling group. In this example, a connection to AutoScaling service is first established by calling *boto.ec2.autoscale.connect_to_region* function.

The EC2 region, AWS access key and AWS secret key are passed to this function. After connecting to AutoScaling service, a new launch configuration is created by calling *conn.create_launch_configuration*. Launch configuration contains instructions on how to launch new instances including the AMI-ID, instance type, security groups, etc. After creating a launch configuration, it is then associated with a new AutoScaling group. AutoScaling group is created by calling *conn.create_auto_scaling_group*. The settings for AutoScaling group include maximum and minimum number of instances in the group, launch configuration, availability zones, optional load balancer to use with the group, etc. After creating an AutoScaling group, the policies for scaling up and scaling down are defined. In this example, a scale up policy with adjustment type *ChangeInCapacity* and *scaling_adjustment* = 1 is defined. Similarly a scale down policy with adjustment type *ChangeInCapacity* and *scaling_adjustment* = −1 is defined. With the scaling policies defined, the next step is to create Amazon CloudWatch alarms that trigger these policies. In this example, alarms for scaling up and scaling down are created. The scale up alarm is defined using the *CPUUtilization* metric with the *Average* statistic and threshold greater 70% for a period of 60 sec. The scale up policy created previously is associated with this alarm. This alarm is triggered when the average CPU utilization of the instances in the group becomes greater than 70% for more than 60 seconds. The scale down alarm is defined in a similar manner with a threshold less than 50%.

■ **Box 8.25: Python program for creating an AutoScaling group**

```python
import boto.ec2.autoscale
from boto.ec2.autoscale import LaunchConfiguration
from boto.ec2.autoscale import AutoScalingGroup
from boto.ec2.cloudwatch import MetricAlarm
from boto.ec2.autoscale import ScalingPolicy
import boto.ec2.cloudwatch

ACCESS_KEY="<enter access key>"
SECRET_KEY="<enter secret key>"

REGION="us-east-1"
AMI_ID = "ami-d0f89fb9"
EC2_KEY_HANDLE = "<enter key handle>"
INSTANCE_TYPE="t1.micro"
SECGROUP_HANDLE="default"

print "Connecting to Autoscaling Service"

conn = boto.ec2.autoscale.connect_to_region(REGION,
     aws_access_key_id=ACCESS_KEY,
     aws_secret_access_key=SECRET_KEY)


print "Creating launch configuration"


lc = LaunchConfiguration(name='My-Launch-Config-2',
        image_id=AMI_ID,
        key_name=EC2_KEY_HANDLE,
        instance_type=INSTANCE_TYPE,
        security_groups = [ SECGROUP_HANDLE, ])


conn.create_launch_configuration(lc)

print "Creating auto-scaling group"

ag = AutoScalingGroup(group_name='My-Group',
        availability_zones=['us-east-1b'],
        launch_config=lc, min_size=1, max_size=2,
        connection=conn)

conn.create_auto_scaling_group(ag)

print "Creating auto-scaling policies"

scale_up_policy = ScalingPolicy(name='scale_up',
```

```
                    adjustment_type='ChangeInCapacity',
              as_name='My-Group',
               scaling_adjustment=1,
              cooldown=180)

  scale_down_policy = ScalingPolicy(name='scale_down',
              adjustment_type='ChangeInCapacity',
              as_name='My-Group',
               scaling_adjustment=-1,
              cooldown=180)


conn.create_scaling_policy(scale_up_policy)
conn.create_scaling_policy(scale_down_policy)


scale_up_policy = conn.get_all_policies( as_group='My-Group',
policy_names=['scale_up'])[0]
scale_down_policy = conn.get_all_policies( as_group='My-Group',
policy_names=['scale_down'])[0]

print "Connecting to CloudWatch"

cloudwatch = boto.ec2.cloudwatch.connect_to_region(REGION,
        aws_access_key_id=ACCESS_KEY,
         aws_secret_access_key=SECRET_KEY)

alarm_dimensions = "AutoScalingGroupName":  'My-Group'

print "Creating scale-up alarm"

scale_up_alarm = MetricAlarm(
     name='scale_up_on_cpu', namespace='AWS/EC2',
     metric='CPUUtilization', statistic='Average',
     comparison='>', threshold='70',
     period='60', evaluation_periods=2,
     alarm_actions=[scale_up_policy.policy_arn] ,
     dimensions=alarm_dimensions)

cloudwatch.create_alarm(scale_up_alarm)

print "Creating scale-down alarm"

scale_down_alarm = MetricAlarm(
     name='scale_down_on_cpu', namespace='AWS/EC2',
     metric='CPUUtilization', statistic='Average',
     comparison='<', threshold='50',
     period='60', evaluation_periods=2,
     alarm_actions=[scale_down_policy.policy_arn],
     dimensions=alarm_dimensions)

cloudwatch.create_alarm(scale_down_alarm)
print "Done!"
```

### 8.6.3   Amazon S3

Amazon S3 is an online cloud-based data storage infrastructure for storing and retrieving a very large amount of data. S3 provides highly reliable, scalable, fast, fully redundant and affordable storage infrastructure. S3 can serve as a raw datastore (or "Thing Tank") for IoT systems for storing raw data, such as sensor data, log data, image, audio and video data.

Let us look at some examples of using S3. Box 8.26 shows the Python code for uploading a file to Amazon S3 cloud storage. In this example, a connection to S3 service is first established by calling *boto.connect_s3* function. The AWS access key and AWS secret key are passed to this function. This example defines two functions *upload_to_s3_bucket_path* and *upload_to_s3_bucket_root*. The *upload_to_s3_bucket_path* function uploads the file to the S3 bucket specified at the specified path. The *upload_to_s3_bucket_root* function uploads the file to the S3 bucket root.

■ **Box 8.26:  Python program for uploading a file to an S3 bucket**

```python
import boto.s3

ACCESS_KEY="<enter access key>"
SECRET_KEY="<enter secret key>"

conn = boto.connect_s3(aws_access_key_id=ACCESS_KEY,
    aws_secret_access_key=SECRET_KEY)

def percent_cb(complete, total):
  print ('.')

def upload_to_s3_bucket_path(bucketname, path, filename):
  mybucket = conn.get_bucket(bucketname)
  fullkeyname=os.path.join(path,filename)
  key = mybucket.new_key(fullkeyname)
  key.set_contents_from_filename(filename, cb=percent_cb, num_cb=10)

def upload_to_s3_bucket_root(bucketname, filename):
  mybucket = conn.get_bucket(bucketname)
  key = mybucket.new_key(filename)
  key.set_contents_from_filename(filename, cb=percent_cb, num_cb=10)

upload_to_s3_bucket_path('mybucket2013', 'data', 'file.txt')
```

### 8.6.4   Amazon RDS

Amazon RDS is a web service that allows you to create instances of MySQL, Oracle or Microsoft SQL Server in the cloud. With RDS, developers can easily set up, operate, and scale a relational database in the cloud.

RDS can serve as a scalable datastore for IoT systems. With RDS, IoT system developers can store any amount of data in scalable relational databases. Let us look at some examples of using RDS. Box 8.27 shows the Python code for launching an Amazon RDS instance. In this example, a connection to RDS service is first established by calling *boto.rds.connect_to_region* function. The RDS region, AWS access key and AWS secret key are passed to this function. After connecting to RDS service, the *conn.create_dbinstance* function is called to launch a new RDS instance. The input parameters to this function include the instance ID, database size, instance type, database username, database password, database port, database engine (e.g. MySQL5.1), database name, security groups, etc. The program shown in Box 8.27 waits till the status of the RDS instance becomes *available* and then prints the instance details such as instance ID, create time, or instance end point.

■ Box 8.27:  Python program for launching an RDS instance

```python
import boto.rds
from time import sleep

ACCESS_KEY="<enter access key>"
SECRET_KEY="<enter secret key>"

REGION="us-east-1"
INSTANCE_TYPE="db.t1.micro"
ID = "MySQL-db-instance"
USERNAME = 'root'
PASSWORD = 'password'
DB_PORT = 3306
DB_SIZE = 5
DB_ENGINE = 'MySQL5.1'
DB_NAME = 'mytestdb'
SECGROUP_HANDLE="default"

print "Connecting to RDS"

conn = boto.rds.connect_to_region(REGION,
   aws_access_key_id=ACCESS_KEY,
   aws_secret_access_key=SECRET_KEY)

print "Creating an RDS instance"

db = conn.create_dbinstance(ID, DB_SIZE, INSTANCE_TYPE,
USERNAME, PASSWORD, port=DB_PORT, engine=DB_ENGINE,
db_name=DB_NAME, security_groups = [
SECGROUP_HANDLE, ] )
print db

print "Waiting for instance to be up and running"

status = db.status
while not status == 'available':
   sleep(10)
   status = db.status

if status == 'available':
   print " \n RDS Instance is now running.  Instance details are:"
   print "Intance ID: " + str(db.id)
   print "Intance State:  " + str(db.status)
   print "Intance Create Time:  " + str(db.create_time)
   print "Engine:  " + str(db.engine)
   print "Allocated Storage:  " + str(db.allocated_storage)
```

```
print "Endpoint:   " + str(db.endpoint)
```

Box 8.28 shows the Python code for creating a MySQL table, writing and reading from the table. This example uses the MySQLdb Python package. To connect to the MySQL RDS instance, the *MySQLdb.connect* function is called and the end point of the RDS instance, database username, password and port are passed to this function. After the connection to the RDS instance is established, a cursor to the database is obtained by calling *conn.cursor*. Next, a new database table named *TemperatureData* is created with *Id* as primary key and other columns. After creating the table some values are inserted. To execute the SQL commands for database manipulation, the commands are passed to the *cursor.execute* function.

■ **Box 8.28: Python program for creating a MySQL table, writing and reading from the table**

```
import MySQLdb

USERNAME = 'root'
PASSWORD = 'password'
DB_NAME = 'mytestdb'

print "Connecting to RDS instance"

conn = MySQLdb.connect (host =
"mysql-db-instance-3.c35qdifuf9ko.us-east-1.rds.amazonaws.com",
user = USERNAME,
passwd = PASSWORD,
db = DB_NAME,
port = 3306)

print "Connected to RDS instance"

cursor = conn.cursor ()
cursor.execute ("SELECT VERSION()")
row = cursor.fetchone ()
print "server version:", row[0]

cursor.execute ("CREATE TABLE TemperatureData(Id INT PRIMARY KEY,
Timestamp TEXT, Data TEXT) ")
cursor.execute ("INSERT INTO TemperatureData VALUES(1,
'1393926310', '20')")
cursor.execute ("INSERT INTO TemperatureData VALUES(2,
'1393926457', '25')")

cursor.execute("SELECT * FROM TemperatureData")
rows = cursor.fetchall()

for row in rows:
   print row

cursor.close ()
conn.close ()
```

### 8.6.5  Amazon DynamoDB

Amazon DynamoDB is a fully-managed, scalable, high performance No-SQL database service. DynamoDB can serve as a scalable datastore for IoT systems. With DynamoDB, IoT system developers can store any amount of data and serve any level of requests for the data.

Let us look at some examples of using DynamoDB. Box 8.29 shows the Python code for creating a DynamoDB table. In this example, a connection to DynamoDB service is first established by calling
*boto.dynamodb.connect_to_region*. The DynamoDB region, AWS access key and AWS secret key are passed to this function. After connecting to DynamoDB service, a schema for the new table is created by calling *conn.create_schema*. The schema includes the hash key and range key names and types. A DynamoDB table is then created by calling *conn.create_table* function with the table schema, read units and write units as input parameters.

---

■ **Box 8.29: Python program for creating a DynamoDB table**

```
import boto.dynamodb
import time
from datetime import date

ACCESS_KEY="<enter access key>"
SECRET_KEY="<enter secret key>"
REGION="us-east-1"

print "Connecting to DynamoDB"

conn = boto.dynamodb.connect_to_region(REGION,
    aws_access_key_id=ACCESS_KEY,
    aws_secret_access_key=SECRET_KEY)

table_schema = conn.create_schema(
    hash_key_name='msgid',
    hash_key_proto_value=str,
    range_key_name='date',
    range_key_proto_value=str
    )

print "Creating table with schema:"
print table_schema


table = conn.create_table(
    name='my-test-table',
    schema=table_schema,
    read_units=1,
    write_units=1
    )

print "Creating table:"
print table
```

---

```
print "Done!"
```

Box 8.30 shows the Python code for writing and reading from a DynamoDB table. After establishing a connection with DynamoDB service, the *conn.get_table* is called to retrieve an existing table. The data written in this example consists of a JSON message with keys - *Body*, *CreatedBy* and *Time*. After creating the JSON message, a new DynamoDB table item is created by calling *table.new_item* and the hash key and range key is specified. The data item is finally committed to DynamoDB by calling *item.put*. To read data from DynamoDB, the *table.get_item* function is used with the hash key and range key as input parameters.

■ **Box 8.30: Python program for writing and reading from a DynamoDB table**

```
import boto.dynamodb
import time
from datetime import date

ACCESS_KEY="<enter access key>"
SECRET_KEY="<enter secret key>"
REGION="us-east-1"

print "Connecting to DynamoDB"

conn = boto.dynamodb.connect_to_region(REGION,
   aws_access_key_id=ACCESS_KEY,
   aws_secret_access_key=SECRET_KEY)

print "Listing available tables"
tables_list = conn.list_tables()
print tables_list

print "my-test-table description"
desc = conn.describe_table('my-test-table')
print desc

msg_datetime = time.asctime(time.localtime(time.time()))

print "Writing data"

table = conn.get_table("my-test-table")

hash_attribute = "Entry/" + str(date.today())

item_data =
   'Body':  'Test message',
   'CreatedBy':  'Vijay',
   'Time':  msg_datetime,


item = table.new_item(
   hash_key=hash_attribute,
   range_key=str(date.today()),
   attrs=item_data
)
```

```
item.put()

print "Reading data"

table = conn.get_table('my-test-table')

read_data = table.get_item(
    hash_key=hash_attribute,
    range_key=str(date.today())
    )

print read_data
print "Done!"
```

### 8.6.6  Amazon Kinesis

Amazon Kinesis is a fully managed commercial service that allows real-time processing of streaming data. Kinesis scales automatically to handle high volume streaming data coming from large number of sources. The streaming data collected by Kinesis can be processed by applications running on Amazon EC2 instances or any other compute instance that can connect to Kinesis. Kinesis is well suited for IoT systems that generate massive scale data and have strict real-time requirements for processing the data. Kinesis allows rapid and continuous data intake and support data blobs of size upto 50Kb. The data producers (e.g. IoT devices) write data records to Kinesis streams. A data record comprises of a sequence number, a partition key and the data blob. Data records in a Kinesis stream are distributed in shards. Each shard provides a fixed unit of capacity and a stream can have multiple shards. A single shard of throughput allows capturing 1MB per second of data, at up to 1,000 PUT transactions per second and allows applications to read data at up to 2 MB per second.

Box 8.31 shows a Python program for writing to a Kinesis stream. This example follows a similar structure as the controller program in Box 8.4 that sends temperature data from an IoT device to the cloud. In this example a connection to the Kinesis service is first established and then a new Kinesis stream is either created (if not existing) or described. The data is written to the Kinesis stream using the *kinesis.put_record* function.

■ **Box 8.31: Python program for writing to a Kinesis stream**

```
import json
import time
import datetime
import boto.kinesis
from boto.kinesis.exceptions import ResourceNotFoundException
from random import randint

ACCESS_KEY = "<enter access key>"
SECRET_KEY = "<enter secret key>"

kinesis = boto.connect_kinesis(aws_access_key_id=ACCESS_KEY,
aws_secret_access_key=SECRET_KEY)
streamName = "temperature"
partitionKey = "IoTExample"
```

```
shardCount = 1
global stream


def readTempSensor():
#Return random value
   return randint(20,30)


#Controller main function
def runController():
   temperature = readTempSensor()
   timestamp = datetime.datetime.utcnow()
   record=str(timestamp)+":"+str(temperature)
   print "Putting record in stream:  " + record
   response = kinesis.put_record( stream_name=streamName,
data=record, partition_key=partitionKey)
   print ("-= put seqNum:", response['SequenceNumber'])

def get_or_create_stream(stream_name, shard_count):
   stream = None
   try:
      stream = kinesis.describe_stream(stream_name)
      print (json.dumps(stream, sort_keys=True, indent=2, separators=(',',
': ')))
   except ResourceNotFoundException as rnfe:
      while (stream is None) or (stream['StreamStatus'] is not 'ACTIVE'):
         print ('Could not find ACTIVE stream:0 trying to create.'.format(
            stream_name))
         stream = kinesis.create_stream(stream_name, shard_count)
         time.sleep(0.5)

   return stream


def setupController():
   global stream
   stream = get_or_create_stream(streamName, shardCount)

setupController()
while True:
   runController()
   time.sleep(1)
```

Box 8.32 shows a Python program for reading from a Kinesis stream. In this example a shard iterator is obtained using the *kinesis.get_shard_iterator* function. The shard iterator specifies the position in the shard from which you want to start reading data records sequentially. The data is read using the *kinesis.get_records* function which returns one or more data records from a shard.

■ **Box 8.32: Python program for reading from a Kinesis stream**

```
import json
import time
```

```
import boto.kinesis
from boto.kinesis.exceptions import ResourceNotFoundException
from boto.kinesis.exceptions import
ProvisionedThroughputExceededException
from boto.kinesis.exceptions import
ProvisionedThroughputExceededException

ACCESS_KEY = "<enter access key>"
SECRET_KEY = "<enter secret key>"

kinesis = boto.connect_kinesis(aws_access_key_id=ACCESS_KEY,
aws_secret_access_key=SECRET_KEY)
streamName = "temperature"
partitionKey = "IoTExample"
shardCount = 1
iterator_type='LATEST'

stream = kinesis.describe_stream(streamName)
print (json.dumps(stream, sort_keys=True, indent=2,
separators=(',', ': ')))
shards = stream['StreamDescription']['Shards']
print ('# Shard Count:', len(shards))

def processRecords(records):
  for record in records:
    text = record['Data'].lower()
    print 'Processing record with data: ' + text

i=0
response = kinesis.get_shard_iterator(streamName, shards[0]['ShardId'],
'TRIM_HORIZON', starting_sequence_number=None)
next_iterator = response['ShardIterator']
print ('Getting next records using iterator: ', next_iterator)
while i<10:
  try:
    response = kinesis.get_records(next_iterator, limit=1)
    #print response
    if len(response['Records']) > 0:
      #print 'Number of records fetched:' +
str(len(response['Records']))
      processRecords(response['Records'] )

    next_iterator = response['NextShardIterator']
    time.sleep(1)
    i=i+1

  except ProvisionedThroughputExceededException as ptee:
    print (ptee.message)
    time.sleep(5)
```

### 8.6.7 Amazon SQS

Amazon SQS offers a highly scalable and reliable hosted queue for storing messages as they travel between distinct components of applications. SQS guarantees only that messages arrive, not that they arrive in the same order in which they were put in the queue. Though, at first look, Amazon SQS may seem to be similar to Amazon Kinesis, however, both are intended for very different types of applications. While Kinesis is meant for real-time applications that involve high data ingress and egress rates, SQS is simply a queue system that stores and releases messages in a scalable manner.

SQS can be used in distributed IoT applications in which various application components need to exchange messages. Let us look at some examples of using SQS. Box 8.33 shows the Python code for creating an SQS queue. In this example, a connection to SQS service is first established by calling *boto.sqs.connect_to_region*. The AWS region, access key and secret key are passed to this function. After connecting to SQS service, *conn.create_queue* is called to create a new queue with queue name as input parameter. The function *conn.get_all_queues* is used to retrieve all SQS queues.

■ **Box 8.33: Python program for creating an SQS queue**

```python
import boto.sqs

ACCESS_KEY="<enter access key>"
SECRET_KEY="<enter secret key>"
REGION="us-east-1"

print "Connecting to SQS"

conn = boto.sqs.connect_to_region(
    REGION,
    aws_access_key_id=ACCESS_KEY,
    aws_secret_access_key=SECRET_KEY)

queue_name = 'mytestqueue'

print "Creating queue with name:  " + queue_name
q = conn.create_queue(queue_name)

print "Created queue with name:  " + queue_name

print " \n Getting all queues"

rs = conn.get_all_queues()

for item in rs:
  print item
```

Box 8.34 shows the Python code for writing to an SQS queue. After connecting to an SQS queue, the *queue.write* is called with the message as input parameter.

■ **Box 8.34: Python program for writing to an SQS queue**

```python
import boto.sqs
from boto.sqs.message import Message
import time
```

```
ACCESS_KEY="<enter access key>"
SECRET_KEY="<enter secret key>"

REGION="us-east-1"

print "Connecting to SQS"

conn = boto.sqs.connect_to_region(
    REGION,
    aws_access_key_id=ACCESS_KEY,
    aws_secret_access_key=SECRET_KEY)

queue_name = 'mytestqueue'

print "Connecting to queue:  " + queue_name
q = conn.get_all_queues(prefix=queue_name)

msg_datetime = time.asctime(time.localtime(time.time()))

msg = "Test message generated on:  " + msg_datetime
print "Writing to queue:  " + msg

m = Message()
m.set_body(msg)
status = q[0].write(m)

print "Message written to queue"

count = q[0].count()

print "Total messages in queue:  " + str(count)
```

Box 8.35 shows the Python code for reading from an SQS queue. After connecting to an SQS queue, the *queue.read* is called to read a message from a queue.

### ■ Box 8.35:  Python program for reading from an SQS queue

```
import boto.sqs
from boto.sqs.message import Message

ACCESS_KEY="<enter access key>"
SECRET_KEY="<enter secret key>"

REGION="us-east-1"

print "Connecting to SQS"

conn = boto.sqs.connect_to_region(
    REGION,
    aws_access_key_id=ACCESS_KEY,
    aws_secret_access_key=SECRET_KEY)

queue_name = 'mytestqueue'
```

```
print "Connecting to queue:   " + queue_name
q = conn.get_all_queues(prefix=queue_name)

count = q[0].count()

print "Total messages in queue:   " + str(count)

print "Reading message from queue"

for i in range(count):
  m = q[0].read()
  print "Message %d:   %s" % (i+1,str(m.get_body()))
  q[0].delete_message(m)

print "Read %d messages from queue" % (count)
```

### 8.6.8  Amazon EMR

Amazon EMR is a web service that utilizes Hadoop framework running on Amazon EC2 and Amazon S3. EMR allows processing of massive scale data, hence, suitable for IoT applications that generate large volumes of data that needs to be analyzed. Data processing jobs are formulated with the MapReduce parallel data processing model.

MapReduce is a parallel data processing model for processing and analysis of massive scale data [85]. MapReduce model has two phases: Map and Reduce. MapReduce programs are written in a functional programming style to create Map and Reduce functions. The input data to the map and reduce phases is in the form of key-value pairs.

Consider an IoT system that collects data from a machine (or sensor data) which is logged in a cloud storage (such as Amazon S3) and analyzed on hourly basis to generate alerts if a certain sequence occurred more than a predefined number of times. Since the scale of data involved in such applications can be massive, MapReduce is an ideal choice for processing such data.

Let us look at a MapReduce example that finds the number of occurrences of a sequence from a log. Box 8.36 shows the Python code for launching an Elastic MapReduce job. In this example, a connection to EMR service is first established by calling *boto.emr.connect_to_region*. The AWS region, access key and secret key are passed to this function. After connecting to EMR service, a jobflow step is created. There are two types of steps - streaming and custom jar. To create a streaming job an object of the *StreamingStep* class is created by specifying the job name, locations of the mapper, reducer, input and output. The job flow is then started using the *conn.run_jobflow* function with streaming step object as input. When the MapReduce job completes, the output can be obtained from the output location on the S3 bucket specified while creating the streaming step.

■ **Box 8.36: Python program for launching an EMR job**

```
import boto.emr
from boto.emr.step import StreamingStep
from time import sleep

ACCESS_KEY="<enter access key>"
```

```
SECRET_KEY="<enter secret key>"
REGION="us-east-1"

print "Connecting to EMR"

conn = boto.emr.connect_to_region(REGION,
      aws_access_key_id=ACCESS_KEY,
      aws_secret_access_key=SECRET_KEY)

print "Creating streaming step"

step = StreamingStep(name='Sequence Count',
      mapper='s3n://mybucket/seqCountMapper.py',
      reducer='s3n://mybucket/seqCountReducer.py',
      input='s3n://mybucket/data/',
      output='s3n://mybucket/seqcountoutput/')


print "Creating job flow"

jobid = conn.run_jobflow(name='Sequence Count Jobflow',
      log_uri='s3n://mybucket/wordcount_logs',
      steps=[step])

print "Submitted job flow"

print "Waiting for job flow to complete"

status = conn.describe_jobflow(jobid)
print status.state

while status.state != 'COMPLETED' or status.state != 'FAILED':
   sleep(10)
   status = conn.describe_jobflow(jobid)

print "Job status:  " + str(status.state)

print "Done!"
```

Box 8.37 shows the sequence count mapper program in Python. The mapper reads the data from standard input (stdin) and for each line in input in which the sequence occurs, the mapper emits a key-value pair where key is the sequence and value is equal to 1.

### ■ Box 8.37: Sequence count Mapper in Python

```
#!/usr/bin/env python
import sys

#Enter the sequence to search
seq='123'
for line in sys.stdin:
   line = line.strip()
   if seq in line:
```

```
print '%st%s' % (seq, 1)
```

Box 8.38 shows the sequence count reducer program in Python. The key-value pairs emitted by the map phase are shuffled to the reducers and grouped by the key. The reducer reads the key-value pairs grouped by the same key from the standard input (stdin) and sums up the occurrences to compute the count for each sequence.

■ **Box 8.38: Sequence count Reducer in Python**

```
#!/usr/bin/env python
from operator import itemgetter
import sys

current_seq = None
current_count = 0
seq = None

for line in sys.stdin:
   line = line.strip()
   seq, count = line.split('t', 1)
   current_count += count

   try:
      count = int(count)
   except ValueError:
      continue

   if current_seq == seq:
      current_count += count
else:
   if current_seq:
      print '%st%s' % (current_seq, current_count)
   current_count = count
   current_seq = seq

if current_seq == seq:
   print '%st%s' % (current_seq, current_count)
```

## 8.7  SkyNet IoT Messaging Platform

SkyNet is an open source instant messaging platform for Internet of Things. The SkyNet API supports both HTTP REST and real-time WebSockets. SkyNet allows you to register devices (or nodes) on the network. A device can be anything including sensors, smart home devices, cloud resources, drones, etc. Each device is assigned a UUID and a secret token. Devices or client applications can subscribe to other devices and receive/send messages.

Box 8.39 shows the commands to setup SkyNet on a Linux machine. Box 8.40 shows a sample configuration for SkyNet. Box 8.41 shows examples of using SkyNet. The first step is to create a device on SkyNet. The POST request to create a device returns the UUID and token of the created device. The box also shows examples of updating a device, retrieving last 10 events related to a device, subscribing to a device and sending a message to a device. Box 8.42 shows the code for a Python client that performs various functions such as subscribing to a device, sending a message and retrieving the service status.

### ■ Box 8.39: Commands for Setting up SkyNet

```
#Install DB Redis:
sudo apt-get install redis-server

#Install MongoDB:
sudo apt-key adv -keyserver keyserver.ubuntu.com -recv 7F0CEB10
echo 'deb http://downloads-distro.mongodb.org/repo/ubuntu-upstart
dist 10gen' |
sudo tee /etc/apt/sources.list.d/10gen.list
sudo apt-get update
sudo apt-get install mongodb-10gen

#Install dependencies
sudo apt-get install git
sudo apt-get install software-properties-common
sudo apt-get install npm

#Install Node.JS
sudo apt-get update
sudo apt-get install -y python-software-properties python g++ make
sudo add-apt-repository ppa:chris-lea/node.js
sudo apt-get update
sudo apt-get install nodejs

#Install Skynet:
git clone https://github.com/skynetim/skynet.git
npm config set registry http://registry.npmjs.org/
npm install
```

### ■ Box 8.40: Sample SkyNet configuration file

```
module.exports = {
   databaseUrl:  "mongodb://localhost:27017/skynet",
   port:  3000,
   log:  true,
   rateLimit:  10, // 10 transactions per user per secend
   redisHost:  "127.0.0.1",
   redisPort:  "6379"
};
```

### ■ Box 8.41: Using the SkyNet REST API

```
#Creating a device
$curl -X POST -d "name=mydevicename&token=mytoken&color=green"
http://localhost:3000/devices
```

```
{"name":"mydevicename","token":"mytoken","ipAddress":"127.0.0.1",
"uuid":"myuuid","timestamp":1394181626324,"channel":"main",
"online":false,"_id":"531985fa16ac510d4c000006","eventCode":400}


--------------------
#Listing devices
$curl http://localhost:3000/devices/myuuid

{"name":"mydevicename","ipAddress":"127.0.0.1","uuid":"myuuid",
"timestamp":1394181626324, "channel":"main","online":false,
"_id":"531985fa16ac510d4c000006", "eventCode":500}


--------------------
#Update a device
$curl -X PUT -d "token=mytoken&color=red"
http://localhost:3000/devices/myuuid

#Get last 10 events for a device
$curl -X GET http://localhost:3000/events/myuuid?token=mytoken

{"events":[{"color":"red","fromUuid":"myuuid",
"timestamp":1394181722052, "eventCode":300,"id":"mytoken"},{
"name":"mydevicename","ipAddress":"127.0.0.1" ,
"uuid":"myuuid",
"timestamp":1394181626324, "channel":"main","online":false,
"eventCode":500, "id":"531985fa16ac510d4c000006"}]}


--------------------
#Subscribing to a device
$curl -X GET http://localhost:3000/subscribe/myuuid?token=mytoken


--------------------
#Sending a message
$curl -X POST -d '{"devices":  "myuuid", "message":
{"color":"red"}}' http://localhost:3000/messages
```

■ **Box 8.42: Python client for SkyNet**

```python
from socketIO_client import SocketIO

HOST='<enter host IP>'
PORT=3000
UUID='<enter UUID>'
TOKEN='<enter Token>'

def on_status_response(*args):
   print 'Status:  ', args

def on_ready_response(*args):
   print 'Ready:  ', args

def on_noready_response(*args):
   print 'Not Ready:  ', args
```

```
def on_sub_response(*args):
  print 'Subscribed:  ', args

def on_msg_response(*args):
  print 'Message Received:  ', args

def on_whoami_response(*args):
  print 'Who Am I : ', args

def on_id_response(*args):
  print 'Websocket connecting to Skynet with
socket id:  ' + args[0]['socketid']
  print 'Sending arguments:  ', type(args), args
  socketIO.emit('identity', 'uuid':UUID, 'socketid':
args[0]['socketid'], 'token':TOKEN)

def on_connect(*args):
  print 'Requesting websocket connection to Skynet'
  socketIO.on('identify', on_id_response)
  socketIO.on('ready', on_ready_response)
  socketIO.on('notReady', on_noready_response)

socketIO = SocketIO(HOST, PORT)
socketIO.on('connect', on_connect)

socketIO.emit('status', on_status_response)
socketIO.emit('subscribe', 'uuid':UUID,'token':  TOKEN, on_sub_response)

socketIO.emit('whoami', 'uuid':UUID, on_whoami_response)

socketIO.emit('message', 'devices':  UUID, 'message':  'color':'purple')

socketIO.on('message', on_msg_response)

socketIO.wait()
```

## Summary

In this chapter you learned about various cloud computing services and their applications for IoT. You learned about the WAMP protocol and the AutoBahn framework. WAMP is a sub-protocol of Websocket which provides publish-subscribe and RPC messaging patterns. You learned about the Xively Platform-as-a-Service that can be used for creating solutions for Internet of Things. Xively platform comprises of a message bus for real-time message management and routing, data services for time series archiving, directory services that provides a searchable directory of objects and business services for device provisioning and management. You learned how to send data to and retrieve data from Xively.

You learned about Django which is an open source web application framework for developing web applications in Python. Django is based on the Model-Template-View architecture. You also learned how to develop a Django application made up of model, view and templates. You learned how to develop a RESTful web API.

You learned about various commercial cloud services offered by Amazon. Amazon EC2 is a computing service from Amazon. You learned how to programmatically launch an Amazon EC2 instance. Amazon AutoScaling allows automatically scaling Amazon EC2 capacity up or down according to user defined conditions. You also learned how to programmatically create an AutoScaling group, define AutoScaling policies and CloudWatch alarms for triggering the AutoScaling policies. Amazon S3 is an online cloud-based data storage from Amazon. You learned how to programmatically upload a file to an S3 bucket. Amazon RDS is a cloud-based relational database service. You learned how to programmatically launch an RDS instance, view running instances, connect to an instance, create a MySQL table, write and read from the table on the RDS instance. Amazon DynamoDB is a No-SQL database service. You learned how to programmatically create a DynamoDB table, write and read from a DynamoDB table. Amazon SQS is a scalable queuing service from Amazon. You learned how to programmatically create an SQS queue, write messages to a queue and read messages from a queue. Amazon EMR is a MapReduce web service. You learned how to programmatically create an EMR job. Finally, you learned about the SkyNet messaging platform for IoT.

## Review Questions

1. What is the difference between a Xively data stream and a channel?
2. Describe the architecture of a Django application.
3. What is the function of URL patterns in Django?
4. What is the purpose of an Amazon AutoScaling group? Describe the steps involved in creating an AutoScaling group.
5. What is Amazon DynamoDB? Describe an application that can benefit from Amazon DynamoDB.
6. Describe the use of Amazon Kinesis for IoT.
7. What are the uses of messaging queues? What are the message formats supported by Amazon SQS?
8. What does a MapReduce job comprise of?
9. What protocols does the SkyNet messaging platform support?

# 9 - Case Studies Illustrating IoT Design

This Chapter Covers
IoT case studies on:
- Smart Lighting
- Home Intrusion Detection
- Smart Parking
- Weather Monitoring System
- Weather Reporting Bot
- Air Pollution Monitoring
- Forest Fire Detection
- Smart Irrigation
- IoT Printer

## 9.1    Introduction

In Chapter-2 you learned about the applications of Internet of Things for homes, cities, environment, energy systems, retail, logistics, industry, agriculture and health. This chapter provides concrete implementations of several of these applications helping you understand how sophisticated applications are designed and deployed. The case studies are based on the IoT design methodology described in Chapter-5. The IoT device used for the case studies is the Raspberry Pi mini-computer. The case studies are implemented in Python and use the Django framework. You learned about basics of Python and Django in Chapters 6 and 8, respectively. However, principles you have learned are not limited to these particular languages or platforms.

## 9.2    Home Automation

### 9.2.1   Smart Lighting

A design of a smart home automation system was described in Chapter-5 using the IoT design methodology. A concrete
implementation of the system based on Django framework is described in this section. The purpose of the home automation system is to control the lights in a typical home remotely using a web application.

The system includes auto and manual modes. In auto mode, the system measures the light in a room and switches on the light when it gets dark. In manual mode, the system provides the option of manually and remotely switching on/off the light.

Figure 9.1 shows the deployment design of the home automation system. As explained in Chapter-5, the system has two REST services (mode and state) and a controller native service. Figures 9.2 and 9.3 show specifications of the mode and state REST services of the home automation system. The Mode service is a RESTful web service that sets mode to auto or manual (PUT request), or retrieves the current mode (GET request) . The mode is updated to/retrieved from the database. The State service is a RESTful web service that sets the light appliance state to on/off (PUT request), or retrieves the current light state (GET request). The state is updated to/retrieved from the status database.

---

**■ Box 9.1: Django model for mode and state REST services - models.py**

```
from django.db import models

class Mode(models.Model):
    name = models.CharField(max_length=50)

class State(models.Model):
    name = models.CharField(max_length=50)
```

---

To start with the implementation of the system, we first map services to Django models. Box 9.1 shows the model fields for the REST services (state - on/off and mode - auto/manual).

---

**■ Box 9.2: Serializers for mode and state REST services - serializers.py**

---

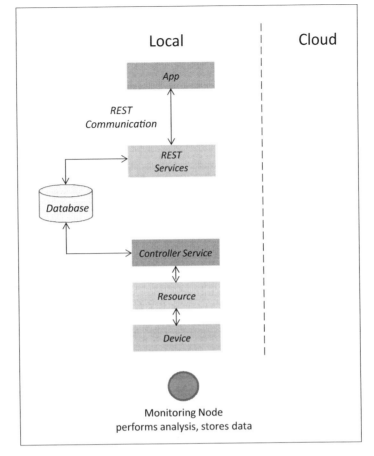

Figure 9.1: Deployment design of the home automation IoT system

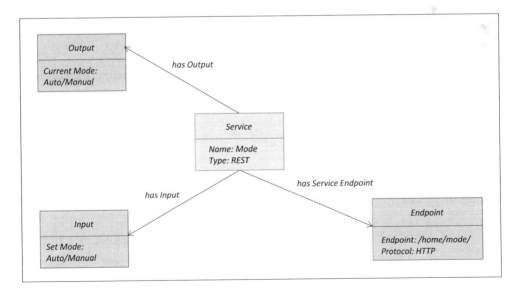

Figure 9.2: Service specification for home automation IoT system - mode service

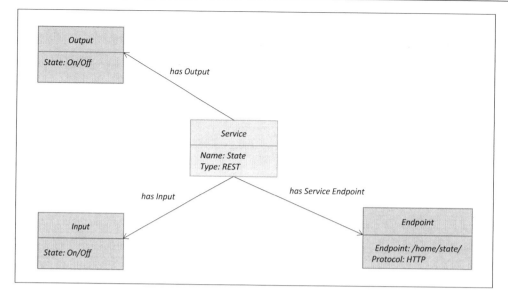

Figure 9.3: Service specification for home automation IoT system - state service

```
from myapp.models import Mode, State
from rest_framework import serializers

class ModeSerializer(serializers.HyperlinkedModelSerializer):
    class Meta:
        model = Mode
        fields = ('url', 'name')

class StateSerializer(serializers.HyperlinkedModelSerializer):
    class Meta:
        model = State
        fields = ('url', 'name')
```

After implementing the Django model, we implement the model serializers. Serializers allow complex data (such as model instances) to be converted to native Python datatypes that can then be easily rendered into JSON, XML or other content types. Box 9.2 shows the serializers for mode and state REST services.

After implementing the serializers, we write ViewSets for the Django models. ViewSets combine the logic for a set of related views in a single class. Box 9.3 shows the Django views for REST services and home automation application. The ViewSets for the models (ModeViewSet and StateViewSet) are included in the views file. The application view (home) is described later in this section.

■ **Box 9.3: Django views for REST services and home automation application - views.py**

```
from myapp.models import Mode, State
from rest_framework import viewsets
from django.shortcuts import render_to_response
from django.template import RequestContext
```

```python
from myapp.serializers import ModeSerializer, StateSerializer
import requests
import json

class ModeViewSet(viewsets.ModelViewSet):
    queryset = Mode.objects.all()
    serializer_class = ModeSerializer

class StateViewSet(viewsets.ModelViewSet):
    queryset = State.objects.all()
    serializer_class = StateSerializer

def home(request):
    out=""
    currentmode='auto'
    currentstate='off'

    if 'on' in request.POST:
        values = "name": "on"
        r=requests.put('http://127.0.0.1:8000/state/1/',
        data=values, auth=('myuser', 'password'))
        result=r.text
        output = json.loads(result)
        out=output['name']
    if 'off' in request.POST:
        values = "name": "off"
        r=requests.put('http://127.0.0.1:8000/state/1/',
        data=values, auth=('myuser', 'password'))
        result=r.text
        output = json.loads(result)
        out=output['name']
    if 'auto' in request.POST:
        values = "name": "auto"
        r=requests.put('http://127.0.0.1:8000/mode/1/',
        data=values, auth=('myuser', 'password'))
        result=r.text
        output = json.loads(result)
        out=output['name']
    if 'manual' in request.POST:
        values = "name": "manual"
        r=requests.put('http://127.0.0.1:8000/mode/1/',
        data=values, auth=('myuser', 'password'))
        result=r.text
        output = json.loads(result)
        out=output['name']

    r=requests.get('http://127.0.0.1:8000/mode/1/',
    auth=('myuser', 'password'))
    result=r.text
    output = json.loads(result)
    currentmode=output['name']

    r=requests.get('http://127.0.0.1:8000/state/1/',
    auth=('myuser', 'password'))
    result=r.text
```

```
output = json.loads(result)
currentstate=output['name']

return render_to_response('lights.html','r':out,
'currentmode':currentmode, 'currentstate':currentstate,
context_instance=RequestContext(request))
```

Box 9.4 shows the URL patterns for the REST services and home automation application. Since ViewSets are used instead of views for the REST services, we can automatically generate the URL configuration by simply registering the viewsets with a router class. Routers automatically determine how the URLs for an application should be mapped to the logic that deals with handling incoming requests.

■ **Box 9.4: Django URL patterns for REST services and home automation application - urls.py**

```
from django.conf.urls import patterns, include, url
from django.contrib import admin
from rest_framework import routers
from myapp import views

admin.autodiscover()

router = routers.DefaultRouter()
router.register(r'mode', views.ModeViewSet)
router.register(r'state', views.StateViewSet)

urlpatterns = patterns('',
    url(r'^', include(router.urls)),
    url(r'^api-auth/', include('rest_framework.urls',
    namespace='rest_framework')),
    url(r'^admin/', include(admin.site.urls)),
    url(r'^home/', 'myapp.views.home'),
)
```

Box 9.5 shows the code for the Django template for the home automation application.

■ **Box 9.5: Django template for home automation application - index.html**

```
<!DOCTYPE html>
<html>
<head>

</head>
<body>
<p>{{r}}<p>
<h3>State</h3>
<form action="" method="post">{% csrf_token %}
<input type="submit" name="on" value="on" />
<input type="submit" name="off" value="off" />
</form>
<br>
```

```
<h3>Mode</h3>
<form action="" method="post">{% csrf_token %}
<input type="submit" name="auto" value="auto" />
<input type="submit" name="manual" value="manual" />
</form>

</body>
</html>
```

Figure 9.4 shows a screenshot of the home automation web application.

Figure 9.4: Home automation web application screenshot

Figure 9.5 shows a schematic diagram of the home automation IoT system. The devices and components used in this example are Raspberry Pi mini computer, LDR sensor and relay switch actuator.

Figure 9.6 shows the specification of the controller native service that runs on Raspberry Pi. When in auto mode, the controller service monitors the light level and switches the light on/off and updates the status in the status database. When in manual mode, the controller service, retrieves the current state from the database and switches the light on/off. A Python implementation of the controller service is shown in Box 9.6.

■ **Box 9.6: Python code for controller native service - controller.py**

```
import time
import datetime
import sqlite3
import spidev
import RPi.GPIO as GPIO

#Initialize SQLite
con = sqlite3.connect('database.sqlite')
cur = con.cursor()

#LDR channel on MCP3008
LIGHT_CHANNEL = 0

#GPIO Setup
GPIO.setmode(GPIO.BCM)
```

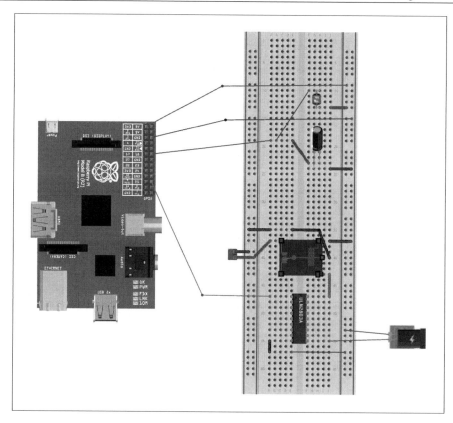

Figure 9.5: Schematic diagram of the home automation IoT system showing the device, sensor and actuator integrated

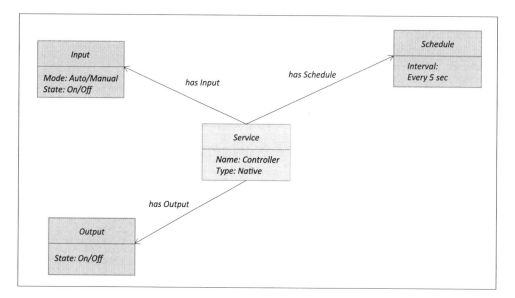

Figure 9.6: Controller service of the home automation IoT system

```
LIGHT_PIN = 25

# Open SPI bus
spi = spidev.SpiDev()
spi.open(0,0)

#Light Level Threshold
threshold=200

#Function to read LDR connected to MCP3008
def readLDR():
   light_level = ReadChannel(LIGHT_CHANNEL)
   lux = ConvertLux(light_level,2)
   return lux

#Function to convert LDR reading to Lux
def ConvertLux(data,places):
   R=10 #10k-ohm resistor connected to LDR
   volts = (data * 3.3) / 1023
   volts = round(volts,places)
   lux=500*(3.3-volts)/(R*volts)
   return lux

# Function to read SPI data from MCP3008 chip
def ReadChannel(channel):
   adc = spi.xfer2([1,(8+channel)<<4,0])
   data = ((adc[1]&3) << 8) + adc[2]
   return data

#Get current state from DB
def getCurrentMode():
   cur.execute('SELECT * FROM myapp_mode')
   data = cur.fetchone()      #(1, u'auto')
   return data[1]


#Get current state from DB
def getCurrentState():
   cur.execute('SELECT * FROM myapp_state')
   data = cur.fetchone()      #(1, u'on')
   return data[1]

#Store current state in DB
def setCurrentState(val):
   query='UPDATE myapp_state set name="'+val+'"'
   cur.execute(query)

def switchOnLight(PIN):
   GPIO.setup(PIN, GPIO.OUT)
   GPIO.output(PIN, True)

def switchOffLight(PIN):
   GPIO.setup(PIN, GPIO.OUT)
   GPIO.output(PIN, False)
```

```
def runManualMode():
  #Get current state from DB
  currentState=getCurrentState()
  if currentState=='on':
    switchOnLight(LIGHT_PIN)
  elif currentState=='off':
    switchOffLight(LIGHT_PIN)

def runAutoMode():
  #Read LDR
  lightlevel=readLDR()

  if lightlevel < ldr_threshold:
    switchOnLight(LIGHT_PIN)
  else:
    switchOffLight(LIGHT_PIN)

  print 'Manual'+' - '+getCurrentState()

#Controller main function
def runController():
  currentMode=getCurrentMode()
  if currentMode=='auto':
    runAutoMode()
  elif currentMode=='manual':
    runManualMode()

  return true

while True:
  runController()
  time.sleep(5)
```

## 9.2.2  Home Intrusion Detection

You got an overview of home intrusion detection systems in Chapter-2. A concrete implementation of a home intrusion detection system is described in this section. The purpose of the home intrusion detection system is to detect intrusions using sensors (such as PIR sensors and door sensors) and raise alerts, if necessary.

Figure 9.7 shows the process diagram for the home intrusion detection system. Each room in the home has a PIR motion sensor and each door has a door sensor. These sensors can detect motion or opening of doors. Each sensor is read at regular intervals and the motion detection or door opening events are stored and alerts are sent.

Figure 9.8 shows the domain model for the home intrusion detection system. The domain model includes physical entities for room and door and the corresponding virtual entities. The device in this example is a single-board mini computer which has PIR and door sensors attached to it. The domain model also includes the services involved in the system.

Figure 9.9 shows the information model for the home intrusion detection system. The information model defines the attributes of room and door virtual entities and their possible values. The room virtual entity has an attribute 'motion' and the door virtual entity has an attribute 'state'.

The next step is to define the service specifications for the system.  The services are

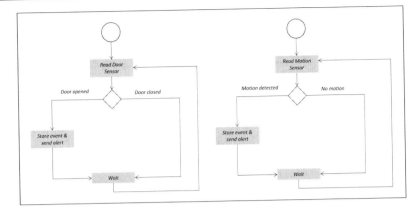

Figure 9.7: Process specification of the home intrusion detection IoT system

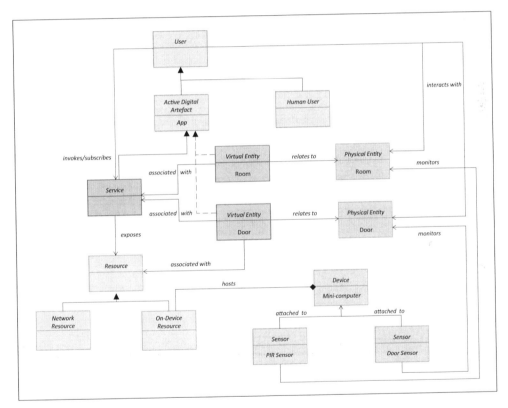

Figure 9.8: Domain model of the home intrusion detection IoT system

derived from the process specification and the information model. The system has three services - (1) a RESTful web service that retrieves the current state of a door from the database or sets the current state of a door to open/closed, (2) A RESTful web service that retrieves the current motion in a room or sets the motion of a room to yes/no, (3) a native controller service that runs on the device and reads the PIR and door sensors and calls the REST services for updating the state of rooms and doors in the database. Figures 9.10, Figures 9.11 and 9.12 show specifications of the web services and the controller service.

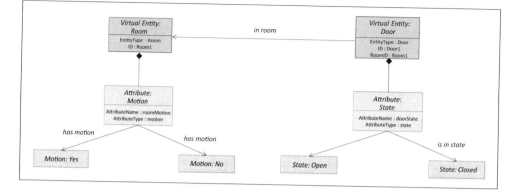

Figure 9.9: Information model of the home intrusion detection IoT system

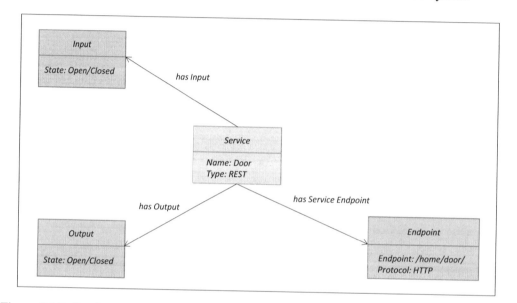

Figure 9.10: Service specification for the home intrusion detection IoT system - door service

Figure 9.13 shows the deployment design for the home intrusion detection system. Recall that this is a level-2 IoT system.

The functional view and the operational view specifications for home intrusion detection system are shown in Figure 9.14. Various options pertaining to the system deployment and operation and their mapping to the corresponding functional groups is shown in Figure 9.14. The system uses Django framework for web application and REST service. The Django web application is backed by a MySQL database. The IoT device used for this example is Raspberry Pi along with the PIR and door sensors. Figure 9.15 shows a schematic diagram of the home intrusion detection system and Figure 9.16 shows how the sensors are deployed in a parking.

Let us now look at the implementation of the web application and services for the system. Box 9.7 shows the model fields for the room and door REST service. After implementing the Django model, we implement the model serializers that allows model instances to be converted to native Python datatypes. Box 9.8 shows the serializers for room and door REST

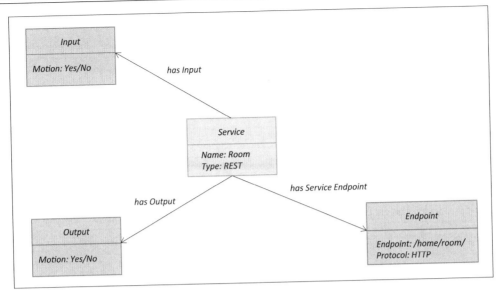

Figure 9.11: Service specification for the home intrusion detection IoT system - room service

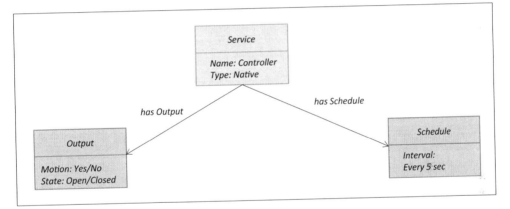

Figure 9.12: Controller service of the home intrusion detection IoT system

services.

■ Box 9.7: Django model for room and door REST services - models.py

```
from django.db import models

class Room(models.Model):
    name = models.CharField(max_length=50)
    state = models.CharField(max_length=50)
    timestamp = models.CharField(max_length=50)
    pin = models.CharField(max_length=5)

class Door(models.Model):
    name = models.CharField(max_length=50)
    state = models.CharField(max_length=50)
```

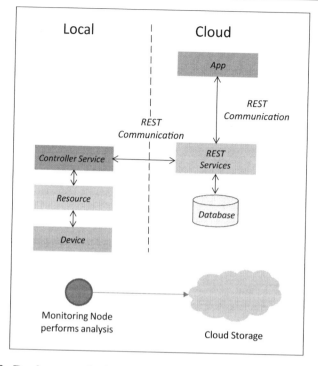

Figure 9.13: Deployment design for the home intrusion detection IoT system

```
timestamp = models.CharField(max_length=50)
pin = models.CharField(max_length=5)
```

■ **Box 9.8: Serializers for room and door REST services - serializers.py**

```
from myapp.models import Room, Door
from rest_framework import serializers

class RoomSerializer(serializers.HyperlinkedModelSerializer):
    class Meta:
        model = Room
        fields = ('url', 'name', 'state', 'timestamp', 'pin')

class DoorSerializer(serializers.HyperlinkedModelSerializer):
    class Meta:
        model = Door
        fields = ('url', 'name', 'state', 'timestamp', 'pin')
```

Box 9.9 shows the Django views for REST services and home intrusion detection application. The ViewSets for the models (RoomViewSet and RoomViewSet) are included in the views file. The *home* view renders the content for the home intrusion detection application home page that displays the status of each room. Notice that a request is sent to the state REST service to obtain the state of a room.

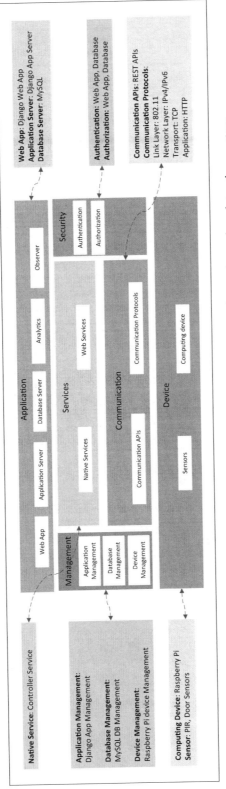

Figure 9.14: Functional & operational view specifications for home intrusion detection system

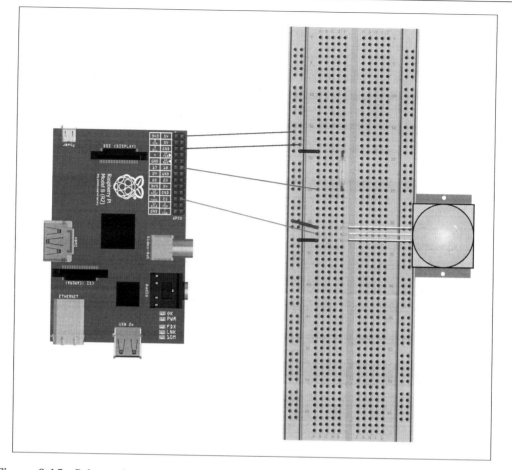

Figure 9.15: Schematic diagram of the home intrusion detection IoT system prototype, showing the device and ultrasonic sensor

**■ Box 9.9: Django views for REST services and home intrusion detection application - views.py**

```python
from myapp.models import Room, Door
from rest_framework import viewsets
from django.shortcuts import render_to_response
from django.template import RequestContext
from myapp.serializers import RoomSerializer, DoorSerializer
import requests
import json

class RoomViewSet(viewsets.ModelViewSet):
    queryset = Room.objects.all()
    serializer_class = RoomSerializer

class DoorViewSet(viewsets.ModelViewSet):
    queryset = Door.objects.all()
    serializer_class = DoorSerializer
```

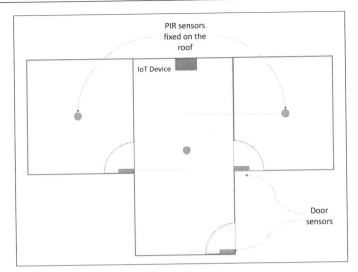

Figure 9.16: Deployment of sensors for home intrusion detection system

```python
def home(request):
    r=requests.get('http://127.0.0.1:8000/room/', auth=('username',
'password'))
    result=r.text
    output = json.loads(result)
    roomCount = output['count']

    r=requests.get('http://127.0.0.1:8000/door/', auth=('username',
'password'))
    result=r.text
    output = json.loads(result)
    doorCount = output['count']

    roomsDict={}
    for i in range (0, roomCount):
        r=requests.get('http://127.0.0.1:8000/room/'+str(i+1)+'/',
        auth=('username', 'password'))
        result=r.text
        output = json.loads(result)
        roomName=output['name']
        roomState=output['state']
        roomTimestamp=output['timestamp']
        roomsDict[roomName] = [roomState, roomTimestamp]

    doorsDict={}
    for i in range (0, doorCount):
        r=requests.get('http://127.0.0.1:8000/door/'+str(i+1)+'/',
        auth=('username', 'password'))
        result=r.text
        output = json.loads(result)
        doorName=output['name']
        doorState=output['state']
```

```
        doorTimestamp=output['timestamp']
        doorsDict[doorName] = [doorState, doorTimestamp]

    return render_to_response('index.html',
    {'roomsDict':roomsDict, 'doorsDict':doorsDict},
    context_instance=RequestContext(request))
```

Box 9.10 shows the URL patterns for the REST services and home intrusion detection application. Since ViewSets are used instead of views for the REST services, we can automatically generate the URL configuration by simply registering the viewsets with a router class.

### ■ Box 9.10: Django URL patterns for REST services and home intrusion detection application - urls.py

```python
from django.conf.urls import patterns, include, url
from django.contrib import admin
from rest_framework import routers
from myapp import views

admin.autodiscover()

router = routers.DefaultRouter()
router.register(r'room', views.RoomViewSet)
router.register(r'door', views.DoorViewSet)

urlpatterns = patterns('',
    url(r'^', include(router.urls)),
    url(r'^api-auth/', include('rest_framework.urls',
        namespace='rest_framework')),
    url(r'^admin/', include(admin.site.urls)),
    url(r'^home/', 'myapp.views.home'),
)
```

Box 9.11 shows the code for the Django template for the home intrusion detection application. This template is rendered by the *home* view. Figure 9.17 shows a screenshot of the home intrusion detection web application.

### ■ Box 9.11: Django template for home intrusion detection application - index.html

```html
<html>
<head>
<meta charset="utf-8">
<meta http-equiv="X-UA-Compatible" content="IE=edge,chrome=1">
<title>Home Intrusion Detection App</title>
<link rel="stylesheet" href="/static/css/style.css">
</head>
<body>

<div class="app-container">
```

```
<header class="app-header clearfix">
<h1 class="app-logo js-app-title icon-home">Dashboard</h1>
<div class="app-state"><span class="app-loading-loader">
</span></div>
<center>
<h4>Home #:  123</h4>
</center>
</header>

<div role="main" class="app-content clearfix">
<div class="app-loading"><span class="app-loading-loader">
</span></div>
<div class="app-content-inner">

<form class="dashboard-control js-form clearfix">
<fieldset>
<div class="field clearfix">
<center><h4>Rooms</h4></center>
<table width = "90%" border="1">
{% for key,val in roomsDict.items %}
<tr>
<td width="50%">{{key}}
<br>
<center>
{% if val.0 == 'no' %}
<img src="/static/img/g.png">
{% else %}
<img src="/static/img/r.png">
{% endif %}
<br>
<p>Last Updated:  {{val.1}}</p>
</center>
</td>
</tr>
{% endfor %}
</table>
</div></div>
</fieldset>
</form></div>
<br>

<div role="main" class="app-content clearfix">
<div class="app-loading"><span class="app-loading-loader">
</span></div>
<div class="app-content-inner">

<form class="dashboard-control js-form clearfix">
<fieldset>
<div class="field clearfix">
<center><h4>Doors</h4></center>
<table width = "90%" border="1">
{% for key,val in doorsDict.items %}
<tr>
<td width="50%">{{key}}
```

```
<br>
<center>
{% if val.0 == 'closed' %}
<img src="/static/img/g.png">
{% else %}
<img src="/static/img/r.png">
{% endif %}
<br>
<p>Last Updated:  {{val.1}}</p>
</center>
</td>
</tr>
{% endfor %}
</table>
</div>
</div>
</fieldset>
</form>
</div>
</div>
<script src="https://ajax.googleapis.com/ajax/libs/
jquery/1.8.2/jquery.min.js"></script>
<script src="/static/js/script.js"></script>

</body> </html>
```

A Python implementation of the controller service native service that runs on Raspberry Pi, is shown in Box 9.12. The *runController* function is called every second and the readings of the PIR and door sensors are obtained. The current states of the room and door are then updated by sending a PUT request to the corresponding REST services.

■ **Box 9.12: Python code for controller native service - intrusion detection - controller.py**

```python
import RPi.GPIO as GPIO
import time
import sys

GPIO.setmode(GPIO.BCM)

global PIR_SENSOR_PIN

global DOOR_SENSOR_PIN
def readingPIRSensor():

    if GPIO.input(PIR_SENSOR_PIN):
        return 1
    else:
        return 0

def readingDoorSensor():
    if GPIO.input(DOOR_SENSOR_PIN):
```

```
          return 1
      else:
          return 0


def runController():
    pirState = readingPIRSensor()
    if pinState == 1:
        setPIRState('yes')
    else:
        setPIRState('no')

    doorState = readingDoorSensor()
    if doorState == 1:
        setDoorState('open')
    else:
        setDoorState('closed')


def setPIRState(val):
    values = {"state":  val, "timestamp":  str(time.time())}
    r=requests.put('http://127.0.0.1:8000/room/1/', data=values,
    auth=('username', 'password'))
def setDoorState(val):
    values = {"state":  val, "timestamp":  str(time.time())}
    r=requests.put('http://127.0.0.1:8000/door/1/', data=values,
    auth=('username', 'password'))


def setupController():
    r=requests.get('http://127.0.0.1:8000/config/1/', data=values,
    auth=('username', 'password'))
    configStr=r.text
    config = json.loads(configStr)
    global PIR_SENSOR_PIN = config['room1']
    global DOOR_SENSOR_PIN = config['door1']
    GPIO.setup(PIR_SENSOR_PIN,GPIO.IN)
    GPIO.setup(DOOR_SENSOR_PIN,GPIO.IN, pull_up_down=GPIO.PUD_UP)


setupController()
while True:
    runController()
    time.sleep(1)
```

## 9.3 Cities

### 9.3.1 Smart Parking

You got an overview of smart parking systems in Chapter-2. A concrete implementation of a smart parking IoT system is described in this section.

The purpose of a smart parking system is to detect the number of empty parking slots and send the information over the Internet to smart parking application backends. These applications can be accessed by drivers from smartphones, tablets or from in-car navigation systems. In smart parking, sensors are used for each parking slot, to detect whether the slot is empty or occupied. This information is aggregated by a local controller and then sent over

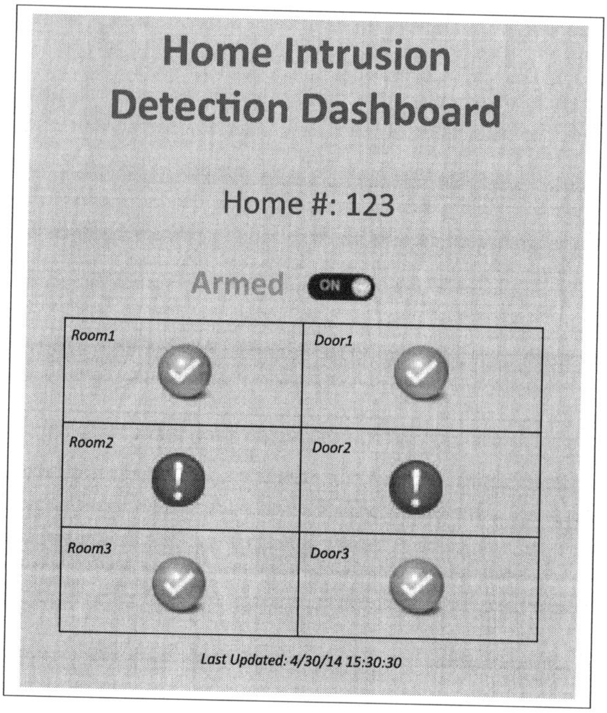

Figure 9.17: Home intrusion detection web application screenshot

the Internet to a server.

Figure 9.18 shows the process diagram for the smart parking system. Each parking slot has an ultrasonic sensor fixed above, which can detect the presence of a vehicle in the slot. Each sensor is read at regular intervals and the state of the parking slot (empty or occupied) is updated in a database.

Figure 9.19 shows the domain model for the smart parking system. The domain model includes a physical entity for the parking slot and the corresponding virtual entity. The device in this example is a single-board mini computer which has ultrasonic sensor attached to it. The domain model also includes the services involved in the system.

Figure 9.20 shows the information model for the smart parking system. The information model defines the attribute (state) of the parking slot virtual entity with two possible values (empty or occupied).

The next step is to define the service specifications for the system. The services are derived from the process specification and the information model. The smart parking system has two services - (1) a service that monitors the parking slots (using ultrasonic sensors) and updates the status in a database on the cloud (REST web service), (2) a service that retrieves the current state of the parking slots (controller native service). Figures 9.21 and 9.22 show specifications of the controller and state services of the smart parking system.

The functional view and the operational view specifications for smart parking system are similar to the specifications for the home intrusion detection system shown in Figure 9.14. The system uses Django framework for web application and REST service - both of which you learned about from earlier chapters of this book. The Django web application is supported

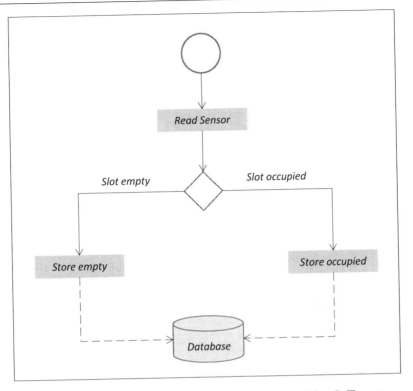

Figure 9.18: Process specification for the smart parking IoT system

by a MySQL database. The IoT device used for this example is Raspberry Pi along with the ultrasonic sensors. Figure 9.23 shows how the sensors are deployed in a parking and Figure 9.24 shows a schematic diagram of the smart parking system.

Let us now look at the implementation of the web application and services for the smart parking system. Box 9.13 shows the model fields for the state REST service. After implementing the Django model, we implement the model serializer which allows model instances to be converted to native Python datatypes. Box 9.14 shows the serializer for state REST service.

■ **Box 9.13: Django model for REST service - models.py**

```
from django.db import models

class State(models.Model):
    name = models.CharField(max_length=50)
```

■ **Box 9.14: Serializer for REST service - serializers.py**

```
from myapp.models import State
from rest_framework import serializers
```

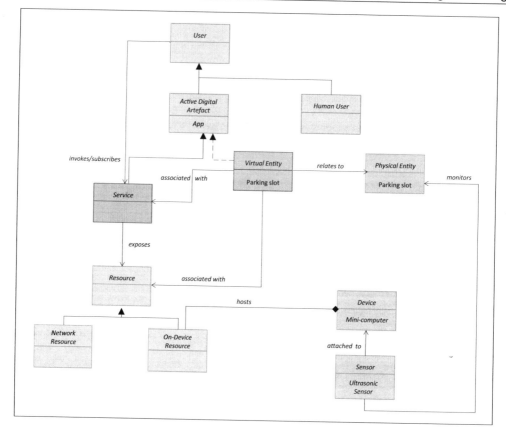

Figure 9.19: Domain model of the smart parking IoT system

```
class StateSerializer(serializers.HyperlinkedModelSerializer):
    class Meta:
        model = State
        fields = ('url', 'name')
```

Box 9.15 shows the Django views for REST services and smart parking application. The ViewSets for the model (StateViewSet) are included in the views file. The *home* view renders the content for the smart parking application home page that displays the status of the parking slots. Notice that a request is sent to the state REST service to obtain the state of a parking slot. The code shown in this example is for a trivial case of a one-slot parking.

■ **Box 9.15: Django views for REST service and smart parking application - views.py**

```
from myapp.models import State
from rest_framework import viewsets
from django.shortcuts import render_to_response
from django.template import RequestContext
from myapp.serializers import StateSerializer
import requests
import json
```

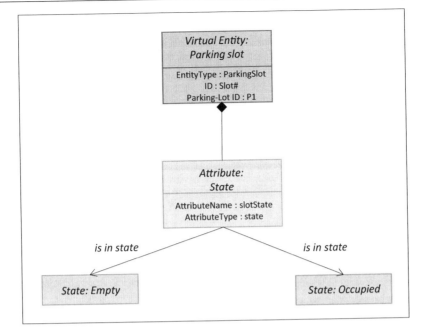

Figure 9.20: Information model of the smart parking IoT system

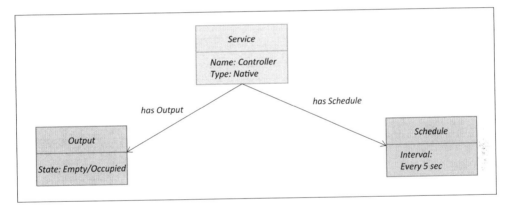

Figure 9.21: Controller service of the smart parking IoT system

```
class StateViewSet(viewsets.ModelViewSet):
   queryset = State.objects.all()
   serializer_class = StateSerializer

def home(request):
    currentstate='off'
    r=requests.get('http://127.0.0.1:8000/state/1/',
    auth=('username', 'password'))
    result=r.text
    output = json.loads(result)
    currentstate=output['name']
```

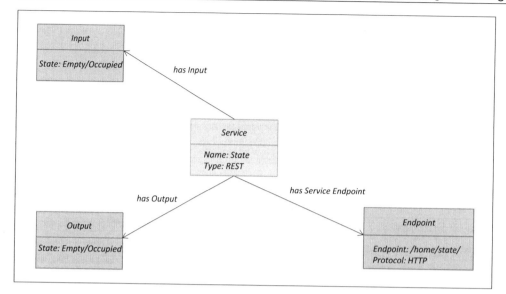

Figure 9.22: Service specification for the smart parking IoT system - state service

```
if currentstate=='empty':
    occupiedCount=0
    emptyCount=1
else:
    occupiedCount=1
    emptyCount=0

return render_to_response('index.html',
{'currentstate':currentstate, 'occupiedCount':
occupiedCount, 'emptyCount':  emptyCount},
context_instance=RequestContext(request))
```

Box 9.16 shows the URL patterns for the REST service and smart parking application. Since ViewSets are used instead of views for the REST service, we can automatically generate the URL configuration by simply registering the viewsets with a router class.

■ **Box 9.16:  Django URL patterns for REST service and smart parking application - urls.py**

```
from django.conf.urls import patterns, include, url
from django.contrib import admin
from rest_framework import routers
from myapp import views

admin.autodiscover()

router = routers.DefaultRouter()
router.register(r'state', views.StateViewSet)

urlpatterns = patterns('',
    url(r'^', include(router.urls)),
```

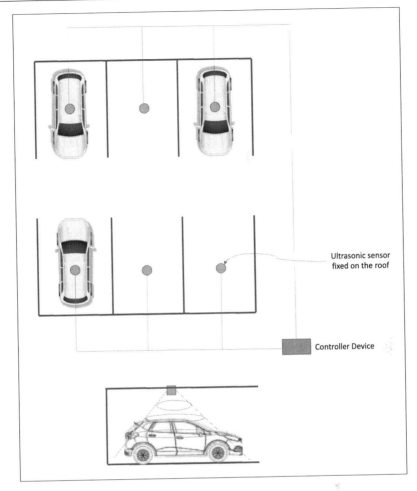

Figure 9.23: Deployment of sensors for smart parking system

```
    url(r'∧api-auth/', include('rest_framework.urls',
  namespace='rest_framework')),
    url(r'∧admin/', include(admin.site.urls)),
    url(r'∧home/', 'myapp.views.home'),
)
```

Box 9.17 shows the code for the Django template for the smart parking application. This template is rendered by the *home* view.

### ■ Box 9.17: Django template for smart parking application - index.html

```
<html>
<head>
<meta charset="utf-8">
<meta http-equiv="X-UA-Compatible" content="IE=edge,chrome=1">
<title>Smart Parking App</title>
<link rel="stylesheet" href="/static/css/style.css">
```

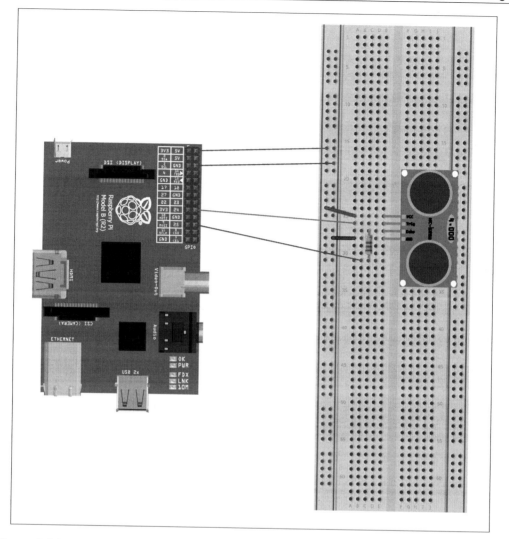

Figure 9.24: Schematic diagram of the smart parking IoT system prototype, showing the device and ultrasonic sensor

```
</head>
<body>
<div class="app-container">
<header class="app-header clearfix">
<h1 class="app-logo js-app-title icon-home">Smart Parking
Dashboard</h1>
<div class="app-state"><span
class="app-loading-loader"></span></div>
<center>
<h4>Parking Lot #:   123</h4>
<h4>Empty: {{emptyCount}} Occupied:   {{occupiedCount}}</h4>
</center>
</header>
<div role="main" class="app-content clearfix">
```

```
<div class="app-loading"><span class="app-loading-loader"></span></div>
<div class="app-content-inner">
<form class="dashboard-control js-form clearfix">
<fieldset>

<div class="field clearfix">
<table width = "90%" border="1">
<tr>
<td width="100%">1
<br>
<center>
{% if currentstate == 'empty' %}
<img src="/static/img/empty.png">
{% else %}
<img src="/static/img/occupied.png">
{% endif %}
</center>
</td>
</tr>
</table>
</div>
</div>
</fieldset>
</form>
</div></div></div>

<script src="https://ajax.googleapis.com/ajax/libs/
jquery/1.8.2/jquery.min.js"></script>
<script src="/static/js/script.js"></script>
</body></html>
```

Figure 9.25 shows a screenshot of the smart parking web application.

A Python implementation of the controller service native service that runs on Raspberry Pi, is shown in Box 9.18. The *runController* function is called every second and the reading of the ultrasonic sensor is obtained. If the distance returned by the sensor is less than a threshold, the slot is considered to be occupied. The current state of the slot is then updated by sending a PUT request to the state REST service.

■ **Box 9.18: Python code for controller native service - smart parking - controller.py**

```
import RPi.GPIO as GPIO
import time
import sys

GPIO.setmode(GPIO.BCM)
SENSOR_PIN = 27
TRIGGER_PIN=17
threshold = 10000

def readUltrasonicSensor():
   GPIO.setup(TRIGGER_PIN,GPIO.OUT)
   GPIO.setup(SENSOR_PIN,GPIO.IN)
```

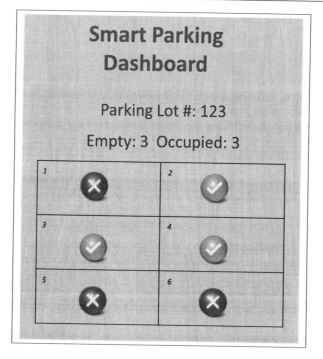

Figure 9.25: Samrt Parking web application screenshot

```
    GPIO.output(TRIGGER_PIN, GPIO.LOW)
    time.sleep(0.3)
    GPIO.output(TRIGGER_PIN, True)
    time.sleep(0.00001)
    GPIO.output(TRIGGER_PIN, False)
    while GPIO.input(SENSOR_PIN) == 0:
       signaloff = time.time()

    while GPIO.input(SENSOR_PIN) == 1:
       signalon = time.time()

    timepassed = signalon - signaloff
    distance = timepassed * 17000
    if distance < threshold:
       return 1
    else:
       return 0

def runController():
   pinState = readUltrasonicSensor()
   if pinState == 1:
      setCurrentState('occupied')
   else:
      setCurrentState('empty')

def setCurrentState(val):
   values = {"name":  val}
   r=requests.put('http://127.0.0.1:8000/state/1/',
```

```
        data=values, auth=('username', 'password'))

while True:
    runController()
    time.sleep(1)
```

## 9.4  Environment

### 9.4.1  Weather Monitoring System

**REST-based Implementation**

A design of a weather monitoring IoT system was described in Chapter-5 using the IoT design methodology. A concrete implementation of the system based on Django framework is described in this section. The purpose of the weather monitoring system is to collect data on environmental conditions such as temperature, pressure, humidity and light in an area using multiple end nodes. The end nodes send the data to the cloud where the data is aggregated and analyzed.

Figure 9.26 shows the deployment design for the system. The system consists of multiple nodes placed in different locations for monitoring temperature, humidity and pressure in an area. The end nodes are equipped with various sensors (such as temperature, pressure, humidity and light). The end nodes send the data to the cloud and the data is stored in a cloud database. The analysis of data is done in the cloud to aggregate the data and make predictions. A cloud-based application is used for visualizing the data. The centralized controller can send control commands to the end nodes, for example, to configure the monitoring interval on the end nodes.

Figure 9.27 shows a schematic diagram of the weather monitoring system. The devices and components used in this example are Raspberry Pi mini computer, temperature and humidity sensor (DHT22), pressure and temperature sensor (BMP085) and LDR sensor. An analog-to-digital (A/D) converter (MCP3008) is used for converting the analog input from LDR to digital.

Figure 9.28 shows the specification of the controller service for the weather monitoring system. The controller service runs as a native service on the device and monitors temperature, pressure, humidity and light every 10 seconds. The controller service calls the REST service to store these measurements in the cloud. This example uses the Xively Platform-as-a-Service for storing data. In the *setupController* function, new Xively datastreams are created for temperature, pressure, humidity and light data. The *runController* function is called every 10 seconds and the sensor readings are obtained.

■ **Box 9.19:  Python code for controller native service - controller.py**

```
import time
import datetime
import sys
import json
import requests
import xively
```

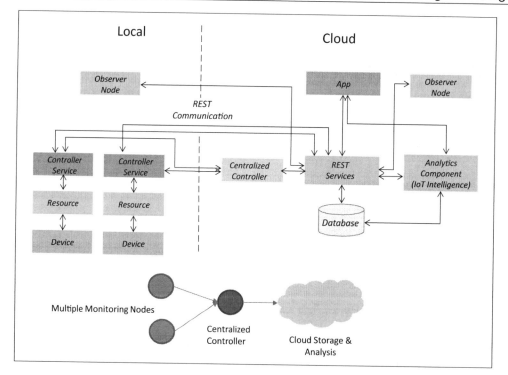

Figure 9.26: Deployment design of the weather monitoring IoT system

```
import subprocess
from random import randint
import dhtreader
from Adafruit_BMP085 import BMP085
import spidev

global temp_datastream
global pressure_datastream
global humidity_datastream
global light_datastream

#Initialize DHT22 Temperature/Humidity Sensor
dev_type = 22
dht_pin = 24
dhtreader.init()

# Initialise BMP085 Temperature/Pressure Sensor
bmp = BMP085(0x77)

#LDR channel on MCP3008
light_channel = 0

# Open SPI bus
spi = spidev.SpiDev()
spi.open(0,0)
```

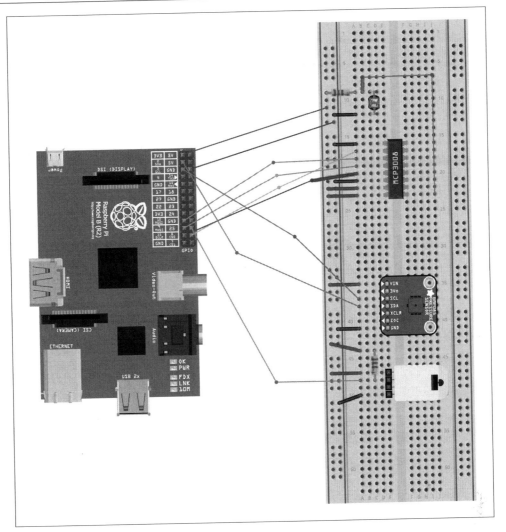

Figure 9.27: Schematic diagram of a weather monitoring end-node showing the device and sensors

```
#Initialize Xively Feed
FEED_ID = "<enter feed-id>"
API_KEY = "<enter apr-key>"
api = xively.XivelyAPIClient(API_KEY)

# Function to read SPI data from MCP3008 chip
def ReadChannel(channel):
    adc = spi.xfer2([1,(8+channel)<<4,0])
    data = ((adc[1]&3) << 8) + adc[2]
    return data

#Function to convert LDR reading to Lux
def ConvertLux(data,places):
    R=10 #10k-ohm resistor connected to LDR
```

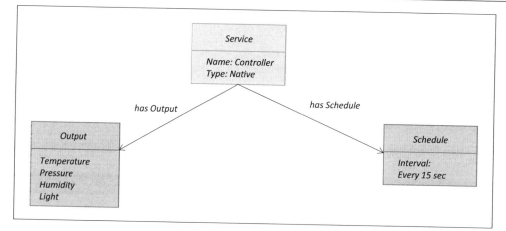

Figure 9.28: Controller service of the weather monitoring IoT system

```
   volts = (data * 3.3) / 1023
   volts = round(volts,places)
   lux=500*(3.3-volts)/(R*volts)
   return lux


#Read temperature & humidity from DHT22 sensor
def read_DHT22_Sensor():
   temp, humidity = dhtreader.read(dev_type, dht_pin)
   return temp, humidity


#Read LDR connected to MCP3008
def readLDR():
   light_level = ReadChannel(light_channel)
   lux = ConvertLux(light_level,2)
   return lux


#Read temperature & pressure from BMP085 sensor
def read_BMP085_Sensor():
   temp = bmp.readTemperature()
   pressure = bmp.readPressure()
   return temp, pressure


#Controller main function
def runController():
   global temp_datastream
   global pressure_datastream
   global humidity_datastream
   global light_datastream

   temp1, humidity=read_DHT22_Sensor()
   temp2, pressure=read_BMP085_Sensor()
   temp=(temp1+temp2)/2 #take avg

   light=readLDR()

   temp_datastream.current_value = temperature
```

```python
    temp_datastream.at = datetime.datetime.utcnow()

    pressure_datastream.current_value = pressure
    pressure_datastream.at = datetime.datetime.utcnow()

    humidity_datastream.current_value = humidity
    humidity_datastream.at = datetime.datetime.utcnow()

    light_datastream.current_value = light
    light_datastream.at = datetime.datetime.utcnow()

    print "Updating Xively feed with Temperature:  %s" % temperature
    try:
        temp_datastream.update()
    except requests.HTTPError as e:
        print "HTTPError({0}):  {1}".format(e.errno, e.strerror)

    print "Updating Xively feed with Humidity:  %s" % humidity
    try:
        pressure_datastream.update()
    except requests.HTTPError as e:
        print "HTTPError({0}):  {1}".format(e.errno, e.strerror)

    print "Updating Xively feed with Pressure:  %s" % pressure
    try:
        humidity_datastream.update()
    except requests.HTTPError as e:
        print "HTTPError({0}):  {1}".format(e.errno, e.strerror)

    print "Updating Xively feed with Light:  %s" % light
    try:
        light_datastream.update()
    except requests.HTTPError as e:
        print "HTTPError({0}):  {1}".format(e.errno, e.strerror)

#Get existing or create new Xively data stream for temperature
def get_tempdatastream(feed):
    try:
        datastream = feed.datastreams.get("temperature")
        return datastream
    except:
        datastream =
        feed.datastreams.create("temperature", tags="temperature")
        return datastream

#Get existing or create new Xively data stream for pressure
def get_pressuredatastream(feed):
    try:
        datastream = feed.datastreams.get("pressure")
        return datastream
    except:
        datastream = feed.datastreams.create("pressure", tags="pressure")
        return datastream
```

```
#Get existing or create new Xively data stream for humidity
def get_humiditydatastream(feed):
    try:
        datastream = feed.datastreams.get("humidity")
        return datastream
    except:
        datastream = feed.datastreams.create("humidity", tags="humidity")
        return datastream

#Get existing or create new Xively data stream for light
def get_lightdatastream(feed):
    try:
        datastream = feed.datastreams.get("light")
        return datastream
    except:
        datastream = feed.datastreams.create("light", tags="light")
        return datastream

#Controller setup function
def setupController():
    global temp_datastream
    global pressure_datastream
    global humidity_datastream
    global light_datastream

    feed = api.feeds.get(FEED_ID)

    feed.location.lat="30.733315"
    feed.location.lon="76.779418"
    feed.tags="Weather"
    feed.update()

    temp_datastream = get_tempdatastream(feed)
    temp_datastream.max_value = None
    temp_datastream.min_value = None

    pressure_datastream = get_pressuredatastream(feed)
    pressure_datastream.max_value = None
    pressure_datastream.min_value = None

    humidity_datastream = get_humiditydatastream(feed)
    humidity_datastream.max_value = None
    humidity_datastream.min_value = None

    light_datastream = get_lightdatastream(feed)
    light_datastream.max_value = None
    light_datastream.min_value = None


setupController()
while True:
    runController()
    time.sleep(10)
```

Box 9.20 shows the HTML and JavaScript code for the web page that displays the weather information for a location. The web page uses the Xively JavaScript library [128] to fetch the weather data from the Xively cloud.

■ **Box 9.20:** **Code for a web page for displaying weather information**

```html
<!DOCTYPE html>
<html lang="en">
<head>
<meta charset="utf-8">
<meta http-equiv="Content-Type" content="text/html; charset=iso-8859-1">
<link href="readable.css" rel="stylesheet">
<style>
body {
padding-top:  80px;
}
</style>
<link href="bootstrap-responsive.css" rel="stylesheet">

<!-[if lt IE 9]>
<script src="http://html5shim.googlecode.com/svn/trunk/html5.js">
</script>
<![endif]-> <style type="text/css">
hr {
margin:  0 0;
}
#map_canvas {
width:  100%;
height:  100%;
min-height:  100%;
display:  block;
border-radius:  10px;
-webkit-border-radius:  10px;
}

.well {
width:  100%;
height:  100%;
min-height:  100%;
}

.alert {
border:  1px solid rgba(229,223,59,0.78);
}
</style>
<script type="text/javascript"
src="http://maps.google.com/maps/api/js?sensor=false"></script>

<script type="text/javascript">
function initialize() {
var latlng = new google.maps.LatLng(30.733315,76.779418);
var settings = {
zoom:  11,
center:  latlng,
```

```
mapTypeControl: false,
mapTypeControlOptions: {style:
google.maps.MapTypeControlStyle.DROPDOWN_MENU},
navigationControl: true,
navigationControlOptions: {style:
google.maps.NavigationControlStyle.SMALL},
mapTypeId: google.maps.MapTypeId.TERRAIN
};

var map = new google.maps.Map(document.getElementById("map_canvas"),
settings);

var wespiMarker = new google.maps.Marker({
position: latlng,
map: map,
title:"Location"
});
startws ();

}

</script>
<title>Weather Station</title>
</head>
<body onload="initialize()">
<div class="container">
<div class="row" style="height:20px"> </div>
<div class="row"> <div class="span12">
<center><h1>Weather Station</h1></center>
<br>
<h3>CityName</h3>
</div></div>
<div class="row">
<div class="span6">
<div class='row'>
<div class='span3'><h4>Temperature</h4></div>
<div class='span3'>
<h4 id='temperature'></h4></div></div><hr/>
<div class='row'>
<div class='span3'><h4>Humidity</h4></div>
<div class='span3'> <h4 id='humidity'></h4></div></div><hr/>
<div class='row'>
<div class='span3'><h4>Pressure</h4></div>
<div class='span3'> <h4 id='pressure'></h4></div></div><hr/>
<div class='row'>
<div class='span3'><h4>Light sensor</h4></div>
<div class='span3'> <h4 id='light'></h4></div></div></div>
<div class="span6" style="height:435px">
<b>Location:</b> CityName | <b>Exposure:</b> outdoor |
<b>Disposition:</b> fixed<div class="well">
<div id = "map_canvas">
</div>
</div>
</div>
```

```
</div>
</div>
<script
src="http://ajax.googleapis.com/ajax/libs/jquery/1.8.3/jquery.min.js">
</script>
<script
src="http://d23cj0cdvyoxg0.cloudfront.net/xivelyjs-1.0.4.min.js">
</script>
<script>
$(document).ready(function($) {
xively.setKey( "<enter api key>" );
var feedID = <enter feed-id>, // Feed ID
temp_datastreamID = "temperature";
pressure_datastreamID = "pressure";
humidity_datastreamID = "humidity";
light_datastreamID = "light";

temp_selector = "#temperature";
pressure_selector = "#pressure";
humidity_selector = "#humidity";
light_selector = "#light";

// Get datastream data from Xively
xively.datastream.get (feedID, temp_datastreamID, function(datastream) {
// Display the current value from the datastream
$(temp_selector).html( datastream["current_value"].concat(" C") );
});

xively.datastream.get (feedID,
pressure_datastreamID, function ( datastream ) {
$(pressure_selector).html( datastream["current_value"].concat(" mb") );
});

xively.datastream.get (feedID,
humidity_datastreamID, function ( datastream ) {
$(humidity_selector).html( datastream["current_value"].concat(" %") );
});

xively.datastream.get (feedID,
light_datastreamID, function ( datastream ) {
$(light_selector).html( datastream["current_value"].concat(" L") );
});

});
</script>

</body>
</html>
```

An alternative to using the Xively JavaScript API, is to use the Xively Python library with a Django application. Box 9.21 shows the code for a Django view that retrieves data from the Xively cloud.

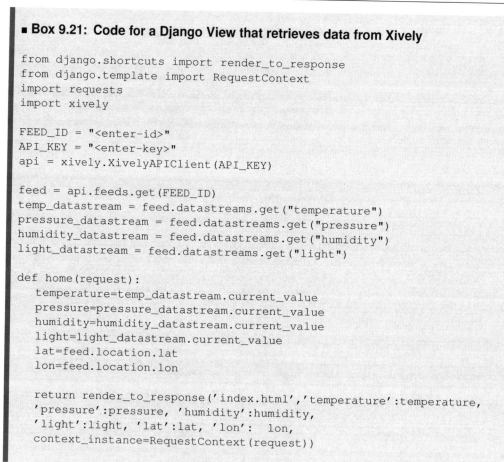

■ **Box 9.21: Code for a Django View that retrieves data from Xively**

```
from django.shortcuts import render_to_response
from django.template import RequestContext
import requests
import xively


FEED_ID = "<enter-id>"
API_KEY = "<enter-key>"
api = xively.XivelyAPIClient(API_KEY)

feed = api.feeds.get(FEED_ID)
temp_datastream = feed.datastreams.get("temperature")
pressure_datastream = feed.datastreams.get("pressure")
humidity_datastream = feed.datastreams.get("humidity")
light_datastream = feed.datastreams.get("light")

def home(request):
    temperature=temp_datastream.current_value
    pressure=pressure_datastream.current_value
    humidity=humidity_datastream.current_value
    light=light_datastream.current_value
    lat=feed.location.lat
    lon=feed.location.lon

    return render_to_response('index.html','temperature':temperature,
    'pressure':pressure, 'humidity':humidity,
    'light':light, 'lat':lat, 'lon':  lon,
    context_instance=RequestContext(request))
```

Figure 9.29 shows a screenshot of the weather monitoring web application.

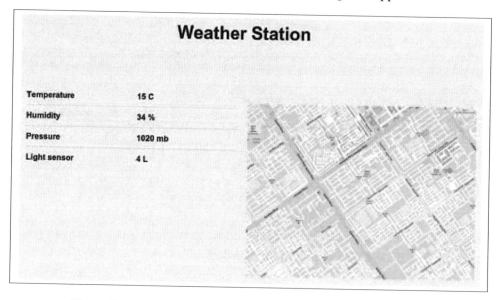

Figure 9.29: Screenshot of weather monitoring web application

## WebSocket-based Implementation

The previous section described a REST-based implementation of the weather monitoring IoT system. In this section you will learn about an alternative implementation of the weather monitoring IoT system based on WebSocket.

The WebSocket implementation is based the Web Application Messaging Protocol (WAMP) which is a sub-protocol of WebSocket. You learned about Autobahn, an open source implementation of WAMP in Chapter 8. The deployment design for the WebSocket implementation is the same as shown in Figure 9.26.

Figure 9.30 shows the communication between various components of the WebSocket implementation. The controller in the WebSocket implementation is a WAMP application component that runs over a WebSocket transport client on the IoT device. WAMP application router runs on a WebSocket transport server on the server instance in the cloud. The role of the Client on the device in this example is that of a Publisher, while the role of the Router is that of a Broker. Publisher publishes messages to the topics managed by the Broker. Subscribers subscribe to topics they are interested in with Brokers. Brokers route events incoming from Publishers to Subscribers that are subscribed to respective topics. Brokers decouple the Publisher and Subscriber. In this example, the Publisher and Subscriber run application code. The Publisher application component is the controller component, the source code of which is shown in Box 9.22. The Subscriber application component is the web frontend, the source code of which is shown in Box 9.23. The analytics component runs on a separate instance and subscribes to the topics managed by the Broker. Box 9.25 shows the code for a dummy analytics component. The communication between Publisher - Broker and Broker - Subscribers happens over a WAMP-WebSocket session.

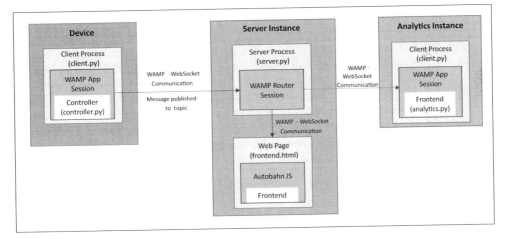

Figure 9.30: Components in the Websocket implementation

### ■ Box 9.22: Controller code for WebSocket implementation - weathercontroller.py

```
from twisted.internet import reactor
from twisted.internet.defer import inlineCallbacks
from autobahn.twisted.util import sleep
```

```python
from autobahn.twisted.wamp import ApplicationSession
import dhtreader
from Adafruit_BMP085 import BMP085
import spidev

#Initialize DHT22 Temperature/Humidity Sensor
dev_type = 22
dht_pin = 24
dhtreader.init()

# Initialise BMP085 Temperature/Pressure Sensor
bmp = BMP085(0x77)

#LDR channel on MCP3008
light_channel = 0

# Open SPI bus
spi = spidev.SpiDev()
spi.open(0,0)

# Function to read SPI data from MCP3008 chip
def ReadChannel(channel):
    adc = spi.xfer2([1, (8+channel)<<4,0])
    data = ((adc[1]&3) << 8) + adc[2]
    return data

#Function to convert LDR reading to Lux
def ConvertLux(data,places):
    R=10 #10k-ohm resistor connected to LDR
    volts = (data * 3.3) / 1023
    volts = round(volts,places)
    lux=500*(3.3-volts)/(R*volts)
    return lux

#Function to read temperature & humidity from DHT22 sensor
def read_DHT22_Sensor():
    temp, humidity = dhtreader.read(dev_type, dht_pin)
    return temp, humidity

#Function to read LDR connected to MCP3008
def readLDR():
    light_level = ReadChannel(light_channel)
    lux = ConvertLux(light_level,2)
    return lux

#Function to read temperature & pressure from BMP085 sensor
def read_BMP085_Sensor():
    temp = bmp.readTemperature()
    pressure = bmp.readPressure()
    return temp, pressure

#Controller main function
def runController():
    temp1, humidity=read_DHT22_Sensor()
```

```
   temp2, pressure=read_BMP085_Sensor()
   temperature=(temp1+temp2)/2 #take avg
   light=readLDR()

   datalist = [temperature, humidity, pressure, light]

   return datalist


#An application component that publishes sensor data every second.
class Component(ApplicationSession):
   @inlineCallbacks
   def onJoin(self, details):
      while True:
         datalist = runcontroller()
         self.publish('com.myapp.topic1', datalist)
         yield sleep(1)
```

■ **Box 9.23:  Code for a web page for displaying weather information
- WebSocket implementation - frontend.html**

```
<!DOCTYPE html>
<html lang="en">
<head>
<meta charset="utf-8">
<meta http-equiv="Content-Type" content="text/html; charset=iso-8859-1">
<title>Weather Station</title>
<!- Le styles ->
<link href="readable.css" rel="stylesheet">
<style>
body {
padding-top:  80px;
}
</style>
<link href="bootstrap-responsive.css" rel="stylesheet">
<!- HTML5 shim, for IE6-8 support of HTML5 elements ->
<!-[if lt IE 9]>
<script
src="http://html5shim.googlecode.com/svn/trunk/html5.js">
</script>
<![endif]-> <style type="text/css">
hr {
margin:  0 0;
}
#map_canvas {
width:  100%;
height:  100%;
min-height:  100%;
display:  block;
border-radius:  10px;
-webkit-border-radius:  10px;
}
```

```
.well {
width:  100%;
height:  100%;
min-height:  100%;
}

.alert {
border:  1px solid rgba(229,223,59,0.78);
}
</style>
<script type="text/javascript"
src="http://maps.google.com/maps/api/js?sensor=false"></script>

<script type="text/javascript">
function initialize() {
var latlng = new google.maps.LatLng(30.733315,76.779418);
var settings = {
zoom:  11,
center:  latlng,
mapTypeControl:  false,
mapTypeControlOptions:  {style:
google.maps.MapTypeControlStyle.DROPDOWN_MENU},
navigationControl:  true,
navigationControlOptions:  {style:
google.maps.NavigationControlStyle.SMALL},
mapTypeId:  google.maps.MapTypeId.TERRAIN
};

var map = new google.maps.Map(
document.getElementById("map_canvas"), settings);

var wespiMarker = new google.maps.Marker({
position:  latlng,
map:  map,
title:"CityName, Country"
});

}
</script>
<script
src="https://autobahn.s3.amazonaws.com/autobahnjs/
latest/autobahn.min.jgz"> </script>
</head>
<body onload="initialize()">
<div class="container">
<div class="row" style="height:20px"> </div>
<div class="row"> <div class="span12">
<center><h1>Weather Station</h1></center>
<br>
<h3>CityName</h3>
</div></div>
<div class="row">
<div class="span6">
<div class='row'>
```

```
<div class='span3'><h4>Temperature</h4></div>
<div class='span3'> <h4 id='temperature'></h4>
</div></div><hr/><div class='row'>
<div class='span3'><h4>Humidity</h4></div>
<div class='span3'> <h4 id='humidity'></h4></div>
</div><hr/><div class='row'>
<div class='span3'><h4>Pressure</h4></div>
<div class='span3'> <h4 id='pressure'></h4></div>
</div><hr/><div class='row'>
<div class='span3'><h4>Light sensor</h4></div>
<div class='span3'> <h4 id='light'></h4></div></div></div>
<div class="span6" style="height:435px">
<b>Location:</b> CityName, Country | <b>
Exposure:</b> outdoor | <b>Disposition:</b> fixed
<div class="well">
<div id = "map_canvas">
</div>
</div>

<script
src="http://ajax.googleapis.com/ajax/libs/jquery/1.8.3/jquery.min.js">
</script>

<script>
try {
var autobahn = require('autobahn');
} catch (e) {
// when running in browser, AutobahnJS will
// be included without a module system
}

var connection = new autobahn.Connection({
url: 'ws://127.0.0.1:8080/ws',
realm: 'realm1'}
);

connection.onopen = function (session) {

var received = 0;
temp_selector = "#temperature";
pressure_selector = "#pressure";
humidity_selector = "#humidity";
light_selector = "#light";

function onevent1(args) {
//console.log("Got event:", args);

$(temp_selector).html( args[0][0].concat(" C") );
$(pressure_selector).html( args[0][1].concat(" mb") );
$(humidity_selector).html( args[0][2].concat(" %") );
$(light_selector).html( args[0][3].concat(" L") );
}

session.subscribe('com.myapp.topic1', onevent1);
```

```
};
connection.open();
</script>
</body>
</html>
```

### ■ Box 9.24: Commands for running WebSocket implementation of weather monitoring example

```
#Setup Autobahn-Python
sudo apt-get install python-twisted python-dev
sudo apt-get install python-pip
sudo pip install -upgrade twisted
sudo pip install -upgrade autobahn

#Clone AutobahnPython
git clone https://github.com/tavendo/AutobahnPython.git

#Create weathercontroller.py as shown in Box 9.22

#Run the application router on a WebSocket transport server

python AutobahnPython/examples/twisted/wamp/basic/server.py

#Run controller component over a WebSocket transport client
python AutobahnPython/examples/twisted/wamp/basic/client.py -component
"weathercontroller.Component"

#Create frontend.html as shown in Box 9.23
#Open frontend.html in a Browser
#Sensor readings would be updated in the web page shown in Figure 9.29
```

### ■ Box 9.25: Code for a dummy analytics component - WebSocket implementation - analytics.py

```
from twisted.internet import reactor
from twisted.internet.defer import inlineCallbacks
from autobahn.twisted.wamp import ApplicationSession

#Placeholder for analysis function
def analyzeData(data):
    return true

#An application component that subscribes and receives events
class Component(ApplicationSession):
    @inlineCallbacks
    def onJoin(self, details):

    self.received = 0

    def on_event(data):
```

```
      print "Temperature:   " + data[0] + "; Humidity:   " + data[1]
      + "; Pressure:   " + data[2] + "; Light:   " + data[3]


   #Placeholder for analysis function
   analyzeData(data)

   yield self.subscribe(on_event, 'com.myapp.topic1')


def onDisconnect(self):
   reactor.stop()
```

### 9.4.2 Weather Reporting Bot

This case study is about a weather reporting bot which reports weather information by sending tweets on Twitter. Figure 9.31 shows a schematic of the weather monitoring end-node. The end-node is comprised of a Raspberry Pi mini-computer, temperature, humidity, pressure and light sensors. In addition to the sensors, a USB webcam is also attached to the device.

Box 9.26 shows the Python code for the controller service that runs on the end-node. The controller service obtains the temperature, humidity, pressure and light readings from the sensors, every 30 minutes. At at the same time an image is captured from the webcam attached to the device. The sensor readings and the captured image is then sent as a tweet on Twitter. To send tweets the controller service uses a Python library for Twitter called *tweepy*. With tweepy you can use the Twitter REST API to send tweets. Before using the Twitter API, you would need to setup a Twitter developer account and then create a new application (with read-write permissions). Upon creating the application you will get the API key, API secret and access tokens. These credentials and tokens are used in the controller service.

■ **Box 9.26: Python code for weather reporting bot that tweets weather updates to Twitter**

```
import time
import datetime
import sys
from random import randint
import dhtreader
from Adafruit_BMP085 import BMP085
import spidev
from SimpleCV import Camera
from time import sleep
import tweepy


#Initialize USB webcam
myCamera = Camera(prop_set={'width':320, 'height':  240})

#Twitter Application Credentials
CONSUMER_KEY ="<enter>"
CONSUMER_SECRET = "<enter>"
ACCESS_KEY = "<enter>"
```

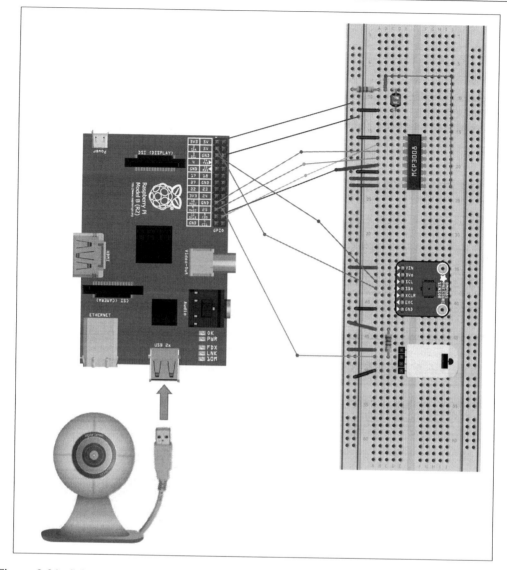

Figure 9.31: Schematic diagram of a weather reporting bot end-node showing the device and sensors

```
ACCESS_SECRET = "<enter>"

auth = tweepy.OAuthHandler(CONSUMER_KEY, CONSUMER_SECRET)
auth.set_access_token(ACCESS_KEY, ACCESS_SECRET)
api = tweepy.API(auth)


#Initialize DHT22 Temperature/Humidity Sensor
dev_type = 22
dht_pin = 24
dhtreader.init()
```

```python
# Initialise BMP085 Temperature/Pressure Sensor
bmp = BMP085(0x77)

#LDR channel on MCP3008
light_channel = 0

# Open SPI bus
spi = spidev.SpiDev()
spi.open(0,0)

#Initialize Xively Feed
FEED_ID = "<enter>"
API_KEY = "<enter>"
api = xively.XivelyAPIClient(API_KEY)

# Function to read SPI data from MCP3008 chip
def ReadChannel(channel):
   adc = spi.xfer2([1,(8+channel)<<4,0])
   data = ((adc[1]&3) << 8) + adc[2]
   return data

#Function to convert LDR reading to Lux
def ConvertLux(data,places):
   R=10 #10k-ohm resistor connected to LDR
   volts = (data * 3.3) / 1023
   volts = round(volts,places)
   lux=500*(3.3-volts)/(R*volts)
   return lux

#Function to read temperature & humidity from DHT22 sensor
def read_DHT22_Sensor():
   temp, humidity = dhtreader.read(dev_type, dht_pin)
   return temp, humidity

#Function to read LDR connected to MCP3008
def readLDR():
   light_level = ReadChannel(light_channel)
   lux = ConvertLux(light_level,2)
   return lux

#Function to read temperature & pressure from BMP085 sensor
def read_BMP085_Sensor():
   temp = bmp.readTemperature()
   pressure = bmp.readPressure()
   return temp, pressure

#Controller main function
def runController():

   #Get sensor readings
   temp1, humidity=read_DHT22_Sensor()
   temp2, pressure=read_BMP085_Sensor()
   temperature=(temp1+temp2)/2 #take avg
   light=readLDR()
```

```
#Capture Image
frame = myCamera.getImage()
frame.save("weather.jpg")

status = "Weather Update at:  " +
datetime.datetime.now().strftime('%Y/%m/%d %H:%M:%S') +
    " - Temperature:  "+ temperature + ", Humidity:  "+
    humidity + ", Pressure:  "+ pressure + ", Light:  "+ light

photo_path = '/home/pi/weather.jpg'

#Tweet weather information with photo
api.update_with_media(photo_path, status=status)


setupController()
while True:
   runController()
   time.sleep(1800)
```

Figure 9.32 shows a screenshot of a tweet sent by the weather reporting bot on Twitter.

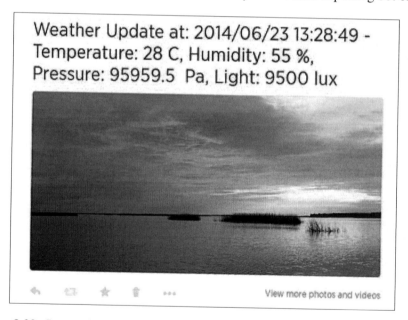

Figure 9.32: Screenshot of a weather update tweeted by the weather reporting bot

### 9.4.3   Air Pollution Monitoring

IoT based air pollution monitoring systems can monitor emission of harmful gases by factories and automobiles using gaseous and meteorological sensors. This section provides an implementation of an air pollution monitoring IoT system. The deployment design for the system is similar to the deployment shown in Figure 9.26. The system design steps are similar to the weather monitoring system described in the previous section. Therefore only the schematic design and the controller implementation is provided.

The system consists of multiple nodes placed in different locations for monitoring air pollution in an area. The end nodes are equipped with $CO$ and $NO_2$ sensors. The end nodes send the data to the cloud and the data is stored in a cloud database. A cloud-based application is used for visualizing the data.

Figure 9.33 shows a schematic diagram of air pollution monitoring end-node. The end node includes a Raspberry Pi mini-computer, MICS-2710 $NO_2$ sensor and MICS-5525 $CO$ sensor. An A/D converter (MCP3008) is used for converting the analog inputs from the sensors to digital.

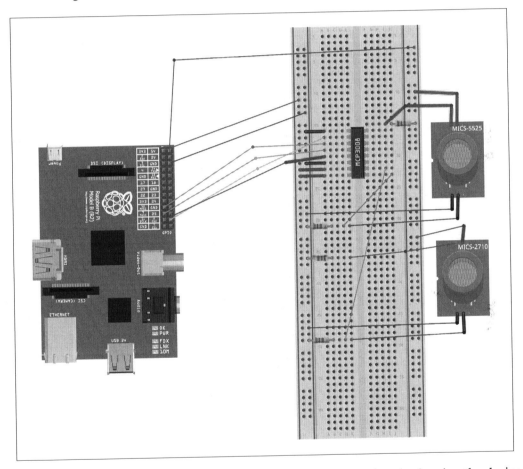

Figure 9.33: Schematic diagram of air pollution monitoring end-node showing the device and sensors

Box 9.27 shows the implementation of the native controller service for air pollution monitoring system. The controller service runs as a native service on the device and obtains the sensor readings every 10 seconds. The controller service calls the Xively REST service to store these measurements in the cloud.

**■ Box 9.27: Python code for controller native service - air pollution monitoring system**

```python
import time
import datetime
import sys
import json
import requests
import xively
import spidev

global NO2_datastream
global CO_datastream

#Sensor channel on MCP3008
CO_CHANNEL = 0
NO2_CHANNEL = 1

vin=5
r0=10000
pullup = 10000

#Conversions based on Rs/Ro vs ppm plots of the sensors
CO_Conversions = [((0,100),(0,0.25)),((100,133),(0.25,0.325)),
((133,167),(0.325,0.475)),((167,200),(0.475,0.575)),((200,233),
(0.575,0.665)),((233,267),(0.666,0.75))]
NO2_Conversions = [((0,100),(0,0.25)),((100,133),(0.25,0.325)),
((133,167),(0.325,0.475)),((167,200),(0.475,0.575)),((200,233),
(0.575,0.665)),((233,267),(0.666,0.75))]

# Open SPI bus
spi = spidev.SpiDev()
spi.open(0,0)

#Initialize Xively Feed
FEED_ID = "467475686"
API_KEY = "OzMuaKpacvlDNgOrXl6SA3WNb9n83BfT51MfEEkLVHHZiEDB"
api = xively.XivelyAPIClient(API_KEY)

# Function to read SPI data from MCP3008 chip
def ReadChannel(channel):
    adc = spi.xfer2([1,(8+channel)<<4,0])
    data = ((adc[1]&3) << 8) + adc[2]
    return data

def get_resistance(channel):
    result = ReadChannel(channel)
    if result == 0:
        resistance = 0
    else:
        resistance = (vin/result - 1)*pullup
    return resistance

def converttoppm(rs,conversions):
```

```
     rsper = 100*(float(rs)/r0)
     for a in conversions:
          if a[0][0]>=rsper>a[0][1]:
               mid, hi = rsper-a[0][0],a[0][1]-a[0][0]
               sf = float(mid)/hi
               ppm = sf * (a[1][1]-a[1][0]) + a[1][0]
                return ppm
     return 0

def get_NO2():
   rs = get_resistance(NO2_CHANNEL)
   ppm = converttoppm(rs,NO2_Conversions)
   return ppm

def get_CO():
   rs = get_resistance(CO_CHANNEL)
   ppm = converttoppm(rs,CO_Conversions)
   return ppm

#Controller main function
def runController():
   global NO2_datastream
   global CO_datastream

   NO2_reading=get_NO2()
   CO_reading=get_CO()

   NO2_datastream.current_value = NO2_reading
   NO2_datastream.at = datetime.datetime.utcnow()

   CO_datastream.current_value = CO_reading
   CO_datastream.at = datetime.datetime.utcnow()


   print "Updating Xively feed with CO: %s" % CO
   try:
      CO_datastream.update()
   except requests.HTTPError as e:
      print "HTTPError({0}):  {1}".format(e.errno, e.strerror)

   print "Updating Xively feed with NO2:  %s" % NO2
   try:
      NO2_datastream.update()
   except requests.HTTPError as e:
      print "HTTPError({0}):  {1}".format(e.errno, e.strerror)


#Function to get existing or create new Xively data stream for NO2
def get_NO2datastream(feed):
   try:
      datastream = feed.datastreams.get("NO2")
      return datastream
   except:
      datastream = feed.datastreams.create("NO2", tags="NO2")
      return datastream
```

```
#Function to get existing or create new Xively data stream for CO
def get_COdatastream(feed):
    try:
        datastream = feed.datastreams.get("CO")
        return datastream
    except:
        datastream = feed.datastreams.create("CO", tags="CO")
        return datastream

#Controller setup function
def setupController():
    global NO2_datastream
    global CO_datastream

    feed = api.feeds.get(FEED_ID)

    feed.location.lat="30.733315"
    feed.location.lon="76.779418"
    feed.tags="Pollution"
    feed.update()

    NO2_datastream = get_NO2datastream(feed)
    NO2_datastream.max_value = None
    NO2_datastream.min_value = None

    CO_datastream = get_COdatastream(feed)
    CO_datastream.max_value = None
    CO_datastream.min_value = None


setupController()
while True:
    runController()
    time.sleep(10)
```

### 9.4.4  Forest Fire Detection

IoT based forest fire detection systems use a number of monitoring nodes deployed at different locations in a forest. Each monitoring node collects measurements on ambient conditions (such as temperature and humidity) to predict whether a fire has broken out.

An implementation of a forest fire detection system is described in this section. The system is based on a level-5 IoT deployment with multiple end nodes and one coordinator node. The end nodes perform sensing and the coordinator node collects data from the end nodes and sends to the cloud.

Figure 9.34 shows a schematic diagram of forest fire detection end-node. The end node includes a Raspberry Pi mini-computer and DHT-22 temperature and humidity sensor. An XBee module is used for wireless communication between the end-node and the coordinator node. Figure 9.35 shows a schematic diagram of the coordinator node.

Boxes 9.28 and 9.29 show the implementations of the native controller services for the end node and coordinator node respectively. The controller service on the end node obtains the sensor readings every 10 seconds and writes the data to the XBee module which sends the data to the coordinator node. The controller service on the coordinator node receives the data from all end nodes and calls the Xively REST service to store these measurements in the cloud.

The XBee modules can be configured to communicate with each other using a Windows based application called X-CTU [127]. All XBee modules should have the same network ID and channel. The XBee module for the coordinator node has to be configured as a coordinator and the rest of the modules have to be configured as end devices or routers.

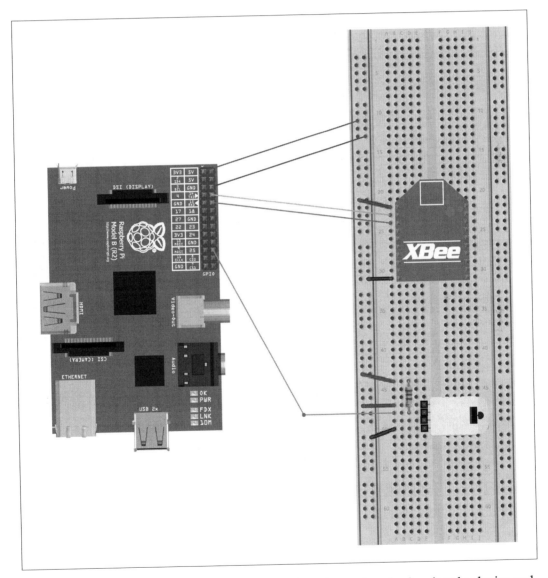

Figure 9.34: Schematic diagram of a forest fire detection end-node showing the device and sensor

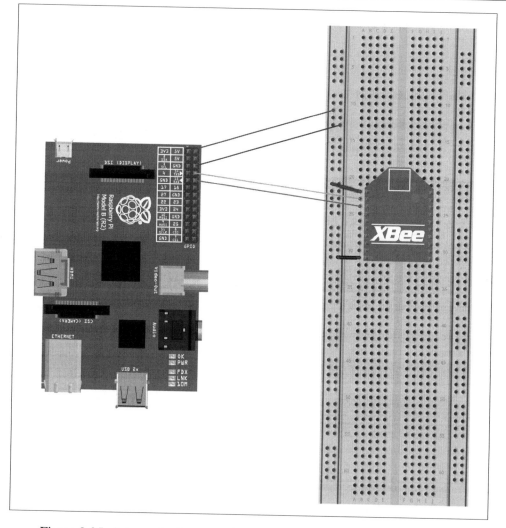

Figure 9.35: Schematic diagram of a forest fire detection coordinator node

■ **Box 9.28: Python code for controller service on end-node - forest fire detection system**

```
import time
import datetime
import serial
import dhtreader

#Set Router ID
RouteID='123'

#Initialize DHT22 Temperature/Humidity Sensor
dev_type = 22
dht_pin = 24
dhtreader.init()
```

```
#Function to read temperature & humidity from DHT22 sensor
def read_DHT22_Sensor():
    temp, humidity = dhtreader.read(dev_type, dht_pin)
    return temp, humidity


def write_xbee(data):
    xbee=serial.Serial(port='/dev/ttyAMA0',baudrate='9600')
    xbee.write(data)


#Controller main function
def runController():
    temperature, humidity=read_DHT22_Sensor()
    timestamp = str(datetime.datetime.utcnow())

    data= RouteID + "|"+ timestamp + "|"+
        temperature + "|" + humidity + "| "
    write_xbee(data)

while True:
    runController()
    time.sleep(10)
```

■ **Box 9.29: Python code for controller service on coordinator - forest fire detection system**

```
import time
import datetime
import sys
import json
import requests
import xively

global temp_datastream = []
global humidity_datastream = []


#Set number of routers
numRouters=2

#Map router ID's to sequence numbers
routerIDs={'123':'1','345':'2'}

#Initialize Xively Feed
FEED_ID = "enter feed id"
API_KEY = "enter key"
api = xively.XivelyAPIClient(API_KEY)


def read_xbee():
```

```
    xbee=serial.Serial(port='/dev/ttyAMA0', 9600,timeout=1)
    data = xbee.readline()
    return data

#Controller main function
def runController():
   global temp_datastream
   global humidity_datastream

   data=read_xbee()
   dataArr=data.split('|')

   id = dataArr[0]
   i = routerIDs[id]
   timestamp = dataArr[1]
   temperature = dataArr[2]
   humidity = dataArr[3]

   temp_datastream[i].current_value = temperature
   temp_datastream[i].at = timestamp

   humidity_datastream[i].current_value = humidity
   humidity_datastream[i].at = timestamp

   print "Updating Xively feed with Temperature:  %s" % temperature
   try:
       temp_datastream[i].update()
   except requests.HTTPError as e:
       print "HTTPError({0}):  {1}".format(e.errno, e.strerror)

   print "Updating Xively feed with Humidity:  %s" % humidity
   try:
       pressure_datastream[i].update()
   except requests.HTTPError as e:
       print "HTTPError({0}):  {1}".format(e.errno, e.strerror)


#Function to get existing or create new Xively data stream
def get_tempdatastream(feed,id):
   try:
      datastream = feed.datastreams.get("temperature"+str(id))
      return datastream
   except:
      datastream = feed.datastreams.create("temperature"+str(id),
tags="temperature")
      return datastream

#Function to get existing or create new Xively data stream for humidity
def get_humiditydatastream(feed,id):
   try:
      datastream = feed.datastreams.get("humidity"+str(id))
      return datastream
   except:
      datastream = feed.datastreams.create(
```

```
            "humidity"+str(id), tags="humidity")
        return datastream

#Controller setup function
def setupController():
    global temp_datastream
    global humidity_datastream

    feed = api.feeds.get(FEED_ID)

    feed.tags="Weather"
    feed.update()

    for i in range(1,numRouters+1):
        temp_datastream[i] = get_tempdatastream(feed,i)
        temp_datastream[i].max_value = None
        temp_datastream[i].min_value = None

        humidity_datastream[i] = get_humiditydatastream(feed,i)
        humidity_datastream[i].max_value = None
        humidity_datastream[i].min_value = None


setupController()
while True:
    runController()
    time.sleep(10)
```

## 9.5  Agriculture

### 9.5.1  Smart Irrigation

Smart irrigation systems use IoT devices and soil moisture sensors to determine the amount of moisture in the soil and release the flow of water through the irrigation pipes only when the moisture levels go below a predefined threshold. Data on the moisture levels is also collected in the cloud where it is analyzed to plan watering schedules.

An implementation of a smart irrigation system is described in this section. The deployment design for the system is similar to the deployment shown in Figure 9.26. The system consists of multiple nodes placed in different locations for monitoring soil moisture in a field. The end nodes send the data to the cloud and the data is stored in a cloud database. A cloud-based application is used for visualizing the data. Figure 9.36 shows a schematic diagram of smart irrigation system end-node. The end node includes a Raspberry Pi mini-computer and soil moisture sensor. A solenoid valve is used to control the flow of water through the irrigation pipe. When the moisture level goes below a threshold, the valve is opened to release water. Box 9.30 shows the Python code for the controller native service for the smart irrigation system.

> ■ **Box 9.30: Python code for controller native service - smart irrigation system**

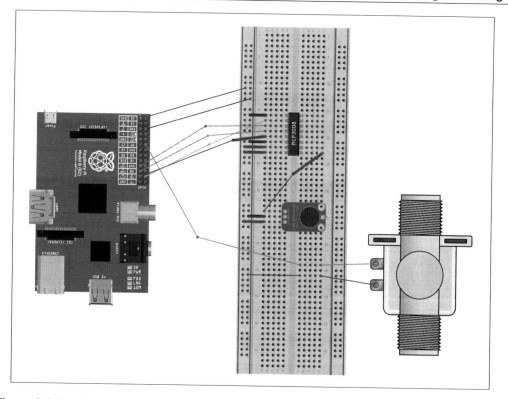

Figure 9.36: Schematic diagram of a smart irrigation system end-node showing the device and sensor

```
import time
import datetime
import sys
import json
import requests
import xively
import subprocess
import spidev

global mositure_datastream
#LDR channel on MCP3008
mositure_channel = 0

GPIO.setmode(GPIO.BCM)
TRIGGER_PIN=18
threshold = 10

# Open SPI bus
spi = spidev.SpiDev()
spi.open(0,0)

#Initialize Xively Feed
FEED_ID = "enter feed id"
API_KEY = "enter key"
```

```python
api = xively.XivelyAPIClient(API_KEY)

# Function to read SPI data from MCP3008 chip
def ReadChannel(channel):
    adc = spi.xfer2([1,(8+channel)<<4,0])
    data = ((adc[1]&3) << 8) + adc[2]
    return data

#Function to read sensor connected to MCP3008
def readMositure():
    level = ReadChannel(mositure_channel)
    return level


#Controller main function
def runController():
    global mositure_datastream

    level=readMositure()

    #Check moisture level
    if (level<threshold):
        GPIO.output(TRIGGER_PIN, True)
    else:
        GPIO.output(TRIGGER_PIN, False)

    mositure_datastream.current_value = level
    mositure_datastream.at = datetime.datetime.utcnow()

    print "Updating Xively feed with mositure:  %s" % mositure
    try:
        mositure_datastream.update()
    except requests.HTTPError as e:
        print "HTTPError({0}):  {1}".format(e.errno, e.strerror)


#Function to get existing or create new Xively data stream
def get_mosituredatastream(feed):
    try:
        datastream = feed.datastreams.get("mositure")
        return datastream
    except:
        datastream = feed.datastreams.create("mositure", tags="mositure")
        return datastream


#Controller setup function
def setupController():
    global mositure_datastream

    feed = api.feeds.get(FEED_ID)

    feed.location.lat="30.733315"
    feed.location.lon="76.779418"
```

```
    feed.tags="Soil Moisture"
    feed.update()

    mositure_datastream = get_mosituredatastream(feed)
    mositure_datastream.max_value = None
    mositure_datastream.min_value = None

setupController()
while True:
    runController()
    time.sleep(10)
```

## 9.6   Productivity Applications

### 9.6.1   IoT Printer

This case study is about an IoT printer that prints a daily briefing every morning. The daily briefing comprises of the current weather information, weather predictions for the day and the user's schedule for the day (obtained from the user's Google Calendar account).

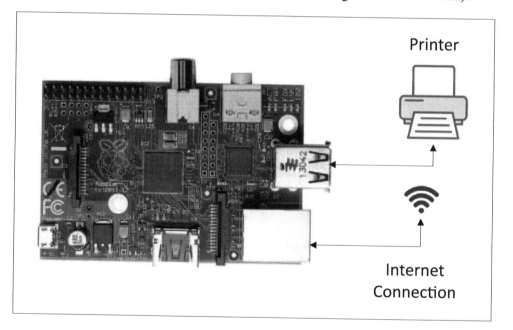

Figure 9.37: Connecting a printer to Raspberry Pi

Box 9.31 shows the code for the service that runs on the mini-computer which is connected to the printer.

■ **Box 9.31: Python code for IoT printer**

```
import gflags
import httplib2
import datetime
```

```
from apiclient.discovery import build
from oauth2client.file import Storage
from oauth2client.client import OAuth2WebServerFlow
from oauth2client.tools import run
import pywapi
import popen2


#Get weather information from weather.com
weather_com_result = pywapi.get_weather_from_weather_com('INXX0096')

#Write information to file
fp= file('dailybrieding.txt','w')
fp.write(str(datetime.datetime.now().strftime("%A - %D"))+'\n')


fp.write("WEATHER INFORMATION \n")
fp.write( "Current conditions:\n")
fp.write( "Condition:   "+
weather_com_result['current_conditions']['text']+'\n')
fp.write( "Temperature:   " +
weather_com_result['current_conditions']['temperature']+'\n')
fp.write( "Humidity:   " +
weather_com_result['current_conditions']['humidity']+'\n')


fp.write( "Today's Forecast:\n")
fp.write( "Forecast:   " +
weather_com_result["forecasts"][0]["day"]["brief_text"]+'\n')
fp.write( "Temperature:  Max:   " +
weather_com_result["forecasts"][0]["high"] + ",
          Min:  " + weather_com_result["forecasts"][0]["low"]+'\n')
fp.write( "Humidity:   " +
weather_com_result["forecasts"][0]["day"]["humidity"]+'\n')
fp.write( "Precipitation chances:   " +
weather_com_result["forecasts"][0]["day"]["chance_precip"]+'\n')


    fp.write( "TODAY'S CALENDAR:\n")


#Get calendar information

FLAGS = gflags.FLAGS

# Client_id and client_secret from Google Developers Console
FLOW = OAuth2WebServerFlow(
   client_id='<enter id>',
   client_secret='<enter secret>',
   scope='https://www.googleapis.com/auth/calendar',
   user_agent='MyTestApp/1')

# Credentials will get written back to a file.
storage = Storage('calendar.dat')
credentials = storage.get()
if credentials is None or credentials.invalid == True:
credentials = run(FLOW, storage)
```

```
# Create an httplib2.Http object to handle HTTP requests and authorize
# with good Credentials.
http = httplib2.Http()
http = credentials.authorize(http)

# Build a service object for interacting with the API.
service = build(serviceName='calendar', version='v3', http=http,
    developerKey='<enter key>')

startdatetime =
str(datetime.datetime.now().strftime("%Y-%m-%dT00:00:00+05:30"))
enddatetime =
str(datetime.datetime.now().strftime("%Y-%m-%dT23:59:59+05:30"))

page_token = None
while True:
   events = service.events().list(calendarId='primary',
   pageToken=page_token, timeMin=startdatetime,
   timeMax=enddatetime).execute()
for event in events['items']:
   fp.write("Event:   "+ event['summary'] +
   " From:   "+ event['start']['dateTime'] + " To:   " +
    event['end']['dateTime']+'\n')
   page_token = events.get('nextPageToken')
   if not page_token:
   break

fp.close()

#Print the weather and calendar information file
popen2.popen4("lpr -P Xerox-Phaser-3117 dailybrieding.txt")
```

Box 9.32 shows an example of a daily briefing printed by the IoT printer.

**■ Box 9.32: Example of a daily briefing printed by the IoT printer**

```
   Friday - 06/20/14

WEATHER INFORMATION

Current conditions:
Condition:  Widespread Dust
Temperature:  42
Humidity:  25

Today's Forecast:
Forecast:
Temperature:  Max:  42, Min:  32
Humidity:  0
Precipitation chances:  0
-------------------
```

```
TODAY'S CALENDAR:

Event:  Team Meeting
From:   2014-06-20T15:30:00+05:30 To:  2014-06-20T16:30:00+05:30
```

## Summary

In this chapter you learned about various applications of IoT and fully developed case studies. This provided you with a solid foundation, hopefully, that will assist you in designing and implementing various levels of IoT systems. From the smart lighting case study you learned how to implement a level-1 IoT system comprising of a local controller, device and application. Services were implemented using the Django REST framework. From the intrusion detection system case study, you learned about designing the process specification, domain model, information model, service specifications, functional and operational view specifications for a level-2 IoT system. From the weather monitoring system case study you learned about two alternative approaches of implementing the services for an IoT system - one based on REST and other based on WebSocket. The weather monitoring system described is a level-6 IoT system with multiple independent end nodes which perform sensing and send data to the cloud. The REST implementation was done using the Django REST framework and the WebSocket implementation was done using the AutoBahn framework. From the air pollution monitoring, forest fire detection and smart irrigation case studies you learned how to interface various types of sensors with an IoT device and process the sensor data.

## Lab Exercises

1. Design and implement a fire alarm IoT system, using a Raspberry Pi device, temperature, $CO_2$ and $CO$ sensors. Follow the steps below:
   - Define the process specification of the system. The system should collect and analyze the sensor data and send email alerts when a fire is detected.
   - Define a domain model.
   - Define service specifications.
   - Design a deployment of the system. The system can be a level-1 IoT system.
   - Define the functional and operational view specifications.
   - Implement the web services and controller service.
2. For the fire alarm IoT system in exercise-1, identify the configuration and state data. Define a YANG module for the system.
3. Rework the home automation case study to make it a level-2 IoT system.
4. Extend the functionality of the home intrusion detection IoT system to send email alerts when an intrusion is detected.
5. Extend the functionality of the home intrusion detection IoT system by interfacing a webcam. Implement a function in the controller to capture an image from the webcam and send it as an attachment in the email alert when an intrusion is detected.
6. Box 9.25 shown the code for a dummy analytics component of weather monitoring system. Implement the analytics component to compute the hourly maximum and minimum values of temperature and humidity.

7. Implement the air pollution monitoring system using the WebSocket approach.
8. Implement the analytics component for the forest fire detection system.

# Part III

# ADVANCED TOPICS

# 10 - Data Analytics for IoT

## This Chapter Covers

- Overview of MapReduce parallel programming model
- Overview of Hadoop
- Case study on batch data analysis using Hadoop
- Case study on real-time data analysis using Hadoop
- Overview of Apache Oozie
- Overview of Apache Spark
- Overview of Apache Storm
- Case study on using Apache Storm for real-time data analysis

## 10.1   Introduction

The volume, velocity and variety of data generated by data-intensive IoT systems is so large that it is difficult to store, manage, process and analyze the data using traditional databases and data processing tools. Analysis of data can be done with aggregation methods (such as computing mean, maximum, minimum, counts, etc.) or using machine learning methods such as clustering and classification. Clustering is used to grouping similar data items together such that, data items which are more similar to each other (with respect to some similarity criteria) than other data items are put in one cluster. Classification is used for categorizing objects into predefined categories.

In this chapter, you will learn about various frameworks for data analysis including Apache Hadoop, Apache Oozie, Apache Spark and Apache Storm. Case studies on batch and real-time data analysis for a forest fire detection system are described. Before going into the specifics of the data analysis tools, let us look at the IoT system and the requirements for data analysis.

Figure 10.1 shows the deployment design of a forest fire detection system with multiple end nodes which are deployed in a forest. The end nodes are equipped with sensors for measuring temperature, humidity, light and carbon monoxide ($CO$) at various locations in the forest. Each end node sends data independently to the cloud using REST-based communication. The data collected in the cloud is analyzed to predict whether fire has broken out in the forest.

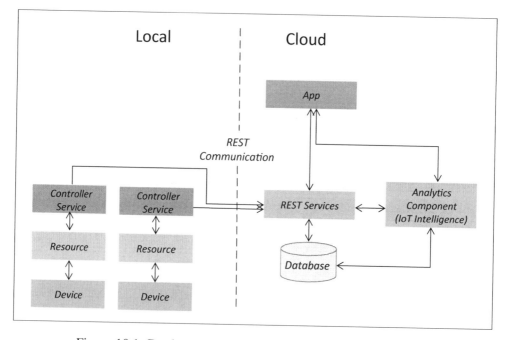

Figure 10.1: Deployment design of forest fire detection system

Figure 10.2 shows an example of the data collected for forest fire detection. Each row in the table shows timestamped readings of temperature, humidity, light and $CO$ sensors. By analyzing the sensor readings in real-time (each row of table), predictions can be made about the occurrence of a forest fire. The sensor readings can also be aggregated on a various timescales (minute, hourly, daily or monthly) to determine the mean, maximum and minimum readings. This data can help in developing prediction models.

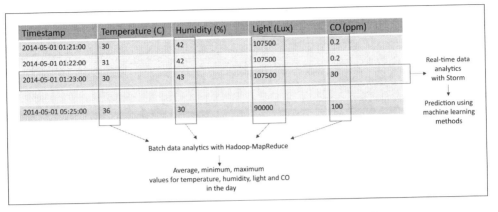

Figure 10.2: Data analysis for forest fire detection

Figure 10.3 shows a schematic diagram of forest fire detection end node. The end node is based on a Raspberry Pi device and uses DHT22 temperature and humidity sensor, light dependent resistor and MICS5525 *CO* sensor. Box 10.1 shows the Python code for the native controller service than runs on the end nodes. This example uses the Xively PaaS for storing data. In the *setupController* function new Xively datastreams are created for temperature, humidity, light and *CO* data. The *runController* function is called every second and the sensor readings are obtained. The Xively REST API is used for sending data to the Xively cloud.

■ **Box 10.1: Controller service for forest fire detection system - controller.py**

```python
import time
import datetime
import requests
import xively
import dhtreader
import spidev

global temp_datastream
global CO_datastream
global humidity_datastream
global light_datastream


#Initialize Xively Feed
FEED_ID = "<enter feed ID>"
API_KEY = "<enter API key>"
api = xively.XivelyAPIClient(API_KEY)

#Configure these pin numbers for DHT22
DEV_TYPE = 22
DHT_PIN = 24
```

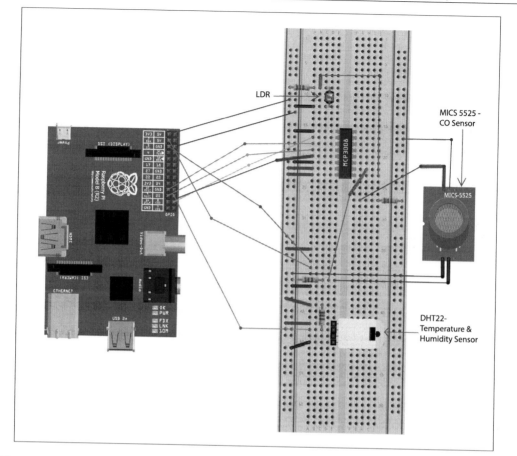

Figure 10.3: Schematic diagram of forest fire detection end node showing Raspberry Pi device and sensors

```
#Initialize DHT22
dhtreader.init()

#LDR channel on MCP3008
LIGHT_CHANNEL = 0

# Open SPI bus
spi = spidev.SpiDev()
spi.open(0,0)

#MICS5525 CO sensor channel on MCP3008
CO_CHANNEL = 1

#Conversions based on Rs/Ro vs ppm plot of MICS5525 CO sensor
CO_Conversions = [((0,100),(0,0.25)), ((100,133),(0.25,0.325)),
     ((133,167),(0.325,0.475)), ((167,200),(0.475, 0.575)),
     ((200,233),(0.575,0.665)), ((233,267),(0.666,0.75)) ]

#Read temperature & humidity from DHT22 sensor
```

```python
def read_DHT22_Sensor():
   temperature, humidity = dhtreader.read(DEV_TYPE, DHT_PIN)
   return temperature, humidity

#Read LDR connected to MCP3008
def readLDR():
   light_level = ReadChannel(LIGHT_CHANNEL)
   lux = ConvertLux(light_level,2)
   return lux

#Convert LDR reading to Lux
def ConvertLux(data,places):
   R=10 #10k-ohm resistor connected to LDR
   volts = (data * 3.3) / 1023
   volts = round(volts,places)
   lux=500*(3.3-volts)/(R*volts)
   return lux

# Read SPI data from MCP3008 chip
def ReadChannel(channel):
   adc = spi.xfer2([1,(8+channel)<<4,0])
   data = ((adc[1]&3) << 8) + adc[2]
   return data

#Read MICS5525 CO sensor connected to MCP3008
def readCOSensor():
   result = ReadChannel(CO_CHANNEL)
   if result == 0:
     resistance = 0
   else:
     resistance = (vin/result - 1)*pullup
   ppmresult = converttoppm(resistance, CO_Conversions)
   return ppmresult

#Convert resistance reading to PPM
def converttoppm(rs,conversions):
   rsper = 100*(float(rs)/r0)
   for a in conversions:
     if a[0][0]>=rsper>a[0][1]:
       mid,hi = rsper-a[0][0],a[0][1]-a[0][0]
       sf = float(mid)/hi
       ppm = sf * (a[1][1]-a[1][0]) + a[1][0]
       return ppm
   return 0

#Controller main function
def runController():
   global temp_datastream
   global CO_datastream
   global humidity_datastream
   global light_datastream

   temperature, humidity=read_DHT22_Sensor()
```

```
   light=readLDR()
   CO_reading = readCOSensor()

   temp_datastream.current_value = temperature
   temp_datastream.at = datetime.datetime.utcnow()

   humidity_datastream.current_value = humidity
   humidity_datastream.at = datetime.datetime.utcnow()

   light_datastream.current_value = light
   light_datastream.at = datetime.datetime.utcnow()

   CO_datastream.current_value = CO_reading
   CO_datastream.at = datetime.datetime.utcnow()

   try:
       temp_datastream.update()
   except requests.HTTPError as e:
       print "HTTPError({0}): {1}".format(e.errno, e.strerror)

   try:
       humidity_datastream.update()
   except requests.HTTPError as e:
       print "HTTPError({0}): {1}".format(e.errno, e.strerror)

   try:
       light_datastream.update()
   except requests.HTTPError as e:
       print "HTTPError({0}): {1}".format(e.errno, e.strerror)

   try:
       CO_datastream.update()
   except requests.HTTPError as e:
       print "HTTPError({0}): {1}".format(e.errno, e.strerror)

#Get existing or create new Xively data stream for temperature
def get_tempdatastream(feed):
   try:
      datastream = feed.datastreams.get("temperature")
      return datastream
   except:
      datastream = feed.datastreams.create("temperature",
tags="temperature")
      return datastream

#Get existing or create new Xively data stream for CO
def get_COdatastream(feed):
   try:
      datastream = feed.datastreams.get("CO")
      return datastream
   except:
      datastream = feed.datastreams.create("CO", tags="CO")
      return datastream
```

```python
#Get existing or create new Xively data stream for humidity
def get_humiditydatastream(feed):
   try:
      datastream = feed.datastreams.get("humidity")
      return datastream
   except:
      datastream = feed.datastreams.create("humidity", tags="humidity")
      return datastream

#Get existing or create new Xively data stream for light
def get_lightdatastream(feed):
   try:
      datastream = feed.datastreams.get("light")
      return datastream
   except:
      datastream = feed.datastreams.create("light", tags="light")
      return datastream

#Controller setup function
def setupController():
   global temp_datastream
   global CO_datastream
   global humidity_datastream
   global light_datastream

   feed = api.feeds.get(FEED_ID)
   feed.update()

   temp_datastream = get_tempdatastream(feed)
   temp_datastream.max_value = None
   temp_datastream.min_value = None

   humidity_datastream = get_humiditydatastream(feed)
   humidity_datastream.max_value = None
   humidity_datastream.min_value = None

   light_datastream = get_lightdatastream(feed)
   light_datastream.max_value = None
   light_datastream.min_value = None

   CO_datastream = get_COdatastream(feed)
   CO_datastream.max_value = None
   CO_datastream.min_value = None

setupController()
while True:
   runController()
   time.sleep(1)
```

## 10.2 Apache Hadoop

Apache Hadoop [130] is an open source framework for distributed batch processing of big data. MapReduce is parallel programming model [85] suitable for analysis of big data. MapReduce algorithms allow large scale computations to be parallelized across a large cluster of servers.

### 10.2.1 MapReduce Programming Model

MapReduce is a widely used parallel data processing model for processing and analysis of massive scale data [85]. MapReduce model has two phases: Map and Reduce. MapReduce programs are written in a functional programming style to create Map and Reduce functions. The input data to the map and reduce phases is in the form of key-value pairs. Run-time systems for MapReduce are typically large clusters built of commodity hardware. The MapReduce run-time systems take care of tasks such partitioning the data, scheduling of jobs and communication between nodes in the cluster. This makes it easier for programmers to analyze massive scale data without worrying about tasks such as data partitioning and scheduling. Figure 10.4 shows the flow of data for a MapReduce job. MapReduce programs take a set of input key-value pairs and produce a set of output key-value pairs. In the Map phase, data is read from a distributed file system, partitioned among a set of computing nodes in the cluster, and sent to the nodes as a set of key-value pairs. The Map tasks process the input records independently of each other and produce intermediate results as key-value pairs. The intermediate results are stored on the local disk of the node running the Map task. When all the Map tasks are completed, the Reduce phase begins in which the intermediate data with the same key is aggregated. An optional Combine task can be used to perform data aggregation on the intermediate data of the same key for the output of the mapper before transferring the output to the Reduce task.

MapReduce programs take advantage of locality of data and the data processing takes place on the nodes where the data resides. In traditional approaches for data analysis, data is moved to the compute nodes which results in delay in data transmission between the nodes in a cluster. MapReduce programming model moves the computation to where the data resides thus decreasing the transmission of data and improving efficiency. MapReduce programming model is well suited for parallel processing of massive scale data in which the data analysis tasks can be accomplished by independent map and reduce operations.

### 10.2.2 Hadoop MapReduce Job Execution

In this section you will learn about the MapReduce job execution workflow and the steps involved in job submission, job initialization, task selection and task execution. Figure 10.5 shows the components of a Hadoop cluster. A Hadoop cluster comprises of a Master node, backup node and a number of slave nodes. The master node runs the NameNode and JobTracker processes and the slave nodes run the DataNode and TaskTracker components of Hadoop. The backup node runs the Secondary NameNode process. The functions of the key processes of Hadoop are described as follows:

#### NameNode

NameNode keeps the directory tree of all files in the file system, and tracks where across the cluster the file data is kept. It does not store the data of these files itself. Client

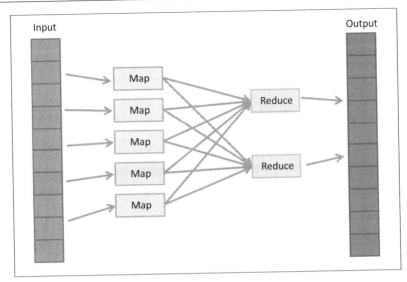

Figure 10.4: Data flow in MapReduce

applications talk to the NameNode whenever they wish to locate a file, or when they want to add/copy/move/delete a file. The NameNode responds to the successful requests by returning a list of relevant DataNode servers where the data lives. NameNode serves as both directory namespace manager and 'inode table' for the Hadoop DFS. There is a single NameNode running in any DFS deployment.

**Secondary NameNode**

HDFS is not currently a high availability system. The NameNode is a Single Point of Failure for the HDFS Cluster. When the NameNode goes down, the file system goes offline. An optional Secondary NameNode which is hosted on a separate machine creates checkpoints of the namespace.

**JobTracker**

The JobTracker is the service within Hadoop that distributes MapReduce tasks to specific nodes in the cluster, ideally the nodes that have the data, or at least are in the same rack.

**TaskTracker**

TaskTracker is a node in a Hadoop cluster that accepts Map, Reduce and Shuffle tasks from the JobTracker. Each TaskTracker has a defined number of slots which indicate the number of tasks that it can accept. When the JobTracker tries to find a TaskTracker to schedule a map or reduce task it first looks for an empty slot on the same node that hosts the DataNode containing the data. If an empty slot is not found on the same node, the JobTracker looks for an empty slot on a node in the same rack.

**DataNode**

A DataNode stores data in an HDFS file system. A functional HDFS filesystem has more than one DataNode, with data replicated across them. DataNodes connect to the NameNode on startup. DataNodes respond to requests from the NameNode for filesystem operations. Client applications can talk directly to a DataNode, once the NameNode has provided the location of the data. Similarly, MapReduce operations assigned to TaskTracker instances near a DataNode, talk directly to the DataNode to access the files. TaskTracker instances can be deployed on the same servers that host DataNode instances, so that MapReduce operations are performed close to the data.

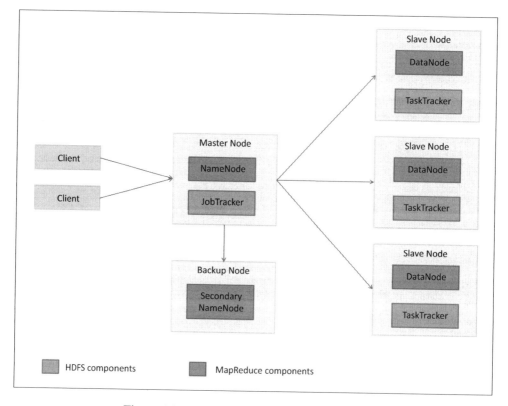

Figure 10.5: Components of a Hadoop cluster

## 10.2.3  MapReduce Job Execution Workflow

Figure 10.6 shows the MapReduce job execution workflow for Hadoop MapReduce framework. The job execution starts when the client applications submit jobs to the Job tracker. The JobTracker returns a JobID to the client application. The JobTracker talks to the NameNode to determine the location of the data. The JobTracker locates TaskTracker nodes with available slots at/or near the data. The TaskTrackers send out heartbeat messages to the JobTracker, usually every few minutes, to reassure the JobTracker that they are still alive. These messages also inform the JobTracker of the number of available slots, so the JobTracker can stay up to date with where in the cluster, new work can be delegated. The JobTracker submits the work to the TaskTracker nodes when they poll for tasks. To choose a task for a TaskTracker, the JobTracker uses various scheduling algorithms. The default scheduling algorithm in Hadoop is FIFO (first-in, first-out). In FIFO scheduling a work queue is maintained and JobTracker pulls the oldest job first for scheduling. There is no notion of the job priority or size of the job in FIFO scheduling.

The TaskTracker nodes are monitored using the heartbeat signals that are sent by the TaskTrackers to JobTracker. The TaskTracker spawns a separate JVM process for each task

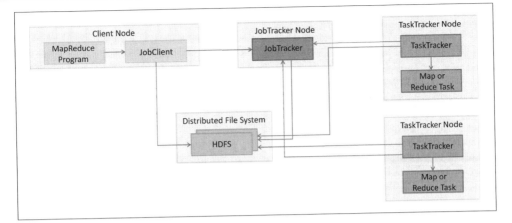

Figure 10.6: Hadoop MapReduce job execution

so that any task failure does not bring down the TaskTracker. The TaskTracker monitors these spawned processes while capturing the output and exit codes. When the process finishes, successfully or not, the TaskTracker notifies the JobTracker. When a task fails the TaskTracker notifies the JobTracker and the JobTracker decides whether to resubmit the job to some other TaskTracker or mark that specific record as something to avoid. The JobTracker can blacklist a TaskTracker as unreliable if there are repeated task failures. When the job is completed, the JobTracker updates its status. Client applications can poll the JobTracker for status of the jobs.

### 10.2.4  Hadoop Cluster Setup

In this section you will learn how to setup a Hadoop cluster. The Hadoop open source framework is written in Java and has been designed to work with commodity hardware. The Hadoop filesystem HDFS is highly fault-tolerant. While the preferred operating system to host Hadoop is Linux, it can also be set up on Windows-like operating systems with a Cygwin environment.

A multi-node Hadoop cluster configuration will be described in this section comprising of one master node that runs the NameNode and JobTracker and two slave nodes that run the TaskTracker and DataNode. The hardware used for the Hadoop cluster described in this section consists of three Amazon EC2 (*m1.Large*) instances running Ubuntu Linux.

The steps involved in setting up a Hadoop cluster are described as follows:

**Install Java**

Hadoop requires Java 6 or later version. Box 10.2 lists the commands for installing Java 7.

**Install Hadoop**

To setup a Hadoop cluster, the Hadoop setup tarball is downloaded and unpacked on all the nodes. The Hadoop version used for the cluster example in this section is 1.0.4. Box 10.3 lists the commands for installing Hadoop.

### ■ Box 10.2: Commands for installing Java

```
# Set the properties
sudo apt-get -q -y install python-software-properties
sudo add-apt-repository -y ppa:webupd8team/java
sudo apt-get -q -y update

#State that you accepted the license
echo debconf shared/accepted-oracle-license-v1-1 select true |
sudo debconf-set-selections
echo debconf shared/accepted-oracle-license-v1-1 seen true |
sudo debconf-set-selections

#Install Oracle Java 7 sudo apt-get -q -y install oracle-java7-installer

#Update environment variable
sudo bash -c "echo JAVA_HOME=/usr/lib/jvm/java-7-oracle/
>> /etc/environment"
```

### ■ Box 10.3: Commands for installing and configuring Hadoop

```
$wget http://apache.techartifact.com/mirror/hadoop/common/hadoop-1.0.4/
hadoop-1.0.4.tar.gz
$tar xzf hadoop-1.0.4.tar.gz
#Change hostname of node
#sudo hostname master
#sudo hostname slave1
#sudo hostname slave2

#Modify /etc/hosts file and add private IPs of Master and Slave nodes:
$sudo vim /etc/hosts
#<private_IP_master> master
#<private_IP_slave1> slave1
#<private_IP_slave2> slave2

$ssh-keygen -t rsa -f /.ssh/id_rsa
$sudo cat /.ssh/id_rsa.pub >> /.ssh/authorized_keys

#Open authorized keys file and copy authorized keys of each node
$sudo vim /.ssh/authorized_keys

#Save host key fingerprints by connecting to every node using SSH
#ssh master
#ssh slave1
#ssh slave2
```

## Networking

After unpacking the Hadoop setup package on all the nodes of the cluster, the next step is to configure the network such that all the nodes can connect to each other over the network. To make the addressing of nodes simple, assign simple host names to nodes (such master, slave1

| File Name | Description |
|---|---|
| core-site.xml | Configuration parameters for Hadoop core which are common to MapReduce and HDFS |
| mapred-site.xml | Configuration parameters for MapReduce daemons – JobTracker and TaskTracker |
| hdfs-site.sml | Configuration parameters for HDFS daemons – NameNode and Secondary NameNode and DataNode |
| hadoop-env.sh | Environment variables for Hadoop daemons |
| masters | List of nodes that run a Secondary NameNode |
| slaves | List of nodes that run TaskTracker and DataNode |
| log4j.properties | Logging properties for the Hadoop daemons |
| mapred-queue-acls.xml | Access control lists |

Table 10.1: Hadoop configuration files

and slave2). The /etc/hosts file is edited on all nodes and IP addresses and host names of all the nodes are added.

Hadoop control scripts use SSH for cluster-wide operations such as starting and stopping NameNode, DataNode, JobTracker, TaskTracker and other daemons on the nodes in the cluster. For the control scripts to work, all the nodes in the cluster must be able to connect to each other via a password-less SSH login. To enable this, public/private RSA key pair is generated on each node. The private key is stored in the file /.ssh/id_rsa and public key is stored in the file /.ssh/id_rsa.pub. The public SSH key of each node is copied to the /.ssh/authorized_keys file of every other node. This can be done by manually editing the /.ssh/authorized_keys file on each node or using the ssh-copy-id command. The final step to setup the networking is to save host key fingerprints of each node to the known_hosts file of every other node. This is done by connecting from each node to every other node by SSH.

### Configure Hadoop

With the Hadoop setup package unpacked on all nodes and networking of nodes setup, the next step is to configure the Hadoop cluster. Hadoop is configured using a number of configuration files listed in Table 10.1. Boxes 10.4, 10.5, 10.6 and 10.7 show the sample configuration settings for the Hadoop configuration files core-site.xml, mapred-site.xml, hdfs-site.xml, masters/slaves files respectively.

■ **Box 10.4: Sample configuration – core-site.xml**

```
<?xml version="1.0"?>
<configuration>
<property>
<name>fs.default.name</name>
<value>hdfs://master:54310</value>
</property>
</configuration>
```

■ Box 10.5:  Sample configuration hdfs-site.xml

```
<?xml version="1.0"?>
<configuration>
<property>
<name>dfs.replication</name>
<value>2</value>
</property>
</configuration>
```

■ Box 10.6:  Sample configuration mapred-site.xml

```
<?xml version="1.0"?>
<configuration>
<property>
<name>mapred.job.tracker</name>
<value>master:54311</value>
</property>
</configuration>
```

■ Box 10.7:  Sample configuration masters and slave files

```
$cd hadoop/conf/

#Open the masters file and add hostname of master node
$vim masters
#master

#Open the masters file and add hostname of slave nodes
$vim slaves
#slave1
#slave2
```

■ Box 10.8:  Starting and stopping Hadoop cluster

```
$cd hadoop-1.0.4
#Format NameNode
$bin/hadoop namenode -format

#Start HDFS daemons
$bin/start-dfs.sh

#Start MapReduce daemons
$bin/start-mapred.sh

#Check status of daemons
```

```
$jps

#Stopping Hadoop cluster
# bin/stop-mapred.sh
$bin/stop-dfs.sh
```

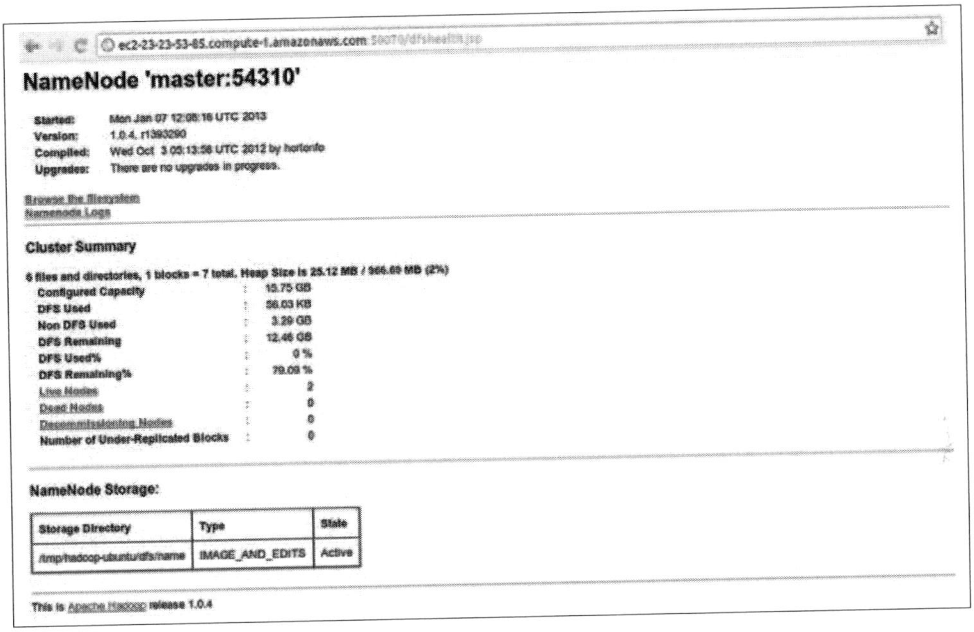

Figure 10.7: Hadoop NameNode status page

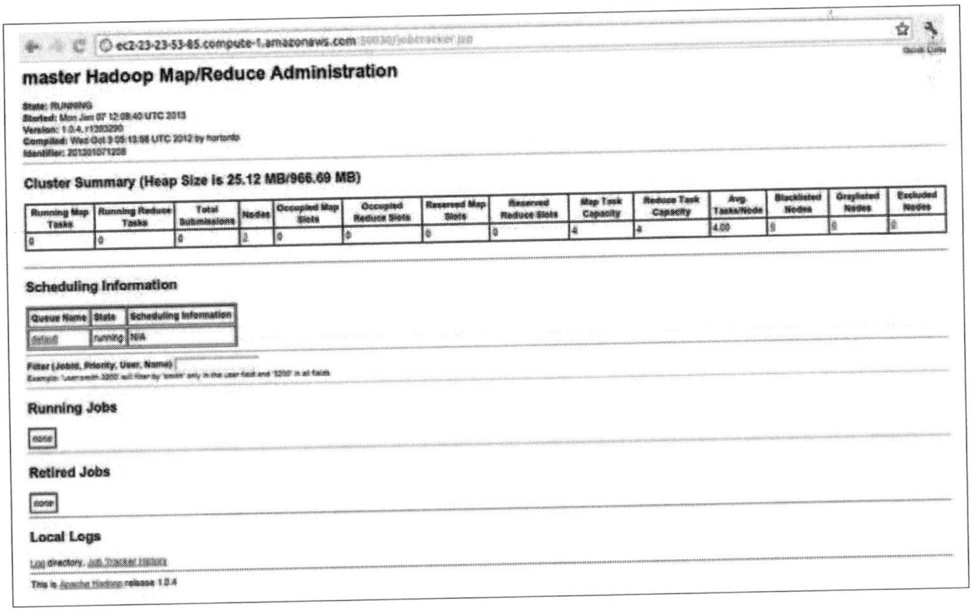

Figure 10.8: Hadoop MapReduce administration page

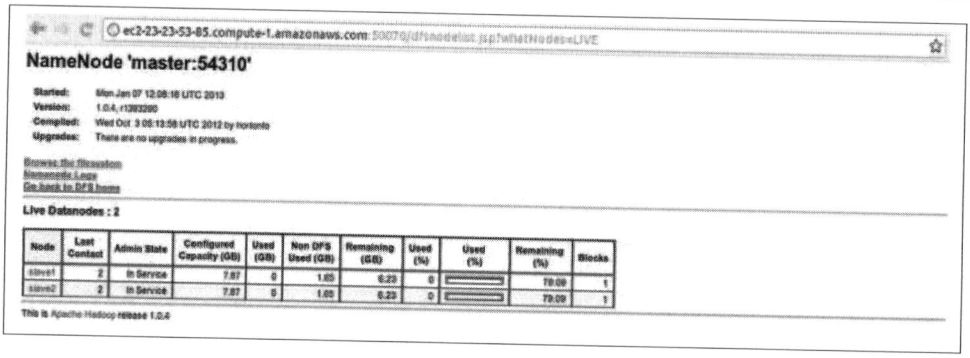

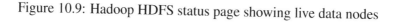

Figure 10.9: Hadoop HDFS status page showing live data nodes

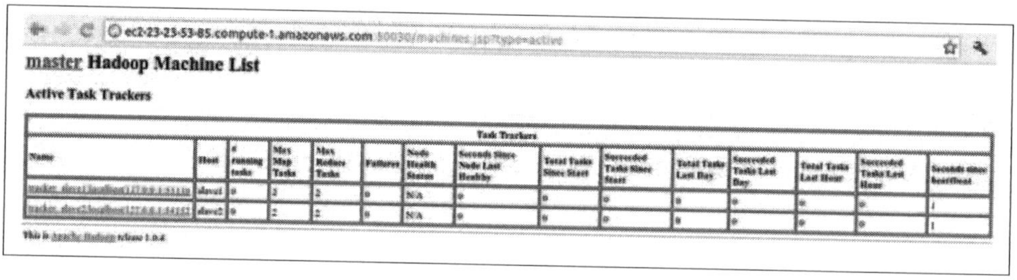

Figure 10.10: Hadoop MapReduce status page showing active TaskTrackers

## Starting and Stopping Hadoop Cluster

Having installed and configured Hadoop the next step is to start the Hadoop cluster. Box 10.8 lists the commands for starting and stopping the Hadoop cluster.

If the Hadoop cluster is correctly installed, configured and started, the status of the Hadoop daemons can be viewed using the administration web-pages for the daemons. Hadoop publishes the status of HDFS and MapReduce jobs to an internally running web server on the master node of the Hadoop cluster. The default addresses of the web UIs are as follows:
NameNode - http://<NameNodeHostName>:50070/
JobTracker - http://<JobTrackerHostName>:50030/
Figure 10.7 shows the Hadoop NameNode status page which provides information about NameNode uptime, the number of live, dead, and decommissioned nodes, host and port information, safe mode status, heap information, audit logs, garbage collection metrics, total load, file operations, and CPU usage.

Figure 10.8 shows the MapReduce administration page which provides host and port information, start time, tracker counts, heap information, scheduling information, current running jobs, retired jobs, job history log, service daemon logs, thread stacks, and a cluster utilization summary.

Figure 10.9 shows the status page of the live data nodes of the Hadoop cluster. The status page shows two live data nodes – slave1 and slave2.

Figure 10.10 shows the status page of the active TaskTrackers of the Hadoop cluster. The status page shows two active TaskTrackers that run on the slave1 and slave2 nodes of the cluster.

## 10.3   Using Hadoop MapReduce for Batch Data Analysis

Figure 10.11 shows a Hadoop MapReduce workflow for batch analysis of IoT data. Batch analysis is done to aggregate data (computing mean, maximum, minimum, etc.) on various timescales. The data collector retrieves the sensor data collected in the cloud database and creates a raw data file in a form suitable for processing by Hadoop. For the forest fire detection example, the raw data file consists of the raw sensor readings along with the timestamps as shown below:

"2014-04-29 10:15:32",37,44,31,6

:

"2014-04-30 10:15:32",84,58,23,2

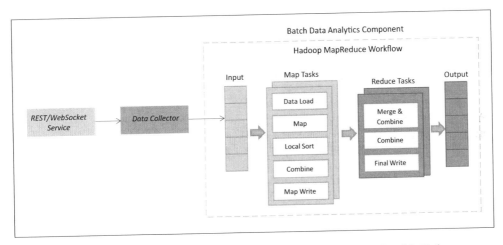

Figure 10.11: Using Hadoop MapReduce for batch analysis of IoT data

Box 10.9 shows the map program for the batch analysis of sensor data. The map program reads the data from standard input (*stdin*) and splits the data into timestamp and individual sensor readings. The map program emits key-value pairs where key is a portion of the timestamp (that depends on the timescale on which the data is to be aggregated) and the value is a comma separated string of sensor readings.

■ **Box 10.9: Map program - forestMapper.py**

```
#!/usr/bin/env python
import sys

#Calculates mean temperature, humidity, light and CO2
# Input data format:
#"2014-04-29 10:15:32",37,44,31,6
#Output:
#"2014-04-29 10:15 [48.75, 31.25, 29.0, 16.5]"

#Input comes from STDIN (standard input)
for line in sys.stdin:
    # remove leading and trailing whitespace
```

```
line = line.strip()
data = line.split(',')
l=len(data)

#For aggregation by minute
key=str(data[0][0:17])

value=data[1]+','+data[2]+','+data[3]+','+data[4]
print '%s \t%s' % (key, value)
```

Box 10.10 shows the reduce program for the batch analysis of sensor data. The key-value pairs emitted by the map program are shuffled to the reducer and grouped by the key. The reducer reads the key-value pairs grouped by the same key from standard input and computes the means of temperature, humidity, light and CO readings.

### ■ Box 10.10: Reduce program - forestReducer.py

```
#!/usr/bin/env python
from operator import itemgetter
import sys
import numpy as np

current_key = None
current_vals_list = []
word = None

#Input comes from STDIN
for line in sys.stdin:
  # remove leading and trailing whitespace
  line = line.strip()

#Parse the input from mapper
  key, values = line.split('\t', 1)
  list_of_values = values.split(',')

#Convert to list of strings to list of int
  list_of_values = [int(i) for i in list_of_values]

  if current_key == key:
    current_vals_list.append(list_of_values)
  else:
    if current_key:
      l = len(current_vals_list)+ 1
      b = np.array(current_vals_list)
      meanval = [np.mean(b[0:l,0]),np.mean(b[0:l,1]),
      np.mean(b[0:l,2]), np.mean(b[0:l,3])]
      print '%s%s' % (current_key, str(meanval))

    current_vals_list = []
    current_vals_list.append(list_of_values)
    current_key = key

#Output the last key if needed
```

```
if current_key == key:
  l = len(current_vals_list)+ 1
  b = np.array(current_vals_list)
  meanval = [np.mean(b[0:l,0]),np.mean(b[0:l,1]),
     np.mean(b[0:l,2]), np.mean(b[0:l,3])]
  print '%s%s' % (current_key, str(meanval))
```

■ **Box 10.11: Running MapReduce program on Hadoop cluster**

```
#Testing locally
$cat data.txt | python forestMapper.py | python forestReducer.py

#Running on Hadoop cluster
#Copy data file to HDFS sudo -u user1 bin/hadoop dfs -copyFromLocal
data.txt input

#Run MapReduce job bin/hadoop jar
contrib/streaming/hadoop-*streaming*.jar
-mapper forestMapper.py -reducer forestReducer.py
-file /home/ubuntu/hadoop/forestMapper.py
-file /home/ubuntu/hadoop/forestReducer.py
-input input/* -output output

#View output bin/hadoop dfs -ls output
bin/hadoop dfs -cat output/part-00000
```

### 10.3.1  Hadoop YARN

Hadoop YARN is the next generation architecture of Hadoop (version 2.x). In the YARN architecture, the original processing engine of Hadoop (MapReduce) has been separated from the resource management (which is now part of YARN) as shown in Figure 10.12. This makes YARN effectively an operating system for Hadoop that supports different processing engines on a Hadoop cluster such as MapReduce for batch processing, Apache Tez [131] for interactive queries, Apache Storm [134] for stream processing, etc.

Figure 10.13 shows the MapReduce job execution workflow for next generation Hadoop MapReduce framework (MR2). The next generation MapReduce architecture divides the two major functions of the JobTracker - resource management and job life-cycle management - into separate components – ResourceManager and ApplicationMaster. The key components of YARN are described as follows:

- **Resource Manager (RM):** RM manages the global assignment of compute resources to applications. RM consists of two main services:
  - Scheduler: Scheduler is a pluggable service that manages and enforces the resource scheduling policy in the cluster.
  - Applications Manager (AsM): AsM manages the running Application Masters in the cluster. AsM is responsible for starting application masters and for monitoring and restarting them on different nodes in case of failures.
- **Application Master (AM):** A per-application AM manages the application's life cycle. AM is responsible for negotiating resources from the RM and working with the

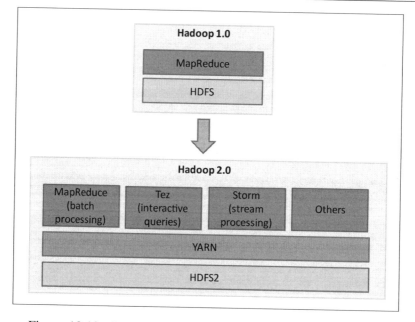

Figure 10.12: Comparison of Hadoop 1.x and 2.x architectures

NMs to execute and monitor the tasks.

- **Node Manager (NM):** A per-machine NM manages the user processes on that machine.
- **Containers:** Container is a bundle of resources allocated by RM (memory, CPU, network, etc.). A container is a conceptual entity that grants an application the privilege to use a certain amount of resources on a given machine to run a component task. Each node has an NM that spawns multiple containers based on the resource allocations made by the RM.

Figure 10.13 shows a YARN cluster with a Resource Manager node and three Node Manager nodes. There are as many Application Masters running as there are applications (jobs). Each application's AM manages the application tasks such as starting, monitoring and restarting tasks in case of failures. Each application has multiple tasks. Each task runs in a separate container. Containers in YARN architecture are similar to task slots in Hadoop MapReduce 1.x (MR1). However, unlike MR1 which differentiates between map and reduce slots, each container in YARN can be used for both map and reduce tasks. The resource allocation model in MR1 consists of a predefined number of map slots and reduce slots. This static allocation of slots results in low cluster utilization. The resource allocation model of YARN is more flexible with introduction of resource containers which improve cluster utilization.

To better understand the YARN job execution workflow let us analyze the interactions between the main components on YARN. Figure 10.14 shows the interactions between a Client and Resource Manager. Job execution begins with the submission of a new application request by the client to the RM. The RM then responds with a unique application ID and information about cluster resource capabilities that the client will need in requesting resources for running the application's AM. Using the information received from the RM, the client

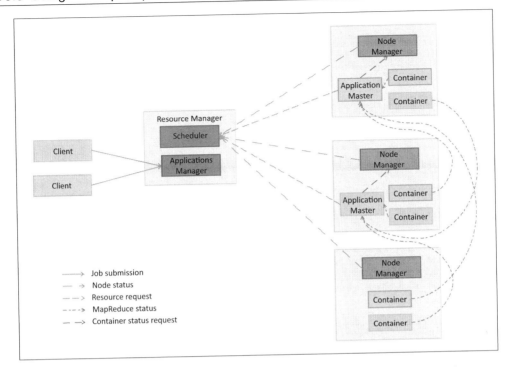

Figure 10.13: Hadoop MapReduce Next Generation (YARN) job execution

constructs and submits an Application Submission Context which contains information such as scheduler queue, priority and user information. The Application Submission Context also contains a Container Launch Context which contains the application's jar, job files, security tokens and any resource requirements. The client can query the RM for application reports. The client can also "force kill" an application by sending a request to the RM.

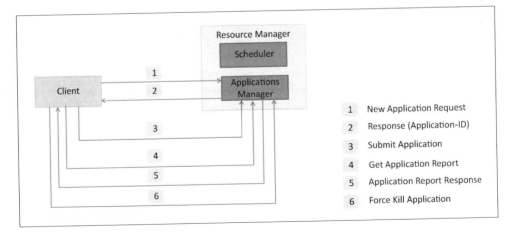

Figure 10.14: Client – Resource Manager interaction

Figure 10.15 shows the interactions between Resource Manager and Application Master. Upon receiving an application submission context from a client, the RM finds an available container meeting the resource requirements for running the AM for the application. On

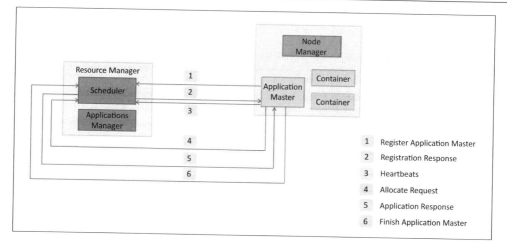

Figure 10.15: Resource Manager – Application Master interaction

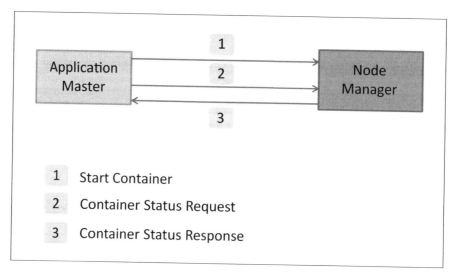

Figure 10.16: Application Master- Node Manager interaction

finding a suitable container, the RM contacts the NM for the container to start the AM process on its node. When the AM is launched it registers itself with the RM. The registration process consists of handshaking that conveys information such as the RPC port that the AM will be listening on, the tracking URL for monitoring the application's status and progress, etc. The registration response from the RM contains information for the AM that is used in calculating and requesting any resource requests for the application's individual tasks (such as minimum and maximum resource capabilities for the cluster). The AM relays heartbeat and progress information to the RM. The AM sends resource allocation requests to the RM that contains a list of requested containers, and may also contain a list of released containers by the AM. Upon receiving the allocation request, the scheduler component of the RM computes a list of containers that satisfy the request and sends back an allocation response. Upon receiving the resource list, the AM contacts the associated NMs for starting the containers. When the job finishes, the AM sends a Finish Application message to the RM.

Figure 10.16 shows the interactions between the an Application Master and Node Manager. Based on the resource list received from the RM, the AM requests the hosting NM for each container to start the container. The AM can request and receive a container status report from the Node Manager.

**Setting up Hadoop YARN cluster**

In the previous section you learned how to setup a Hadoop 1.x cluster. This section describes the steps involved in setting up Hadoop YARN cluster. The initial steps of setting up the hosts, installing Java and configuring the networking are the same as in Hadoop 1.x. The next step is to download the Hadoop YARN setup package and unpack it on all nodes as follows:

```
wget http://mirror.cc.columbia.edu/pub/software/apache/
hadoop/common/stable2/hadoop-2.2.0.tar.gz

tar -xzf hadoop-2.2.0.tar.gz
```

Add the following lines to the /.bashrc file:

```
export HADOOP_HOME=/home/ubuntu/hadoop-2.2.0
export HADOOP_MAPRED_HOME=$HADOOP_HOME
export HADOOP_COMMON_HOME=$HADOOP_HOME
export HADOOP_HDFS_HOME=$HADOOP_HOME
export YARN_HOME=$HADOOP_HOME
export HADOOP_CONF_DIR=$HADOOP_HOME/etc/hadoop
export YARN_CONF_DIR=$HADOOP_HOME/etc/hadoop
```

Add the following lines to the etc/hadoop/yarn-env.sh file:

```
export JAVA_HOME=/usr/lib/jvm/java-7-oracle/
export HADOOP_HOME=/home/ubuntu/hadoop-2.2.0
export HADOOP_MAPRED_HOME=$HADOOP_HOME
export HADOOP_COMMON_HOME=$HADOOP_HOME
export HADOOP_HDFS_HOME=$HADOOP_HOME
export YARN_HOME=$HADOOP_HOME
export HADOOP_CONF_DIR=$HADOOP_HOME/etc/hadoop
export YARN_CONF_DIR=$HADOOP_HOME/etc/hadoop
```

Next, create temporary folder in HADOOP_HOME:

```
$ mkdir -p $HADOOP_HOME/tmp
```

Next, add the slave hostnames to the etc/hadoop/slaves file on master machine:

```
slave1
slave2
slave3
```

The next step is to edit the Hadoop configuration files. Boxes 10.12, 10.13, 10.14 and 10.15 show the sample configuration settings for the Hadoop configuration files - core-site.xml, hdfs-site.xml, mapred-site.xml, yarn-site.xml files respectively.

■ **Box 10.12: Sample configuration – core-site.xml**

```xml
<?xml version="1.0" encoding="UTF-8"?>
<?xml-stylesheet type="text/xsl" href="configuration.xsl"?>
   <configuration>
   <property>
      <name>fs.default.name</name>
      <value>hdfs://master:9000</value>
   </property>
   <property>
      <name>hadoop.tmp.dir</name>
      <value>/home/ubuntu/hadoop-2.2.0/tmp</value>
   </property>
</configuration>
```

■ **Box 10.13: Sample configuration hdfs-site.xml**

```xml
<?xml version="1.0" encoding="UTF-8"?>
<?xml-stylesheet type="text/xsl" href="configuration.xsl"?>
   <configuration>
   <property>
      <name>dfs.replication</name>
      <value>2</value>
   </property>
   <property>
      <name>dfs.permissions</name>
      <value>false</value>
   </property>
</configuration>
```

■ **Box 10.14: Sample configuration mapred-site.xml**

```xml
<?xml version="1.0"?>
<configuration>
   <property>
      <name>mapreduce.framework.name</name>
      <value>yarn</value>
   </property>
</configuration>
```

■ **Box 10.15: Sample configuration yarn-site.xml**

```xml
<?xml version="1.0"?>
<configuration>
  <property>
     <name>yarn.nodemanager.aux-services</name>
     <value>mapreduce.shuffle</value>
  </property>
  <property>
     <name>yarn.nodemanager.aux-services.mapreduce.shuffle.class</name>
     <value>org.apache.hadoop.mapred.ShuffleHandler</value>
  </property>
  <property>
     <name>yarn.resourcemanager.resource-tracker.address</name>
     <value>master:8025</value>
  </property>
  <property>
     <name>yarn.resourcemanager.scheduler.address</name>
     <value>master:8030</value>
  </property>
  <property>
     <name>yarn.resourcemanager.address</name>
     <value>master:8040</value>
  </property>
</configuration>
```

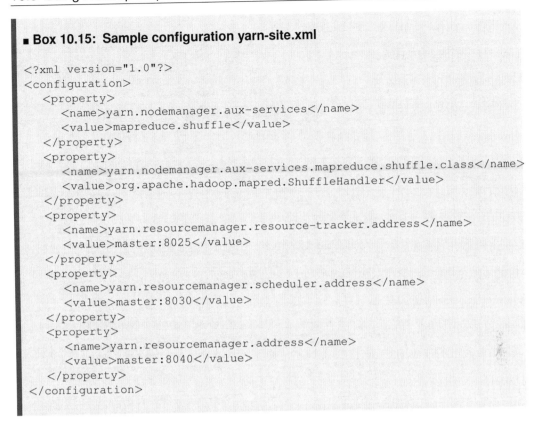

Figure 10.17: Screenshot of Hadoop Namenode dashboard

Box 10.16 shows the commands for starting/stopping Hadoop YARN cluster.

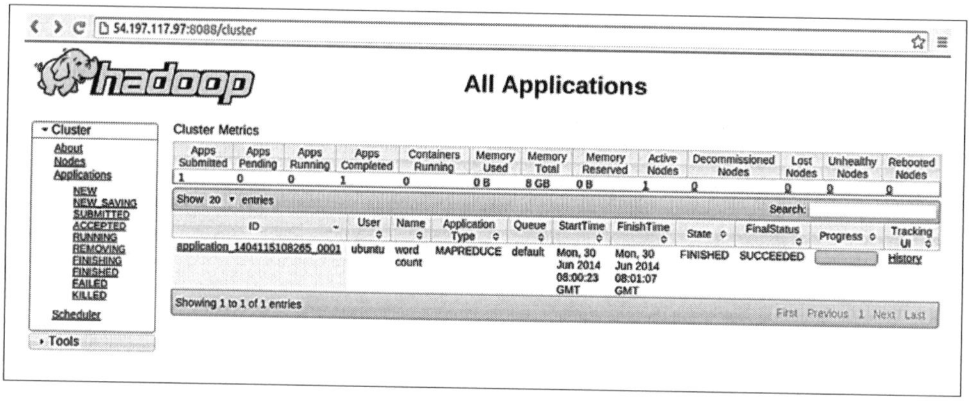

Figure 10.18: Screenshot of YARN cluster dashboard

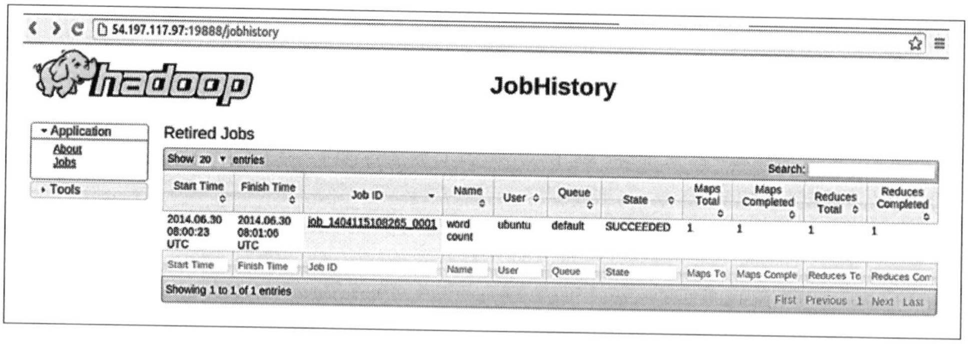

Figure 10.19: Screenshot of job history server dashboard

■ **Box 10.16: Starting and stopping Hadoop YARN cluster**

```
$cd hadoop-1.0.4
#Format NameNode
bin/hadoop namenode -format

sbin/hadoop-daemon.sh start namenode
sbin/hadoop-daemons.sh start datanode
sbin/yarn-daemon.sh start resourcemanager
sbin/yarn-daemons.sh start nodemanager
sbin/mr-jobhistory-daemon.sh start historyserver


sbin/mr-jobhistory-daemon.sh stop historyserver
sbin/yarn-daemons.sh stop nodemanager
sbin/yarn-daemon.sh stop resourcemanager
sbin/hadoop-daemons.sh stop datanode
sbin/hadoop-daemon.sh stop namenode
```

Figures 10.17, 10.18 and 10.19 show the screenshots of the Hadoop Namenode, YARN cluster and job history server dashboards.

## 10.4 Apache Oozie

In the previous section you learned about the Hadoop framework and how the MapReduce jobs can be used for analyzing IoT data. Many IoT applications require more than one MapReduce job to be chained to perform data analysis. This can be accomplished using Apache Oozie system. Oozie is a workflow scheduler system that allows managing Hadoop jobs. With Oozie, you can create workflows which are a collection of actions (such as MapReduce jobs) arranged as Direct Acyclic Graphs (DAG). Control dependencies exists between the actions in a workflow. Thus an action is executed only when the preceding action is completed. An Oozie workflow specifies a sequence of actions that need to be executed using an XML-based Process Definition Language called hPDL. Oozie supports various types of actions such as Hadoop MapReduce, Hadoop file system, Pig, Java, Email , Shell , Hive, Sqoop, SSH and custom actions.

### 10.4.1 Setting up Oozie

Oozie requires a Hadoop installation and can be setup up on either a single node or a cluster of two or more nodes. Before setting up Hadoop create a new user and group as follows:

```
■ sudo addgroup hadoop
sudo adduser -ingroup hadoop hduser
sudo adduser hduser sudo
```

Next, follow the steps for setting up Hadoop described in the previous section. After setting up Hadoop install the packages required for setting up Oozie as follows:

```
■ sudo apt-get install maven
sudo apt-get install zip
sudo apt-get install unzip
```

Next, download and build Oozie using the following commands:

```
■ wget http://supergsego.com/apache/oozie/3.3.2/oozie-3.3.2.tar.gz
tar xvzf oozie-3.3.2.tar.gz
cd oozie-3.3.2/bin
./mkdistro.sh -DskipTests
```

Create a new directory named 'oozie' and copy the built binaries. Also copy the jar files from 'hadooplibs' directory to the libext directory as follows:

```
■ cd /home/hduser
mkdir oozie
cp -R oozie-3.3.2/distro/target/oozie-3.3.2-distro/oozie-3.3.2/* oozie
cd /home/hduser/oozie
mkdir libext

cp /home/hduser/oozie-3.3.2/hadooplibs/hadoop-1/target/hadooplibs/
hadooplib-1.1.1.oozie-3.3.2/* /home/hduser/oozie/libext/
```

Download Ext2Js to the 'libext' directory. This is required for the Oozie web console:

```
■ cd /home/hduser/oozie/libext/
wget http://extjs.com/deploy/ext-2.2.zip
```

Prepare the Oozie WAR file as follows:

```
■ #Prepare the WAR file
./bin/oozie-setup.sh prepare-war
```

Next, create sharelib on HDFS as follows:

```
■ #Create sharelib on HDFS
./bin/oozie-setup.sh sharelib create -fs hdfs://master:54310
```

Next, create the OozieDB as follows:

```
■ ./bin/ooziedb.sh create -sqlfile oozie.sql -run
```

Finally use the following command to start Oozie server:

```
■ #Start Oozie
./bin/oozied.sh start
```

The status of Oozie can be checked from command line or the web console as follows:

```
■ #To check the status of Oozie from command line:
./bin/oozie admin -oozie http://master:11000/oozie -status
#Oozie Web Console URL:
http://localhost:11000/oozie
```

To setup the Oozie client, copy the client tar file to the 'oozie-client' and add the path in .bashrc file as follows:

```
■ #Oozie Client Setup cd /home/hduser/
cp /home/hduser/oozie/oozie-client-3.3.2.tar.gz /home/hduser/
tar xvzf oozie-client-3.3.2.tar.gz

#Add to PATH in .bashrc
sudo vim .bashrc
export PATH=$PATH:/home/hduser/oozie-client-3.3.2/bin
```

## 10.4.2   Oozie Workflows for IoT Data Analysis

Let us look at an example of analyzing machine diagnosis data. Assuming that the data received from a machine has the following structure (including time stamp and the status/error code):

```
■ #timestamp, status/error "2014-07-01 20:03:18",115
"2014-07-01 20:04:15",106
```

```
:
"2014-07-01 20:10:15",110
```

The goal of the analysis job is to find the counts of each status/error code and produce an output with a structure as shown below:

```
■ #status/error, count 111, 6
112, 7
113, 12
```

Figure 10.20 shows a representation of the Oozie workflow comprising of Hadoop streaming MapReduce job action and Email actions that notify the success or failure of the job.

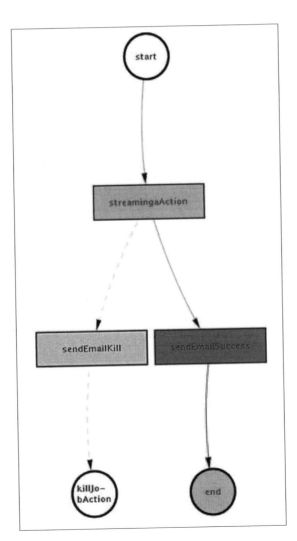

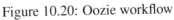
Figure 10.20: Oozie workflow

Boxes 10.17 and 10.18 show the map and reduce programs which are executed in the workflow. The map program parses the status/error code from each line in the input and emits key-value pairs where key is the status/error code and value is 1. The reduce program receives the key-value pairs emitted by the map program aggregated by the same key. For each key, the reduce program calculates the count and emits key-value pairs where key is the status/error code and the value is the count.

■ **Box 10.17: Map program for computing counts of machine status/error codes**

```python
#!/usr/bin/env python
import sys

#Data format
#"2014-07-01 20:03:18",115

# input comes from STDIN (standard input)
for line in sys.stdin:
    # remove leading and trailing whitespace
    line = line.strip()
    # split the line into words
    data = line.split(',')
    print '%s%s' % (data[1], 1)
```

■ **Box 10.18: Reduce program for computing counts of machine status/error codes**

```python
#!/usr/bin/env python
from operator import itemgetter
import sys

current_key = None
current_count = 0
key = None

# input comes from STDIN
for line in sys.stdin:
    line = line.strip()

    key, count = line.split(',', 1)
    count = int(count)

    if current_key == key:
        current_count += count
    else:
        if current_key:
            unpackedKey = current_key.split(',')
            print '%s%s' % (current_key, current_count)
        current_count = count
        current_key = key

if current_key == key:
```

```
unpackedKey = current_key.split(',')
print '%s%s' % (current_key, current_count)
```

Box 10.20 shows the specification for the Oozie workflow shown in Figure 10.20. Oozie workflow has been parameterized with variables within the workflow definition. The values of these variables are provided in the job properties file shown in Box 10.19

■ **Box 10.19: Job properties file for Oozie workflow**

```
nameNode=hdfs://master:54310
jobTracker=master:54311
queueName=default

oozie.libpath=${nameNode}/user/hduser/share/lib
oozie.use.system.libpath=true
oozie.wf.rerun.failnodes=true

oozieProjectRoot=${nameNode}/user/hduser/oozieProject
appPath=${oozieProjectRoot}/pythonApplication
oozie.wf.application.path=${appPath}
oozieLibPath=${oozie.libpath}

inputDir=${oozieProjectRoot}/pythonApplication/data/
outputDir=${appPath}/output
```

■ **Box 10.20: Oozie workflow for computing counts of machine status/error codes**

```
<workflow-app name="PythonOozieApp" xmlns="uri:oozie:workflow:0.1">
 <start to="streamingaAction"/>
  <action name="streamingaAction">
<map-reduce>
    <job-tracker>${jobTracker}</job-tracker>
    <name-node>${nameNode}</name-node>
    <prepare>
     <delete path="${outputDir}"/>
    </prepare>
    <streaming>
     <mapper>python Mapper.py</mapper>
     <reducer>python Reducer.py</reducer>
    </streaming>
    <configuration>
<property>
<name>oozie.libpath</name>
    <value>${oozieLibPath}/mapreduce-streaming</value>
   </property>
     <property>
      <name>mapred.input.dir</name>
      <value>${inputDir}</value>
     </property>
     <property>
      <name>mapred.output.dir</name>
```

```
            <value>${outputDir}</value>
         </property>
   <property>
            <name>mapred.reduce.tasks</name>
            <value>1</value>
         </property>
        </configuration>
   <file>${appPath}/Mapper.py#Mapper.py</file>
   <file>${appPath}/Reducer.py#Reducer.py</file>
     </map-reduce>
  <ok to="sendEmailSuccess"/>
  <error to="sendEmailKill"/>
     </action>

  <action name="sendEmailSuccess">
     <email xmlns="uri:oozie:email-action:0.1">
        <to>${emailToAddress}</to>
        <subject>Status of workflow ${wf:id()}</subject>
        <body>The workflow ${wf:id()} completed successfully</body>
     </email>
     <ok to="end"/>
     <error to="end"/>
    </action>
   <action name="sendEmailKill">
     <email xmlns="uri:oozie:email-action:0.1">
      <to>${emailToAddress}</to>
      <subject>Status of workflow ${wf:id()}</subject>
      <body>The workflow ${wf:id()} had issues and was killed.
The error message is:  ${wf:errorMessage(wf:lastErrorNode())}</body>
     </email>
     <ok to="killJobAction"/>
     <error to="killJobAction"/>
    </action>

   <kill name="killJobAction">
     <message>"Killed job due to error:
${wf:errorMessage(wf:lastErrorNode())}"</message>
    </kill>
   <end name="end" />
  </workflow-app>
```

Let us now look at a more complicated workflow which has two MapReduce jobs. Extending the example described earlier in this section, let us say we want to find the status/error code with the maximum count. The MapReduce job in the earlier workflow computed the counts for each status/error code. A second MapReduce job, which consumes the output of the first MapReduce job computes the maximum count. The map and reduce programs for the second MapReduce job are shown in Boxes 10.21 and 10.22.

Figure 10.21 shows a DAG representation of the Oozie workflow for computing machine status/error code with maximum count. The specification of the workflow is shown in Box 10.23.

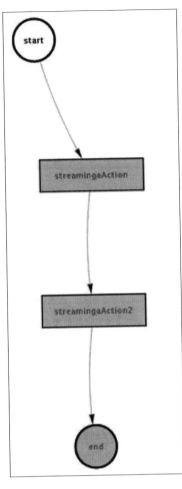

Figure 10.21: Oozie workflow for computing machine status/error code with maximum count

■ **Box 10.21: Map program for computing machine status/error code with maximum count**

```python
#!/usr/bin/env python
import sys

#Data format
#"2014-07-01 20:03:18",115

# input comes from STDIN (standard input)
for line in sys.stdin:
    # remove leading and trailing whitespace
    line = line.strip()
    # split the line into words
    data = line.split(',')

    #For aggregation by minute
    print '%s%s' % (data[0], data[1])
```

**■ Box 10.22: Reduce program for computing machine status/error code with maximum count**

```python
#!/usr/bin/env python
from operator import itemgetter
import sys

current_key = None
current_count = 0
key = None
maxcount=0
maxcountkey=None

# input comes from STDIN
for line in sys.stdin:
  # remove leading and trailing whitespace
  line = line.strip()

  # parse the input we got from mapper.py
  key, count = line.split('	', 1)

  # convert count to int
  count = int(count)

  if count>maxcount:
    maxcount=count
    maxcountkey=key
    print '%s%s' % (maxcountkey, maxcount)
```

**■ Box 10.23: Oozie workflow for computing machine status/error code with maximum count**

```xml
<workflow-app name="PythonOozieApp" xmlns="uri:oozie:workflow:0.1">
 <start to="streamingaAction"/>
  <action name="streamingaAction">
<map-reduce>
    <job-tracker>${jobTracker}</job-tracker>
    <name-node>${nameNode}</name-node>
    <prepare>
     <delete path="${outputDir}"/>
    </prepare>
    <streaming>
     <mapper>python Mapper.py</mapper>
     <reducer>python Reducer.py</reducer>
    </streaming>
    <configuration>
<property>
<name>oozie.libpath</name>
    <value>${oozieLibPath}/mapreduce-streaming</value>
   </property>
    <property>
```

```
            <name>mapred.input.dir</name>
            <value>${inputDir}</value>
        </property>
        <property>
            <name>mapred.output.dir</name>
            <value>${outputDir}</value>
        </property>
<property>
            <name>mapred.reduce.tasks</name>
            <value>1</value>
        </property>
    </configuration>
<file>${appPath}/Mapper.py#Mapper.py</file>
<file>${appPath}/Reducer.py#Reducer.py</file>
  </map-reduce>
    <ok to="streamingaAction2"/>
    <error to="killJobAction"/>
  </action>

<action name="streamingaAction2">
<map-reduce>
    <job-tracker>${jobTracker}</job-tracker>
    <name-node>${nameNode}</name-node>
    <streaming>
     <mapper>python Mapper1.py</mapper>
     <reducer>python Reducer1.py</reducer>
    </streaming>
    <configuration>
<property>
<name>oozie.libpath</name>
    <value>${oozieLibPath}/mapreduce-streaming</value>
  </property>
        <property>
         <name>mapred.input.dir</name>
         <value>${outputDir}</value>
        </property>
        <property>
         <name>mapred.output.dir</name>
         <value>${outputDir}/output2</value>
        </property>
<property>
        <name>mapred.reduce.tasks</name>
        <value>1</value>
        </property>
    </configuration>
<file>${appPath}/Mapper1.py#Mapper1.py</file>
<file>${appPath}/Reducer1.py#Reducer1.py</file>
  </map-reduce>
    <ok to="end"/>
    <error to="killJobAction"/>
  </action>

  <kill name="killJobAction">
    <message>"Killed job due to error:
```

```
${wf:errorMessage(wf:lastErrorNode())}"</message>
  </kill>
  <end name="end" />
</workflow-app>
```

Figure 10.22 shows a screenshot of the Oozie web console which can be used to monitor the status of Oozie workflows.

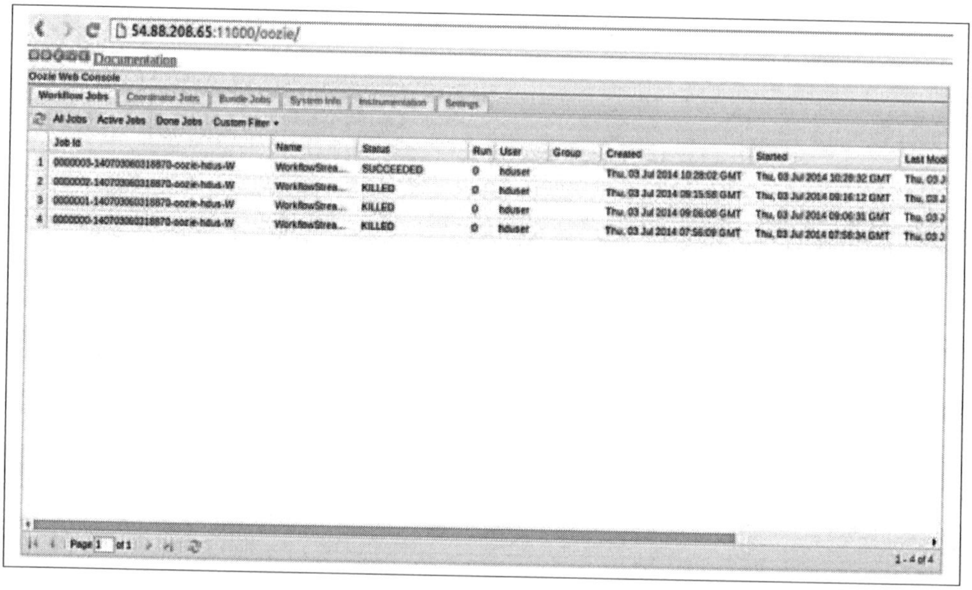

Figure 10.22: Screenshot of Oozie web console

## 10.5   Apache Spark

Apache Spark is yet another open source cluster computing framework for data analytics [121]. However, Spark supports in-memory cluster computing and promises to be faster than Hadoop. Spark supports various high-level tools for data analysis such as Spark Streaming for streaming jobs, Spark SQL for analysis of structured data, MLlib machine learning library for Spark, GraphX for graph processing and Shark (Hive on Spark). Spark allows real-time, batch and interactive queries and provides APIs for Scala, Java and Python languages.

Figure 10.24 shows the components of a Spark cluster. Each Spark application consists of a driver program and is coordinated by a *SparkContext* object. Spark supports various cluster managers including Spark's standalone cluster manager, Apache Mesos and Hadoop YARN. The cluster manager allocates resources for applications on the worker nodes. The executors which are allocated on the worker nodes run the application code as multiple tasks. Applications are isolated from each other and run within their own executor processes on the worker nodes. Spark provides data abstraction called resilient distributed dataset (RDD) which is a collection of elements partitioned across the nodes of the cluster. The RDD elements can be operated on in parallel in the cluster. RDDs support two types of operations - transformations and actions. Transformations are used to create a new dataset from an existing one. Actions return a value to the driver program after running a computation on the

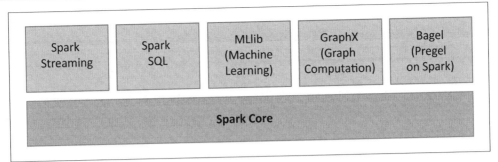

Figure 10.23: Spark tools

dataset. Spark API allows chaining together transformations and actions.

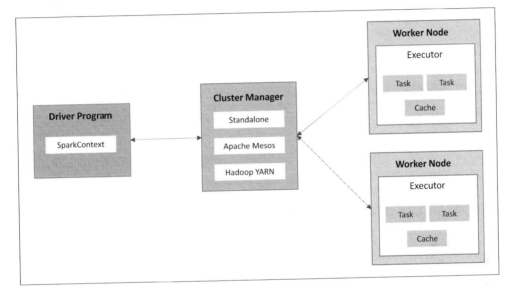

Figure 10.24: Components of a Spark cluster

Spark comes with a spark-ec2 script (in the spark/ec2 directory) which makes it easy to setup Spark cluster on Amazon EC2. With spark-ec2 script you can easily launch, manage and shutdown Spark cluster on Amazon EC2. To start a Spark cluster use the following command:

```
./spark-ec2 -k <keypair> -i <key-file> -s <num-slaves>
launch <cluster-name> -instance-type=<INSTANCE_TYPE>
```

Spark cluster setup on EC2 is configured to use HDFS as its default filesystem. To analyze contents of a file, the file should be first copied to HDFS using the following command:

```
bin/hadoop fs -put file.txt file.txt
```

Spark supports a shell mode with which you can interactively run commands for analyzing data. To launch the Spark Python shell, run the following command:

```
■ ./bin/pyspark
```

When you launch a PySpark shell, a SparkContext is created in the variable called sc. The following commands show how to load a text file and count the number of lines from the PySpark shell.

```
■ textFile = sc.textFile("file.txt")
textFile.count()
```

Let us now look at a standalone Spark application that computes word counts in a file. Box 10.24 shows a Python program for computing word count. The program uses the map and reduce functions. The *flatMap* and *map* transformation take as input a function which is applied to each element of the dataset. While the *flatMap* function can map each input item to zero or more output items, the *map* function maps each input item to another item. The transformations take as input, functions which are applied to the data elements. The input functions can be in the form of Python lambda expressions or local functions. In the word count example *flatMap* takes as input a lambda expression that splits each line of the file into words. The *map* transformation outputs key value pairs where key is a word and value is 1. The *reduceByKey* transformation aggregates values of each key using the function specified (*add* function in this example). Finally the *collect* action is used to return all the elements of the result as an array.

**■ Box 10.24: Apache Spark Python program for computing word count**

```
from operator import add
from pyspark import SparkContext

sc = SparkContext(appName="WordCountApp")
lines = sc.textFile("file.txt")
counts = lines.flatMap(lambda x:
x.split(' ')).map(lambda x:  (x, 1)).reduceByKey(add)

output = counts.collect()

for (word, count) in output:
   print "%s:  %i" % (word, count)
```

Let us look at another Spark application for batch analysis of data. Taking the example of analysis of forest fire detection sensor data described in the previous section, let us look at a Spark application that aggregates the time-stamped sensor data and finds hourly maximum values for temperature, humidity, light and $CO_2$. The Python code for the Spark application is shown in Box 10.25. The sensor data is loaded as a text file. Each line of the text file contains time-stamped sensor data. The lines are first split by applying the *map* transformation to access the individual sensor readings. In the next step, a *map* transformation is applied which outputs key-value pairs where key is a timestamp (excluding the minutes and seconds part) and value is a sensor reading. Finally the *reduceByKey* transformation is applied to find the maximum sensor reading.

■ Box 10.25: Apache Spark Python program for computing maximum values for sensor readings

```
#Data format:
#"2014-06-25 10:47:44",26,36,2860,274
from pyspark import SparkContext

sc = SparkContext(appName="MyApp")
textFile = sc.textFile("data.txt")

splitlines = textFile.map(lambda line:  line.split(','))

maxtemp = splitlines.map(lambda line:
(line[0][0:17],int(line[1]))).reduceByKey(lambda a, b:
a if (a > b) else b).collect()

maxhumdity = splitlines.map(lambda line:
(line[0][0:17],int(line[2]))).reduceByKey(lambda a, b:
a if (a > b) else b).collect()

maxlight = splitlines.map(lambda line:
(line[0][0:17],int(line[3]))).reduceByKey(lambda a, b:
a if (a > b) else b).collect()

maxco = splitlines.map(lambda line:
(line[0][0:17],int(line[4]))).reduceByKey(lambda a, b:
a if (a > b) else b).collect()

print "Maximum temperature"
for item in maxtemp:
   print item

print "Maximum humidity"
for item in maxhumdity:
   print item

print "Maximum light"
for item in maxlight:
   print item

print "Maximum CO2"
for item in maxco:
   print item
```

Box 10.26 shows an example of using Spark for data filtering. This example uses the sensor data from forest fire detection IoT system.

■ Box 10.26: Apache Spark Python program for filtering sensor readings

```
#Data format:
#"2014-06-25 10:47:44",26,36,2860,274

from pyspark import SparkContext
```

```
sc = SparkContext(appName="App")
textFile = sc.textFile("data.txt")

splitlines = textFile.map(lambda line:  line.split(','))

splitlines.filter(lambda line:  int(line[1])>10).collect()

splitlines.filter(lambda line:
int(line[1])>20 and int(line[2])>20 and
int(line[3])>6000 and int(line[4])>200).collect()

#Alternative implementation
def filterfunc(line):
   if int(line[1])>20 and int(line[2])>20
and int(line[3])>6000 and int(line[4])>200:
      return line
   else:
      return "

splitlines.filter(filterfunc).collect()
```

Spark includes a machine learning library, MLlib, which includes implementations of machine learning algorithms for classification, regression, clustering, collaborative filtering and dimensionality reduction. Let us look at examples of using MLlib for clustering and classifying data.

Box 10.27 shows an example of clustering data with k-means clustering algorithm. In this example, the data is loaded from a text file and then parsed using the *parseVector* function. Next, the KMeans object is used to cluster the data into two clusters.

■ **Box 10.27: Apache Spark Python program for clustering data**

```
#Data format:
#26.0,36.0,2860.0,274.0

import numpy as np
from pyspark import SparkContext
from pyspark.mllib.clustering import KMeans

#Specify number of clusters
k = 2

#Specify input data file
inputfile="data.txt"

def parseVector(line):
   return np.array([float(x) for x in line.split(',')])

sc = SparkContext(appName="KMeans")
lines = sc.textFile(inputfile)
```

```
data = lines.map(parseVector)

model = KMeans.train(data, k)
print "Final centers:  " + str(model.clusterCenters)
```

Box 10.28 shows an example of classifying data with Naive Bayes classification algorithm. The training data in this example consists of labeled points where value in the first column is the label. The *parsePoint* function parses the data and creates Spark *LabeledPoint* objects. The labeled points are passed to the *NaiveBayes* object for training a model. Finally, the classification is done by passing the test data (as labeled point) to the trained model.

■ **Box 10.28: Apache Spark Python program for classifying data**

```
#Data format:
#1.0,26.0,36.0,2860.0,274.0

import numpy as np
from pyspark import SparkContext
from pyspark.mllib.regression import LabeledPoint
from pyspark.mllib.classification import NaiveBayes


# Parse a line of text into an MLlib LabeledPoint object
def parsePoint(line):
    values = [float(s) for s in line.split(',')]
    return LabeledPoint(values[0], values[1:])


sc = SparkContext(appName="App")
points = sc.textFile("nbdata.txt").map(parsePoint)

# Train a naive Bayes model.
model = NaiveBayes.train(points, 1.0)

# Make prediction.
prediction = model.predict([20.0, 40.0, 1000.0, 300.0])
print "Predition is:  " + str(prediction)
```

## 10.6   Apache Storm

Apache Storm is a framework for distributed and fault-tolerant real-time computation [134]. Storm can be used for real-time processing of streams of data. Figure 10.25 shows the components of a Storm cluster. A Storm cluster comprises of Nimbus, Supervisor and Zookeeper. Nimbus is similar to Hadoop's JobTracker and is responsible for distributing code around the cluster, launching works across the cluster and monitoring computation. A Storm cluster has one or more Supervisor nodes on which the worker processes run. Supervisor nodes communicate with Nimbus through Zookeeper. Nimbus sends signals to Supervisor to start or stop workers. Zookeeper is a high performance distributed coordination service for maintaining configuration information, naming, providing distributed synchronization and group services [135]. Zookeeper is required for coordination of the Storm cluster.

A computation job on the Storm cluster is called a "topology" which is a graph of computation. A Storm topology comprises of a number of worker processes that are distributed on the cluster. Each worker process runs a subset of the topology. A topology is composed of Spouts and Bolts. Spout is a source of streams (sequence of tuples), for example, a sensor data stream. The streams emitted by the Spouts are processed by the Bolts. Bolts subscribe to Spouts, consume the streams, process them and emit new streams. A topology can consists of multiple Spouts and Bolts. Figure 10.26 shows a Storm topology with one Spout and three Bolts. Bolts 1 and 2 subscribe to the Spout and consume the streams emitted by the Spout. The outputs of Bolts 1 and 2 are consumed by Bolt-3.

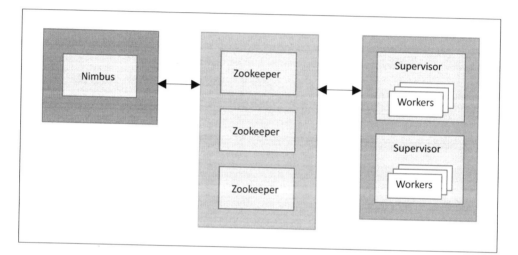

Figure 10.25: Components of a Storm cluster

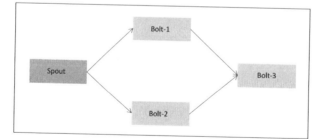

Figure 10.26: Example of a Storm topology

## 10.6.1 Setting up a Storm Cluster

In this section you will learn how to setup a Storm cluster. The cluster setup explained in this section comprises of three Ubuntu Linux instances for Nimbus, Zookeeper and Supervisor. Before starting with the installation, make sure you have three instances running and they can connect securely to each other with SSH. Change the hostnames of the instances to "nimbus", "zookeeper" and "supervisor".

On the instance with hostname "zookeeper", setup Zookeeper by following the instructions in Box 10.29.

### ■ Box 10.29: Zookeeper installation instructions

```
#Create file:
sudo vim /etc/apt/sources.list.d/cloudera.list

#Add this to file:
deb [arch=amd64] http://archive.cloudera.com/cdh4/ubuntu/precise/amd64/
cdh precise-cdh4 contrib
deb-src http://archive.cloudera.com/cdh4/ubuntu/precise/amd64/cdh
precise-cdh4 contrib

sudo apt-get -q -y update

sudo apt-get install zookeeper zookeeper-server

cd /usr/lib/zookeeper/bin/
sudo ./zkServer.sh start

#Check if zookeeper is working:
echo ruok | nc zookeeper 2181
echo stat | nc zookeeper 2181
```

On the instances with hostnames "nimbus" and "supervisor", install Storm by following the instructions shown in Box 10.30.

### ■ Box 10.30: Apache Storm installation instructions

```
#INSTALL REQUIRED PACKAGES
sudo apt-get -q -y install build-essential
sudo apt-get -q -y install uuid-dev
sudo apt-get -q -y install git
sudo apt-get -q -y install pkg-config libtool autoconf automake
sudo apt-get -q -y install unzip

#-------------
#ZEROMQ INSTALLATION
wget http://download.zeromq.org/zeromq-2.1.7.tar.gz
tar -xzf zeromq-2.1.7.tar.gz
cd zeromq-2.1.7
./configure
make
sudo make install

#-----------
#JZMQ INSTALLATION

export JAVA_HOME=/usr/lib/jvm/java-7-oracle

git clone https://github.com/nathanmarz/jzmq.git
```

```
cd jzmq
cd src

touch classdist_noinst.stamp
CLASSPATH=.:./.:$CLASSPATH javac -d .  org/zeromq/ZMQ.java
org/zeromq/ZMQException.java org/zeromq/ZMQQueue.java
org/zeromq/ZMQForwarder.java org/zeromq/ZMQStreamer.java

cd ..
./autogen.sh
./configure
make
sudo make install

#------------
#STORM INSTALLATION

wget https://dl.dropbox.com/u/133901206/storm-0.8.2.zip
unzip storm-0.8.2.zip
sudo ln -s storm-0.8.2 storm

vim .bashrc
PATH=$PATH:"/home/ubuntu/storm"
source .bashrc
```

After installing Storm, edit the configuration file and enter the IP addresses of the Nimbus and Zookeeper nodes as shown in Box 10.31. You can then launch Nimbus and Storm UI. The Storm UI can be viewed in the broswer at the address http://<IP-address-of-Nimubs>:8080. Figures 10.27 and 10.28 show screenshots of the Storm UI. The commands for submitting topologies to Storm are shown in Box 10.31.

### ■ Box 10.31: Intructions for configuring and running Storm and submitting topologies to Storm

```
#Set storm/config/storm.yaml as follows:
#---------
storm.zookeeper.servers:
- "192.168.1.20" #IP Address of Zookeeper node

nimbus.host:  "nimbus"
- "192.168.1.21" #IP Address of Nimbus node

storm.local.dir:  "/home/ubuntu/stormlocal"
#---------

#Create storm local dir:
cd /home/ubuntu
mkdir stormlocal

#Launch nimbus:
cd storm
bin/storm nimbus
```

```
#Launch UI:
bin/storm ui

#Submit topology:
bin/storm jar storm-starter-0.0.1-SNAPSHOT.jar storm.starter.MyTopology
my-topology

#Kill topology
storm -kill my-topology
```

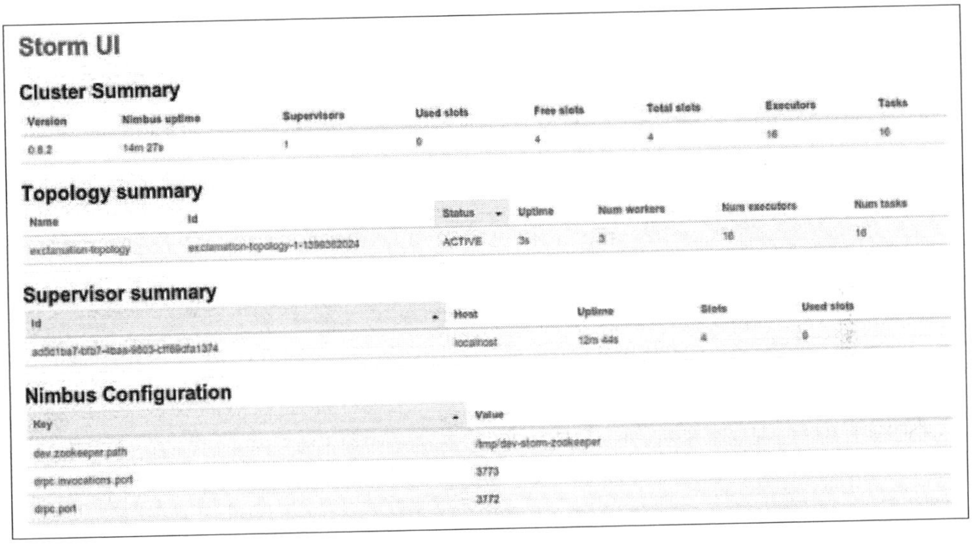

Figure 10.27: Screenshot of Storm UI showing cluster, topology and supervisor summary

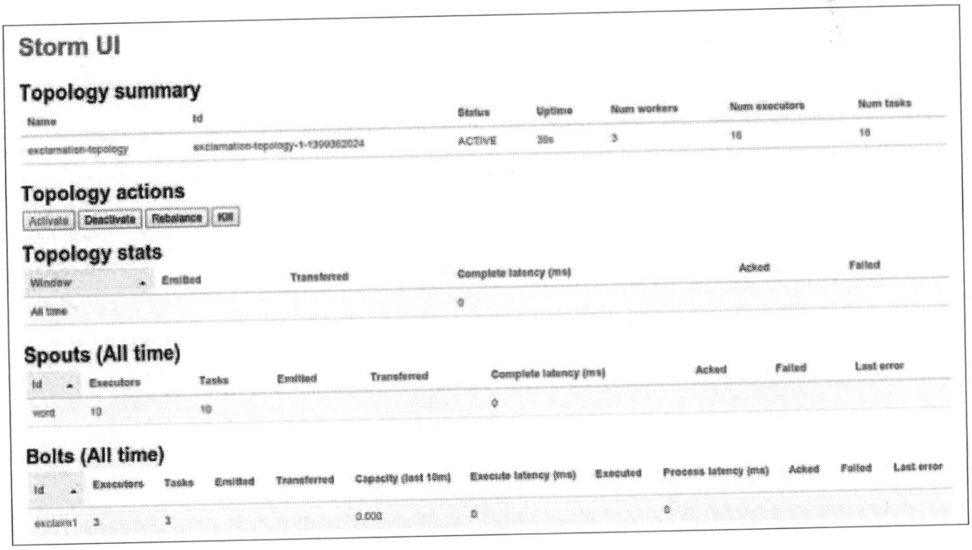

Figure 10.28: Screenshot of Storm UI showing details of a topology

## 10.7   Using Apache Storm for Real-time Data Analysis

Apache Storm can be used for real-time analysis of data. Figure 10.29 shows workflow for real-time analysis of sensor data using Storm.

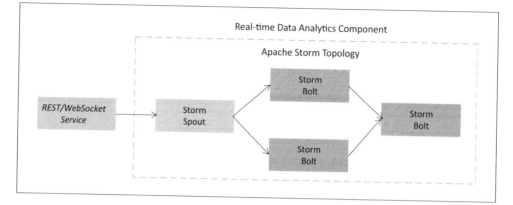

Figure 10.29: Using Apache Storm for real-time analysis of IoT data

### 10.7.1   REST-based approach

This section describes an example of real-time sensor data analysis for forest fire detection using a REST-based approach. The deployment design for the WebSocket implementation is shown in Figure 10.30(a).

The Storm topology used in this example comprises of one Spout and one Bolt. The Spout retrieves the sensor data from Xively cloud and the emits streams of sensor readings. The Bolt processes the data and makes the predictions using a Decision Tree based machine learning classifier.

Decision Trees are a supervised learning method that use a tree created from simple decision rules learned from the training data as a predictive model. The predictive model is in the form of a tree that can be used to predict the value of a target variable based on several attribute variables. Each node in the tree corresponds to one attribute in the dataset on which the "split" is performed. Each leaf in a decision tree represents a value of the target variable. The learning process involves recursively splitting on the attributes until all the samples in the child node have the same value of the target variable or splitting further results in no further information gain. To select the best attribute for splitting at each stage, different metrics can be used.

Before the classifier can be used in the Bolt, the classifier has to be trained. Box 10.32 shows the Python code for training and saving the classifier. The classifier file is then included in the Storm project. Figure 10.31 shows the decision tree generated for the forest fire detection example. The tree shows the attributes on which splitting is done at each step and the split values. Also shown in the figure are the error, total number of samples at each node and the number of samples in each class (in the value array). For example, the first split is done on the second column (attribute X[1] - Humidity) and the total number of samples in the training set is 440. On the first split, there are 248 samples in first class and 192 samples in the second class.

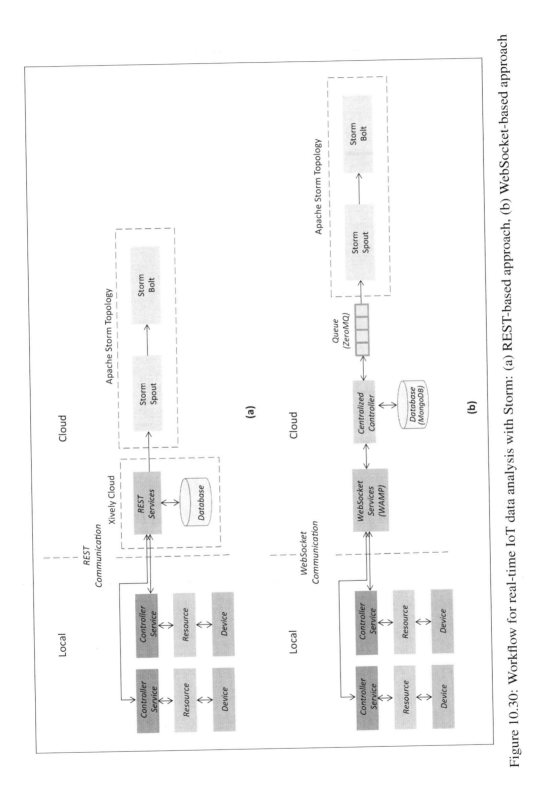

Figure 10.30: Workflow for real-time IoT data analysis with Storm: (a) REST-based approach, (b) WebSocket-based approach

■ **Box 10.32: Training and saving Decision Tree classifier for forest fire detection**

```python
import numpy as np
from sklearn.tree import DecisionTreeClassifier
import csv as csv
import cPickle

#Load the traning data from CSV file
#Format of data in traning file:
# Target, Temperature, Humidity, Light, CO
# Target value is 1 if occurrence is positive and -1 for negative
csv_file_object = csv.reader(open('forest_train.csv', 'rb'))
train_data=[]
for row in csv_file_object:
   train_data.append(row)

train_data = np.array(train_data)

X_train = train_data[0::,1::]
y_train = train_data[0::,0]


#Train the classifier
clf= DecisionTreeClassifier(max_depth=None, min_samples_split=1,
   random_state=0)
clf = clf.fit(X_train, y_train)

#Save the classifier
print "Saving classifier"
with open('dumped_dt_classifier.pkl', 'wb') as fid:
   cPickle.dump(clf, fid)
```

To use the saved Decision Tree classifier for predictions, the next step is to create a new Storm project. Box 10.33 shows the commands for creating a Storm project and Box 10.34 shows a sample configuration file for the project.

■ **Box 10.33: Creating a Storm project**

```
#Create empty project with maven:
$ mvn archetype:generate -DgroupId=com.forest.app -DartifactId=forest-app
-DarchetypeArtifactId=maven-archetype-quickstart -DinteractiveMode=false
```

■ **Box 10.34: Configuration file for forest fire detection Storm app - pom.xml**

```xml
<project xmlns="http://maven.apache.org/POM/4.0.0"
xmlns:xsi="http://www.w3.org/2001/XMLSchema-instance"
xsi:schemaLocation="http://maven.apache.org/POM/4.0.0
http://maven.apache.org/xsd/maven-4.0.0.xsd">
<modelVersion>4.0.0</modelVersion>
<groupId>com.forest.app</groupId>
```

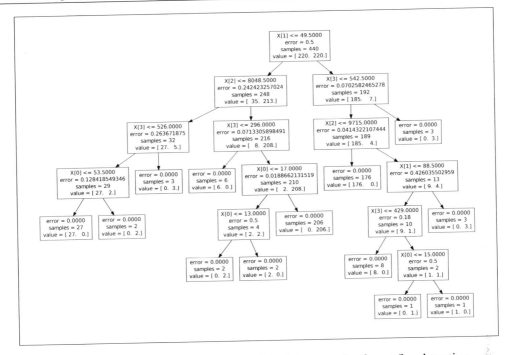

Figure 10.31: Example of a generated decision tree for forest fire detection

```
<artifactId>forest-app</artifactId>
<packaging>jar</packaging>
<version>1.0-SNAPSHOT</version>
<name>forest-app</name>
<url>http://maven.apache.org</url>

<build>
<resources>
<resource>
<directory>${basedir}/multilang</directory>
</resource>
</resources>

<plugins>
<plugin>
<groupId>org.apache.maven.plugins</groupId>
<artifactId>maven-compiler-plugin</artifactId>
<version>2.3.2</version>
<configuration>
<source>1.6</source>
<target>1.6</target>
<compilerVersion>1.6</compilerVersion>
</configuration>
</plugin>
</plugins>
</build>

<repositories>
```

```
<repository>
<id>clojars.org</id>
<url>http://clojars.org/repo</url>
</repository>
</repositories>

<dependencies>
<dependency>
<groupId>storm</groupId>
<artifactId>storm</artifactId>
<version>0.8.0</version>
</dependency>
</dependencies>

</project>
```

After creating the project, within the project directory create directories (/multilang/resources) and then create Python programs for Spout and Bolt within the resources directory. Box 10.35 shows the Python code for the Storm Spout. The Spout connects to the Xively data streams for temperature, humidity light and *CO* data and retrieves the data. The Spout emits the sensor data as streams of comma separated values.

■ **Box 10.35: Storm spout for forest fire detection - sensorSpout.py**

```python
from storm import Spout, emit, log
import time
import datetime
from random import randrange
import xively


FEED_ID = "<enter feed ID>"
API_KEY = "<enter API key>"
api = xively.XivelyAPIClient(API_KEY)
feed = api.feeds.get(FEED_ID)

def getData():
    #Format of data - "temperature,humidity,light,CO"
    #e.g.  30,20,6952,10
    data = feed.datastreams.get("forest_data").current_value
    return data

class SensorSpout(Spout):

    def nextTuple(self):
        time.sleep(2)
        data = getData()
        emit([data])


SensorSpout().run()
```

Box 10.36 shows the Python code for the Storm Bolt. This Bolt receives the streams of sensor data emitted by the Spout. The Decision Tree classifier saved earlier is used in the Bolt to make predictions.

■ **Box 10.36: Storm bolt for forest fire detection - sensorBolt.py**

```python
import storm
import numpy as np
import cPickle
from sklearn.tree import DecisionTreeClassifier

with open('dumped_dt_classifier.pkl', 'rb') as fid:
    clf = cPickle.load(fid)

class SensorBolt(storm.BasicBolt):
    def process(self, tup):
        data = tup.values[0].split(',')

    test_data=[]
    test_data.append(data)
    test_data = np.array(test_data)
    X_test = test_data[0::,0::]

    output = clf.predict(X_test)
    result= "Predicted:   "+ str(output)

    storm.emit([result])


SensorBolt().run()
```

After the Spout and Bolt programs are created the next step is to create a topology. Box 10.37 shows the Java program for creating a topology. To create a topology an object of the *TopologyBuilder* class is created. The Spout and Bolt are defined using the *setSpout* and *setBolt* methods. These methods take as input a user-specified id, objects to the Spout/Bolt classes, and the amount of parallelism required. Storm has two modes of operation - local and distributed. In the local mode, Storm simulates worker nodes within a local process. The distributed mode runs on the Storm cluster. The program in Box 10.37 shows the code for submitting topology to both local and distributed modes.

With all the project files created, the final step is to build and run the project. Box 10.38 shows the commands for building and running a Storm project.

■ **Box 10.37: Java Program for creating Storm topology for forest fire detection - app.java**

```java
package com.forest.app;

import backtype.storm.Config;
import backtype.storm.LocalCluster;
import backtype.storm.StormSubmitter;
import backtype.storm.task.ShellBolt;
```

```java
import backtype.storm.spout.ShellSpout;
import backtype.storm.topology.IRichBolt;
import backtype.storm.topology.IRichSpout;
import backtype.storm.topology.OutputFieldsDeclarer;
import backtype.storm.topology.TopologyBuilder;
import backtype.storm.tuple.Fields;
import java.util.Map;


public class App {

public static class SensorSpout extends ShellSpout implements IRichSpout
{
   public SensorSpout() {
      super("python", "sensorSpout.py");
   }

   @Override
   public void declareOutputFields(OutputFieldsDeclarer declarer) {
      declarer.declare(new Fields("sensordata"));
   }

   @Override
   public Map<String, Object> getComponentConfiguration() {
      return null;
   }
}

public static class SensorBolt extends ShellBolt implements IRichBolt {
   public SensorBolt() {
      super("python", "sensorBolt.py");
   }

   @Override
   public void declareOutputFields(OutputFieldsDeclarer declarer) {
      declarer.declare(new Fields("sensordata"));
   }

   @Override
   public Map<String, Object> getComponentConfiguration() {
      return null;
   }
}


public static void main(String[] args) throws Exception {

   TopologyBuilder builder = new TopologyBuilder();

   builder.setSpout("spout", new SensorSpout(), 5);
   builder.setBolt("analysis",
   new SensorBolt(), 8).shuffleGrouping("spout");

   Config conf = new Config();
```

```
   conf.setDebug(true);

   if (args != null && args.length > 0) {
      conf.setNumWorkers(3);
      StormSubmitter.submitTopology(args[0], conf,
      builder.createTopology());
   }
   else {
      conf.setMaxTaskParallelism(3);

      LocalCluster cluster = new LocalCluster();
      cluster.submitTopology("forest-fire-detect", conf,
      builder.createTopology());

      Thread.sleep(10000);

      cluster.shutdown();
   }
}
```

■ Box 10.38:  Building and running a Storm project

```
#Create empty project with maven:
$ mvn archetype:generate -DgroupId=com.forest.app
-DartifactId=forest-app -DarchetypeArtifactId=
maven-archetype-quickstart -DinteractiveMode=false


#Build the Project
$cd myproject
$mvn package


#Run the Storm Project:
$mvn exec:java -Dexec.mainClass="com.forest.app.App"
```

## 10.7.2   WebSocket-based approach

The previous section described a REST-based implementation of the forest fire detection system. In this section you will learn about an alternative implementation of the IoT system based on the WebSocket approach. The WebSocket implementation is based on the Web Application Messaging Protocol (WAMP) which is a sub-protocol of WebSocket. You learned about AutoBahn, an open source implementation of WAMP in Chapter 8. The deployment design for the WebSocket implementation is shown in Figure 10.30(b).

Box 10.39 shows the implementation of the native controller service that runs on the Raspberry Pi device. The WAMP Publisher application is a part of the controller component. The sensor data is published by the controller to a topic managed by the WAMP Broker. The WAMP Subscriber component subscribes to the topic managed by the Broker. The Subscriber component is a part of the cloud-based centralized controller, the source code for which is shown in Box 10.40. The centralized controller stores the data in a MongoDB database and also pushes the data to a ZeroMQ queue.

The analysis of data is done by a Storm cluster. A Storm Spout pulls the data to be analyzed from the ZeroMQ queue and emits a stream of tuples. The stream is consumed and processed by the Storm Bolt. Boxes 10.41 and 10.42 show the implementations of the Storm Spout and Bolt for real-time analysis of data. The Storm Bolt uses a Decision Tree classifier for making the predictions.

---

### ■ Box 10.39: Forest fire detection controller service

```python
import time
import datetime
import dhtreader
import spidev
from random import randint
from twisted.internet import reactor
from twisted.internet.defer import inlineCallbacks
from autobahn.twisted.util import sleep
from autobahn.twisted.wamp import ApplicationSession

#Configure these pin numbers for DHT22
DEV_TYPE = 22
DHT_PIN = 24

#Initialize DHT22
dhtreader.init()

#LDR channel on MCP3008
LIGHT_CHANNEL = 0

# Open SPI bus
spi = spidev.SpiDev()
spi.open(0,0)

#MICS5525 CO sensor channel on MCP3008
CO_CHANNEL = 1

#Conversions based on Rs/Ro vs ppm plot of MICS5525 CO sensor
CO_Conversions = [((0,100),(0,0.25)),((100,133),(0.25,0.325)),
    ((133,167),(0.325,0.475)),((167,200),(0.475, 0.575)),
    ((200,233),(0.575,0.665)),((233,267),(0.666,0.75)) ]

#Function to read temperature & humidity from DHT22 sensor
def read_DHT22_Sensor():
    temperature, humidity = dhtreader.read(DEV_TYPE, DHT_PIN)
    return temperature, humidity

#Function to read LDR connected to MCP3008
def readLDR():
    light_level = ReadChannel(LIGHT_CHANNEL)
    lux = ConvertLux(light_level,2)
    return lux

#Function to convert LDR reading to Lux
def ConvertLux(data,places):
    R=10 #10k-ohm resistor connected to LDR
    volts = (data * 3.3) / 1023
```

```
  volts = round(volts,places)
  lux=500*(3.3-volts)/(R*volts)
  return lux

# Function to read SPI data from MCP3008 chip
def ReadChannel(channel):
  adc = spi.xfer2([1,(8+channel)<<4,0])
  data = ((adc[1]&3) << 8) + adc[2]
  return data

#Function to read MICS5525 CO sensor connected to MCP3008
def readCOSensor():
  result = ReadChannel(CO_CHANNEL)
  if result == 0:
    resistance = 0
  else:
    resistance = (vin/result - 1)*pullup
  ppmresult = converttoppm(resistance, CO_Conversions)
  return ppmresult

#Function to convert resistance reading to PPM
def converttoppm(rs,conversions):
  rsper = 100*(float(rs)/r0)
  for a in conversions:
    if a[0][0]>=rsper>a[0][1]:
      mid,hi = rsper-a[0][0],a[0][1]-a[0][0]
      sf = float(mid)/hi
      ppm = sf * (a[1][1]-a[1][0]) + a[1][0]
      return ppm
  return 0


#Controller main function
def runController():
  temperature, humidity=read_DHT22_Sensor()
  light=readLDR()
  CO_reading = readCOSensor()
  timestamp = datetime.datetime.fromtimestamp(time.time()).strftime(
'%Y-%m-%d%H:%M:%S')

  datalist = [timestamp, temperature, humidity, light, CO_reading]
  return datalist

#An application component that publishes an event every second.
class Component(ApplicationSession):
  @inlineCallbacks
  def onJoin(self, details):
    while True:
      datalist = runcontroller()
      self.publish('com.myapp.topic1', datalist)
      yield sleep(1)
```

**■ Box 10.40: Centralized controller for forest fire detection**

```
from twisted.internet import reactor
from twisted.internet.defer import inlineCallbacks
from autobahn.twisted.wamp import ApplicationSession
import zmq
from pymongo import MongoClient
import time
import datetime


client = MongoClient()
client = MongoClient('localhost', 27017)

db = client['mydb']

collection = db['iotcollection']

# ZeroMQ Context
context = zmq.Context()

# Define the socket using the "Context"
sock = context.socket(zmq.PUSH)
sock.bind("tcp://127.0.0.1:5690")


class Component(ApplicationSession):
  @inlineCallbacks
  def onJoin(self, details):
    self.received = 0

  def on_event(data):
    #Inset data in MongoDB
    post={'timestamp': data[0], 'temperature':
    data[1], 'humidity': data[2], 'light': data[3], 'CO': data[4]}
    postid=db.collection.insert(post)

    #Send Data to ZMQ queue for further processing
    sock.send(data)

  #Subscribe to Topic
  yield self.subscribe(on_event, 'com.myapp.topic1')


  def onDisconnect(self):
    reactor.stop()
```

**■ Box 10.41: Storm Spout for forest fire detection**

```
from storm import Spout, emit, log
import time
```

```
import datetime
import zmq

# ZeroMQ Context
context = zmq.Context()
sock = context.socket(zmq.PULL)
sock.connect("tcp://127.0.0.1:5690")


class SensorSpout(Spout):

   def nextTuple(self):
      time.sleep(2)
      data = sock.recv()
      emit([data])


SensorSpout().run()
```

■ **Box 10.42: Storm Bolt for forest fire detection**

```
import storm
import numpy as np
import cPickle
from sklearn.tree import DecisionTreeClassifier

with open('dumped_dt_classifier.pkl', 'rb') as fid:
clf = cPickle.load(fid)

class SensorBolt(storm.BasicBolt):
def process(self, tup):
data = tup.values[0].split(',')

   data_without_timestamp = data[1:]

   test_data=[]
   test_data.append(data_without_timestamp)
   test_data = np.array(test_data)
   X_test = test_data[0::,0::]

   output = clf.predict(X_test)
   result= "Predicted at timestamp:  "+ data[0] + " result:   " +
   str(output)

   storm.emit([result])


SensorBolt().run()
```

## 10.8 Structural Health Monitoring Case Study

Structural Health Monitoring (SHM) systems use a network of sensors to monitor the vibration levels in the structures such as bridges and buildings. The data collected from these sensors is analyzed to assess the health of the structures.

This section provides a case study of an SHM system that uses 3-axis accelerometer sensors for measuring the vibrations in a structure. The accelerometer data is collected and analyzed in the cloud. The deployment design for the WebSocket implementation is shown in Figure 10.30(b). Figure 10.32 shows a schematic of the IoT device for monitoring vibrations in a structure, comprising of Raspberry Pi board and ADXL345 accelerometer module.

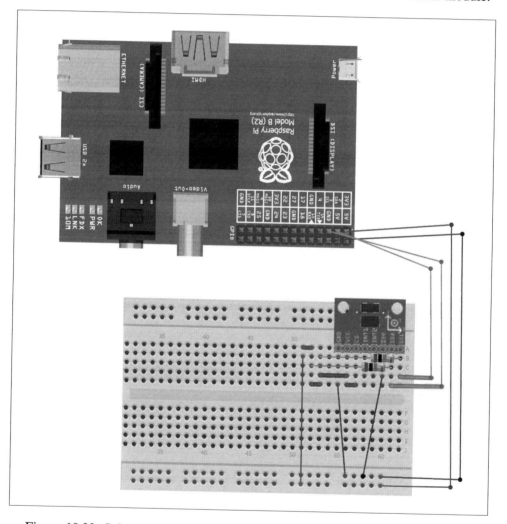

Figure 10.32: Schematic diagram of IoT device for structural health monitoring

Discrete Fourier Transform (DFT) is useful for converting a sampled signal from time domain to frequency domain which makes the analysis of the signal easier. However, for streaming vibration data in which the spectral content changes over time, using DFT cannot reveal the transitions in the spectral content. Short Time Fourier Transform (STFT) is better suited for revealing the changes in the spectral content corresponding to the SHM data. To compute the STFT, windowed sections of the signal are first generated using a window function and then the Fourier Transform of each windowed section is computed.

The STFT of a signal $x[n]$ is given as

$$X[n,\omega] = \sum_{m=-\infty}^{+\infty} x[m] * w[n-m] e^{-j\omega n} \qquad (10.1)$$

where $w[n]$ is a window function. Commonly used window functions are Hann and Hamming windows.

Alternatively, STFT can be interpreted as a filtering operation as follows,

$$X[n,k] = e^{-j\frac{2\pi}{N}kn} \left( x[n] * w[n] e^{-j\frac{2\pi}{N}kn} \right) \qquad (10.2)$$

From STFT, the spectrogram of the signal can be computed which is useful for visualizing the spectrum of frequencies in the signal and their variations with time.

$$Spectogram = |X[n,k]|^2 \qquad (10.3)$$

Box 10.43 shows the implementation of the native controller service for the SHM system. The controller comprises of the WAMP Publisher application which publishes the 3-axis accelerometer data to a topic managed by the WAMP Broker. The WAMP Subscriber component which is a part of the centralized controller subscribes to the topic managed by the Broker and receives the vibration data. Box 10.44 shows an implementation of the centralized controller. The centralized controller stores the vibration in a MongoDB database and also pushes the data to a ZeroMQ queue. The data is analyzed by a Storm cluster. Box 10.45 shows an implementation of the Storm Spout that pulls the data from ZeroMQ queue and emits streams of tuples which are consumed by the Storm Bolt. Box 10.46 shows an implementation of the Storm Bolt which computes the STFT for streams of vibration data.

■ **Box 10.43: SHM native controller service**

```
import time
import datetime
from twisted.internet import reactor
from twisted.internet.defer import inlineCallbacks
from autobahn.twisted.util import sleep
from autobahn.twisted.wamp import ApplicationSession

#Import from ADXL345
#Source: https://github.com/pimoroni/adxl345-python
from adxl345 import ADXL345

adxl345 = ADXL345()
axes = adxl345.getAxes(True)

#Controller main function
def runController():
    timestamp = datetime.datetime.fromtimestamp(
```

```
         time.time()).strftime('%Y-%m-%d %H:%M:%S')
    x=[]
    y=[]
    z=[]

    for i in range(1000):
        x.append(axes['x'])
        y.append(axes['y'])
        z.append(axes['z'])

    datalist = [timestamp, X, Y, Z]
    return datalist

#An application component that publishes an event every second.
class Component(ApplicationSession):
    @inlineCallbacks
    def onJoin(self, details):
        while True:
            datalist = runcontroller()
            self.publish('com.myapp.topic1', datalist)
            yield sleep(1)
```

■ **Box 10.44: SHM centralized controller**

```
from twisted.internet import reactor
from twisted.internet.defer import inlineCallbacks
from autobahn.twisted.wamp import ApplicationSession
import zmq
from pymongo import MongoClient
import time
import datetime


client = MongoClient()
client = MongoClient('localhost', 27017)

db = client['mydb']

collection = db['iotcollection']

# ZeroMQ Context
context = zmq.Context()

# Define the socket using the "Context"
sock = context.socket(zmq.PUSH)
sock.bind("tcp://127.0.0.1:5690")


class Component(ApplicationSession):
    @inlineCallbacks
    def onJoin(self, details):
        self.received = 0
```

```
def on_event(data):
    #Inset data in MongoDB
    post={'timestamp': data[0],
    'X': data[1], 'Y': data[2], 'Z': data[3]}
    postid=db.collection.insert(post)

    #Send Data to ZMQ queue for further processing
    sock.send(data)

#Subscribe to Topic
yield self.subscribe(on_event, 'com.myapp.topic1')


def onDisconnect(self):
    reactor.stop()
```

■ **Box 10.45: Storm Spout for SHM**

```
from storm import Spout, emit, log
import time
import datetime
import zmq

# ZeroMQ Context
context = zmq.Context()
sock = context.socket(zmq.PULL)
sock.connect("tcp://127.0.0.1:5690")


class SensorSpout(Spout):

    def nextTuple(self):
        time.sleep(2)
        data = sock.recv()
        emit([data])

SensorSpout().run()
```

■ **Box 10.46: Storm Bolt for SHM**

```
import storm
import scipy

#Short Time Fourier Transform
def stft(d):
"""
x - signal
fs - sample rate
framesize - frame size
```

```
   hop - hop size (frame size = overlap + hop size)
   """

   #Define analysis window
   framesamp = 200

   #Define the amount of overlap between windows
   hopsamp = 150

   #Define a windowing function
   w = scipy.hamming(framesamp)

   #Generate windowed segments and apply
   #the FFT to each windowed segment
   D = scipy.array([scipy.fft(w*x[i:i+framesamp])
      for i in range(0, len(x)-framesamp, hopsamp)])
   return D


class SensorBolt(storm.BasicBolt):
   def process(self, tup):
      data = tup.values[0].split(',')

      x = data[1]
      y = data[2]
      z = data[3]

      X=stft(x)
      Y=stft(y)
      Z=stft(z)

      output = scipy.absolute(X)
      result= "STFT - X : "+ str(output)

      output = scipy.absolute(Y)
      result= result + "STFT - Y : "+ str(output)

      output = scipy.absolute(Z)
      result= result + "STFT - Z : "+ str(output)

      storm.emit([result])


SensorBolt().run()
```

## Summary

In this chapter you learned about various tools for analyzing IoT data. IoT systems can have varied data analysis requirements. For some IoT systems, the volume of data is so huge that analyzing the data on a single machine is not possible. For such systems, distributed batch data analytics frameworks such as Apache Hadoop can be used for data analysis. For IoT systems which have real-time data analysis requirements, tools such as Apache Storm are useful. For IoT systems which require interactive querying of data, tools such as Apache Spark can be used. Hadoop is an open source framework for distributed batch processing of massive scale data. Hadoop MapReduce provides a data processing model and an execution environment for MapReduce jobs for large scale data processing. Key processes of Hadoop include NameNode, Secondary NameNode, JobTracker, TaskTracker and DataNode. NameNode keeps the directory tree of all files in the file system, and tracks where across the cluster the file data is kept. Secondary NameNode creates checkpoints of the namespace. JobTracker distributes MapReduce tasks to specific nodes in the cluster. TaskTracker accepts Map, Reduce and Shuffle tasks from the JobTracker. DataNode stores data in an HDFS file system. You learned how to setup a Hadoop cluster and run MapReduce jobs on the cluster. You learned about the next generation architecture of Hadoop called YARN. YARN is framework for job scheduling and cluster resource management. Key components of YARN include Resource Manager, Application Master, Node Manager and Containers. You learned about the Oozie workflow scheduler system that allows managing Hadoop jobs. You learned about Apache Spark in-memory cluster computing framework. Spark supports various high-level tools for data analysis such as Spark Streaming for streaming jobs, Spark SQL for analysis of structured data, MLlib machine learning library for Spark, GraphX for graph processing and Shark (Hive on Spark). Finally, you learned about Apache Storm which is a framework for distributed and fault-tolerant real-time computation.

## Lab Exercises

1. In this exercise you will create a multi-node Hadoop cluster on a cloud. Follow the steps below:
   - Create and Amazon Web Services account.
   - From Amazon EC2 console launch two *m1.small* EC2 instances.
   - When the instances start running, note the public DNS addresses of the instances.
   - Connect to the instances using SSH.
   - Run the commands given in Box 10.2 to install Java on each instance.
   - Run the commands given in Box 10.3 to install Hadoop on each instance.
   - Configure Hadoop. Use the templates for core-site.xml, hdfs-site.xml, mapred-site.xml and master and slave files shown in Boxes 10.4 - 10.7.
   - Start the Hadoop cluster using the commands shown in Box 10.8.
   - In a browser open the Hadoop cluster status pages:
     public-DNS-of-hadoop-master:50070
     public-DNS-of-hadoop-master:50030

2. In this exercise you will run a MapReduce job on a Hadoop cluster for aggregating data (computing mean, maximum and minimum) on various timescales. Follow the

steps below:

- Generate synthetic data using the following Python program:

```
■ #Synthetic data generate for forest fire detection system
#Data Format: "2014-06-25 10:47:44",26,36,2860,274

from random import randrange
import time
import datetime

fp= open('forestdata.txt','w')
readings=100

for j in range(0,readings):
    timestamp = datetime.datetime.fromtimestamp(time.time()).
strftime('%Y-%m-%d %H:%M:%S')
    data = timestamp + "," + str(randrange(0,100)) +
"," + str(randrange(0,100))+ "," + str(randrange(0,10000))+
"," + str(randrange(200,400))
    fp.write(data)

fp.close()
```

- Follow the steps in Exercise-1 to create a Hadoop cluster.
- Copy the synthetic data file to the Hadoop master instance. Use scp or copy or wget to download files. Copy the data file to a folder named 'data'.
- Copy the synthetic data file from the Hadoop master node local filesystem to HDFS:
  bin/hadoop dfs -copyFromLocal data/ input
- Create mapper and reducer Python programs as shown in Boxes 10.9 and 10.10.
- Run MapReduce job using the commands given in Box 10.11.

3. Box 10.32 shows the Python code for training and saving Decision Tree classifier for forest fire detection. Modify the code to train and save a Random Forest classifier. Use the classifier in the Storm bolt for forest fire detection.

4. This exercise is about analyzing weather monitoring data using Apache Storm. For the REST and WebSocket implementations of Weather Monitoring system described in Chapter-9, design a Storm topology (including Spout and Bolt) for predicting the current conditions from the weather data collected. The Storm topology should analyze the weather data (temperature, humidity, pressure and light data) in real-time and classify the current conditions to be one of the following - sunny, warm, hot, mild, cool, chilly, cold, freezing, humid, dry. Follow the steps below:

- Save the weather monitoring data to a text or CSV file and manually classify and label the data (50-100 rows). For example:
  #Format of labeled file:

#Label, Timestamp, Temperature, Humidity, Pressure, Light
Hot, 2014-06-25 10:47:44,38,56,102997,2000

- Using the labeled data, train and save the classifier. Try Decision Tree and Random Forest classifiers. Use a program similar to the one shown in Box 10.32.
- Create a Storm project as shown in Box 10.33.
- Implement Spout and Bolt similar to the implementations shown in Boxes 10.35 and 10.36.
- Create a Storm topology with the Spout and Bolt created in the previous step using an implementation similar to the one shown in Box 10.37.
- Build and run the Storm project using the commands shown in Box 10.38.

# 11 - Tools for IoT

This Chapter Covers

- Infrastructure automation & configuration management tools:
  - Chef
  - Puppet
  - NETCONF and YANG case studies
- IoT code generator tool

## 11.1 Introduction

Managing IoT infrastructure and configuring and integrating various components can be complex and challenging task. The complexity of infrastructure grows with increasing number of components (such as load balancers, application server, database servers, etc.). To minimize the manual effort required, a new paradigm of infrastructure-as-a-code has been popularized by infrastructure automation and configuration management tools such as Chef and Puppet.

In the infrastructure-as-a-code paradigm, the computing, storage and network infrastructure is modeling using declarative modeling languages. A modular approach is adopted for modeling the infrastructure to improve code re-usability. The infrastructure models are compiled and run by infrastructure automation tools to generate the desired infrastructure. Infrastructure-as-a-code improves the repeatability of the infrastructure as the same code always produces the same infrastructure. Modular code design along with the automation capabilities improve the scalability of systems. Moreover, in the event of system failures or catastrophic events, the entire infrastructure can be restored from the infrastructure code.

In this chapter you will learn about two popular infrastructure automation tools - Chef and Puppet. Case studies on using these tools for generating infrastructures such as a three-tier deployment, a Hadoop cluster and Storm cluster are described. This chapters also provides case studies on IoT device management with NETCONF and YANG.

## 11.2 Chef

Chef is an infrastructure automation and configuration management framework. Chef adopts the infrastructure-as-a-code paradigm and allows deploying, configuring and integrating various infrastructure components. Figure 11.1 shows the components of the Chef framework. The Chef server stores the information about the infrastructure. The infrastructure code is organized into cookbooks. Cookbooks include recipes (which are written in Ruby language), templates, attributes and resources. The fundamental unit of configuration in a recipe is a resource (such as file, package, user, etc.). Recipes specify which resources to manage, how to manage the resources and also the order in which the resources should be managed.

Chef recipes and cookbooks are authored on a Chef workstation and uploaded to the Chef server. The nodes to be managed run the chef-client. The chef-client connects to the server and obtains information on the desired state for the node. The chef-client performs various tasks such as building the node object, synchronizing cookbooks and applying the cookbooks to bring the node to the desired state.

Chef server comes in two flavors - Enterprise Server and Open Source Server. You can setup either version on your own infrastructure (in-house or in the cloud) or use a Hosted Enterprise Chef Server. Chef provides a free trial of the Hosted Enterprise Chef Server which is a convenient way to get started with Chef. Figure 11.2 shows a screenshot of the Hosted Chef Server.

Before we proceed with examples of using Chef, let us briefly look at the key concepts of the Chef framework:

- **Server:** Server stores all the configuration data for the infrastructure including cookbooks, recipes, roles, attributes, run lists and node objects.

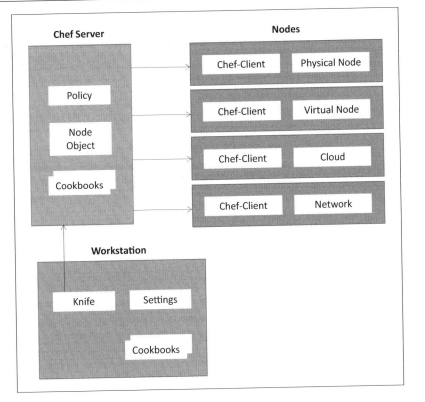

Figure 11.1: Chef components

Figure 11.2: Screenshot of dashboard of hosted Chef server

- **Node:** Node can either be a cloud-based virtual machine instance, a physical node, a virtual node or a network node (such as a switch or router).
- **Cookbook:** Cookbook is a collection of recipes, attributes, templates and resources.
- **Recipe:** Recipe is a configuration element written in Ruby language that specifies various resources to be managed and how to manage the resources.
- **Resource:** Resource is a fundamental unit of configuration ( such as a package, file, user, etc). Recipes include information on resources to manage and the desired state of the resources.
- **Provider:** While resource specification tells which resource to manage and the desired

state of the resource, the specification is abstract in nature and does not describe the steps to manage the resource. Provider describes the steps to bring the resource to the desired state.

- **Attributes:** Attributes are used to provide specific details. Attributes are included in cookbooks, roles, environments and node objects.
- **Templates:** Templates are included in cookbooks and are used for complex configurations. Templates are written in ERB template language which is a feature of Ruby.
- **Policy:** Policy includes roles, environments and data-bags. Roles define the types of servers or patterns that should be applied to all the nodes in a role. For example, all nodes in a role - "Application Server" have the same configuration details (of an application server). Data-bags are used to store sensitive information such as usernames and passwords. Information stored in data-bags can be accessed by nodes authenticated to the Chef server. Environments denote the processes and worflows (e.g. development, staging, production, etc.).
- **Run Lists:** Run list is an ordered list of recipes and/or roles. The chef-client applies the recipes and roles in the run list in the order in which they appear. Run lists are stored on the Chef server as a part of the node object.
- **Knife:** Knife is a command line utility that provides interface between workstation and server. Using knife you perform tasks such as creating and uploading cookbooks, creating roles and environments, bootstrapping nodes, etc.

### 11.2.1  Setting up Chef

To set up a Chef environment, you will need to set up Chef Server, Workstation and Chef-client on nodes. For Chef Server, you can either setup the Open Source version on your own node or use Hosted Enterprise Chef. For the examples in this Chapter, we recommend signing up for a free trial of Hosted Enterprise Chef. When you create an account on Hosted Enterprise Chef, you will be able to download a starter kit that includes the PEM certificates that allow the workstation to authenticate with the Chef server. Setting up Chef on the workstation is as simple as running a single command as follows (for Linux workstation):

```
■ curl -L https://www.opscode.com/chef/install.sh | sudo bash
```

When you run the above command, Chef's omnibus installer installs all you need to get started with Chef.

With the Server and Workstation set up, the next step is to set up a node to manage with Chef. You can use cloud-based node, or a physical or virtual node. For the examples in this chapter we use Amazon EC2 instances as nodes.

After launching a new Amazon EC2 instance, note the IP address of the instance. The next step is to bootstrap the node. The bootstrapping process installs the Chef client and checks in with the Chef server. To bootstrap an Amazon EC2 node, run the following knife command on the Workstation:

```
■ knife bootstrap <IP-Address> -sudo -x ubuntu -i <keypair.pem>
-N <nodeName>
```

You will require your EC2 keypair (PEM) file on the Workstation for bootstrapping the node. The node name that you specify at the time of bootstrapping will be used in further interactions. You can also view the node with the same name in the Hosted Enterprise Chef dashboard.

## 11.3  Chef Case Studies

### 11.3.1  Multi-tier Application Deployment

In this section you will learn how to create a multi-tier deployment comprising of HAProxy load balancer, Django application server and MongoDB database server. Figure 11.3 shows the steps in creating a three-tier deployment with Chef. In the first step the nodes for the load balancer, application server and database server are provisioned. Next, the software packages for HAProxy, Django and MongoDB are setup on the respective nodes. Finally the nodes are integrated to setup the three-tier deployment.

The first step is to create a cookbook named *threetierdeployment* with the following command:

```
knife cookbook create threetierdeployment
```

Next, launch three Amazon EC2 nodes and bootstrap them using the following commands from the workstation:

```
knife bootstrap <IP Address> -sudo -x ubuntu -i <PEM file name>
-N lbnode

knife bootstrap <IP Address> -sudo -x ubuntu -i <PEM file name>
-N appnode

knife bootstrap <IP Address> -sudo -x ubuntu -i <PEM file name>
-N dbnode
```

After bootstrapping three nodes, create recipes for generating SSH keys, setting up HAProxy, Django and MongoDB. Box 11.1 shows the recipe for generating SSH keys and Box 11.2 shows the recipe for collecting the public keys of all nodes and creating an authorized key file on each node. This ensures that all nodes are able to securely connect to each other.

**Box 11.1: Chef recipe for setting up SSH keys - ssh_keys.rb**

```
require 'chef/shell_out'

# Generate Keys
gen_ssh_keys = Mixlib::ShellOut.new('ssh-keygen -t dsa -P " -f
/home/ubuntu/.ssh/id_dsa', :user => 'ubuntu', :cwd => "/tmp")
gen_ssh_keys.run_command

gen_ssh_keys = Mixlib::ShellOut.new('cat /home/ubuntu/.ssh/id_dsa.pub >>
/home/ubuntu/.ssh/authorized_keys', :user => 'ubuntu', :cwd => "/tmp")
gen_ssh_keys.run_command
```

```
get_pub_key = Mixlib::ShellOut.new('cat /home/ubuntu/.ssh/id_dsa.pub',
:cwd => "/tmp")
get_pub_key.run_command

# Set node public key
node.set["public_key"] = get_pub_key.stdout
```

■ **Box 11.2: Chef recipe for setting up authorized keys - authorzed_keys.rb**

```
require 'chef/shell_out'

authorized_keys = ''

# Search all nodes within the cluster
nodes = search(:node, "role:hadoop_cluster_role")

auth_keys = Mixlib::ShellOut.new('cat /home/ubuntu/.ssh/authorized_keys',
:cwd => "/tmp")
auth_keys.run_command

authorized_keys << auth_keys.stdout

# Collect public keys of all nodes
nodes.each do |node|
authorized_keys << node['public_key']
end

# Create 'authorized_keys' file
e = file "/home/ubuntu/.ssh/authorized_keys" do
content authorized_keys
action :create
end
```

Box 11.3 shows the recipe for setting up HAProxy. The recipe defines a package resource name 'haproxy' with the action for the resource set to 'install'. The recipe also defines a template resource for the haproxy.cfg file. The ERB template file for haproxy.cfg is shown in Box 11.4.

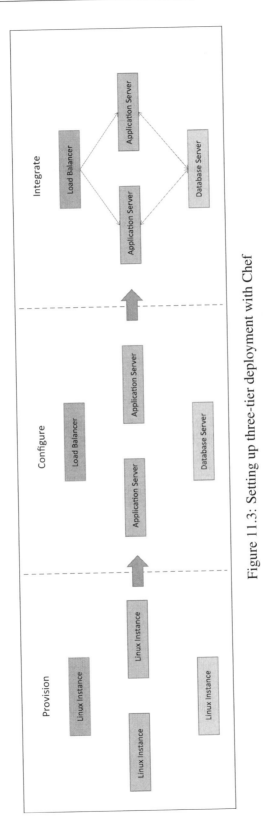

Figure 11.3: Setting up three-tier deployment with Chef

**■ Box 11.3: Chef recipe for setting up HAProxy - setup_haproxy.rb**

```ruby
#Setup haproxy
package "haproxy" do
    action :install
end


#Search all nodes to be load balanced
nodes = search(:node, "role:load_balance_role").sort_by
|h| h[:hostname]

#Setup haproxy.cfg file
template "/etc/haproxy/haproxy.cfg" do
    source "haproxy.cfg.erb"
    owner "root"
    group "root"
    mode 00644
    notifies :reload, "service[haproxy]"
    variables(
    :lbnodes => nodes
    )
end

#Service to start/restart haproxy
service "haproxy" do
    supports :restart => true, :status => true, :reload => true
    action [:enable, :start]
end
```

**■ Box 11.4: Chef template file for HAProxy - haproxy.config.erb**

```
global
    log 127.0.0.1 local0
    log 127.0.0.1 local1 notice
    maxconn 4096
    daemon

defaults
    log global
    mode http
    option httplog
    option dontlognull
    retries 3
    option redispatch
    maxconn 2000
    contimeout 5000
    clitimeout 50000
    srvtimeout 50000

listen mywebfarm
```

```
    bind *:8080
    mode http
    stats enable
    stats auth admin:123456
    balance roundrobin
    option httpclose
    option forwardfor
    option httpchk

    <% @hosts.each do |hosts| %>
    server <%= hosts[:hostname] %>
<%= hosts[:hostname] %>:80    check inter 3000 rise 2 fall 3 maxconn 255
    <% end %>
```

Box 11.5 shows the recipe for setting up Django.

**■ Box 11.5: Chef recipe for setting up Django - setup_django.rb**

```
package "python-django" do
   action :install
end
```

Box 11.6 shows the recipe for setting up MongoDB.

**■ Box 11.6: Chef recipe for setting up MongoDB - setup_mongo.rb**

```
require 'chef/shell_out'

setup_mongodb = Mixlib::ShellOut.new("apt-key adv -keyserver
keyserver.ubuntu.com -recv 7F0CEB10", :cwd => '/tmp')
setup_mongodb.run_command

setup_mongodb = Mixlib::ShellOut.new("echo deb
http://downloads-distro.mongodb.org/repo/ubuntu-upstart dist 10gen|
sudo tee /etc/apt/sources.list.d/10gen.list", :cwd => '/tmp')
setup_mongodb.run_command

setup_mongodb = Mixlib::ShellOut.new("apt-get update", :cwd => '/tmp')
setup_mongodb.run_command

setup_mongodb = Mixlib::ShellOut.new("apt-get install mongodb-10gen",
:cwd => '/tmp')
setup_mongodb.run_command
```

After creating the recipes, the next step is to upload the cookbook. To upload the cookbook run the following command:

```
■ knife cookbook upload threetierdeployment
```

The next step is to create run lists for all the nodes as follows:

```
■ knife node run_list add lbnode
'recipe[threetierdeployment::ssh_keys],
recipe[threetierdeployment::authorzed_keys],
recipe[threetierdeployment::setup_haproxy]'

knife node run_list add appnode
'recipe[threetierdeployment::ssh_keys],
recipe[threetierdeployment::authorzed_keys],
recipe[threetierdeployment::setup_django]'

knife node run_list add dbnode
'recipe[threetierdeployment::ssh_keys],
recipe[threetierdeployment::authorzed_keys],
recipe[threetierdeployment::setup_mongo]'
```

Finally, the chef-client is run on all nodes from the workstation as follows:

```
■ knife ssh <IP Address> 'sudo chef-client' -m -x ubuntu
-i <PEM file name>
```

## 11.3.2  Hadoop Cluster

This section describes a case study on setting up a Hadoop cluster using Chef. You already learned about the steps in setting up a Hadoop cluster in Chapter 10. Let us build on this knowledge. Figure 11.4 shows the steps involved in setting up a Hadoop cluster with Chef. In the first step the instances for Hadoop master and slave nodes are provisioned. Next, Hadoop package is setup on the master and slave nodes. Finally, the Hadoop configuration files are updated and the nodes are integrated to setup the cluster.

The first step is to create a cookbook named *hadoop* with the following command:

```
■ knife cookbook create hadoop
```

Next, launch two Amazon EC2 nodes (one master and one slave node) and bootstrap them using the following commands from the workstation:

```
■ knife bootstrap <IP Address> -sudo -x ubuntu -i <PEM file name>
-N masternode

knife bootstrap <IP Address> -sudo -x ubuntu -i <PEM file name>
-N slavenode
```

After bootstrapping the nodes, create recipes for generating SSH keys, setting up hosts, installing Java and setting up Hadpop. Box 11.1 shows the recipe for generating SSH keys and Box 11.2 shows the recipe for collecting the public keys of all nodes and creating an authorized key file on each node. This ensures that all nodes are able to securely connect to each other.

Box 11.7 shows the Chef recipe for setting up hosts. In this recipe the '/etc/hosts' file is created using the template in Box 11.8. All IP addresses and host names of nodes in the Chef role ('hadoop_cluster_role') are added to the hosts file.

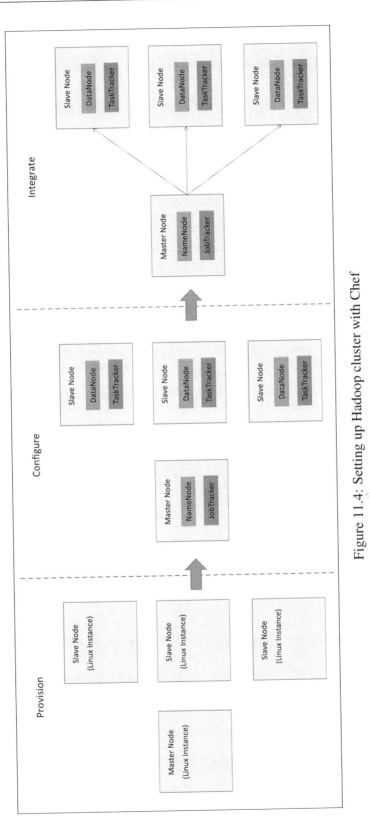

Figure 11.4: Setting up Hadoop cluster with Chef

■ **Box 11.7: Chef recipe for setting up hosts - setup_hosts.rb**

```
require 'chef/shell_out'

# Backup original /etc/hosts
backup_hosts = Mixlib::ShellOut.new("cp /etc/hosts /etc/hosts.original")
backup_hosts.run_command

#Search all nodes within Hadoop Cluster
nodes = search(:node, "role:hadoop_cluster_role")

# Update /etc/hosts
template "/etc/hosts" do
source "hosts.erb"
owner "root"
group "root"
mode 0644
variables(
:hosts => nodes.sort_by { |h| h[:hostname] }
)
end
```

■ **Box 11.8: Chef template - hosts.erb**

```
127.0.0.1 localhost

<% @hosts.each do |hosts| %>
<%= hosts[:ipaddress] %> <%= hosts[:fqdn] %> <%= hosts[:hostname] %>
<% end %>

# The following lines are desirable for IPv6 capable hosts
::1 ip6-localhost ip6-loopback
fe00::0 ip6-localnet
ff00::0 ip6-mcastprefix
ff02::1 ip6-allnodes
ff02::2 ip6-allrouters
ff02::3 ip6-allhosts
```

The recipe for installing Java-7 is shown in Box 11.9.

■ **Box 11.9: Chef recipe for setting up Java-7 - setup_java.rb**

```
require 'chef/shell_out'

# Set the properties
java_command = Mixlib::ShellOut.new("apt-get -q -y install
python-software-properties", :cwd => '/tmp')
java_command.run_command

java_command = Mixlib::ShellOut.new("add-apt-repository -y
ppa:webupd8team/java", :cwd => '/tmp')
```

```
java_command.run_command

java_command = Mixlib::ShellOut.new("apt-get -q -y update",
:cwd => '/tmp')
java_command.run_command

# State that you accepted the license
java_command = Mixlib::ShellOut.new("echo debconf
shared/accepted-oracle-license-v1-1 select true |
sudo debconf-set-selections",
:cwd => '/tmp')
java_command.run_command

java_command = Mixlib::ShellOut.new("echo debconf
shared/accepted-oracle-license-v1-1 seen true |
sudo debconf-set-selections",
:cwd => '/tmp')
java_command.run_command

# Install Oracle Java 7
java_command = Mixlib::ShellOut.new("apt-get -q -y install
oracle-java7-installer", :cwd => '/tmp')
java_command.run_command

# Update environment variable
java_command = Mixlib::ShellOut.new("bash -c ëcho
JAVA_HOME=/usr/lib/jvm/java-7-oracle/ > >
/etc/environment", :cwd =>'/tmp')
java_command.run_command
```

Box 11.10 shows the Chef recipe for setting up Hadoop. In this recipe, the Hadoop package is downloaded and Hadoop configuration files (hdfs-site.xml, core-site.xml and mapred-site.xml) are created using the templates shown in Boxes 11.11, 11.12 and 11.13.

■ **Box 11.10: Chef recipe for setting up Hadoop**

```
require 'chef/shell_out'

# Download Hadoop package
download_hadoop = Mixlib::ShellOut.new("wget
#{node['hadoop_package_uri']}", :cwd => '/home/ubuntu')
download_hadoop.run_command

# Extract Hadoop package
download_hadoop = Mixlib::ShellOut.new("tar -xzf
#{node['hadoop_release']}.tar.gz", :cwd => '/home/ubuntu')
download_hadoop.run_command

download_hadoop = Mixlib::ShellOut.new("chown -R ubuntu:ubuntu
#{node['hadoop_release']}", :cwd => '/home/ubuntu')
download_hadoop.run_command
```

```
# Setup configuration files
template "/home/ubuntu/#{node['hadoop_release']}/conf/hdfs-site.xml" do
owner 'ubuntu'
group 'ubuntu'
source "hdfs-site.xml.erb"
variables ({
:hdfs_replication => node['hdfs_replication'],
:hadoop_namenode_dir => node['hadoop_namenode_dir'],
:hadoop_datanode_dir => node['hadoop_datanode_dir']
})
end

template "/home/ubuntu/#{node['hadoop_release']}/conf/core-site.xml" do
owner 'ubuntu'
group 'ubuntu'
source "core-site.xml.erb"
variables ({ :hadoop_namenode => node['hadoop_master'] })
end

template "/home/ubuntu/#{node['hadoop_release']}/conf/mapred-site.xml" do
owner 'ubuntu'
group 'ubuntu'
source "mapred-site.xml.erb"
variables ({
:hadoop_jobtracker => node['hadoop_master'],
:hadoop_tasktracker_local_dir => node['hadoop_tasktracker_local_dir']
})
end

# Set JAVA_HOME
set_java_home = Mixlib::ShellOut.new("sed -i ö:#.*JAVA_HOME=.*$:export
JAVA_HOME=/usr/lib/jvm/java-7-oracle/:göonf/hadoop-env.sh",
:cwd => "/home/ubuntu/#{node['hadoop_release']}")
set_java_home.run_command
```

■ **Box 11.11: Chef template - core-site.xml.erb**

```
<?xml version="1.0"?>
<?xml-stylesheet type="text/xsl" href="configuration.xsl"?>

<configuration>
<property>
<name>mapred.job.tracker</name>
<value><%= @hadoop_jobtracker %>:54311</value>
<description></description>
</property>
</configuration>
```

### ■ Box 11.12:  Chef template - hdfs-site.xml.erb

```
  <?xml version="1.0"?>
<?xml-stylesheet type="text/xsl" href="configuration.xsl"?>

<configuration>
<property>
<name>dfs.replication</name>
<value><%= @hdfs_replication %></value>
<description></description>
</property>
</configuration>
```

### ■ Box 11.13:  Chef template - mapred-site.xml.erb

```
<?xml version="1.0"?>
<?xml-stylesheet type="text/xsl" href="configuration.xsl"?>

<configuration>
<property>
<name>fs.default.name</name>
<value>hdfs://<%= @hadoop_namenode %>:54310</value>
<description></description>
</property>
</configuration>
```

Box 11.14 shows Chef recipe for setting up Hadoop master node. In this recipe the master and slave configuration files are created and the hostnames of the master and slave are added to these files. Boxes 11.15 and 11.16 show the master and slave templates files used for configuring the Hadoop master node.

### ■ Box 11.14:  Chef recipe for setting up Hadoop master

```
require 'chef/shell_out'

#Search all nodes within Hadoop Cluster
nodes = search(:node, "role:hadoop_cluster_role").sort_by {
|h| h[:hostname] }

# Update conf/masters
template "/home/ubuntu/#{node['hadoop_release']}/conf/masters" do
source "masters.erb"
owner node['hadoop_user']
group node['hadoop_user']
mode 0644
variables(
:hadoop_master => node['hadoop_master']
)
```

```
end


# Update conf/slaves
template "/home/ubuntu/#{node['hadoop_release']}/conf/slaves" do
source "slaves.erb"
owner node['hadoop_user']
group node['hadoop_user']
mode 0644
variables(
:hosts => nodes
)
end
```

■ **Box 11.15: Chef template - masters.erb**

```
<%= @hadoop_master %>
```

■ **Box 11.16: Chef template - slaves.erb**

```
<% @hosts.each do |hosts| %>
<%= hosts[:hostname] %>
<% end %>
```

Box 11.17 shows the attributes for the Hadoop cookbook. These attributes are used in the recipes in the cookbook.

■ **Box 11.17: Chef cookbook attributes**

```
default['hadoop_user'] = 'ubuntu'
default['hadoop_user_password'] = 'password'
default['hadoop_user_home'] = "/home/ubuntu"
default['hadoop_home'] = '/home/ubuntu'
default['public_key'] = "
default['hadoop_cluster_role'] = 'hadoop'
default['hadoop_master'] = "
default['hdfs_replication'] = 2
default['hadoop_package_uri'] =
'http://archive.apache.org/dist/hadoop/core/hadoop-1.0.4/
hadoop-1.0.4.tar.gz'
default['hadoop_release'] = 'hadoop-1.0.4'
```

With the all the recipes for the Hadoop cookbook created the next step is to define roles. Boxes 11.18 and 11.19 show the Chef roles for setting up Hadoop cluster and Hadoop master node. The roles contain definitions of the run lists.

■ **Box 11.18: Chef role for setting up Hadoop cluster**

```
    name "hadoop_cluster_role"
description "Setup cluster nodes"
run_list [
"recipe[hadoop::setup_hosts]",
"recipe[hadoop::ssh_keys]",
"recipe[hadoop::authorized_nodes]",
"recipe[hadoop::setup_java]",
"recipe[hadoop::setup_hadoop]"
]
```

■ **Box 11.19: Chef role for setting up Hadoop master**

```
name "hadoop_master_role"
description "Setup hadoop master node"
run_list [
"recipe[hadoop::setup_master]"
]
```

The Hadoop cookbook is then uploaded to the Chef server using the following command:

```
■ knife cookbook upload hadoop
```

To create roles on the server from the role files use the following commands:

```
■ knife role from file hadoop_cluster_role.rb
knife role from file hadoop_master_role.rb
```

The roles are then added to the run lists of the master and slave nodes as follows:

```
■ knife node run_list add masternode 'role[hadoop_cluster_role]'
knife node run_list add masternode 'role[hadoop_master_role]'
knife node run_list add slavenode 'role[hadoop_cluster_role]'
```

Finally, the chef-client is run on the master and slave nodes (from the workstation) as follows:

```
■ knife ssh <IP Address> 'sudo chef-client' -m -x ubuntu -i <PEM File>
knife ssh <IP Address> 'sudo chef-client' -m -x ubuntu -i <PEM File>
```

### 11.3.3 Storm Cluster

In this section you will learn how to setup an Apache Storm cluster with Chef. The first step is to create a cookbook named hadoop with the following command:

```
knife cookbook create storm
```

Next, launch three Amazon EC2 nodes (for Nimbus, Zookeeper and Supervisor) and bootstrap them using the following commands from the workstation:

```
knife bootstrap <nimbus-IP-address> -sudo -x
ubuntu -i mykeypair.pem -N nimbusnode

knife bootstrap <supervisor-IP-address> -sudo -x
ubuntu -i mykeypair.pem -N supervisornode

knife bootstrap <zookeeper-IP-address> -sudo -x
ubuntu -i mykeypair.pem -N zookeepernode
```

After bootstrapping the nodes, create recipes for generating SSH keys, setting up hosts, installing Java, setting up Zookeeper and setting up Storm. You can reuse the recipes for generating SSH keys, setting up hosts, and installing Java from the Hadoop cookbook described in the previous section. Box 11.20 shows the recipe for setting up Zookeeper.

#### ■ Box 11.20: Chef recipe for setting up Zookeeper - setup_zookeeper.rb

```
setup_zk = Mixlib::ShellOut.new("echo deb [arch=amd64]
http://archive.cloudera.com/cdh4/ubuntu/precise/amd64/cdh precise-cdh4
contrib>> /etc/apt/sources.list.d/cloudera.list", :cwd => '/home/ubuntu')
setup_zk.run_command

setup_zk = Mixlib::ShellOut.new("echo
deb-src http://archive.cloudera.com/cdh4/ubuntu/precise/amd64/cdh
precise-cdh4 contrib>> /etc/apt/sources.list.d/cloudera.list",
:cwd => '/home/ubuntu') setup_zk.run_command

setup_zk = Mixlib::ShellOut.new("apt-get -q -y update",
:cwd => '/home/ubuntu')
setup_zk.run_command

setup_zk = Mixlib::ShellOut.new("apt-get install -q -y
zookeeper zookeeper-server", :cwd => '/home/ubuntu')
setup_zk.run_command

setup_zk = Mixlib::ShellOut.new("./zkServer.sh start",
:cwd => '/usr/lib/zookeeper/bin/')
setup_zk.run_command
```

Box 11.21 shows the recipe for setting up Storm. In this recipe, the dependencies are first installed. Next, the packages for ZeroMQ and JZMQ are installed. The Storm package is then downloaded and installed.

### ■ Box 11.21: Chef recipe for setting up Storm - setup_storm.eb

```
require 'chef/shell_out'

download_depend = Mixlib::ShellOut.new("apt-get install
build-essential uuid-dev git pkg-config libtool autoconf automake",
:cwd => '/home/ubuntu')
download_depend.run_command

download_depend = Mixlib::ShellOut.new("apt-get install
unzip", :cwd => '/home/ubuntu')
download_depend.run_command

download_depend = Mixlib::ShellOut.new("wget
http://download.zeromq.org/zeromq-2.1.7.tar.gz", :cwd => '/home/ubuntu')
download_depend.run_command

download_depend = Mixlib::ShellOut.new("tar -xzf
zeromq-2.1.7.tar.gz", :cwd => '/home/ubuntu')
download_depend.run_command

download_depend = Mixlib::ShellOut.new("./configure",
:cwd => '/home/ubuntu/zeromq-2.1.7')
download_depend.run_command

download_depend = Mixlib::ShellOut.new("make",
:cwd => '/home/ubuntu/zeromq-2.1.7')
download_depend.run_command

download_depend = Mixlib::ShellOut.new("make install",
:cwd => '/home/ubuntu/zeromq-2.1.7')
download_depend.run_command

download_depend = Mixlib::ShellOut.new("export
JAVA_HOME=/usr/lib/jvm/java-7-oracle", :cwd => '/home/ubuntu')
download_depend.run_command

download_depend = Mixlib::ShellOut.new("git clone
https://github.com/nathanmarz/jzmq.git", :cwd => '/home/ubuntu')
download_depend.run_command

download_depend = Mixlib::ShellOut.new("touch
classdist_noinst.stamp", :cwd => '/home/ubuntu/jzmq/src')
download_depend.run_command

download_depend = Mixlib::ShellOut.new("CLASSPATH=
.:../.:$CLASSPATH javac -d .
org/zeromq/ZMQ.java org/zeromq/ZMQException.java
org/zeromq/ZMQQueue.java
org/zeromq/ZMQForwarder.java org/zeromq/ZMQStreamer.java",
:cwd => '/home/ubuntu/jzmq/src')
download_depend.run_command

download_depend = Mixlib::ShellOut.new("./autogen.sh",
```

```
:cwd => '/home/ubuntu/jzmq')
download_depend.run_command

download_depend = Mixlib::ShellOut.new("./configure",
:cwd => '/home/ubuntu/jzmq')
download_depend.run_command

download_depend = Mixlib::ShellOut.new("make",
:cwd => '/home/ubuntu/jzmq')
download_depend.run_command

download_depend = Mixlib::ShellOut.new("make install",
:cwd => '/home/ubuntu/jzmq')
download_depend.run_command

download_storm = Mixlib::ShellOut.new("wget
https://dl.dropbox.com/u/133901206/storm-0.8.2.zip",
:cwd => '/home/ubuntu')
download_storm.run_command

download_storm = Mixlib::ShellOut.new("unzip storm-0.8.2.zip",
:cwd => '/home/ubuntu')
download_storm.run_command

download_storm = Mixlib::ShellOut.new("ln -s storm-0.8.2 storm",
:cwd => '/home/ubuntu')
download_storm.run_command

download_storm = Mixlib::ShellOut.new("chown -R ubuntu:ubuntu storm",
:cwd => '/home/ubuntu')
download_storm.run_command


# setup local directory
directory '/home/ubuntu/stormlocal' do
owner "ubuntu"
group "ubuntu"
action :create
recursive true
end
```

With the all the recipes for the Storm cookbook now created the next step is to define roles. Boxes 11.22, 11.23 and 11.24 show the Chef roles for setting up a cluster for Storm, setting up Zookeeper and setting up Storm respectively.

### ■ Box 11.22: Chef role for setting up Storm cluster

```
name "storm_cluster_role"
description "Setup cluster nodes"
run_list [
  "recipe[storm::setup_hosts]",
  "recipe[storm::ssh_keys]",
  "recipe[storm::authorized_nodes]",
```

```
    "recipe[storm::setup_java]"
]
```

### ■ Box 11.23: Chef role for setting up Zookeeper

```
name "storm_zookeeper_role"
description "Setup zookeeper node"
run_list [
    "recipe[storm::setup_zookeeper]"
]
```

### ■ Box 11.24: Chef role for setting up nodes for Storm cluster

```
name "storm_setup_role"
description "Setup storm nodes"
run_list [
    "recipe[storm::setup_storm]"
]
```

The Storm cookbook is then uploaded to the Chef server using the following command:

```
■ knife cookbook upload storm
```

To create roles on the server from the role files use the following commands:

```
■ knife role from file storm_cluster_role.rb
knife role from file storm_zookeeper_role.rb
knife role from file storm_setup_role.rb
```

The roles are then added to the run lists of the Nimbus, Zookeeper and Supervisor nodes as follows:

```
■ knife node run_list add nimbusnode 'role[storm_cluster_role]'
knife node run_list add nimbusnode 'role[storm_setup_role]'

knife node run_list add supervisornode 'role[storm_cluster_role]'
knife node run_list add supervisornode 'role[storm_setup_role]'

knife node run_list add zookeepernode 'role[storm_cluster_role]'
knife node run_list add zookeepernode 'role[storm_zookeeper_role]'
```

Finally, the chef-client is run on the nimbus, zookeeper and supervisor nodes (from the workstation) as follows:

```
■ knife ssh <nimbus-IP-address> 'sudo chef-client'
-m -x ubuntu -i mykeypair.pem

knife ssh <supervisor-IP-address> 'sudo chef-client'
-m -x ubuntu -i mykeypair.pem

knife ssh <zookeeper-IP-address> 'sudo chef-client'
-m -x ubuntu -i mykeypair.pem
```

## 11.4  Puppet

Puppet (like Chef) is also a configuration management tool that can be used to manage configurations on a variety of platforms. Figure 11.5 shows the deployment model for Puppet. Puppet is usually deployed in a client-server model. The server runs the Puppet Master and the client runs the Puppet Agents. Like the Chef-server, the Puppet Master maintains the configuration information for the clients. The puppet agents connect to the master to obtain information on the desired state. Puppet agents on the clients make changes if the current state is different from the desired state. Puppet agents can be configured to automatically check for new or updated configuration from the master at regular intervals. Like Chef, Puppet also uses a declarative modeling language for defining the configurations.

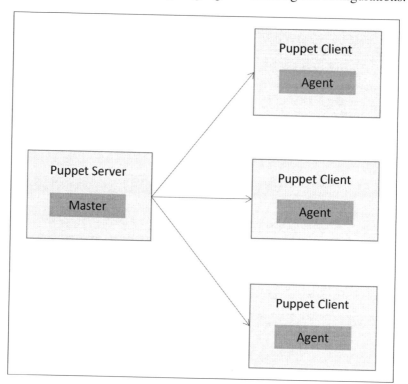

Figure 11.5: Puppet master and agents

Let us now look at the key concepts of Puppet:

- **Resource:** Resource is a fundamental unit of configuration. For example, file, user, package, service, etc. Similar resources are grouped together into resource types.

- **Resource Abstraction Layer (RAL):** Resource descriptions in a configuration are abstract in nature and not tied to a specific OS. RAL allows separation of resource descriptions from their implementations. RAL consists of high-level modules (types) and platform-specific implementations (providers).
- **Class:** Classes define a collection of resources which are managed together as a single unit.
- **Manifest:** Manifests are Puppet programs (with .pp extension). Manifests include various types of logic such as resource descriptions, classes, conditional statements, etc. Manifests can be applied using the 'puppet apply' command, which enforces the desired state as defined in the manifest file.
- **Module:** Instead of defining the entire logic in a single manifest file, Puppet allows you to split the logic in multiple files which are organized as a module. A module consists of multiple files containing the class definitions. Classes group the resource definitions. The classes defined in modules can be included in the manifest file which is applied to bring the systems into the desired state.

Box 11.25 shows the commands for setting up Puppet server and client.

■ **Box 11.25: Setting up Puppet server and client**

```
#Step 1:  Enable the Puppet Labs Package Repository
wget https://apt.puppetlabs.com/puppetlabs-release-trusty.deb
sudo dpkg -i puppetlabs-release-trusty.deb
sudo apt-get update


#Step 2:  Install Puppet on the Puppet Master Server
sudo apt-get install puppetmaster-passenger


#Step 3:  Install Puppet on Agent Nodes
sudo apt-get install puppet



#Post-install configuration

#Change hostnames of server and client
sudo hostname puppet
sudo hostname puppet-client


#Both master and client:
#Edit the /etc/hosts file and add hostnames and IP addresses
of server and clients

sudo vim /etc/hosts
-----/etc/hosts-----
<server-IP-address> puppet
<client-IP-address> puppet-client
----------------


#Edit puppet.conf on server and clients and add server hostname
```

```
sudo vim /etc/puppet/puppet.conf
-------puppet.conf----
[main]
server=puppet
-----------------


#Request certificate from client:
sudo puppet agent -test -ca_server=puppet -waitforcert 60

#Accept certificate on master
sudo puppet cert list
sudo puppet cert sign -all
```

## 11.5   Puppet Case Study - Multi-tier Deployment

In this section you will learn how to create a multi-tier deployment comprising of HAProxy load balancer, Django application server and MongoDB database server, with Puppet.

Create a puppet module with the following directory structure and the files on the Puppet master node:

```
■ -/etc
|-puppet
|  |-modules
|  |  |-threetierdeployment
|  |  |  |-manifests
|  |  |  |  |-init.pp
|  |  |  |  |-haproxy.pp
|  |  |  |  |-django.pp
|  |  |  |  |-mongodb.pp
|  |  |  |-templates
|  |  |  |  |-haproxy.cfg.erb
```

Box 11.26 shows the haproxy class which contains a package resource definition for installing HAProxy and a file resource for configuration file (haproxy.cfg). The template for the configuration file is shown in Box 11.27.

### ■ Box 11.26:  Puppet module - haproxy class - haproxy.pp

```
class haproxy(
   $global_options = {
     'chroot' => '/var/lib/haproxy',
     'pidfile' => '/var/run/haproxy.pid',
     'maxconn' => '4000',
     'user' => 'haproxy',
     'group' => 'haproxy',
     'daemon' => '',
     'stats' => 'socket /var/lib/haproxy/stats'
   },
   $defaults_options = {
     'log' => 'global',
```

```
   'stats' => 'enable',
   'option' => 'redispatch',
   'retries' => '3',
   'timeout' => [
   'http-request 10s',
   'queue 1m',
   'connect 10s',
   'client 1m',
   'server 1m',
   'check 10s',
   ],
   'maxconn' => '8000'
   },
)
{

package { 'haproxy':
   ensure => present,
}

file { 'haproxy-config':
   path => '/etc/haproxy/haproxy.cfg',
   content => template('/etc/puppet/modules/
threetierdeployment/haproxy.cfg.erb'),
}
}
```

**■ Box 11.27: HAProxy template file - haproxy.cfg.erb**

```
global
<% @global_options.each do |key,val| -%>
<% if val.is_a?(Array) -%>
<% val.each do |item| -%>
<%= key %> <%= item %>
<% end -%>
<% else -%>
<%= key %> <%= val %>
<% end -%>
<% end -%>

defaults
<% @defaults_options.each do |key,val| -%>
<% if val.is_a?(Array) -%>
<% val.each do |item| -%>
<%= key %> <%= item %>
<% end -%>
<% else -%>
<%= key %> <%= val %>
<% end -%>
<% end -%>
```

Box 11.28 shows the django class that contains package resources for python-pip provider and django.

---

■ **Box 11.28: Puppet module - django class - django.pp**

```
class django{

   package { 'python-pip':
    ensure => installed,
   }

   package { 'django':
    ensure => installed,
    provider => 'pip',
    require => Package["python-pip"],
   }
}
```

---

Box 11.29 shows the mongodb class that contains commands for setting up MongoDB.

---

■ **Box 11.29: Puppet module - mongodb class - mongodb.pp**

```
class mongodb{

exec { "cmd1":
   command => "/usr/bin/apt-key adv –keyserver
   keyserver.ubuntu.com –recv 7F0CEB10",
}

exec { "cmd2":
   command => "/bin/echo
'deb http://downloads-distro.mongodb.org/repo/ubuntu-upstart
   dist 10gen' >> /etc/apt/sources.list.d/10gen.list",
require => Exec["cmd1"],

}

exec { "cmd3":
   command => "/usr/bin/apt-get update",
require => Exec["cmd2"],
}

exec { "cmd4":
   command => "/usr/bin/apt-get install mongodb-10gen",
require => Exec["cmd3"],
}
```

---

To apply the Puppet module on the client nodes, run the Puppet agent on each client node as follows:

```
■ sudo puppet agent -t
```

## 11.6 NETCONF-YANG Case Studies

In Chapter-4 you learned about NETCONF and YANG. This section describes detailed case studies on IoT device management using NETCONF-YANG. The case studies use the Netopeer NETCONF tools which were described in Chapter-4.

Box 11.30 provides the commands for installing Netopeer tools.

■ **Box 11.30: Commands for installing Netopeer tools**

```
#Install dependencies sudo apt-get update
sudo apt-get install python-dev
sudo apt-get install python-setuptools
sudo apt-get install xsltproc
sudo apt-get install git
sudo apt-get install libxml2
sudo apt-get install libxslt1-dev
sudo apt-get install libxslt1.1
sudo apt-get install libssh2-1-dev
sudo apt-get install doxygen
sudo apt-get install libevent-dev
sudo apt-get install libreadline-dev
sudo apt-get install libncurses5-dev
sudo apt-get install libncurses5
sudo apt-get install libxml++2.6-dev
sudo apt-get install libcurl4-gnutls-dev
sudo apt-get install libssl-dev openssl
sudo apt-get install libxml2-dev
sudo apt-get install python-libxml2
sudo apt-get install libdbus-1-3 libdbus-1-dev
sudo apt-get install libdbus2.0-cil libdbus2.0-cil-dev


#Install libnetconf git clone https://code.google.com/p/libnetconf/
cd libnetconf
./configure -with-nacm-recovery-uid=1000
make
sudo make install


#Install netopeer git clone https://code.google.com/p/netopeer/
cd netopeer/server
./configure -with-dbus-services
make
sudo make install


cd ../server-sl
./configure
make
sudo make install


cd ../cli
./configure
make
sudo make install
```

```
#Launch netopeer-cli
netopeer-cli
```

## 11.6.1 Steps for IoT device Management with NETCONF-YANG

1. Create a YANG model of the system that defines the configuration and state data of the system.

2. Compile the YANG model with the 'lnctool' which comes with Libnetconf. The 'lnctool' generates a TransAPI module (callbacks C file) and the YIN file. The callbacks C file contains the functions for making the changes on the device. YIN file contains an XML representation of the YANG module.

```
■ lnctool -model iotdevice.yang convert

lnctool -model iotdevice.yang validation

lnctool -model iotdevice.yang transapi -paths iotdevice.paths
```

3. Fill in the IoT device management code in the TransAPI module (callbacks C file). This file includes configuration callbacks, RPC callbacks and state data callbacks.
4. Build the callbacks C file to generate the library file (.so).

```
■ autoreconf
./configure
make
```

5. Load the YANG module (containing the data definitions) and the TransAPI module (.so binary) into the Netopeer server using the Netopeer manager tool.

```
■ sudo netopeer-manager add -name iotdevice
-model iotdevice.yin -datastore /home/ubuntu/iotdevice.xml
```

6. The operator can now connect from the management system to the Netopeer server using the Netopeer CLI.

```
■ netopeer-cli
netconf> connect
Host:  localhost
Password:
```

7. Operator can issue NETCONF commands from the Netopeer CLI. Commands can be issued to change the configuration data, get operational data or execute an RPC on the IoT device.

```
■ netconf> get
:
netconf> get-config running
:
netconf> edit-config running
:
netconf> user-rpc
```

## 11.6.2   Managing Smart Irrigation IoT System with NETCONF-YANG

A case study on building a smart irrigation IoT system was described in Chapter-9. The smart irrigation system uses an IoT device and soil moisture sensors to determine the amount of moisture in the soil and release the flow of water through the irrigation pipes only when the moisture levels go below a predefined threshold.

Let us look at how NETCONF-YANG can be used for managing the smart irrigation system. Box 11.31 shows the YANG module for the smart irrigation system and Figure 11.6 shows a visual representation of the YANG module. The YANG module describes the structure of the configuration and state data of the system, RPCs for starting and stopping the irrigation and the notifications. Leaf nodes *systemID*, *systemLocation* and *systemStatus* are non configurable parameters whereas the leaf node *moistureThreshold* is a configurable parameter. The RPC start-irrigation takes as input the *irrigationDuration* which determines the duration for which the irrigation is done. The *irrigationDone* notification notifies the status of irrigation.

### ■ Box 11.31: YANG Module for Smart Irrigation System

```
module smartirrigation {

 namespace "http://netconfcentral.org/ns/smartirrigation";

 prefix "irrigation";

 description
 "YANG module for Smart Irrigation IoT system";


 revision 2014-07-15 {
  description "Smart Irrigation System";
 }


 container smartirrigation {
  presence
   "Indicates the service is available";

  description
   "Top-level container for all smart irrigation system objects.";

  leaf systemID {
```

```
      type string;
      config false;
      mandatory true;
      description
      "ID of the system";
    }

    leaf systemLocation {
      type string;
      config false;
      mandatory true;
      description
      "The location of the system";
    }


    leaf systemStatus {
      type enumeration {
       enum up {
       value 1;
       description
        "The is powered up";
       }
       enum down {
       value 2;
       description
        "The system is powered down";
       }
       enum irrigating {
       value 3;
       description
        "Irrigation is ON";
       }
      }
    config false;
    mandatory true;
    description
    "This variable indicates the current state of
     the system.";
    }

  leaf moistureThreshold {
   type uint32 {
   range "1 ..  100";
   }
    default 20;
   description
    "This variable controls the soil moisture
threshold above which irrigation is turned on.";
  }
  }

 rpc start-irrigation {
  description
```

```
  "Turn on the irrigation";
 input {
  leaf irrigationDuration {
   type uint32 {
    range "1 ..  60";
   }
   default 15;
   description
   "This variable controls the duration
for which irrigation is turned on.";
  }

 }
}

rpc stop-irrigation {
 description
  "Stop irrigation";
}

notification irrigationDone {
 description
  "Indicates that irrigation has been completed.";

 leaf irrigationStatus {
  description
  "Indicates the final irrigation status";
  type enumeration {
   enum done {
   description
    "The irrigation is done.";
   }
   enum cancelled {
   description
    "The irrigation was stopped.";
   }
   enum error {
   description
    "The irrigation system is broken.";
   }
  }
 }
}
}
```

Upon compiling the YANG module with the 'lnctool', the YIN and TransAPI module files are generated. Box 11.32 shows a YIN version (an XML representation) of the smart irrigation system YANG module.

■ **Box 11.32: YIN version of the Smart Irrigation System YANG module**

```
<?xml version="1.0" encoding="UTF-8"?>
<module xmlns="urn:ietf:params:xml:ns:yang:yin:1"
```

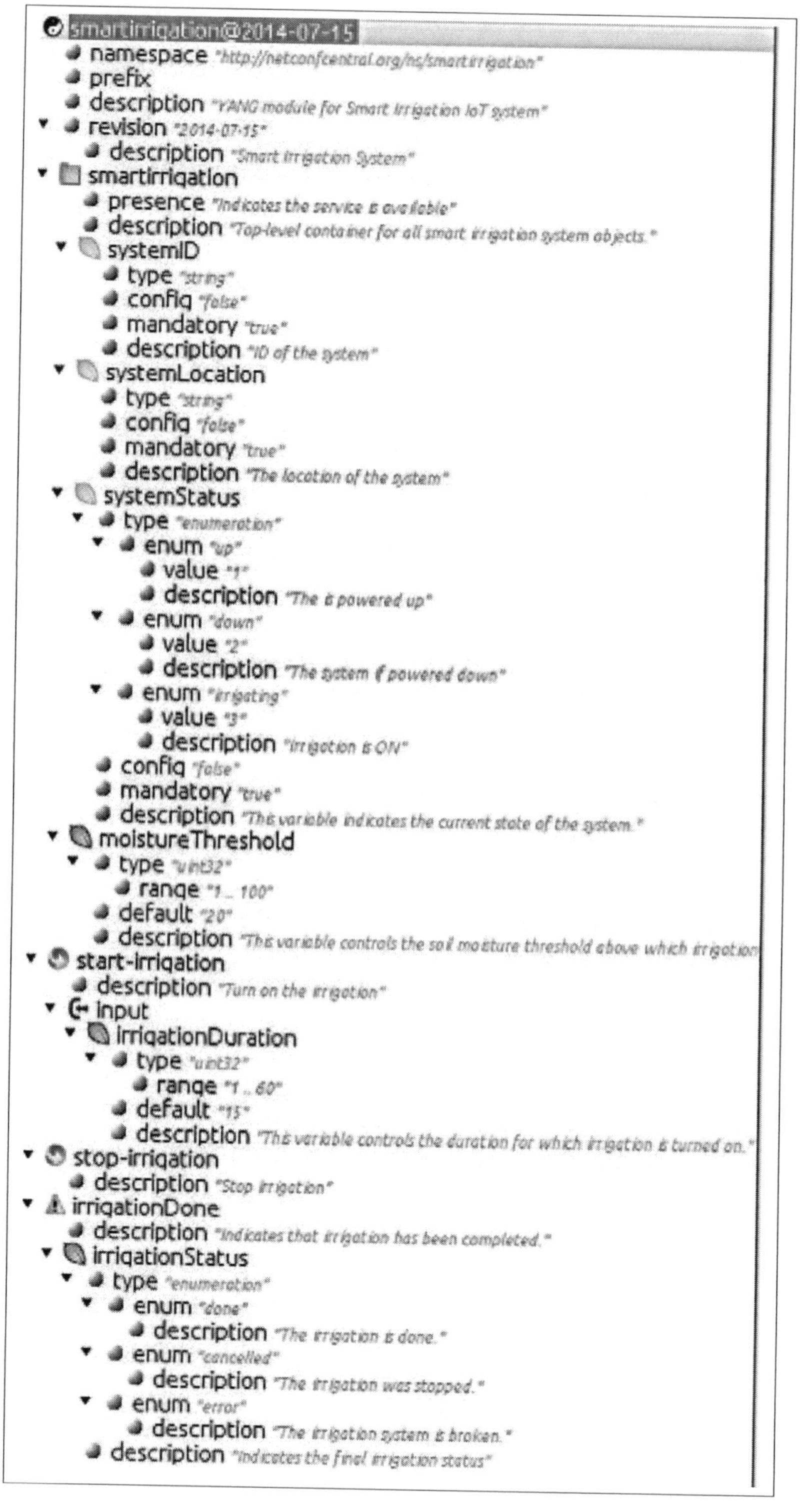

Figure 11.6: Visual representation of YANG Module for smart irrigation IoT system

```
xmlns:toast="http://netconfcentral.org/ns/smartirrigation"
name="smartirrigation">
<namespace uri="http://netconfcentral.org/ns/smartirrigation"/>
<prefix value="toast"/>
<description>
<text>YANG module for Smart Irrigation IoT system</text>
</description>
<revision date="2014-07-15">
<description>
<text>Smart Irrigation System</text>
</description>
</revision>
<container name="smartirrigation">
<presence value="Indicates the service is available"/>
<description>
<text>Top-level container for all objects</text>
</description>
<leaf name="systemID">
<type name="string"/>
<config value="false"/>
<mandatory value="true"/>
<description>
<text>ID of the system</text>
</description>
</leaf>
<leaf name="systemLocation">
<type name="string"/>
<config value="false"/>
<mandatory value="true"/>
<description>
<text>The location of the system</text>
</description>
</leaf>
<leaf name="systemStatus">
<type name="enumeration">
<enum name="up">
<value value="1"/>
<description>
<text>The is powered up</text>
</description>
</enum>
<enum name="down">
<value value="2"/>
<description>
<text>The system if powered down</text>
</description>
</enum>
<enum name="irrigating">
<value value="3"/>
<description>
<text>Irrigation is ON</text>
</description>
</enum>
</type>
```

```
<config value="false"/>
<mandatory value="true"/>
<description>
<text>This variable indicates the current state of
the system.</text>
</description>
</leaf>
<leaf name="moistureThreshold">
<type name="uint32">
<range value="1 ..  100"/>
</type>
<default value="20"/>
<description>
<text>This variable controls the soil moisture threshold above which
irrigation is turned on.</text>
</description>
</leaf>
</container>
<rpc name="start-irrigation">
<description>
<text>Turn on the irrigation</text>
</description>
<input>
<leaf name="irrigationDuration">
<type name="uint32">
<range value="1 ..  60"/>
</type>
<default value="15"/>
<description>
<text>This variable controls the duration for which
irrigation is turned on.</text>
</description>
</leaf>
</input>
</rpc>
<rpc name="stop-irrigation">
<description>
<text>Stop irrigation</text>
</description>
</rpc>
<notification name="irrigationDone">
<description>
<text>Indicates that irrigation has been completed.</text>
</description>
<leaf name="irrigationStatus">
<description>
<text>Indicates the final irrigation status</text>
</description>
<type name="enumeration">
<enum name="done">
<description>
<text>The irrigation is done.</text>
</description>
</enum>
```

```
<enum name="cancelled">
<description>
<text>The irrigation was stopped.</text>
</description>
</enum>
<enum name="error">
<description>
<text>The irrigation system is broken.</text>
</description>
</enum>
</type>
</leaf>
</notification>
</module>
```

Box 11.33 shows the TransAPI module file after implementing the functions in the auto-generated file. The following additions are done to the auto-generated file:

1. A system status structure is added.
2. The 'transapi_init()' function is filled which includes the actions run after the module is loaded. Note that the irrigation status is set to false (0) in this function.
3. The 'get_state_data()' function is filled with the code that generates state information as defined in the data model.
4. The configuration callback function 'callback_smartirrigation_smartirrigation()' is filled which is run when node in path /smartirrigation:smartirrigation changes.
5. RPC message callback functions 'rpc_start_irrigation()' and 'rpc_stop_irrigation()' are filled and the auxiliary function 'irrigate()' is implemented.

■ **Box 11.33: TransAPI C module for Smart Irrigation System**

```
#include <unistd.h>
#include <stdlib.h>
#include <libxml/tree.h>
#include <libnetconf_xml.h>
#include <pthread.h>
#include <time.h>
#include <string.h>
#include <sys/types.h>
#include <sys/ipc.h>
#include <sys/shm.h>


/* TransAPI version which must be compatible with libnetconf */
int transapi_version = 4;

/* Signal to libnetconf that config data were modified by any callback.
 * 0 - data not modified
 * 1 - data have been modified
 */
int config_modified = 0;
```

```
/*
 * Determines the callbacks order.
 * Set this variable before compilation and DO NOT modify it in runtime.
 * TRANSAPI_CLBCKS_LEAF_TO_ROOT (default)
 * TRANSAPI_CLBCKS_ROOT_TO_LEAF
 */
const TRANSAPI_CLBCKS_ORDER_TYPE callbacks_order =
TRANSAPI_CLBCKS_ORDER_DEFAULT;


/*This variable is set by libnetconf to
announce edit-config's error-option
 * Possible values:
 * NC_EDIT_ERROPT_STOP - Following callback after failure are not
executed, all successful callbacks executed till
failure point must be applied to the device.
 * NC_EDIT_ERROPT_CONT - Failed callbacks are skipped, but all
callbacks needed to apply configuration changes are executed
 * NC_EDIT_ERROPT_ROLLBACK - After failure, following callbacks
are not executed, but previous successful callbacks are
executed again with previous configuration data to roll it back.
 */
NC_EDIT_ERROPT_TYPE erropt = NC_EDIT_ERROPT_NOTSET;


/* smart irrigation system status structure */
struct smartirrigation_status {
 int enabled;
 int irrigating;
 pthread_mutex_t smartirrigation_mutex;
};


/* status structure instance, stored in shared memory */
struct smartirrigation_status * status = NULL;


/**
 * @brief Initialize plugin after loaded and
before any other functions are called.

 * This function should not apply any configuration
data to the controlled device.  If no
 * running is returned (it stays *NULL), complete
startup configuration is consequently
 * applied via module callbacks.  When a
running configuration is returned, libnetconf
 * then applies (via module's callbacks)
only the startup configuration data that
 * differ from the returned running configuration data.

 * Please note, that copying startup data to
the running is performed only after the
 * libnetconf's system-wide close.

 * @param[out] running Current configuration of managed device.
```

```
* @return EXIT_SUCCESS or EXIT_FAILURE
*/
int transapi_init(xmlDocPtr * running)
{
 key_t shmkey;
 int shmid;
 int first;

 /* get shared memory key */
 if ((shmkey = ftok ("/proc/self/exe", 1)) == -1) {
  return EXIT_FAILURE;
 }

{ /* get id of shared memory if exist */
 if ((shmid = shmget (shmkey, sizeof(struct smartirrigation_status), 0666))
!= -1)
  first = 0;
{ /* create shared memory */
 } else if ((shmid = shmget (shmkey,
sizeof(struct smartirrigation_status),
IPC_CREAT | 0666)) != -1)
  first = 1;
 } else { /*shared memory can not be found nor created */
  return EXIT_FAILURE;
 }

 /* attach shared memory */
 if ((status = shmat (shmid, NULL, 0)) == (void*)-1) {
  return EXIT_FAILURE;
 }
 /* first run after shared memory removed
(reboot, manually) initiate the mutex */
 if (first) {
  if (pthread_mutex_init (&status->smartirrigation_mutex, NULL)) {
  return EXIT_FAILURE;
  }
  status->irrigating = 0;
 }

 return EXIT_SUCCESS;
}

/**
* @brief Free all resources allocated on plugin
runtime and prepare plugin for removal.
*/
void transapi_close(void)
{
  return;
}

/**
* @brief Retrieve state data from device and return them as XML document
*
```

```
 * @param model Device data model.  libxml2 xmlDocPtr.
 * @param running Running datastore content.  libxml2 xmlDocPtr.
 * @param[out] err Double pointer to error structure.
Fill error when some occurs.
 * @return State data as libxml2 xmlDocPtr or NULL in case of error.
 */
xmlDocPtr get_state_data (xmlDocPtr model,
xmlDocPtr running, struct nc_err **err)
{
  xmlDocPtr state;
  xmlNodePtr root;
  xmlNsPtr ns;

  state = xmlNewDoc(BAD_CAST "1.0");
  root = xmlNewDocNode(state, NULL, BAD_CAST "smartirrigation", NULL);
  xmlDocSetRootElement(state, root);
  ns = xmlNewNs(root, BAD_CAST
"http://netconfcentral.org/ns/smartirrigation", NULL);
  xmlSetNs(root, ns);
  xmlNewChild(root, ns, BAD_CAST "systemID", BAD_CAST "IOT123");
  xmlNewChild(root, ns, BAD_CAST "systemLocation", BAD_CAST "Field-1");

  if (status->enabled == 1){
   xmlNewChild(root, ns, BAD_CAST "systemStatus", BAD_CAST "up");
  }
  else if(status->enabled == 0){
   xmlNewChild(root, ns, BAD_CAST "systemStatus", BAD_CAST "down");
  }
  else if (status->irrigating == 1){
   xmlNewChild(root, ns, BAD_CAST "systemStatus", BAD_CAST "irrigating");
  }

  return (state);
}
/*
 * Mapping prefixes with namespaces.
 * Do NOT modify this structure!
 */
struct ns_pair namespace_mapping[] = {{"smartirrigation",
"http://netconfcentral.org/ns/smartirrigation"}, {NULL, NULL}};

/*
 * CONFIGURATION callbacks
 * Here follows set of callback functions run every time some
change in associated part of running datastore occurs.
 */

/**
 * @brief This callback will be run when node in path
/smartirrigation:smartirrigation changes
 *
 * @param[in] data Double pointer to void.
Its passed to every callback.  You can share data using it.
 * @param[in] op Observed change in path.  XMLDIFF_OP type.
```

```
* @param[in] node Modified node.
if op == XMLDIFF_REM its copy of node removed.
* @param[out] error If callback fails, it can return
libnetconf error structure with a failure description.
*
* @return EXIT_SUCCESS or EXIT_FAILURE
*/
/* !DO NOT ALTER FUNCTION SIGNATURE! */
int callback_smartirrigation_smartirrigation (void ** data,
XMLDIFF_OP op, xmlNodePtr node, struct nc_err** error)
{
 pthread_mutex_lock(&status->smartirrigation_mutex);

 if (op <= 0 || op > (XMLDIFF_MOD | XMLDIFF_CHAIN |
XMLDIFF_ADD | XMLDIFF_REM) || ((op & XMLDIFF_ADD) && (op & XMLDIFF_REM)))
{
   *error = nc_err_new(NC_ERR_OP_FAILED);
   nc_err_set(*error, NC_ERR_PARAM_MSG, "Invalid configuration
data modification for smartirrigation module.");
   return (EXIT_FAILURE);
 } else {
  if (op & XMLDIFF_REM) {
  status->enabled = 0;
  if (status->irrigating != 0) {
  nc_verb_warning("Interrupting ongoing irrigation!");
  status->irrigating = 0;
  }
  } else if (op & XMLDIFF_ADD) {
  status->enabled = 1;
  }
 }

 nc_verb_verbose("Turning smartirrigation %s.",
status->enabled ?  "on" :  "off");

 pthread_mutex_unlock(&status->smartirrigation_mutex);

 return EXIT_SUCCESS;
}

/*
* Structure transapi_config_callbacks provide
mapping between callback and path in configuration datastore.
* It is used by libnetconf library to decide which callbacks will be run.
* DO NOT alter this structure
*/
struct transapi_data_callbacks clbks = {
 .callbacks_count = 1,
 .data = NULL,
 .callbacks = {
  {.path = "/smartirrigation:smartirrigation",
 .func = callback_smartirrigation_smartirrigation}
 }
};
```

```
void * irrigate (void * duration)
{
  /* pretend irrigation */
  sleep (*(int*)duration);

  pthread_mutex_lock (&status->smartirrigation_mutex);

  if (status->irrigating == 0) { /* was canceled */
    pthread_mutex_unlock (&status->smartirrigation_mutex);
  } else { /* still irrigationing */
    /* turn off */
    status->irrigating = 0;
    ncntf_event_new(-1, NCNTF_GENERIC,
"<irrigationDone><irrigationStatus>done</irrigationStatus>
</irrigationDone>");
  }

  pthread_mutex_unlock (&status->smartirrigation_mutex);
  return NULL;
}


/*
 * RPC callbacks
 * Here follows set of callback functions run every
time RPC specific for this device arrives.
 * Every function takes array of inputs as an argument.
On few first lines they are assigned to named variables.
Avoid accessing the array directly.
 * If input was not set in RPC message argument in set to NULL.
 */

nc_reply * rpc_start_irrigation (xmlNodePtr input[])
{
  xmlNodePtr irrigationDuration = input[0];

  struct nc_err * err;
  nc_reply * reply;
  static int duration;
  pthread_t tid;

  if (irrigationDuration == NULL) { /* use default*/
    duration = 15;
  } else { /* duration value */
    duration = atoi ((char*)xmlNodeGetContent(irrigationDuration));
  }

  pthread_mutex_lock(&status->smartirrigation_mutex);

  if (status->enabled == 0) { /* Smart Irrigation system is off */
    reply = nc_reply_error(nc_err_new (NC_ERR_RES_DENIED));
  } else if (status->irrigating) { /* Smart Irrigation system is busy */
```

```
   reply = nc_reply_error (nc_err_new (NC_ERR_IN_USE));
  } else if (duration == 0) { /* duration must be from <1,10> */
   reply = nc_reply_error (nc_err_new (NC_ERR_INVALID_VALUE));
{ /* Smart Irrigation system internal error (cannot turn heater on) */
  } else if (pthread_create (&tid, NULL, irrigate, &duration))
   err = nc_err_new (NC_ERR_OP_FAILED);
   nc_err_set (err, NC_ERR_PARAM_MSG, "Smart Irrigation system is broken!");
   ncntf_event_new(-1, NCNTF_GENERIC,
 "<irrigationDone><irrigationStatus>error</irrigationStatus>
</irrigationDone>");
   reply = nc_reply_error (err);
  } else { /* all ok, start irrigating */
   status->irrigating = 1;
   reply = nc_reply_ok();
   pthread_detach (tid);
  }

  pthread_mutex_unlock(&status->smartirrigation_mutex);
  return reply;


}
nc_reply * rpc_stop_irrigation (xmlNodePtr input[])
{

  nc_reply * reply;
  struct nc_err * err;

  pthread_mutex_lock(&status->smartirrigation_mutex);

  if (status->enabled == 0) {/* smart irrigation system is off */
   reply = nc_reply_error(nc_err_new (NC_ERR_RES_DENIED));
  } else if (status->irrigating == 0) { /* smart irrigation system in not
 irrigating */
   err = nc_err_new (NC_ERR_OP_FAILED);
   nc_err_set (err, NC_ERR_PARAM_MSG,
 "There is no irrigating in progress.");
   reply = nc_reply_error(err);
  } else { /* interrupt irrigation */
   status->irrigating = 0;
   ncntf_event_new(-1, NCNTF_GENERIC,
 "<irrigationDone><irrigationStatus>cancelled</irrigationStatus>
</irrigationDone>");
   reply = nc_reply_ok();
  }

  pthread_mutex_unlock(&status->smartirrigation_mutex);

  return reply;
}
/*
* Structure transapi_rpc_callbacks provide mapping between callbacks and
RPC messages.
* It is used by libnetconf library to decide which callbacks will be run
when RPC arrives.
* DO NOT alter this structure
```

```
*/
struct transapi_rpc_callbacks rpc_clbks = {
 .callbacks_count = 2,
 .callbacks = {
  {.name="start-irrigation",
.func=rpc_start_irrigation,
.arg_count=1, .arg_order={"irrigationDuration"}},
  {.name="stop-irrigation",
.func=rpc_stop_irrigation, .arg_count=0, .arg_order={}}
  }
};
```

After implementing the TransAPI module file, the file is compiled and the binary (.so file) is loaded into the Netopeer-server using the Netopeer-manager as described in the previous section. After loading the module, NETCONF commands can be issued from the Netopeer-cli. For example, to show the current status of the smart irrigation system, use get command as follows:

```
■ netconf> get -filter

Type the filter (close editor by Ctrl-D):
<smartirrigation xmlns="http://netconfcentral.org/ns/smartirrigation"/>

Result:
<smartirrigation xmlns="http://netconfcentral.org/ns/smartirrigation">
<systemID>IOT123</systemID>
<systemLocation>Field-1</systemLocation>
<systemStatus>up</systemStatus>
</smartirrigation>
```

To run the TransAPI module specific RPCs, the user-rpc command is used as follows:

```
■ netconf> user-rpc

Type the content of a RPC operation (close editor by Ctrl-D):
<?xml version="1.0"?>
<start-irrigation xmlns="http://netconfcentral.org/ns/smartirrigation" />
```

### 11.6.3  Managing Home Intrusion Detection IoT System with NETCONF-YANG

A case study on building a home intrusion detection system was described in Chapter-9. The purpose of the home intrusion detection system is to detect intrusions using sensors (such as PIR sensors and door sensors) and raise alerts.

Let us look at how NETCONF-YANG can be used for managing the intrusion detection system. Box 11.34 shows the YANG module for the intrusion detection system and Figure 11.7 shows a visual representation of the YANG module.

The YANG module describes the structure of the configuration and state data of the system, RPCs for arming and disarming the system and the notifications.

Leaf nodes *systemID*, *systemLocation* and *systemStatus* are non-configurable parameters.

The RPC arm-system sets the arming status to active, whereas the RPC disarm-system sets the arming status to inactive. The *systemArmed* notification notifies the system arming status.

■ **Box 11.34: Home Intrusion Detection system YANG module**

```
module intrusiondetection {

  namespace "http://netconfcentral.org/ns/intrusiondetection";

  prefix "intrusion";

  description
    "YANG module for Intrusion Detection IoT system";

  revision 2014-07-15 {
    description "Intrusion Detection System";
  }

grouping room {
  leaf doorsensorID {
    type string;
    description "ID of door sensor in the room";
  }
  leaf motionsensorID {
    type string;
    description
    "ID of motion sensor in the room";
  }
}

  container intrusiondetection {
    presence
      "Indicates the service is available";

    description
      "Top-level container for all system objects.";

    leaf systemID {
      type string;
      config false;
      mandatory true;
      description
      "ID of the system";
    }

    leaf systemLocation {
      type string;
      config false;
      mandatory true;
      description
      "The location of the system";
    }
```

```
    leaf systemStatus {
     type enumeration {
      enum up {
      value 1;
      description
       "The is powered up";
      }
      enum down {
      value 2;
      description
       "The system is powered down";
      }
      enum armed {
      value 3;
      description
       "System is armed";
      }
      enum disarmed {
      value 4;
      description
       "System is disarmed";
      }
     }
     config false;
     mandatory true;
     description
     "This variable indicates the current state of
      the system.";
    }

    container sensors {
    uses room;
    config false;
    }

   }

  rpc arm-system {
   description
    "Arm the system";
  }

  rpc disarm-system {
   description
    "Disarm the system";
  }

  notification systemArmed {
   description
    "Indicates that system has been armed.";

   leaf armStatus {
    description
    "Indicates the system arming status";
```

```
   type enumeration {
    enum armed {
    description
     "The system was armed.";
    }
    enum disarmed {
    description
     "The system was disarmed.";
    }
    enum error {
    description
     "The system is broken.";
    }
   }
  }
 }
}
```

Upon compiling the YANG module with the 'lnctool', the YIN and TransAPI module files are generated. Box 11.35 shows a YIN version of the intrusion detection system YANG module.

■ **Box 11.35: YIN version of the home intrusion detection system YANG module**

```
    <?xml version="1.0" encoding="UTF-8"?>
<module xmlns="urn:ietf:params:xml:ns:yang:yin:1"
xmlns:intrusion="http://netconfcentral.org/ns/intrusiondetection"
name="intrusiondetection">
<namespace uri="http://netconfcentral.org/ns/intrusiondetection"/>
<prefix value="intrusion"/>
<description>
 <text>YANG module for Intrusion Detection IoT system</text>
</description>
<revision date="2014-07-15">
 <description>
  <text>Intrusion Detection System</text>
 </description>
</revision>
<grouping name="room">
 <leaf name="doorsensorID">
  <type name="string"/>
  <description>
  <text>ID of door sensor in the room</text>
  </description>
 </leaf>
 <leaf name="motionsensorID">
  <type name="string"/>
  <description>
  <text>ID of motion sensor in the room</text>
  </description>
 </leaf>
</grouping>
<container name="intrusiondetection">
```

Figure 11.7: Visual representation of YANG Module of home intrusion detection IoT system

```xml
<presence value="Indicates the service is available"/>
<description>
 <text>Top-level container for all system objects.</text>
</description>
<leaf name="systemID">
 <type name="string"/>
 <config value="false"/>
 <mandatory value="true"/>
 <description>
 <text>ID of the system</text>
 </description>
</leaf>
<leaf name="systemLocation">
 <type name="string"/>
 <config value="false"/>
 <mandatory value="true"/>
 <description>
 <text>The location of the system</text>
 </description>
</leaf>
<leaf name="systemStatus">
 <type name="enumeration">
 <enum name="up">
  <value value="1"/>
  <description>
  <text>The is powered up</text>
  </description>
 </enum>
 <enum name="down">
  <value value="2"/>
  <description>
  <text>The system is powered down</text>
  </description>
 </enum>
 <enum name="armed">
  <value value="3"/>
  <description>
  <text>System is armed</text>
  </description>
 </enum>
 <enum name="disarmed">
  <value value="4"/>
  <description>
  <text>System is disarmed</text>
  </description>
 </enum>
 </type>
 <config value="false"/>
 <mandatory value="true"/>
 <description>
 <text>This variable indicates the current state of
the system.</text>
 </description>
 </leaf>
```

```
  <container name="sensors">
   <uses name="room"/>
   <config value="false"/>
  </container>
 </container>
 <rpc name="arm-system">
  <description>
   <text>Arm the system</text>
  </description>
 </rpc>
 <rpc name="disarm-system">
  <description>
   <text>Disarm the system</text>
  </description>
 </rpc>
 <notification name="systemArmed">
  <description>
   <text>Indicates that system has been armed.</text>
  </description>
  <leaf name="armStatus">
   <description>
   <text>Indicates the system arming status</text>
   </description>
   <type name="enumeration">
   <enum name="armed">
    <description>
    <text>The system was armed.</text>
    </description>
   </enum>
   <enum name="disarmed">
    <description>
    <text>The system was disarmed.</text>
    </description>
   </enum>
   <enum name="error">
    <description>
    <text>The system is broken.</text>
    </description>
   </enum>
   </type>
  </leaf>
 </notification>
</module>
```

Box 11.36 shows the TransAPI module file after implementing the functions in the auto-generated file. The following additions are done to the auto-generated file:

1. A system status structure is added.
2. The 'transapi_init()' function is filled which includes the actions run after the module is loaded. Note that the irrigation status is set to false (0) in this function.
3. The 'get_state_data()' function is filled with the code that generates state information as defined in the data model.
4. The configuration callback function 'callback_intrusiondetection_intrusiondetection()'

function is filled which is run when node in path
/intrusiondetection:intrusiondetection changes.
5. RPC message callback functions 'rpc_arm_system()' and 'rpc_disarm_system()' are filled
and the auxiliary function 'armsystem()' is implemented.

■ **Box 11.36: TransAPI C module for Home Intrusion Detection system**

```c
#include <unistd.h>
#include <stdlib.h>
#include <libxml/tree.h>
#include <libnetconf_xml.h>
#include <pthread.h>
#include <time.h>
#include <string.h>
#include <sys/types.h>
#include <sys/ipc.h>
#include <sys/shm.h>

/* TransAPI version which must be compatible with libnetconf */
int transapi_version = 4;

/* Signal to libnetconf that configuration data
were modified by any callback.
* 0 - data not modified
* 1 - data have been modified
*/
int config_modified = 0;

/*
* Determines the callbacks order.
* Set this variable before compilation and DO NOT modify it in runtime.
* TRANSAPI_CLBCKS_LEAF_TO_ROOT (default)
* TRANSAPI_CLBCKS_ROOT_TO_LEAF
*/
const TRANSAPI_CLBCKS_ORDER_TYPE callbacks_order =
TRANSAPI_CLBCKS_ORDER_DEFAULT;

NC_EDIT_ERROPT_TYPE erropt = NC_EDIT_ERROPT_NOTSET;


/* system status structure */
struct intrusiondetection_status {
  int enabled;
  int armed;
  pthread_mutex_t intrusiondetection_mutex;
};

/* status structure instance, stored in shared memory */
struct intrusiondetection_status * status = NULL;


/**
* @brief Initialize plugin after loaded and before any
other functions are called.
```

```
 * @param[out] running Current configuration of managed device.

 * @return EXIT_SUCCESS or EXIT_FAILURE
 */
int transapi_init(xmlDocPtr * running)
{
  key_t shmkey;
  int shmid;
  int first;

  /* get shared memory key */
  if ((shmkey = ftok ("/proc/self/exe", 1)) == -1) {
    return EXIT_FAILURE;
  }

{ /* get id of shared memory if exist */
  if ((shmid = shmget (shmkey,
sizeof(struct intrusiondetection_status), 0666)) != -1)
    first = 0;
{ /* create shared memory */
  } else if ((shmid = shmget (shmkey, sizeof(struct
intrusiondetection_status), IPC_CREAT | 0666)) != -1)
    first = 1;
  } else { /*shared memory can not be found nor created */
    return EXIT_FAILURE;
  }

  /* attach shared memory */
  if ((status = shmat (shmid, NULL, 0)) == (void*)-1) {
    return EXIT_FAILURE;
  }
  /* first run after shared memory removed initiate the mutex */
  if (first) {
    if (pthread_mutex_init (&status->intrusiondetection_mutex, NULL)) {
    return EXIT_FAILURE;
    }
    status->armed = 0;
  }

  return EXIT_SUCCESS;
}

/**
 * @brief Free all resources allocated on
plugin runtime and prepare plugin for removal.
 */
void transapi_close(void)
{
  return;
}

/**
 * @brief Retrieve state data from device and return them as XML document
 *
```

```
* @param model Device data model.  libxml2 xmlDocPtr.
* @param running Running datastore content.  libxml2 xmlDocPtr.
* @param[out] err Double pointer to error structure.
* @return State data as libxml2 xmlDocPtr or NULL in case of error.
*/
xmlDocPtr get_state_data (xmlDocPtr model,
xmlDocPtr running, struct nc_err **err)
{
  xmlDocPtr state;
  xmlNodePtr root;
  xmlNsPtr ns;

  state = xmlNewDoc(BAD_CAST "1.0");
  root = xmlNewDocNode(state, NULL, BAD_CAST "intrusiondetection", NULL);
  xmlDocSetRootElement(state, root);
  ns = xmlNewNs(root, BAD_CAST
"http://netconfcentral.org/ns/intrusiondetection", NULL);
  xmlSetNs(root, ns);
  xmlNewChild(root, ns, BAD_CAST "systemID", BAD_CAST "IOT456");
  xmlNewChild(root, ns, BAD_CAST "systemLocation", BAD_CAST "Home-1");

  if (status->enabled == 1){
    xmlNewChild(root, ns, BAD_CAST "systemStatus", BAD_CAST "up");
  }
  else if(status->enabled == 0){
    xmlNewChild(root, ns, BAD_CAST "systemStatus", BAD_CAST "down");
  }
  else if (status->armed == 1){
    xmlNewChild(root, ns, BAD_CAST "systemStatus", BAD_CAST "armed");
  }
  else if (status->armed == 0){
    xmlNewChild(root, ns, BAD_CAST "systemStatus", BAD_CAST "disarmed");
  }

  return (state);
}
/*
* Mapping prefixes with namespaces.
* Do NOT modify this structure!
*/
struct ns_pair namespace_mapping[] = {{"intrusiondetection",
"http://netconfcentral.org/ns/intrusiondetection"}, {NULL, NULL}};


/*
* CONFIGURATION callbacks
*/


/**
* @brief This callback will be run when node in path
/intrusiondetection:intrusiondetection changes
*
* @param[in] data Double pointer to void.  Its passed to every callback.
* @param[in] op Observed change in path.  XMLDIFF_OP type.
* @param[in] node Modified node.  if op == XMLDIFF_REM its copy
of node removed.
```

```
 * @param[out] error If callback fails, it can return libnetconf
error structure with a failure description.
 *
 * @return EXIT_SUCCESS or EXIT_FAILURE
 */
/* !DO NOT ALTER FUNCTION SIGNATURE! */
int callback_intrusiondetection_intrusiondetection (void ** data,
XMLDIFF_OP op, xmlNodePtr node, struct nc_err** error)
{
  pthread_mutex_lock(&status->intrusiondetection_mutex);

  if (op <= 0 || op > (XMLDIFF_MOD | XMLDIFF_CHAIN
| XMLDIFF_ADD | XMLDIFF_REM) ||
((op & XMLDIFF_ADD) && (op & XMLDIFF_REM))) {
    *error = nc_err_new(NC_ERR_OP_FAILED);
    nc_err_set(*error, NC_ERR_PARAM_MSG,
"Invalid configuration data
modification for intrusiondetection module.");
    return (EXIT_FAILURE);
  } else {
    if (op & XMLDIFF_REM) {
    status->enabled = 0;
    if (status->armed != 0) {
    nc_verb_warning("Disarming system!");
    status->armed = 0;
    }
    } else if (op & XMLDIFF_ADD) {
    status->enabled = 1;
    }
  }

  nc_verb_verbose("Turning intrusiondetection %s.",
status->enabled ?  "up" :  "down");

  pthread_mutex_unlock(&status->intrusiondetection_mutex);

  return EXIT_SUCCESS;
}

/*
 * Structure transapi_config_callbacks provide mapping between callback and
path in configuration datastore.
 * It is used by libnetconf library to decide which callbacks will be run.
 * DO NOT alter this structure
 */
struct transapi_data_callbacks clbks = {
 .callbacks_count = 1,
 .data = NULL,
 .callbacks = {
  {.path = "/intrusiondetection:intrusiondetection",
.func = callback_intrusiondetection_intrusiondetection}
 }
};
```

```
void * armsystem ()
{
 pthread_mutex_lock (&status->intrusiondetection_mutex);

 if (status->armed == 0) { /* was canceled */
  pthread_mutex_unlock (&status->intrusiondetection_mutex);
 } else { /* still arming */
  /* turn off */
  status->armed = 0;
  ncntf_event_new(-1, NCNTF_GENERIC,
"<systemArmed><armStatus>armed</armStatus></systemArmed>");
 }

 pthread_mutex_unlock (&status->intrusiondetection_mutex);
 return NULL;
}


/*
* RPC callbacks
*/

nc_reply * rpc_arm_system (xmlNodePtr input[])
{

  struct nc_err * err;
  nc_reply * reply;
  pthread_t tid;

  pthread_mutex_lock(&status->intrusiondetection_mutex);

  if (status->enabled == 0) { /* Intrusion Detection system is off */
   reply = nc_reply_error(nc_err_new (NC_ERR_RES_DENIED));
  } else if (status->armed) { /* Intrusion Detection system is armed */
   reply = nc_reply_error (nc_err_new (NC_ERR_IN_USE));
{ /* Intrusion Detection system internal error (cannot turn heater on) */
  } else if (pthread_create (&tid, NULL, armsystem, NULL))
   err = nc_err_new (NC_ERR_OP_FAILED);
   nc_err_set (err, NC_ERR_PARAM_MSG,
 "Intrusion Detection system is broken!");
   ncntf_event_new(-1, NCNTF_GENERIC,
 "<systemArmed><armStatus>error</armStatus></systemArmed>");
   reply = nc_reply_error (err);
  } else { /* all ok, start armed */
   status->armed = 1;
   reply = nc_reply_ok();
   pthread_detach (tid);
  }

  pthread_mutex_unlock(&status->intrusiondetection_mutex);
  return reply;
}
 nc_reply * rpc_disarm_system (xmlNodePtr input[])
 {
```

```
  nc_reply * reply;
  struct nc_err * err;

  pthread_mutex_lock(&status->intrusiondetection_mutex);

  if (status->enabled == 0) {/* system is off */
   reply = nc_reply_error(nc_err_new (NC_ERR_RES_DENIED));
  } else if (status->armed == 0) { /* system in not armed */
   err = nc_err_new (NC_ERR_OP_FAILED);
   nc_err_set (err, NC_ERR_PARAM_MSG, "There is no armed in progress.");
   reply = nc_reply_error(err);
  } else { /* disarm */
   status->armed = 0;
   ncntf_event_new(-1, NCNTF_GENERIC,
 "<systemArmed><armStatus>disarmed</armStatus></systemArmed>");
   reply = nc_reply_ok();
  }

  pthread_mutex_unlock(&status->intrusiondetection_mutex);

  return reply;
}
/*
 * Structure transapi_rpc_callbacks provide
mapping between callbacks and RPC messages.
 * It is used by libnetconf library to decide which
callbacks will be run when RPC arrives.
 * DO NOT alter this structure
*/
struct transapi_rpc_callbacks rpc_clbks = {
  .callbacks_count = 2,
  .callbacks = {
   {.name="arm-system", .func=rpc_arm_system,
.arg_count=0, .arg_order={}},
   {.name="disarm-system", .func=rpc_disarm_system,
.arg_count=0, .arg_order={}}
  }
};
```

After implementing the TransAPI module file, the file is compiled and the binary (.so file) is loaded into the Netopeer-server using the Netopeer-manager. After loading the module, NETCONF commands can be issued from the Netopeer-cli. For example, to show the current status of the intrusion detection system, use the get command as follows:

```
■ netconf> get -filter

Type the filter (close editor by Ctrl-D):
<intrusiondetection
xmlns="http://netconfcentral.org/ns/intrusiondetection"/>

Result:
<intrusiondetection
```

```
xmlns="http://netconfcentral.org/ns/intrusiondetection">
<systemID>IOT456</systemID>
<systemLocation>Home-1</systemLocation>
<systemStatus>up</systemStatus>
</intrusiondetection>
```

To run the TransAPI module specific RPCs, the user-rpc command is used as follows:

```
■ netconf> user-rpc

Type the content of a RPC operation (close editor by Ctrl-D):
<?xml version="1.0"?>
<arm-system xmlns="http://netconfcentral.org/ns/intrusiondetection" />
```

## 11.7   IoT Code Generator

The IoT Code Generator, developed by the authors, is a tool for generating IoT device, services and application code similar to the examples in this book. IoT Code Generator is included in the book website. To begin with, the user selects an IoT level for the system for which the code is to be generated. The example shown in this section is of a level-1 IoT system. The next step is to select an IoT device as shown in Figure 11.8.

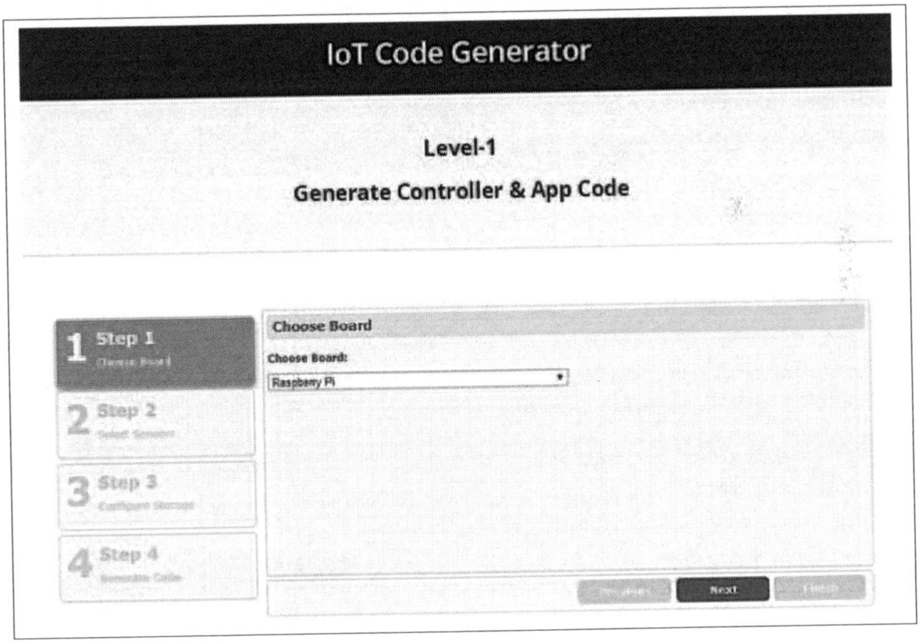

Figure 11.8: Selecting an IoT device or single board mini-computer

In the next step, the sensors are selected as shown in Figure 11.9.

After selecting the sensors, the storage option is selected and configured as shown in Figures 11.10 and 11.11.

On completing the code generation wizard, the code generator generates the controller

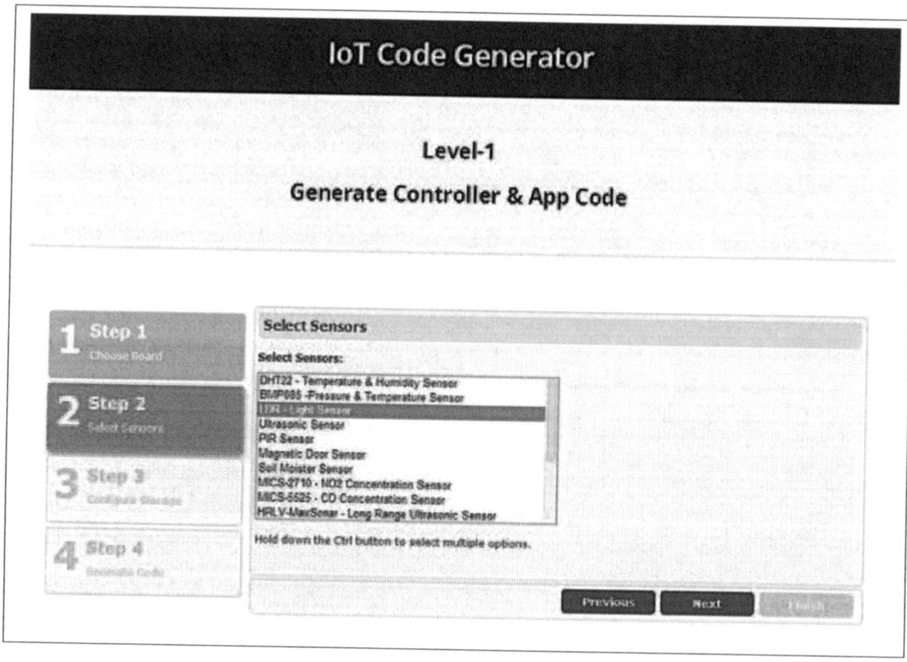

Figure 11.9: Selecting sensors

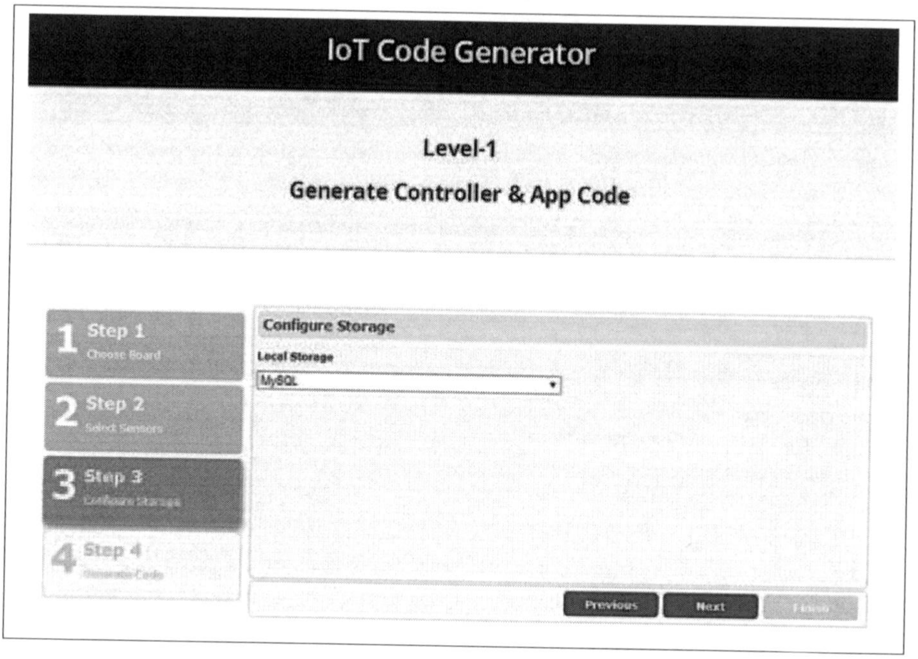

Figure 11.10: Selecting storage option

and application code as shown in Figures 11.12 and 11.13.

The IoT Code Generator has a separate wizard for generating web services code. To generate the services code, the service specifications are uploaded as a text file, in the format described in the wizard. Figures 11.14 and 11.15 show the wizard for generating service

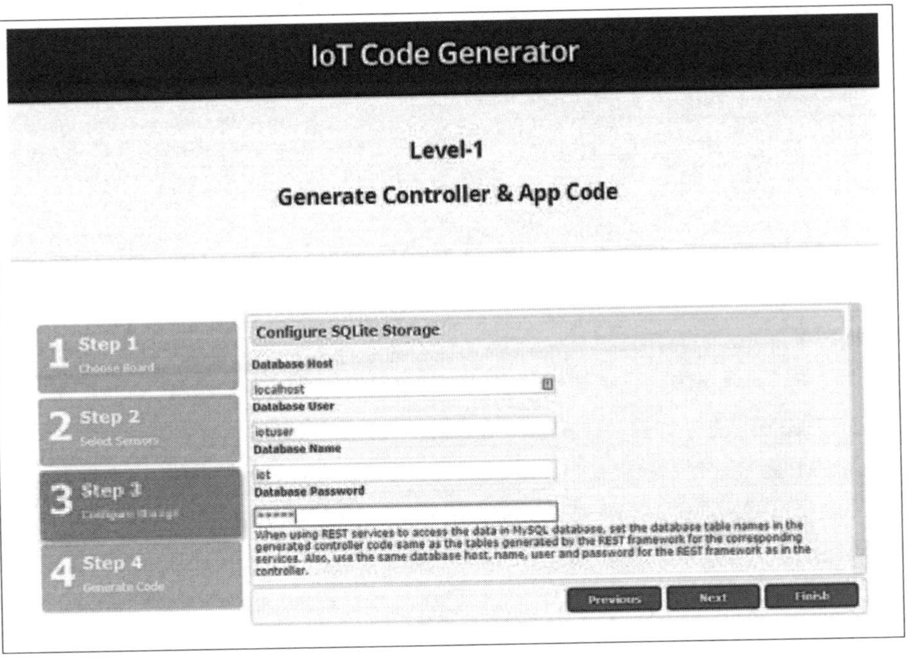

Figure 11.11: Configuring storage

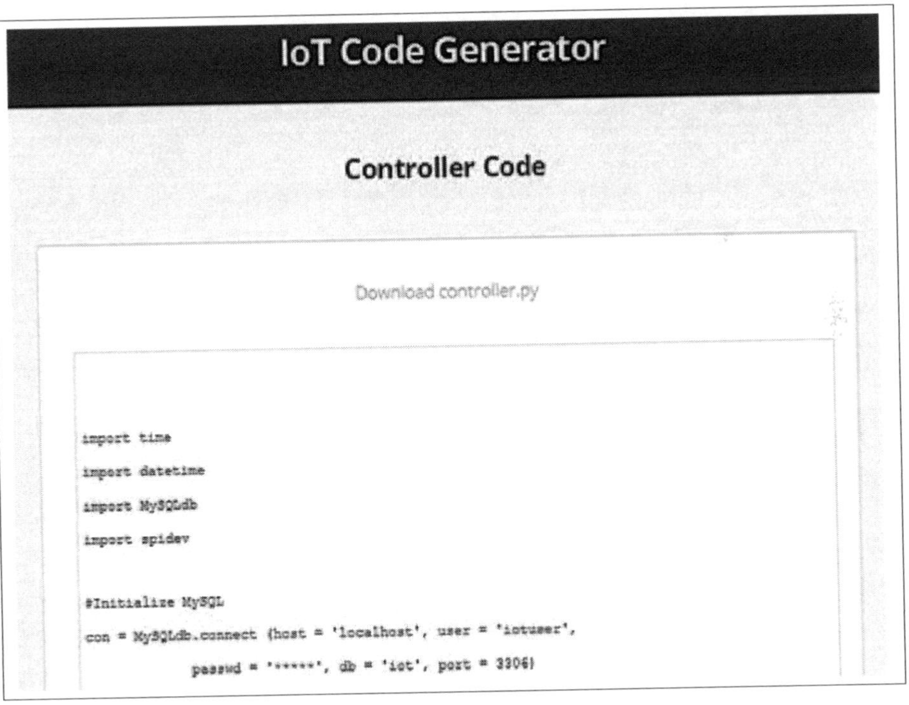

Figure 11.12: Screenshot of IoT code generator showing generated controller code

code.

On completing the service code generation wizard, the code generator generates the service code as shown in Figure 11.16.

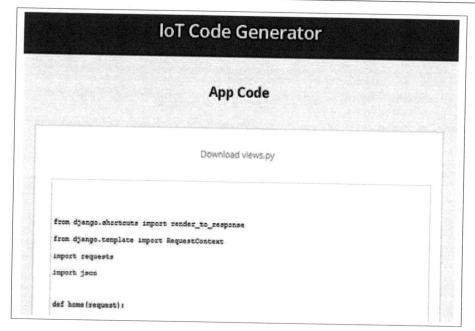

Figure 11.13: Screenshot of IoT code generator showing generated app code

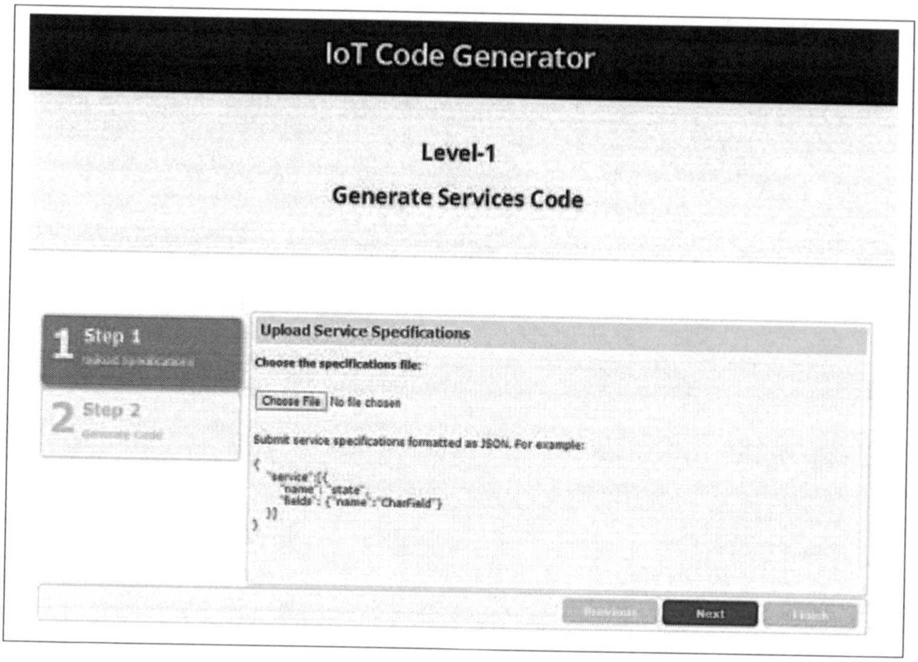

Figure 11.14: Generating services code with IoT code generator

## Summary

In this chapter you learned about various tools for IoT including tools for infrastructure automation, configuration management and code generation. You learned about Chef, which is an infrastructure automation and configuration management framework. Chef adopts the

Figure 11.15: Generating services code with IoT code generator

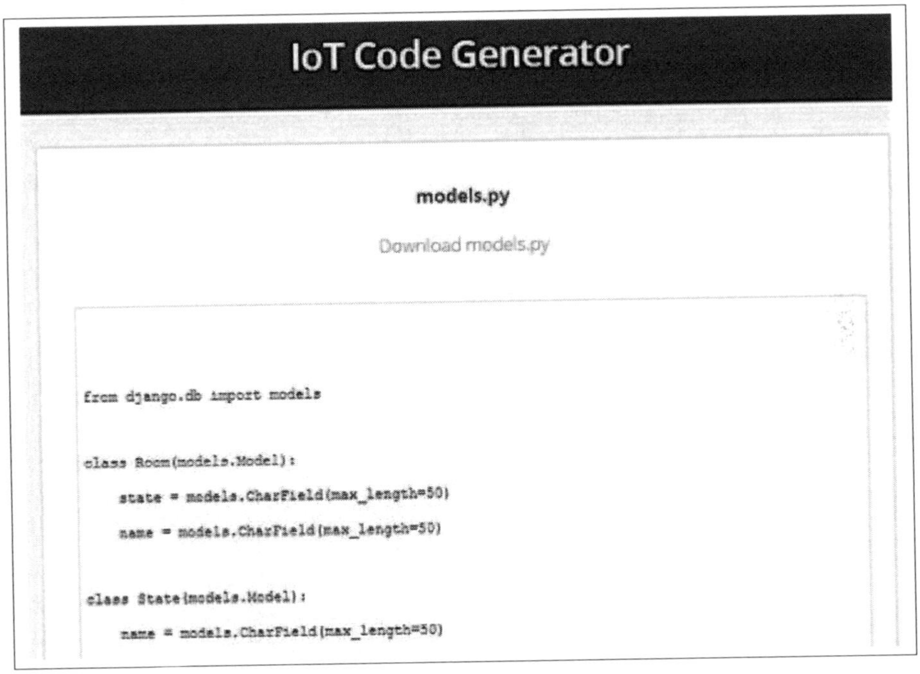

Figure 11.16: Screenshot of IoT code generator showing generated code for services

infrastructure-as-a-code paradigm and allows deploying, configuring and integrating various infrastructure components. You learned about the key components and concepts of Chef including Chef Server, Node, Cookbook, Recipe, Resource, Provider, Attributes, Templates, Policy, Run Lists and Knife. You learned how to develop and run Chef recipes. Puppet is another configuration management tool like Chef. You learned about the key concepts of Puppet including Resource, Resource Abstraction Layer, Class, Manifest and Module. You learned about the steps for IoT device Management with NETCONF-YANG starting from development of a YANG module, compilation of the module, implementation of TransAPI module, loading modules into the NETCONF server and running NETCONF operations. Finally, you learned about the IoT code generation tool which is distributed on this book's website to support students and instructors.

## Lab Exercises

1. Box 11.33 shows the code for the TransAPI C module for Smart Irrigation System. The *rpc_start_irrigation* function in this code is called when a NETCONF RPC is sent from the client to the server to start irrigation. The logic that links the management system with the actual device is implemented in the *irrigate* function. The *irrigate* function in the Box 11.33 provides a dummy code that pretends to turn on the irrigation. Re-implement this function to interface with the actual IoT device described in section 9.5.

2. Write a YANG module for weather monitoring IoT system described in Chapter-9.

3. Implement a TransAPI for weather monitoring IoT system.

4. A forest fire detection system is described in Chapter-9. The system is a level-5 IoT system with multiple end-nodes and one coordinator node. In this exercise you will design a management interface for the system. Follow the steps below:
   - Identify the configuration and state data of the system and write YANG modules for the end nodes and coordinator node.
   - Using the Libnetconf and Netopeer tools compile the YANG modules and generate the TransAPI module templates.
   - Implement the callback functions in the TransAPI module files.
   - Build the TransAPI modules. Load the YANG and TransAPI modules in the NETCONF server.

5. This exercise is about system wide NETCONF transactions for the forest fire detection system. Follow the steps below:
   - Use the YANG and TransAPI modules designed in the previous exercise for this exercise.
   - Clear the candidate datastores on the NETCONF server using the *discard − changes* command from Netopeer-cli. This command reverts the candidate configuration to the current running configuration.
   - Lock the candidate data stores using the *lock* command from Netopeer-cli.
   - Lock the running data stores.
   - Copy running configurations to candidate datastores using the *copy − config* command.
   - Edit the candidate datastores using the *edit − config* command. Make some changes in the existing configurations.
   - Validate the candidate datastores using the *validate* command.
   - Commit candidate configurations to running using the *commit* command.
   - Unlock the candidate data stores using the *unlock* command.

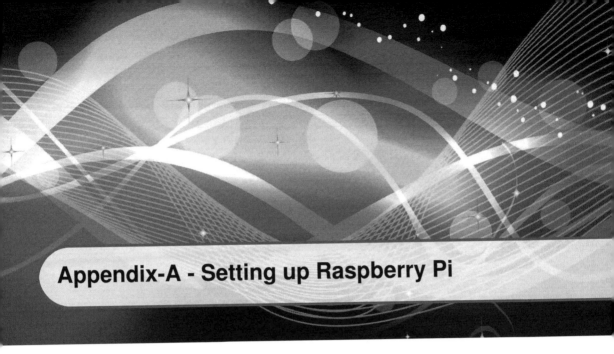

# Appendix-A - Setting up Raspberry Pi

## Setting up Raspberry Pi

The examples and exercises in this book have been developed and tested on Raspberry Pi. This appendix provides the instructions for setting up New Out of Box Software (NOOBS) onto an SD card. To get started, download the latest version of NOOBS from: http://www.raspberrypi.org/downloads

Figure A1.1: NOOBS options on booting from SD card

You will need an SD card of 8GB or more space. Format the SD card as FAT using the the SD Card Association's formatting tool (https://www.sdcard.org/downloads/formatter_4)

Extract the NOOBS zip to the SD card root. Insert the SD card into the SD card slot on Raspberry Pi. Connect a monitor to the HDMI port of Raspberry Pi and a mouse and keyboard to the USB ports. Then power up the Raspberry Pi. On first boot, you will see an options windows as shown in Figure A1.1. This window provides various options for operating systems including Raspbian Linux, Arch Linux, Pidora, RISC OS and RaspBMC. Select Raspbian and click install. After the installation is complete restart Raspberry Pi. After boot you will see the Raspbian desktop as shown in Figure A1.2.

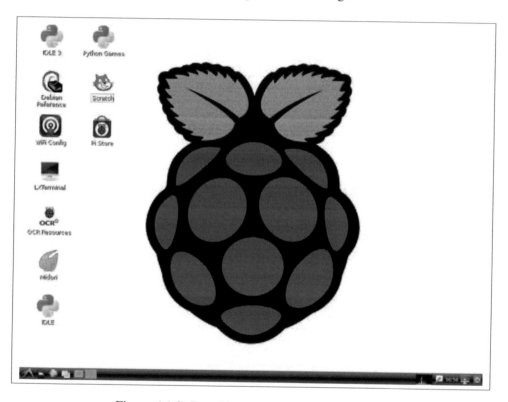

Figure A1.2: Raspbian desktop on Raspberry Pi

For most examples in this book, you will not require a separate display for Raspberry Pi. We recommend either accessing Raspberry Pi using VNC or SSH from your computer which does away with the need for a separate monitor. To use VNC server for accessing Raspberry Pi, make sure the Raspberry Pi is on the same network as your computer. Box A1.1 provides the commands to install and run VNC server on Raspberry Pi.

---

■ **Box A1.1: Installing VNC Server on Raspberry Pi**

#Install VNC server
sudo apt-get install tightvncserver

#Run VNC Server on port 1 (you can set port of your choice):
vncserver :1

---

On your Windows/Linux computer install the VNC viewer (http://www.realvnc.com/download/viewer). Find the IP address of Raspberry Pi by checking the connected devices on your router or by manually scanning the addresses. Connect to the Raspberry Pi using VNC viewer as shown in Figure A1.3.

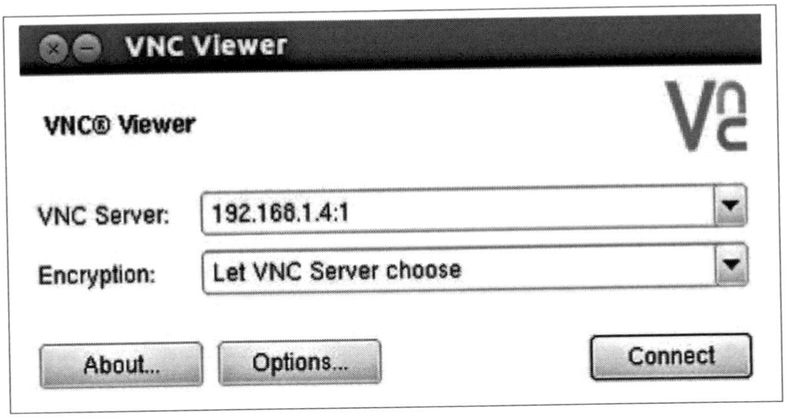

Figure A1.3: Connecting to Raspberry Pi with VNC viewer

You can also connect to Raspberry Pi from your computer by SSH as follows:
ssh pi@<Raspberry-IP-Address>
The default username on Raspbian is 'pi' and password is 'raspberry'.

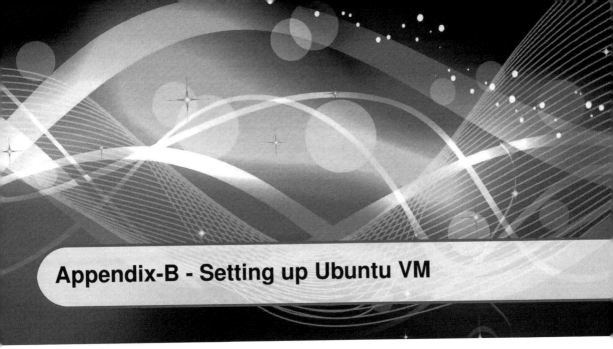

# Appendix-B - Setting up Ubuntu VM

## Setting up Ubuntu Virtual Machine

The examples and exercises in this book have been developed and tested on Ubuntu Linux. This appendix provides the instructions for setting up an Ubuntu Linux virtual machine within other operating systems such as Windows. To set an Ubuntu virtual machine, the VirtualBox [132] software is used. VirtualBox is a virtualization software that allows you to run an entire operating system inside another operating system. VirtualBox runs on Windows, Linux, Macintosh, and Solaris hosts.

Download and install VirtualBox on your local machine. Also download the latest Ubuntu disk image (ISO file) from the Ubuntu website [133]. Launch VitualBox and then click on the New button to create a new virtual machine. Then enter a name for the virtual machine and choose the operating system as shown in Figure A2.1.

Then select the amount of memory to be allocated for the virtual machine.

Allocate a quarter of the RAM on your local machine for a good user experience as shown in Figure A2.2. For examples, if you have 4GB of RAM on your local machine, then allocate 1GB for the virtual machine.

Next, create a new virtual hard disk as shown in Figure A2.3. Select the virtual disk image (VDI) hard drive file type as shown in Figure A2.4. Then choose the fixed size storage for the hard disk as shown in Figure A2.5.

Next select the size of the virtual hard drive as shown in Figure A2.6. For Ubuntu, a virtual hard drive of atleast 4GB is required.

Create the virtual hard disk and then open the settings. In the storage section, click on the "Choose a virtual CD/DVD disk file" and add the downloaded Ubuntu disk image (ISO file) as shown in Figure A2.7.

In the list of virtual machines, in the main window of VirtualBox, double-click your virtual machine to start it as shown in Figure A2.8. When the Ubuntu boots up you will see an option to install Ubuntu as shown in Figure A2.9.

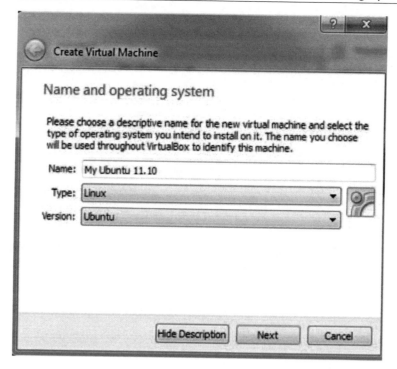

Figure A2.1: Creating a virtual machine with VitualBox

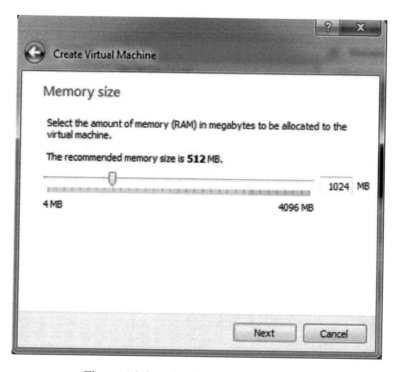

Figure A2.2: Selecting the memory size

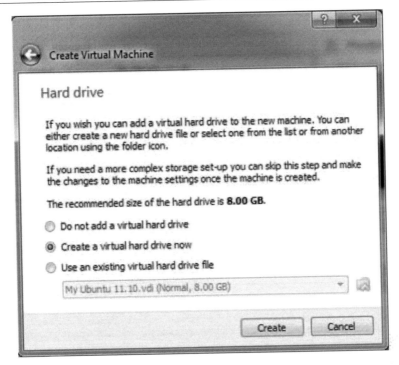

Figure A2.3: Creating a new virtual hard disk

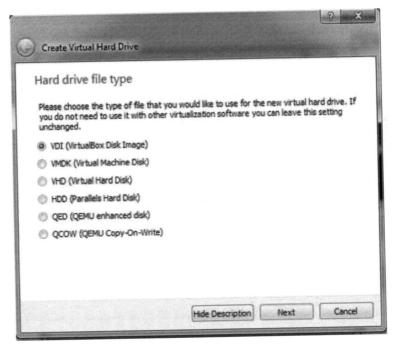

Figure A2.4: Selecting hard drive file type

Click on the Install Ubuntu button and select the installation type as shown in Figure A2.10. Choose the Erase disk option and start the installation as shown in Figures A2.11 and

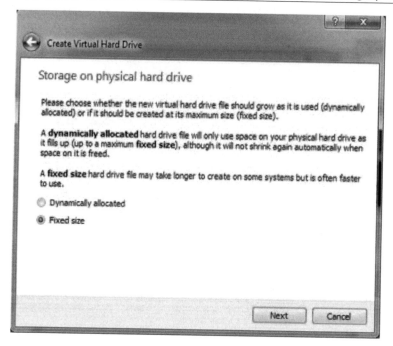

Figure A2.5: Choosing storage type

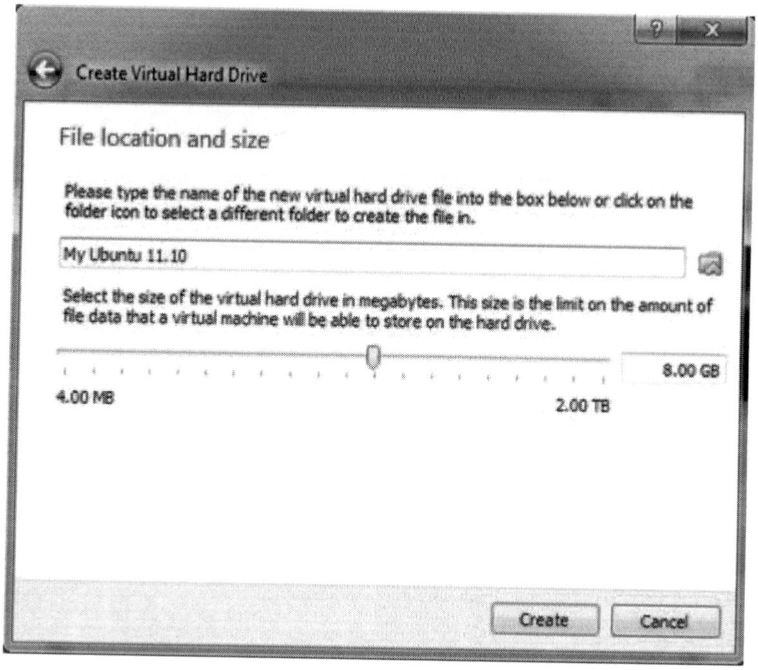

Figure A2.6: Choosing virtual hard drive size

A2.12.

When the installation completes, you will get a message to restart as shown in Figure A2.13. Restart the Ubuntu virtual machine. Ubuntu will boot and present the login screen as

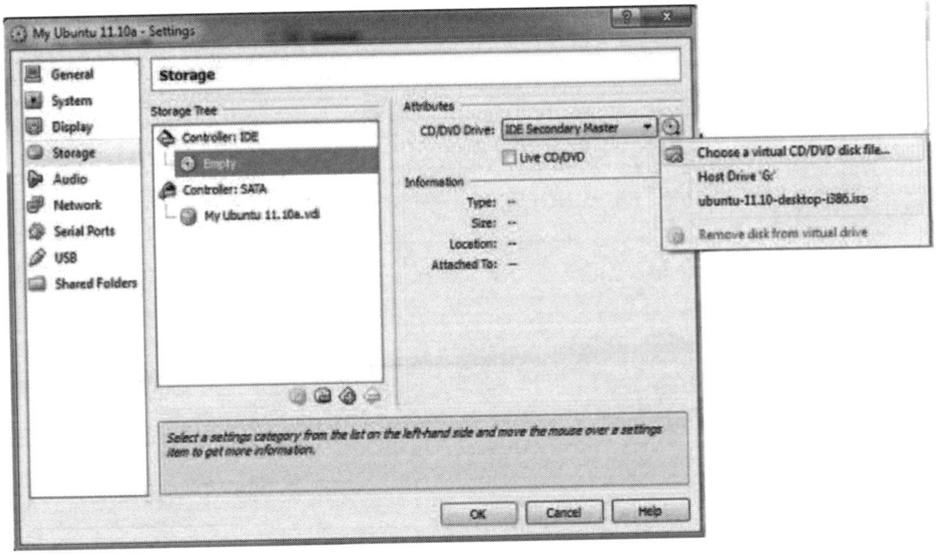

Figure A2.7: Adding Ubuntu disk image to virtual machine

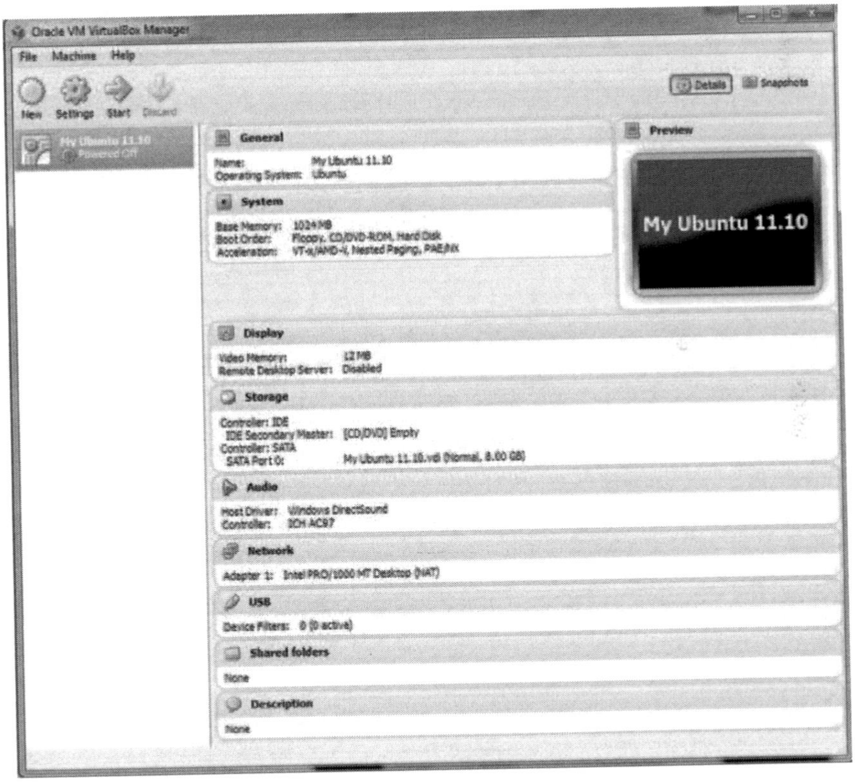

Figure A2.8: VirtualBox main window showing the Ubuntu virtual machine

shown in Figure A2.14. Enter the username and password you provided while installation to login.

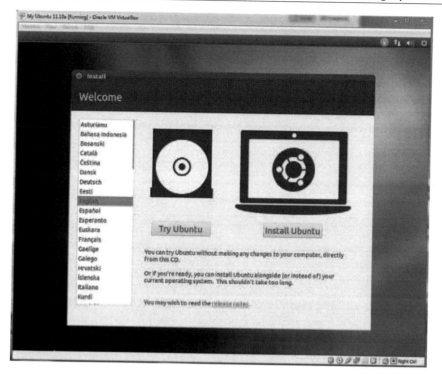

Figure A2.9: Ubuntu virtual machine running in VirtualBox

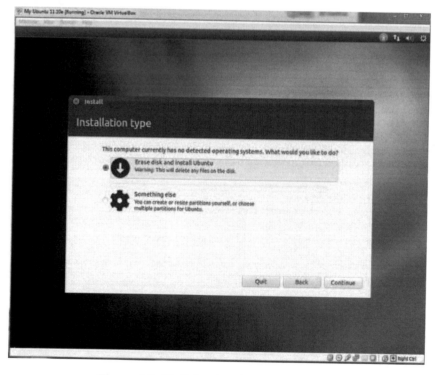

Figure A2.10: Selecting installation type.

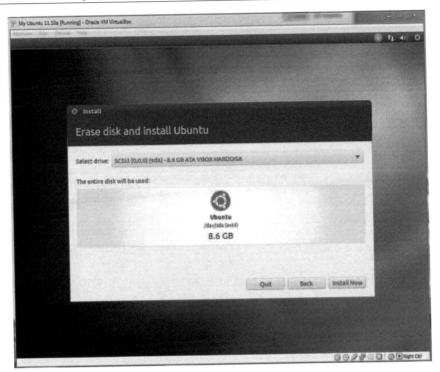

Figure A2.11: Starting installation

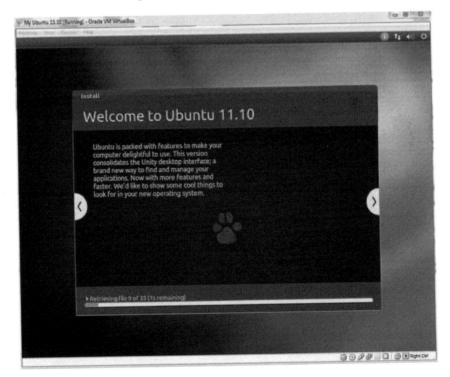

Figure A2.12: Installation in progress

Figure A2.13: Installation complete message

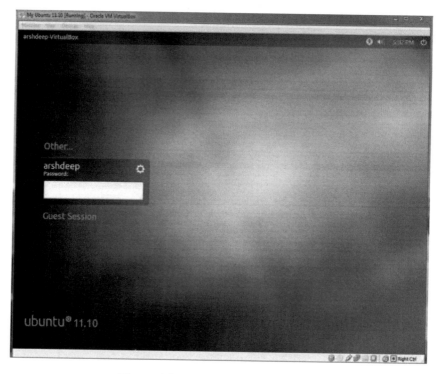

Figure A2.14: Ubuntu login screen

# Appendix-C - Setting up Django

## Setting up Django on Amazon EC2

This section provides instructions for setting up Django on an Amazon EC2 instance. To launch a new instance open the Amazon EC2 console and click on the launch instance button.

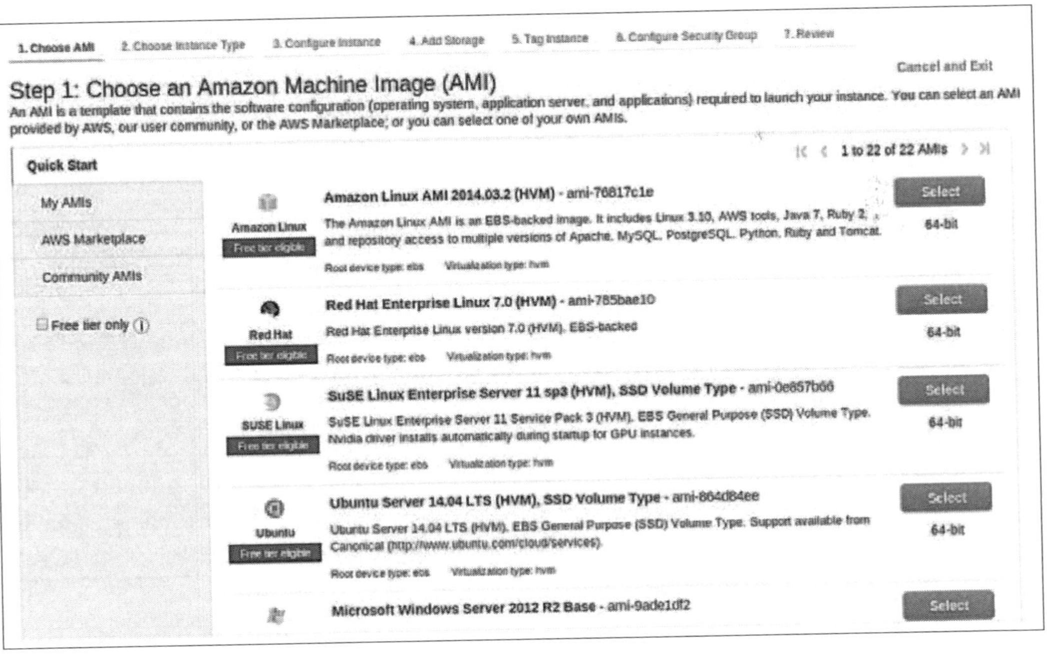

Figure A3.1: Amazon EC2 instance launch wizard showing AMIs

This will open a wizard where you can select the AMI with which you want to launch the instance as shown in Figure A3.1. Select an Ubuntu AMI. When you launch an instance you specify the instance type in the launch wizard as shown in Figure A3.2. In the instance details page you also specify the number of instances to launch based on the selected AMI and availability zones for the instances.

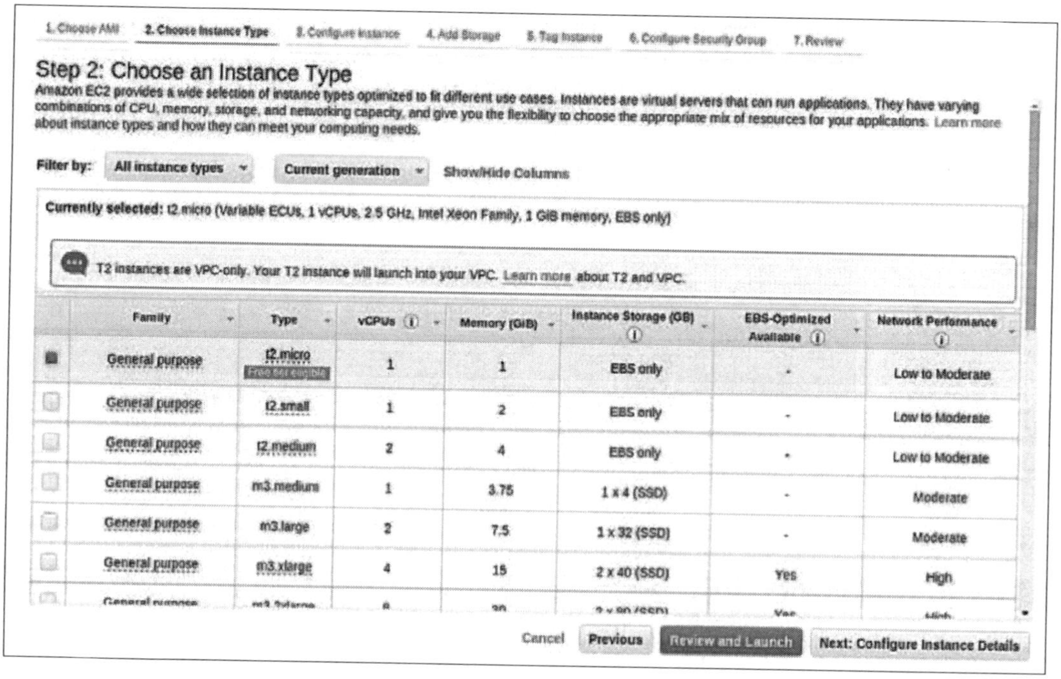

Figure A3.2: Amazon EC2 instance launch wizard showing instance details

Next you specify the advanced instance options and storage device configuration shown in Figures A3.3 and A3.4. Proceed with the default options. In the next step you specify the meta-data tags for the instance as shown in Figure A3.5. These tags are used to simplify the administration of EC2 instances.

Figure A3.6 shows the security groups page of the instance launch wizard. This page allows you to choose an existing security group or create a new security group. Security groups are used to open or block a specific network port for the launched instances. Create a new security group called and open ports 80 (HTTP), 8000 (Django server), 22 (SSH). Figure A3.7 shows the summary of instance to be launched. Clicking on the launch button launches the instance.

The status of the launched instance can be viewed in the EC2 console as shown in Figure A3.8. When an instance is launched its state is pending. It takes a couple of minutes for the instance to come into the running state. When the instance comes into the running state, it is assigned a public DNS, private DNS, public IP and private IP. We will use the public DNS to securely connect to the instance using SSH.

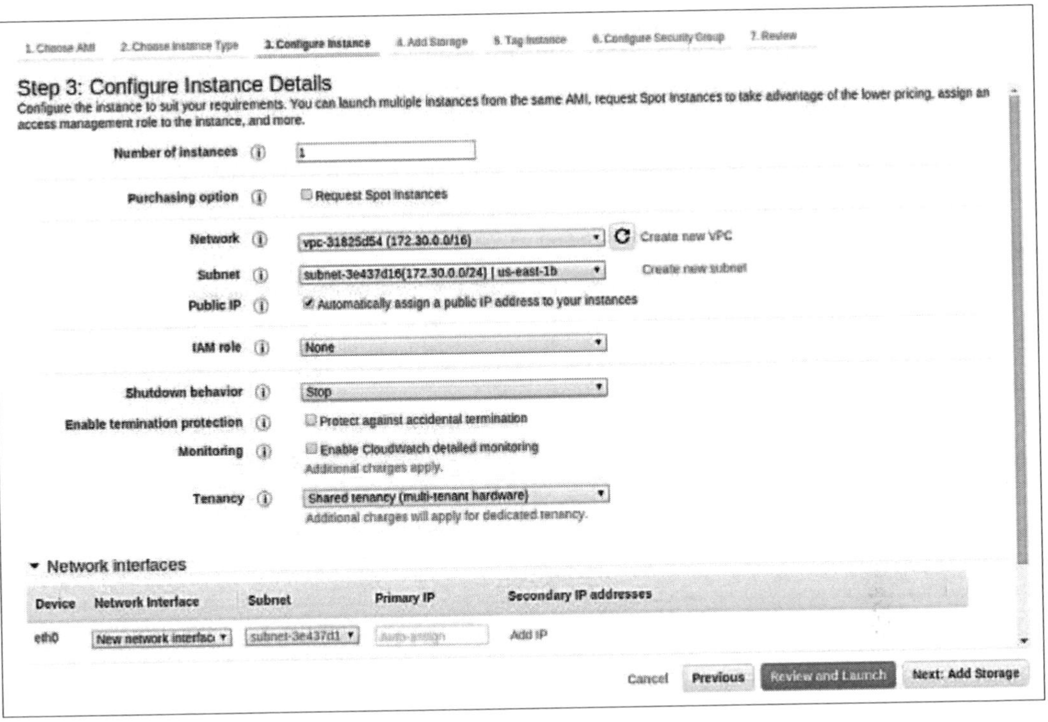

Figure A3.3: Amazon EC2 instance launch wizard showing advanced instance options

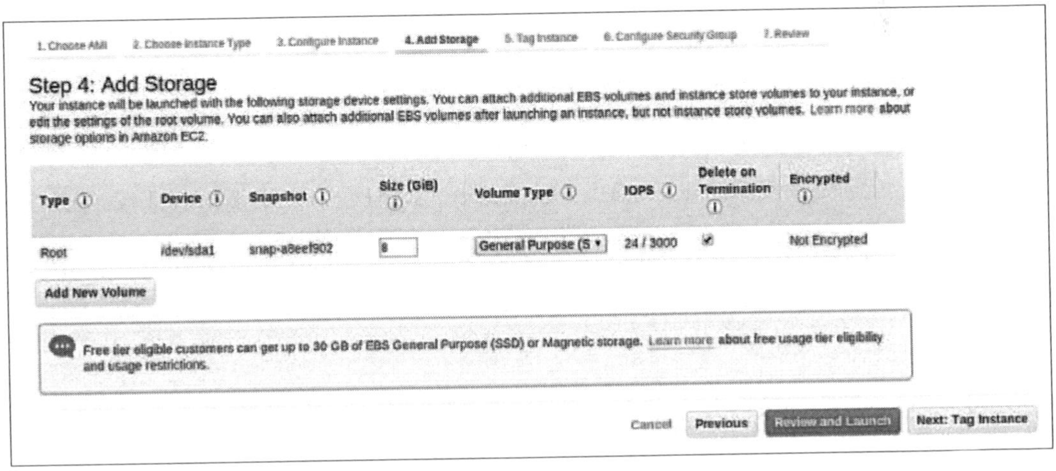

Figure A3.4: Amazon EC2 instance launch wizard showing storage device configuration

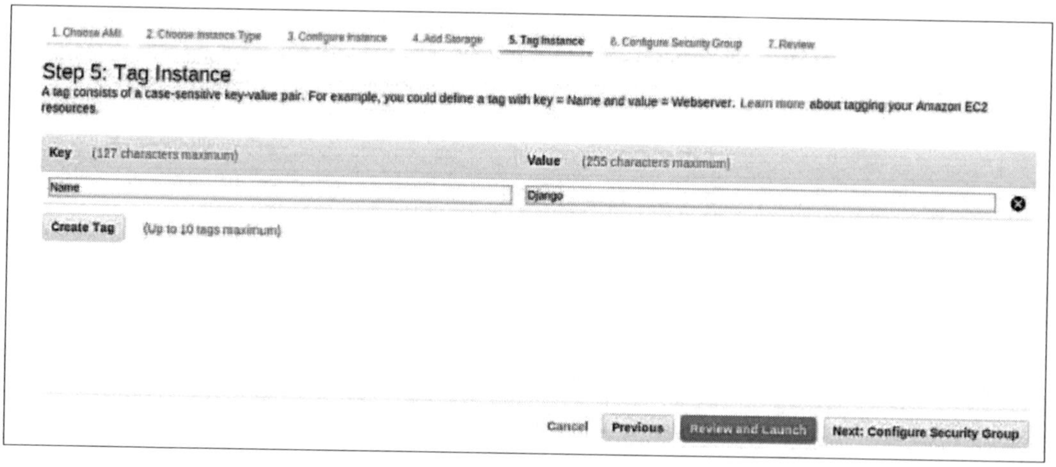

Figure A3.5: Amazon EC2 instance launch wizard showing instance tags

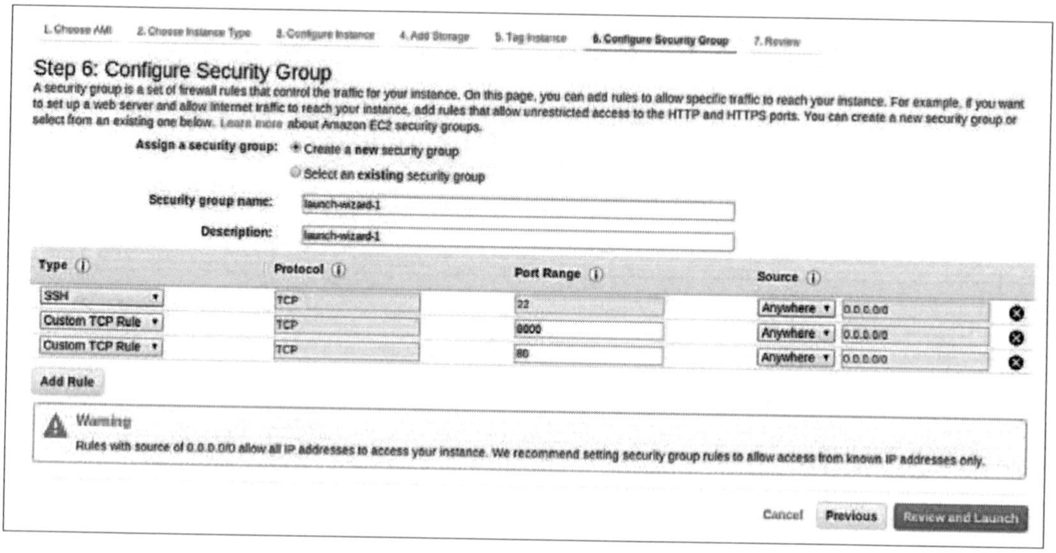

Figure A3.6: Amazon EC2 instance launch wizard showing security groups

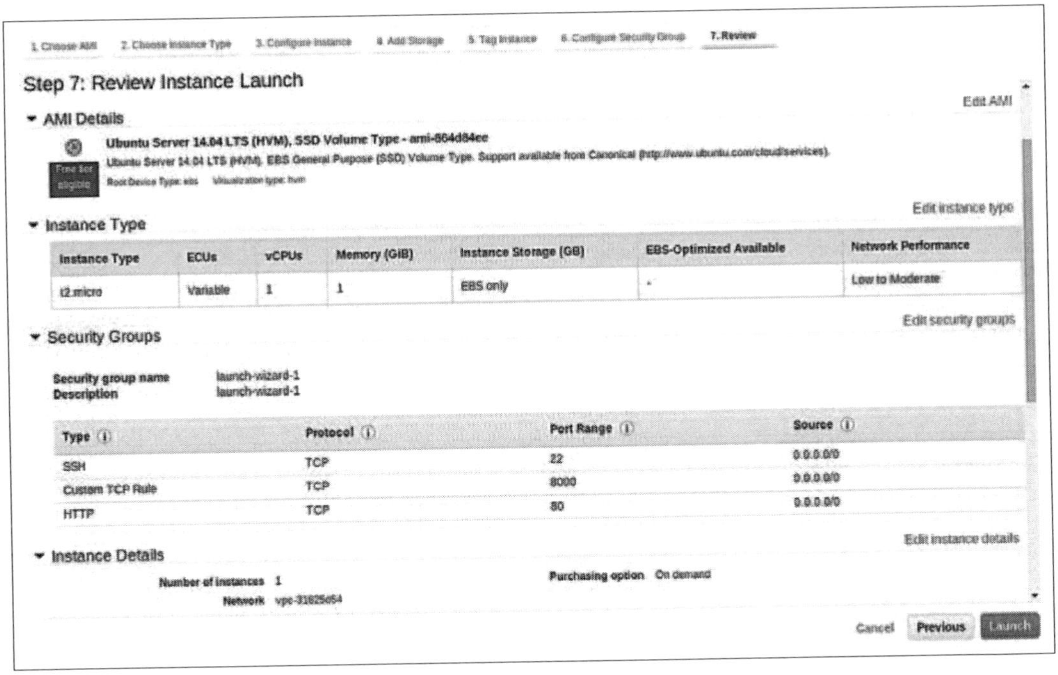

Figure A3.7: Amazon EC2 instance launch wizard showing summary of instance to be launched

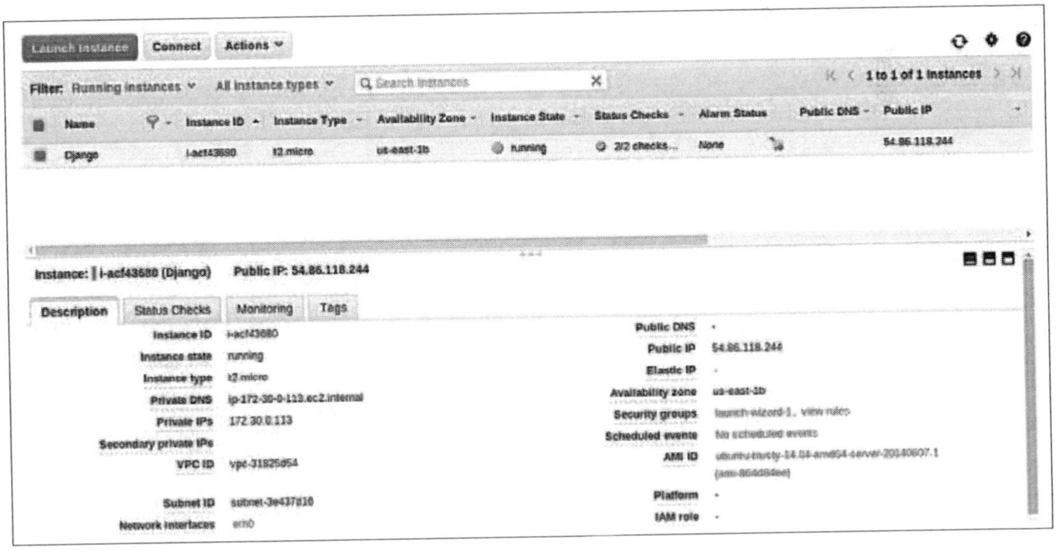

Figure A3.8: Amazon EC2 console showing the launched instance

Connect to the EC2 instance from your local machine using:
ssh -i myKeyPair.pem ubuntu@publicDNS

where publicDNS is the Public DNS of the instance you created.

Box A3.1 provides the commands for installing Django and verifying the Django installation.

■ **Box A3.1: Installing Django**

```
#On EC2 instance run following commands to install Django:
wget https://www.djangoproject.com/m/releases/1.5/Django-1.5.1.tar.gz
tar xzvf Django-1.5.1.tar.gz
cd Django-1.5.1
sudo python setup.py install


#Verifying Django installation
python
>>> import django
>>> django.VERSION
(1, 5, 1, 'final', 0)
```

Box A3.2 provides the commands for creating a blank Django project and running Django server. When you run the Django development server you can see the default Django project page as shown in Figure A3.10.

■ **Box A3.2: Creating a Django project and running Django server**

```
#Create a Django project
django-admin.py startproject myproject

#Starting development server
python manage.py runserver 0.0.0.0:8000

#Django uses port 8000 by default
#The project can be viewed at the URL:
#http://hostname:8000
```

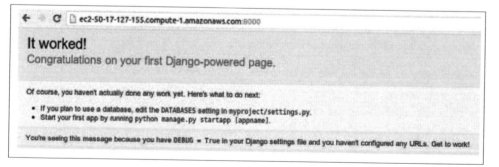

Figure A3.10: Django default project page

# Setting up Django on Google Compute Engine

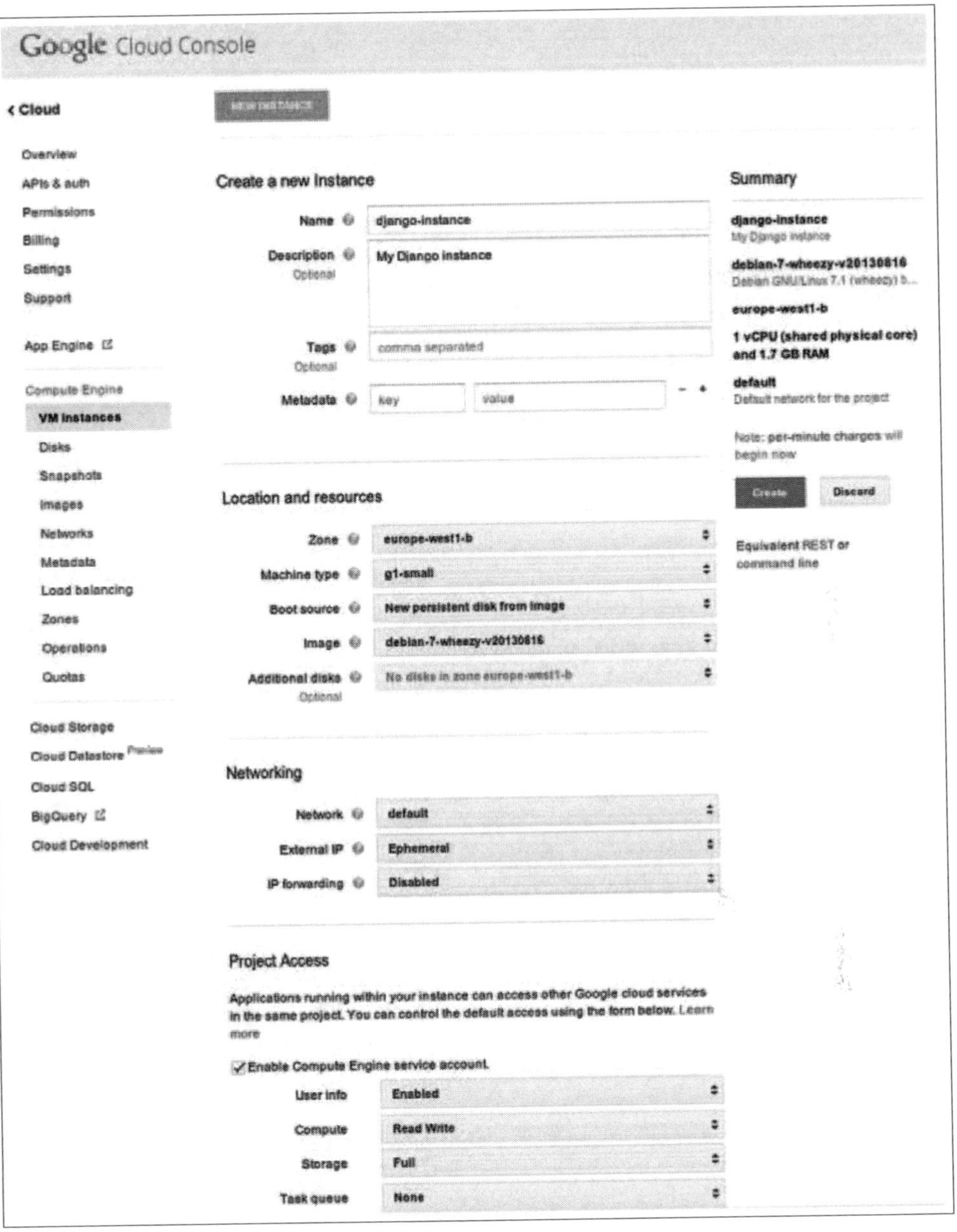

Figure A3.11: Launching a new instance from Google Compute Engine console

This section provides instructions on setting up Django on a Google Compute Engine instance. Figure A3.11 shows a screenshot of the new instance launch page of Google Compute Engine console. After launching the instance, connect to the instance from your local machine using:

```
gcutil getproject –project="myProject" –cache_flag_values
gcutil ssh django-instance
gcutil addfirewall django –description="Incoming HTTP" –allowed="tcp:8000"
```

Run the commands in Box A3.1 to install Django on the GCE instance. Open the instance IP address with port 8000 (http://<instance-IP>:8000) in a browser. You will be able to see the Django default project page.

## Setting up Django on Windows Azure Virtual Machines

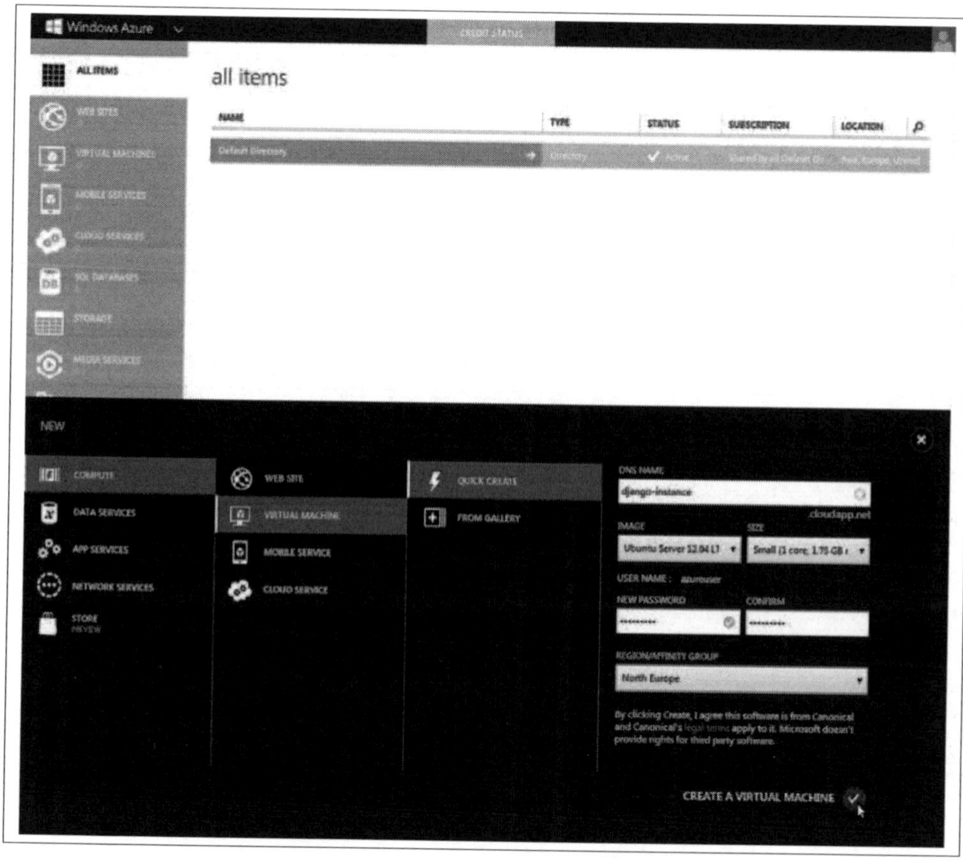

Figure A3.12: Launching a new instance from Windows Azure console

This section provides instructions for setting up Django on a Windows Azure Virtual Machines instance. Figure A3.12 shows a screenshot of the new instance launch wizard of Windows Azure Virtual Machines. After launching the instance, connect to the instance from your local machine using:
ssh <azure-instance-ip>

Enter the username and password you specified while creating the instance to connect to the instance. Run the commands in Box A3.1 to install Django on the Azure VM instance. Open the instance IP address with port 8000 (http://<instance-IP>:8000) in a browser. You will be able to see the Django default project page.

## Taking Django to Production

Although Django comes with a built-in lightweight web-server, it is suited for development purposes only and not recommended for production environments.

The recommended method for taking Django to production is to deploy Django with Apache and mod_wsgi. mod_wsgi is an Apache module which can host any Python WSGI application, including Django [129]. mod_wsgi is suitable for use in hosting high performance production web sites. Box A3.3 shows the commands for installing Apache server with mod-wsgi on an Ubuntu machine.

■ **Box A3.3: Installing Apache server with mod-wsgi**

```
sudo aptitude install apache2 apache2.2-common
apache2-mpm-prefork apache2-utils libexpat1 ssl-cert

sudo aptitude install libapache2-mod-wsgi

sudo service apache2 restart

sudo pip install django-storages boto
```

To provide mod_wsgi the access to a Django application, a wsgi configuration file inside the Django project directory is required. Box A3.4 shows a sample WSGI configuration for a Django project.

■ **Box A3.4: Sample WSGI configuration - wsgi.py**

```
import os
import sys
sys.path.append('/home/ubuntu/myproject/')
os.environ['DJANGO_SETTINGS_MODULE'] = 'myproject.settings'
import django.core.handlers.wsgi
application = django.core.handlers.wsgi.WSGIHandler()
```

Box A3.5 shows a sample WSGI configuration for Apache server. In this configuration the *WSGIScriptAlias* directive tells Apache that all requests below the base URL path specified (e.g. / is the root URL) should be handled by the WSGI application defined in that file.

■ **Box A3.5: Sample Apache server configuration - httpd.conf**

```
WSGIScriptAlias / /home/ubuntu/myproject/myproject/wsgi.py
WSGIPythonPath /home/ubuntu/myproject

<Directory /home/ubuntu/myproject>
<Files wsgi.py>
Order deny,allow
Allow from all
</Files>
</Directory>
```

After configuring the http.conf and wsgi.py files, Apache server must be restarted (/etc/init.d/apache2 restart). If all the configurations are in place, restarting the Apache server would deploy the Django application using mod_wsgi and ready for production.

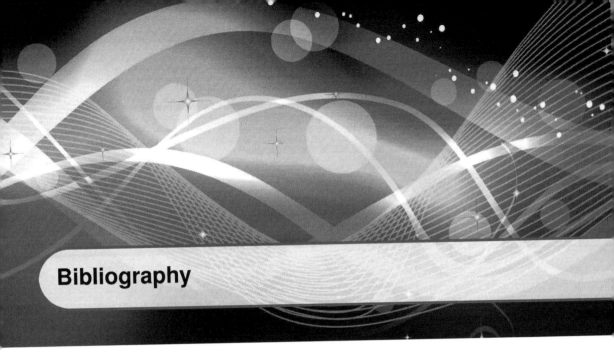

# Bibliography

[1] Ian G Smith, *The Internet of Things 2012 New Horizons*, IERC - Internet of Things European Research Cluster, 2012.

[2] IEEE 802.3 Working Group, http://www.ieee802.org/3, Retrieved 2014.

[3] IEEE 802.11 Working Group, http://www.ieee802.org/11, Retrieved 2014.

[4] IEEE 802.16 Working Group, http://www.ieee802.org/16/, Retrieved 2014.

[5] IEEE 802.11 Working Group, http://www.ieee802.org/15/, Retrieved 2014.

[6] Internet Protocol Specification, http://www.ietf.org/rfc/rfc791.txt, Retrieved 2014.

[7] Internet Protocol, Version 6 (IPv6) Specification, https://www.ietf.org/rfc/rfc2460.txt, Retrieved 2014.

[8] Compression Format for IPv6 Datagrams over IEEE 802.15.4-Based Networks, http://datatracker.ietf.org/doc/rfc6282, Retrieved 2014.

[9] Transmission Control Protocol, www.ietf.org/rfc/rfc793.txt, Retrieved 2014.

[10] User Datagram Protocol, www.ietf.org/rfc/rfc768.txt, Retrieved 2014.

[11] Hypertext Transfer Protocol - HTTP/1.1 , http://tools.ietf.org/html/rfc2616, Retrieved 2014.

[12] Constrained Application Protocol (CoAP), http://tools.ietf.org/html/draft-ietf-core-coap-18, Retrieved 2014.

[13] The WebSocket Protocol, http://tools.ietf.org/html/rfc6455, Retrieved 2014.

[14] MQ Telemetry Transport (MQTT) V3.1 Protocol Specification, http://www.ibm.com/developerworks/webservices/library/ws-mqtt/index.html, Retrieved 2014.

[15] Extensible Messaging and Presence Protocol (XMPP): Core, http://tools.ietf.org/html/rfc6120, Retrieved 2014.

[16] Data Distribution Service for Real-time Systems, OMG Available Specification, http://www.omg.org/spec/DDS/1.2/PDF/, Retrieved 2014.

[17] AMQP v1.0, http://www.amqp.org/sites/amqp.org/files/amqp.pdf, Retrieved 2014.

[18] IPSO Alliance Interop Committee, The IPSO Application Framework, http://www.ipso-alliance.org/wp-content/media/draft-ipso-app-framework-04.pdf, 2012.

[19] T.P. Huynh, Y.K. Tan, K.J. Tseng , *Energy-aware wireless sensor network with ambient intelligence for smart LED lighting system control*, IECON 2011.

[20] S. Bhardwaj, T. Ozcelebi, R. Verhoeven, J. Lukkien, *Smart indoor solid state lighting based on a novel illumination model and implementation*, IEEE Transactions on Consumer Electronics, Vol. 57, Iss. 4, 2011.

[21] OpenRemote, http://www.openremote.org, Retrieved 2014.

[22] Nest, http://www.nest.com, Retrieved 2014.

[23] M. Wang, G. Zhang, C. Zhang, J. Zhang, C. Li, *An IoT-based Appliance Control System for Smart Homes*, ICICIP 2013.

[24] A. Maiti, S. Sivanesan, *Cloud controlled intrusion detection and burglary prevention stratagems in home automation systems*, BCFIC, 2012.

[25] Mong-Fong Horng, Bo-Chao Chang, Bei-Hao Su, *An Intelligent Intrusion Detection System Based on UPnP Technology for Smart Living*, ISDA 2008.

[26] S. Nivedhitha, A.P. Padmavathy, U.S. Susaritha, M.G. Madhan, *Development of Multipurpose Gas Leakage and Fire Detector with Alarm System*, TIIEC, 2013.

[27] International Energy Agency, *Light's Labour's Lost*, OECD/IEA, 2006.

[28] M. Castro1, A.J. Jara1, A.F.G. Skarmeta, *Smart Lighting solutions for Smart Cities*, 27th International Conference on Advanced Information Networking and Applications Workshops, 2013.

[29] E. Polycarpou, L. Lambrinos, E. Protopapadakis, *Smart parking solutions for urban areas*, WoWMoM, 2013.

[30] S.V. Srikanth, Pramod P. J, Dileep K. P, Tapas S, Mahesh U. Patil, Sarat Chandra Babu N, *Design and Implementation of a prototype Smart PARKing (SPARK) System using Wireless Sensor Networks*, International Conference on Advanced Information Networking and Applications Workshops, 2009.

[31] M. Karpiriski, A. Senart, V. Cahill, *Sensor networks for smart roads*, PerCom Workshops, 2006.

[32] H. Zhang, J. Guo, X. Xie, R. Bie, Y, Sun, *Environmental Effect Removal Based Structural Health Monitoring in the Internet of Things*, International Conference on Innovative Mobile and Internet Services in Ubiquitous Computing (IMIS), 2013

[33] Changki Mo, J. Davidson, *Energy harvesting technologies for structural health monitoring applications* IEEE Conference on Technologies for Sustainability (SusTech), 2013.

[34] A. Cammarano, D. Spenza, C. Petrioli, *Energy-harvesting WSNs for structural health monitoring of underground train tunnels* INFOCOM, 2013.

[35] S. Dey, A. Chakraborty, S. Naskar, P. Misra, *Smart city surveillance: Leveraging benefits of cloud data stores* IEEE 37th Conference on Local Computer Networks Workshops, 2012.

[36] A. Attwood, M. Merabti, P. Fergus, O. Abuelmaatti, *Smart Cities Critical Infrastructure Response Framework*, Developments in E-systems Engineering, 2011

[37] S. Djahel, M. Salehie, I. Tal, P. Jamshidi, *Adaptive Traffic Management for Secure and Efficient Emergency Services in Smart Cities* PerCom 2013.

[38] AirPi, http://airpi.es, Retrieved 2014.

[39] A. Foina, A. El-Deeb, *PeWeMoS - Pervasive Weather Monitoring System*, ICPCA, 2008.

[40] M. Masinde, A. Bagula, M. Nzioka, *SenseWeather: Based weather monitoring system for Kenya*, IST-Africa Conference and Exhibition (IST-Africa), 2013.

[41] A. Kadri, E. Yaacoub, M. Mushtaha, A. Abu-Dayya, Wireless sensor network for real-time air pollution monitoring, ICCSPA, 2013.

[42] A.R. Al-Ali, I. Zualkernan, F. Aloul, *A Mobile GPRS-Sensors Array for Air Pollution Monitoring*, IEEE Sensors Journal, 2010.

[43] H.H. Eldien, *Noise mapping in urban environments: Application at Suez city center*, ICCIE, 2009.

[44] L. Ruge, B. Altakrouri, A. Schrader, *SoundOfTheCity - Continuous noise monitoring for a healthy city*, PerComW, 2013.

[45] M. Hefeeda, M. Bagheri, *Wireless Sensor Networks for Early Detection of Forest Fires*, MOBHOC, 2007.

[46] Y. Liu, Y. Gu, G. Chen, Y. Ji, J. Li, *A Novel Accurate Forest Fire Detection System Using Wireless Sensor Networks*, International Conference on Mobile Ad-hoc and Sensor Networks, 2011.

[47] J. Lee ; J.E. Kim ; D. Kim ; P.K. Chong ; J. Kim ; P. Jang *RFMS: Real-time Flood Monitoring System with wireless sensor networks*, MASS, 2008.

[48] Ni-Bin Chang, Da-Hai Guo, *Urban Flash Flood Monitoring, Mapping and Forecasting via a Tailored Sensor Network System* ICNSC, 2006.

[49] Q. Ou, Y. Zhen, X. Li, Y. Zhang, L. Zeng, *Application of Internet of Things in Smart Grid Power Transmission*, International Conference on Mobile, Ubiquitous, and Intelligent Computing, 2012.

[50] OpenPDC, http://openpdc.codeplex.com

[51] A. Bahga, V. Madisetti, *Analyzing Massive Machine Maintenance Data in a Computing Cloud*, IEEE Transactions on Parallel & Distributed Systems, Vol. 23, Iss. 10, Oct 2012.

[52] F.R. Yu, P. Zhang, W. Xiao, P. Choudhury, *Communication systems for grid integration of renewable energy resources*, IEEE Network, Vol 25, Iss 5, 2011.

[53] M.D. Mills-Harris, A. Soylemezoglu, C. Saygin, *RFID data-based inventory management of time-sensitive materials*, IECON, 2005

[54] P. Pourghomi, G. Ghinea, *Managing NFC payment applications through cloud computing*, International Conference for Internet Technology And Secured Transactions, 2012.

[55] Marc Pasquet, J. Reynaud, C. Rosenberger, *Secure payment with NFC mobile phone in the SmartTouch project*, International Symposium on Collaborative Technologies and Systems, 2008.

[56] Cultivar RainCloud, http://ecultivar.com/rain-cloud-product-project/, Retrieved 2014.

[57] C. Akshay, N. Karnwal, K.A. Abhfeeth, R. Khandelwal, T. Govindraju, D. Ezhilarasi, Y. Sujan, *Wireless sensing and control for precision Green house management*, ICST, 2012.

[58] A. Goel, V. Gruhn, *A Fleet Monitoring System for Advanced Tracking of Commercial Vehicles*, IEEE International Conference on Systems, Man and Cybernetics, 2006.

[59] S.T.S. Bukkapatnam, R. Komanduri, *Container Integrity and Condition Monitoring using RF Vibration Sensor Tags*, IEEE International Conference on Automation Science and Engineering, 2007.

[60] S.H. Chen, J.F. Wang, Y. Wei, J. Shang, S.Y. Kao, *The Implementation of Real-Time On-line Vehicle Diagnostics and Early Fault Estimation System*, ICGEC, 2011.

[61] A. Bahga, V. Madisetti, *On a Cloud-Based Information Technology Framework for Data Driven Intelligent Transportation Systems*, Journal of Transportation Technologies, Vol. 3, No. 2, April 2013.

[62] R. Claes, T. Holvoet and D. Weyns, *A Decentralized Approach for Anticipatory Vehicle Routing Using Delegate Multiagent Systems*, IEEE Transactions on Intelligent Transportation Systems, Vol. 12 No. 2, 2011.

[63] D. A. Steil, J. R. Pate, N. A. Kraft, R. K. Smith, B. Dixon, L. Ding and A. Parrish, *Patrol Routing Expression, Execution, Evaluation, and Engagement*, IEEE Transactions on Intelligent Transportation Systems, Vol. 12 No. 1, 2011.

[64] E. Schmitt and H. Jula, *Vehicle Route Guidance Systems: Classification and Comparison*, Proceedings of IEEE ITSC, Toronto, 2006.

[65] A. Pandian, A. Ali, *A review of recent trends in machine diagnosis and prognosis algorithms*, World Congress on Nature & Biologically Inspired Computing, 2009.

[66] Y. Xiang, R. Piedrahita, R.P. Dick, M. Hannigan, Q. Lv, L. Shang, *A Hybrid Sensor System for Indoor Air Quality Monitoring*, IEEE International Conference on Distributed Computing in Sensor Systems, 2013.

[67] S. Bhattacharya, S. Sridevi, R. Pitchiah, *Indoor air quality monitoring using wireless sensor network*, International Conference on Sensing Technology, 2012.

[68] Sony Smartwatch, http://www.sonymobile.com/in/products/accessories/smartwatch/, Retrieved 2014.

[69] Google Glass, www.google.com/glass, Retrieved 2014.

[70] Nike Hyperdunk+ Shoes, http://www.nike.com/us/en_us/c/basketball/nike-basketball-hyperdunk-plus, Retrieved 2014.

[71] Nike Fuelband, http://www.nike.com/us/en_us/c/nikeplus-fuelband, Retrieved 2014.

[72] J.M.L.P. Caldeira, J.J.P.C. Rodrigues, P. Lorenz, *Toward ubiquitous mobility solutions for body sensor networks on healthcare*, IEEE Communications Magazine, 2012.

[73] W.Y. Chung, Y.D. Lee, S.J. Jung *A wireless sensor network compatible wearable u-healthcare monitoring system using integrated ECG, accelerometer and SpO2*, International Conference of the IEEE Engineering in Medicine and Biology Society, 2008.

[74] Fitbit, http://www.fitbit.com/, Retrieved 2014.

[75] IoT-A, *Converged Architectural Reference Model for the IoT v2.0*, http://www.iot-a.eu, Retrieved 2014.

[76] A. Bahga, V. Madisetti, *A Cloud-Based Approach to Interoperable Electronic Health Records (EHRs)*, IEEE Journal of Biomedical and Health Informatics, Vol. 17, Iss. 5, Sep 2013.

[77] Peter Mell, Timothy Grance, *The NIST Definition of Cloud Computing*, NIST Special Publication 800-145, Sep 2011.

[78] Amazon Elastic Compute Cloud, http://aws.amazom.com/ec2, 2012.

[79] Google Compute Engine, https://developers.google.com/compute/, Retrieved 2014.

[80] Windows Azure, http://www.windowsazure.com/, Retrieved 2014.

[81] Google App Engine, http://appengine.google.com, 2012.

[82] Network Functions Virtualization, http://www.etsi.org/technologies-clusters/technologies/nfv, Retrieved 2014.

[83] OpenFlow Switch Specification, https://www.opennetworking.org, Retrieved 2014.

[84] S. Ghemawat, H. Gobioff, S. Leung, *The Google File System*, SOSP 2003.

[85] J. Dean, S. Ghemawat, *MapReduce: Simplified Data Processing on Large Clusters*, OSDI 2004.

[86] Apache Storm, http://storm-project.net, Retrieved 2014.

[87] The Python Standard Library, http://docs.python.org/2/library/, Retrieved 2014.

[88] Roy T. Fielding, Richard N. Taylor, *Principled Design of the Modern Web Architecture*, ACM Transactions on Internet Technology (TOIT), 2002.

[89] Django REST framework, http://django-rest-framework.org/, Retrieved 2014.

[90] Mark Devaney, Bill Cheetham, *Case-Based Reasoning for Gas Turbine Diagnostics*, 18th International FLAIRS Conference, 2005.

[91] Harry Timmerman, *SKF WindCon Condition Monitoring System for Wind Turbines*, New Zealand Wind Energy Conference, 2009.

[92] CSA Trusted Cloud Initiative, https://research.cloudsecurityalliance.org/tci/, 2013.

[93] Keberos, http://web.mit.edu/kerberos/, 2013.

[94] TOTP: Time-Based One-Time Password Algorithm http://tools.ietf.org/html/rfc6238, 2013.

[95] OAuth community site, http://oauth.net/, 2013.

[96] The OAuth 2.0 Authorization Framework, http://tools.ietf.org/html/rfc6749, 2013.

[97] Python OAuth2, https://github.com/simplegeo/python-oauth2, 2013.

[98] A. Bahga, V. Madisetti, *Performance Evaluation Approach for Multi-tier Cloud Applications*, Journal of Software Engineering and Applications, Vol. 6, No. 2, pp. 74-83, Mar 2013.

[99] A. Bahga, V. Madisetti, *Rapid Prototyping of Advanced Cloud-Based Systems*, IEEE Computer, vol. 46, iss. 11, Nov 2013.

[100] AutoBahn, http://autobahn.ws/, Retrieved 2014.

[101] Amazon Web Services, http://aws.amazon.com, Retrieved 2014.

[102] Google Cloud Platform, https://cloud.google.com, Retrieved 2014.

[103] Microsoft Windows Azure, http://www.windowsazure.com, Retrieved 2014.

[104] Raspberry Pi, http://www.raspberrypi.org, Retrieved 2014.

[105] pcDuino, http://www.pcduino.com, Retrieved 2014.

[106] BeagleBone Black, www.beagleboard.org, Retrieved 2014.

[107] Cubieboard, http://cubieboard.org, Retrieved 2014.

[108] boto, http://boto.readthedocs.org/en/latest/, Retrieved 2014.

[109] Python JSON package, http://docs.python.org/library/json.html, Retrieved 2014.

[110] Python email package, http://docs.python.org/2/library/email, Retrieved 2014.

[111] Python HTTPLib, http://code.google.com/p/httplib2/, Retrieved 2014.

[112] Python URLLib, http://docs.python.org/2/howto/urllib2.html, Retrieved 2014.

[113] Python SMTPLib, http://docs.python.org/2/library/smtplib.html, Retrieved 2014.

[114] NumPy, http://www.numpy.org/, Retrieved 2014.

[115] Scikit-learn, http://scikit-learn.org/stable/, Retrieved 2014.

[116] Django, https://docs.djangoproject.com/en/1.5/, Retrieved 2014.

[117] Django Models, https://docs.djangoproject.com/en/1.5/topics/db/models/, Retrieved 2014.

[118] Django Views, https://docs.djangoproject.com/en/1.5/topics/http/views/, Retrieved 2014.

[119] Django Templates, https://docs.djangoproject.com/en/1.5/ref/templates/builtins/, Retrieved 2014.

[120] Django URL dispatcher, https://docs.djangoproject.com/en/1.5/topics/http/urls/, Retrieved 2014.

[121] Apache Spark, http://spark.apache.org, Retrieved 2014.

[122] Overview of the 2002 IAB Network Management Workshop, http://tools.ietf.org/html/rfc3535, Retrieved 2014.

[123] NETCONF Configuration Protocol, http://tools.ietf.org/html/rfc4741, Retrieved 2014.

[124] YANG - A Data Modeling Language for the Network Configuration Protocol (NETCONF), http://tools.ietf.org/html/rfc6020, Retrieved 2014.

[125] Netopeer, https://code.google.com/p/netopeer/, Retrieved 2014.

[126] libnetconf, https://code.google.com/p/libnetconf/, Retrieved 2014.

[127] XCTU, http://www.digi.com/products/wireless-wired-embedded-solutions/zigbee-rf-module /xctu, Retrieved 2014.

[128] Xively-JS, http://xively.github.io/xively-js/, Retrieved 2014.

[129] http://code.google.com/p/modwsgi/, Retrieved 2014.

[130] Apache Hadoop, http://hadoop.apache.org/, Retrieved 2014.

[131] Apache Tez, http://tez.apache.org/, Retrieved 2014.

[132] VirtualBox, https://www.virtualbox.org/, Retrieved 2014.

[133] Ubuntu, https://www.ubuntu.com, Retrieved 2014.

[134] Storm, http://storm.incubator.apache.org/, Retrieved 2014.

[135] Zookeeper, http://zookeeper.apache.org/, Retrieved 2014.

[136] NETCONF-Central, http://www.netconf-central.org/, Retrieved 2014.

[137] YANG-Central, http://www.netconfcentral.org/, Retrieved 2014.

# Index

# Other Book from the Authors

## Cloud Computing: A Hands-On Approach

Recent industry surveys expect the cloud computing services market to be in excess of $20 billion and cloud computing jobs to be in excess of 10 million worldwide in 2014 alone. In addition, since a majority of existing information technology (IT) jobs is focused on maintaining legacy in-house systems, the demand for these kinds of jobs is likely to drop rapidly if cloud computing continues to take hold of the industry.

However, there are very few educational options available in the area of cloud computing beyond vendor-specific training by cloud providers themselves. Cloud computing courses have not found their way (yet) into mainstream college curricula.

This book is written as a textbook on cloud computing for educational programs at colleges. It can also be used by cloud service providers who may be interested in offering a broader perspective of cloud computing to accompany their own customer and employee training programs. The typical reader is expected to have completed a couple of courses in programming using traditional high-level languages at the college-level, and is either a senior or a beginning graduate student in one of the science, technology, engineering or mathematics (STEM) fields. We have tried to write a comprehensive book that transfers knowledge through an immersive "hands-on approach", where the reader is provided the necessary guidance and knowledge to develop working code for real-world cloud applications.

Additional support is available at the book's website: www.cloudcomputingbook.info

### Organization

The book is organized into three main parts. Part I covers technologies that form the foundations of cloud computing. These include topics such as virtualization, load balancing, scalability & elasticity, deployment, and replication. Part II introduces the reader to the design & programming aspects of cloud computing. Case studies on design and implementation of several cloud applications in the areas such as image processing, live streaming and social networks analytics are provided. Part III introduces the reader to specialized aspects of cloud computing including cloud application benchmarking, cloud security, multimedia applications and big data analytics. Case studies in areas such as IT, healthcare, transportation, networking and education are provided.

Made in the USA
Middletown, DE
30 March 2016